READINGS OF THE *LOTUS SŪTRA*

COLUMBIA READINGS OF BUDDHIST LITERATURE

COLUMBIA READINGS OF BUDDHIST LITERATURE

◈ ◈ ◈

SERIES EDITOR

Stephen F. Teiser

This series is published with the sponsorship of the Dharma Drum Foundation for Humanities and Social Science Research

READINGS OF THE *LOTUS SŪTRA*

EDITED BY

Stephen F. Teiser and Jacqueline I. Stone

Columbia University Press

New York

Columbia University Press
Publishers Since 1893
New York Chichester, West Sussex

Library of Congress Cataloging-in-Publication Data
Readings of the *Lotus Sūtra* / Edited by Stephen F. Teiser and Jacqueline I. Stone.

p. cm. — (Columbia readings of Buddhist literature)
Includes bibliographical references and index.
ISBN 978-0-231-14288-5 (cloth : alk. paper) — ISBN 978-0-231-14289-2 (pbk. : alk. paper)
1. Tripiṭaka. Sūtrapiṭaka. Saddharmapuṇḍarīkasūtra—Criticism, interpretation, etc. I. Teiser, Stephen F. II. Stone, Jacqueline Ilyse. III. Title. IV. Series.

BQ2057.R43 2009
294.3'85—dc22 2008040137

♾

Columbia University Press books are printed on permanent and durable acid-free paper.

This book was printed on paper with recycled content.
Printed in the United States of America

c 10 9 8 7 6 5 4 3 2
p 10 9 8 7 6 5 4 3

CONTENTS

FOREWORD

THE SERIES Columbia Readings of Buddhist Literature is intended to offer students and teachers the best scholarship, in a pedagogically useful form, concerning the whole range of Buddhist literature. Each book in the series is crafted to provide for each Buddhist text the essential background knowledge, a series of close readings of the text, and introductions to the ways in which the text has been interpreted throughout the history of Buddhism.

The Dharma Drum Foundation for Research in the Humanities and Social Sciences is delighted to sponsor the series. The foundation supports a wide range of scholarly research, academic exchange, publications, and social work. We believe that *Readings of the "Lotus Sūtra"* is an auspicious beginning for the book series, and we look forward to future volumes that will further the understanding of Buddhist literature.

—Sheng Yen (1930–2009), Founder of Dharma Drum Foundation

PREFACE

THE TURNS of plot, complex philosophy, and rich language and mythology of the *Lotus Sūtra* have made it one of the most popular of all the sacred scriptures of Buddhism. Originally written in a form of the ancient Indian language of Sanskrit, it was later translated into many different languages, and in its Chinese version it has become a vital part of the religious and cultural heritage of China, Korea, and Japan. Few Buddhists in these cultures, past or present, do not know the *Lotus Sūtra*, and it is becoming increasingly well known in the West as well.

The purpose of this book, in accord with the goals of the series that it inaugurates, is to introduce the ways in which this seminal work has been read in the history of Buddhism and to open up perspectives for new readers of the scripture. The contributors to this volume have dedicated substantial research to the interpretation of the *Lotus Sūtra*. In their chapters here they draw on their earlier work, much of it published in monographs or in articles in academic journals, reframing and updating it to provide a fresh, disciplined introduction to the life of the text in various Asian settings. Some chapters focus on the language and doctrines of the *Lotus Sūtra*, offering close readings and philosophical analyses of important problems raised in the text. Other chapters emphasize the various milieus in which the *Lotus* has been understood and trace the development of social movements, schools of thought, art, and poetry inspired by the scripture in East Asia. The first chapter of the book, coauthored by the editors, discusses the origins of the *Lotus Sūtra*, sketches its early Indian background, and also provides an overview of the later history of the *Lotus*.

As editors of this volume on the *Lotus Sūtra*, we have thought hard about how to deal with the complexity of the text and the diversity of its interpretation. We have decided to presuppose as little as possible about the specialized preparation of our readers. We assume only that students opening this book are intelligent and have some motive, whether for personal reasons or because they are enrolled in a course in Buddhism, for reading the text in English translation. Most of the chapters in this book focus on the version of the *Lotus Sūtra* translated from Sanskrit into Chinese by the monk from the ancient central Asian kingdom of Kucha named Kumārajīva, who lived from 344 to 413 (or possibly from 350 to 409). Kumārajīva's Chinese version, supplemented with small additions in the fifth and sixth centuries, was the most influential of all the translations of the *Lotus*. We have chosen one specific modern English translation of Kumārajīva's *Lotus Sūtra* as a point of reference whenever citing the text because of its fidelity to Kumārajīva's Chinese and its consistent rendering of Buddhist technical terms. That translation is *Scripture of the Lotus Blossom of the Fine Dharma* (*The Lotus Sūtra*), originally completed by Leon Hurvitz in 1976 and readily available in a revised edition published in 2009 by Columbia University Press. Our citations of Hurvitz's translation are denoted simply in parentheses by "Hurvitz" plus a page number referring to the 2009 edition. For readers using other translations of the *Lotus Sūtra*, a list of cross-references correlating Hurvitz's pagination with page numbers in the 1976 Hurvitz translation and in another widely used English translation, done by Burton Watson in 1993 (as well as the page of the original Chinese text in the modern scholarly canon), can be found at the end of the book.

Because our goal is to open up the *Lotus Sūtra* to a new generation of readers encountering the text for the first time, our contributors have also taken pains to translate and explain all foreign words at their first occurrence. In keeping with the choices in English translation adopted by Hurvitz, we generally cleave to the meaning of Buddhist terms in Chinese translation, which sometimes differs from the meaning of the original Sanskrit word. We generally refer to time periods by century rather than by dynasty, except when dynastic rule is relevant to the point in question. Similarly, the notes are intended to help students find the best, most up-to-date scholarship written in English on particular topics for further reading or the preparation of term papers. Those who wish to explore more specialized scholarship or works in other languages will find more extensive references in the bibliographies of the sources cited in the notes. In referring to modern East Asian authors, we follow Western convention and place the surname last when citing their English-language publications; otherwise, references to Chinese or Japanese figures follow East Asian convention, giving the surname first.

The editors wish to express their gratitude to the Dharma Drum Foundation, its founder, Venerable Sheng Yen, who passed away when the book was in page proofs, and to the foundation's Chief Executive Officer, Tseng Chi-chun, for their support for this volume and their dedication to the series, Columbia Readings of Buddhist Literature, as a whole. We also want to voice our thanks to Jimmy Yu, whose meticulous work as editorial assistant was crucial in the preparation of the manuscript. We are grateful also to Columbia University Press, especially to our executive editor, Wendy Lochner; to our production editor, Leslie Kriesel; to our copy editor, Mike Ashby; and to Mary Mortensen, who prepared the index. We also extend our thanks to our contributors for their generosity in sharing their insights and polishing their writing. To our families we remain grateful, as always, for their patience and support.

—Stephen F. Teiser and Jacqueline I. Stone

READINGS OF THE *LOTUS SŪTRA*

[1]

INTERPRETING THE *LOTUS SŪTRA*

Stephen F. Teiser and Jacqueline I. Stone

THE *LOTUS SŪTRA* asserts a bold set of claims about the Buddhist religion. Pitting itself against what the text views as immature followers of the Buddha, the *Lotus* champions the cause of the bodhisattva (a being intent upon supreme enlightenment), who seeks salvation for all sentient beings. The text portrays earlier models for the practice of Buddhism as preliminary or incomplete—or effective only after their provisional nature is understood. The *Lotus Sūtra* propounds the doctrine of skillful means, or expedient devices (Skt.: *upāyakauśalya*, or *upāya*), according to which all earlier teachings are temporary measures created by buddhas (fully enlightened beings) to match the individual circumstances of their followers. In the narrative of the *Lotus Sūtra*, buddhas from other realms travel to the scene where the historical Buddha, Śākyamuni, is preaching the *Lotus*, thus demonstrating the sūtra's validity. The text goes on to assert that all buddhas preach the *Lotus* as their final message. Śākyamuni warns of enemies who will malign the teachings of the *Lotus*, and he enjoins devotees of the sūtra to uphold the text by chanting it, reciting the spells it contains, and using the text itself as a template for religious practice.

These claims and others, in concert with the religious and social forces animating Buddhist history, have generated a wide range of interpretation, and it is perhaps no exaggeration to say that the *Lotus Sūtra* has been the most influential Buddhist scripture in East Asia. The goals of this book, the first in a series on great works of Buddhist literature, are to introduce the *Lotus Sūtra* to first-time readers and to survey some of the major issues in how the text has been understood within the rich history of Buddhism. As an introductory text, this book provides suggestions for further reading among the most important studies in English. Furthermore, since the *Lotus Sūtra* was created in ancient India but achieved its greatest influence in China and Japan, most of this book focuses on East Asia.

In the Indian context in which it was originally compiled—perhaps shortly after the beginning of the Common Era—the *Lotus* offered not only a new form of Buddhism but also a sophisticated theory about how its own innovations stood in relation to past and future forms of the religion. Many ideas in the *Lotus* are consistent with teachings of other Mahāyāna movements, which claimed to be more magnificent and more inclusive than preceding forms of Buddhism. That highly charged allegation is crystallized in the general name many such groups used to refer to themselves, Mahāyāna, which means "Great Vehicle." In many contexts the term implies the derogation of other forms of Buddhism as Hīnayāna, meaning "Small Vehicle" or "Lesser Vehicle." Mahāyāna groups agreed also that the highest paradigm for religious practice was the bodhisattva. Rather than aiming for cessation of rebirth (*nirvāṇa*; literally, "extinction" or "blowing out"), a goal attributed to earlier followers of the Buddha, the bodhisattva sought a more expansive result, voluntarily remaining in the realms of suffering to lead all beings to liberation. According to some Mahāyānists, this more exalted objective was not merely a termination of one's own suffering and ignorance but a long-term, selfless dedication to bringing salvation to others. Mahāyāna followers believed that they were returning to the model of religious life established by the historical Buddha, who sacrificed himself in countless incarnations for the benefit of other beings. (The variety of new teachings claiming to represent a "Great Vehicle" are outlined in a later section of this chapter, "The *Lotus Sūtra* and Mahāyāna Movements.")

Of the numerous Mahāyāna sūtras produced in the first centuries of the Common Era, few have provoked more questions than the *Lotus Sūtra*. Some reasons for this diversity of interpretation are internal to the text. For example, the *Lotus* makes extensive use of imagery and parables, which have invited multiple readings. Another puzzling feature of the *Lotus Sūtra* is its self-referential or circular quality. In many places the *Lotus* seems to justify the reasons for believing in the text by referring to the text itself. The main speaker in the scripture, Śākyamuni Buddha, states that only fully awakened beings like himself can understand the *Lotus*—but then he proceeds to preach it to nonbuddhas in the original audience of listeners anyway. In some portions of the sūtra, Śākyamuni portrays the text as a final statement that puts in their place all previous explanations of liberating truth. In other portions, however, he suggests that all teachings have only relative truth. According to this theory, truly effective vehicles of salvation are created in specific historical circumstances, for particular audiences, by buddhas, and hence the truth value of any religious method can be judged only in relation to its context. At one point in the text, the Buddha explains that his own entry into final nirvāṇa was merely a pedagogical device, intended to spur his followers to aspire to their own liberation, and that he is in fact always present, teaching and guiding, even though unenlightened people do not see him. In reaction to such pronouncements, those who hear the Buddha's sermon in the story—like the reader of the text—become quite bewildered, not only confused by the new doctrines but uncertain about how to evaluate the validity of the new teachings and how to assess their legitimacy within Buddhism.

In addition to such ambiguities within the *Lotus* itself, other, contextual factors help account for the multivocality and broad reach of the sūtra throughout the Buddhist cultures of East Asia. We should stress at the outset that interpretation of the *Lotus Sūtra* was very much an East Asian enterprise. Within the Indian cultural sphere, after the *Lotus Sūtra* was produced, it appears to have stimulated relatively little debate, analysis, literary production, or artistic reflection. Similarly, after its translation into Tibetan in the early ninth century—an enterprise requiring in-depth study of the text—the *Lotus Sūtra* did not substantially influence the Himalayan realm. In China, by contrast, the *Lotus Sūtra* blossomed in the cultural soil of the medieval period (lasting roughly from the third to the fourteenth centuries). The ascendancy of the *Lotus Sūtra* in China owes much to the sensibilities of one particular translator of the text, the central Asian monk Kumārajīva (Chinese name: Jiumoluoshi [344–413, or 350–409]). Kumārajīva's writing style in Chinese accorded with the literary tastes of his own day and subsequently became the major standard for the canonical language of East Asian Buddhism. Philosophical, cultural, and institutional factors also help account for the popularity of the *Lotus Sūtra* in East Asia. Without Zhiyi's (538–597) commentaries on the *Lotus*—in effect re-creating the text as a template for doctrinal understanding and meditative practice—it is hard to imagine that the *Lotus Sūtra* would have become a dominant conceptual scheme in China in later centuries. Deities, symbols, and many philosophical principles from the *Lotus Sūtra* also helped shape medieval Chinese religious culture. The text and Chinese forms of Buddhist thought and practice based upon it were also well known in Korea. The most extensive and long-lasting influence of the *Lotus Sūtra*, however, can be seen at the eastern edge of Asia, in Japan. There, official sponsorship was one avenue by which the *Lotus Sūtra* became widely known: by the ninth century, Japanese rulers decreed that the *Lotus Sūtra* be recited in temples for the well-being of the imperial family and the realm. It was also the Buddhist scripture most frequently read and recited by literate lay devotees. Ideas and images drawn from the *Lotus* not only influenced the art and literature of cultural elites but were disseminated across social classes through sermons, edifying tales, public lectures, debates, ritual performances, Noh plays, and even popular songs. It would be little exaggeration to say that, for many premodern Japanese people, the *Lotus Sūtra* was the principal medium for the reception of Buddhism itself.

The remaining pages of this chapter sketch a broader picture of the many ways in which the *Lotus Sūtra* has been interpreted and enacted. The initial sections deal with the composition of the *Lotus Sūtra*, the Indian Buddhist milieu in which the sūtra was compiled, and its place within various Indian Mahāyāna movements. Subsequent sections address the *Lotus Sūtra*'s major claims and the process of the sūtra's translation into Chinese. Still later sections summarize the spread of the *Lotus Sūtra* in East Asia. They introduce religious activities and movements specific to the *Lotus Sūtra*, such as the production of *Lotus* commentaries and miracle tales as well as the Buddhist schools Tiantai (Ja.: Tendai) and Nichiren, which are based on the *Lotus*. A final section then touches on the broader diffusion of symbolism, deities, concepts, and practices related to the *Lotus* into the common religious culture. With this material as background, the individual chapters of the book explore interpretations of the *Lotus Sūtra*, especially in East Asia, in greater depth.

BUDDHIST LITERATURE AND THE COMPOSITION OF THE *LOTUS SŪTRA*

Nobody knows who the original authors of the *Lotus Sūtra* were, nor when they lived, nor what language they spoke. This situation is, however, far from unusual; little is known about the compilers of most Buddhist sūtras. Some discussion of the dynamics of composition and transmission in the Buddhist world will help us better understand the early history of the *Lotus*.

A sūtra is a discourse purporting to contain the words of the historical Buddha as transmitted by the Buddhist community after his death. (Some scholars calculate the years 487 or 486 B.C.E. as the date of the Buddha's death, while others place it in 368 B.C.E.) The etymology of the word *sūtra* has been traced variously to the words for "well said," "aphorism" (hence its extended meaning of discourse or words spoken by the Buddha), and "thread," used to refer to texts or pieces of texts threaded together. In theory, the content of every Buddhist sūtra is made up of words spoken by

Śākyamuni, who is always presented as the originator or creator of the discourse. However, the Buddhist community also played an indispensable (although seemingly invisible) role in the compilation and dissemination of sūtras, since the followers of the Buddha were the ones who heard the sermons firsthand, memorized them, and passed them down to later generations. All sūtras claim, implicitly or explicitly, that they originated as oral teachings heard directly from the Buddha. The words with which most sūtras begin, "Thus have I heard," are supposed to be the prefatory guarantee of authenticity uttered by the Buddha's closest disciple, Ānanda. According to Buddhist tradition, shortly after Śākyamuni died, his monastic followers gathered in the town of Rājagṛha and agreed on every word that the Awakened One had spoken in his preaching. Ānanda recited every discourse or teaching given by the Buddha, while another disciple, Upāli, retold every rule for monastic life instituted by the Buddha as well as the immediate circumstances to which the Buddha was responding when he formulated a particular rule. The discourses were gathered into collections (*nikāyas* or *āgamas*) and known individually as sūtras, while the latter rules and accounts of their promulgation constituted the monastic code known as *vinaya*, a word based on the root for "training" or "discipline." (A third collection of texts, *abhidharma*, or the "higher teaching," was added later, resulting in the common designation of the *tripiṭaka*, "three baskets," containing all Buddhist teachings subdivided into sūtra, vinaya, and abhidharma.)

The Buddhist view of authorship or composition, then, is that sūtras are communal institutions that preserve the words of the Buddha. Traditionally, most Buddhists have accepted the sūtras as the received word of the Buddha, and the modern scholar's question of authorship did not arise. Instead of asking about the identity of the author of such texts, Buddhists have been more interested in questions of audience and pedagogy, such as when, where, to whom, and why Śākyamuni delivered a particular sermon.

The transmission of the Buddha's law or teaching (dharma) involved considerable expansion of the canon. Readers familiar with scriptures of other religious traditions are often surprised at the variety and number of Buddhist scriptures that arose, even before the time of the *Lotus*. Local groups controlled the transmission of the oral canon, and early Buddhists followed the dictum attributed to the Buddha that the dharma be preached in local speech. Such groups were composed predominantly of monks and nuns who specialized in memorizing specific collections of sūtras. Exercising powers of memory and receiving oral training quite different from those of their counterparts in the modern world, guardians of the Buddhist canon certainly acted to prevent change and encourage accuracy in the transmission of the dharma. These standardizing procedures help to explain why there is considerable consistency and overlap in the canons of different groups. On the other hand, monastic communities (*saṅghas*) were decentralized to an astonishing degree in the Indian cultural sphere. Each saṅgha determined its own version of the canon and interacted with its own group of lay supporters. Monastic disagreements and debates between Buddhists and teachers of other religions are well documented in the early sources, as are discussions between monks and a wide range of Buddhist laypeople, ranging from kings and courtesans to merchants and farmers. Even before the *Lotus Sūtra* appeared, then, Indian Buddhism was composed of a host of local Buddhisms, each defined by a saṅgha that maintained its own oral canon in the vernacular and by that community's lay supporters.

Probably around the middle of the first century B.C.E.—at least three centuries after the historical Buddha lived—Buddhist communities began putting their oral traditions into written form.[1] The initial writing down of the canon in Lanka (present-day Sri Lanka) at this time coincided with great changes in the island kingdom's saṅgha as well as consolidating pressures from the state. The general move away from an oral canon had wide-ranging and sometimes surprising effects on the emerging forms of Buddhism. One might expect that the institution of writing would help distance the canon from the spoken language of individual places, resulting in authoritative texts in a more uniform written language that was less accessible to local people. This did, in part, happen. In Sri Lanka, for instance, the canon was recorded not in the local speech (ancient Sinhala) but in Pāli, a literary language based on a form of western Middle Indic. The newly created Mahāyāna sūtra literature was probably composed in various Prakrits, or ancient Indian dialects, and then gradually Sanskritized, often in the variation on classical Sanskrit that modern scholars call Buddhist Hybrid Sanskrit. Texts in written form were easy to transport over long distances and could be useful in forging a consensus or articulating a vision shared between widely separated groups.

Despite these attempts to solidify the word of the Buddha by inscribing it on palm leaf or tree bark, depending on location, the resulting literary products maintained the convention of claiming to be a teaching originally heard directly from the Buddha. That is, even in written form, sūtras preserved the opening phrase "Thus have I heard," which anchored the text to a specific time and place, the existential situation of Śākyamuni speaking to a follower. This is true of the Mahāyāna sūtra literature as well, including the *Lotus Sūtra*.

The decentralization of Buddhist monastic communities and the tendency of the body of Buddhist literature to expand over time in the process of transmission shed some light on why so many questions still surround the compilation of the *Lotus Sūtra*. It may be that, in the early stages of its existence, the *Lotus* existed in different versions; certainly it grew in length, as the last several chapters appear to be later additions. In many ways this early textual history will remain forever unknowable, since the earliest surviving Sanskrit manuscripts of the text, discovered in Khotan in central Asia (modern Xinjiang province, China), were not produced until the sixth through eighth centuries. Even these, however, are but fragments of the whole *Lotus Sūtra*, and they differ from manuscripts discovered in Gilgit (in modern Pakistan) that were copied a little later, and from more complete manuscripts from Nepal copied in the eleventh through nineteenth centuries.

Thus, a gap of several centuries separates the composition of the *Lotus Sūtra* from the earliest surviving Sanskrit manuscripts (sixth century C.E.). To fill in this lacuna and formulate hypotheses about the early stages of the *Lotus*, modern scholars generally rely on two kinds of evidence in addition to the Sanskrit manuscripts.[2] One approach is to reason sideways, as it were, taking knowledge about other early Sanskrit sources and applying it to the *Lotus*. Close study of the degree of Sanskritization that texts have undergone and analysis of the verse sections of Buddhist literature have enabled scholars to offer relative dates for different portions and different versions of the *Lotus*. Expressions like "preachers of the dharma" (*dharmabhāṇaka*) are believed to occur only in later layers of the *Lotus* and other Mahāyāna texts, while concepts such as the veneration of the *Lotus Sūtra* text are thought to be characteristic of layers that are later still. The second kind of evidence used to imagine the early forms of the *Lotus Sūtra* is supplied by translations of the Sanskrit *Lotus Sūtra* into other languages. Chinese versions were produced as early as the third century C.E. (discussed in the next section), and a Tibetan translation was made in the ninth century. In light of all these factors—the proliferation of versions of a single text, the gaps separating the surviving evidence from the time of compilation, and the fragmentary and indirect nature of the evidence—as well as the vitality of faith-based interpretations of the scripture among modern Buddhist groups, the history of the *Lotus Sūtra* will probably always be a hotly contested field.

These difficulties notwithstanding, general but by no means unanimous opinion about the stages of the composition of the *Lotus* has been fairly consistent since at least 1934, when Fuse Kōgaku published, in Japanese, a detailed text-critical analysis of the different versions of the text known at that time.[3] Since then, methods and materials have grown in number, but most scholars still agree that the early *Lotus Sūtra* was composed in three main stages. (The chapter numbers used here refer to the numbering system of the Chinese translation of the *Lotus* produced by Kumārajīva in the early fifth century and put in final form by around the seventh century.) There is general agreement about the sequence of composition but less consensus about the precise time period in which each stage occurred.

In the first stage, Chapters 2 through 9 were composed. During this stage the *Lotus Sūtra* focused on the doctrines of expedient devices and the one, unitary vehicle. These themes are expounded in Chapter 2 and developed through a variety of parables and prophecies of disciples' future buddhahood in Chapters 3 through 9. The second stage, often dated narrowly to around 100 C.E., involved the composition of a new introduction (Chapter 1) and new conclusion (Chapter 22) for the book as a whole. The second stage also included the addition of a series of chapters (10 through 21, but not including 12) explicating the spiritual career of the bodhisattva, different ways to revere the *Lotus Sūtra*, and the constantly abiding and omnipresent nature of the Buddha. The third stage, thought to have occurred around 150 C.E., encompassed Chapters 23 to 28 plus Chapter 12 of the current text. Chapters 23 to 28 recount the biographies of various bodhisattvas and forms of devotion to them. Chapter 12 explains how even those who seem unfit for supreme awakening—Śākyamuni's famously evil cousin Devadatta and a female *nāga* (a nonhuman, dragon or serpentlike species)—can achieve buddhahood.[4]

THE *LOTUS SŪTRA* AND THE INDIAN BUDDHIST WORLDVIEW

Despite the strong claims the *Lotus Sūtra* makes about its unique status, many elements in the scripture are consistent with earlier forms of Indian Buddhism.[5] Concepts of time and space, basic metaphors for understanding Buddhist practice, and many of the attitudes toward Buddhist institutions that appear in the text were not fresh. In order to persuade its audience to assent to its innovations, the *Lotus Sūtra* couched its argument in terms that were already well known.

Space does not allow a full discussion of Indian Buddhism prior to the development of the *Lotus Sūtra* and other Mahāyāna literature, but some basic continuities are important to note here. The *Lotus Sūtra* accepted the social world of Indian Buddhism more broadly, with its division into the "fourfold assembly" of monks, nuns, laymen, and laywomen. The text also perpetuated the worldview of earlier Indian Buddhism.[6] In that view of the universe, ordinary existence is marked by inescapable suffering, and all beings undergo a potentially limitless series of rebirths. Existence as we know it is understood as a process of cyclical change, since one moves from one life to the next continuously, without escape, until liberation is achieved. *Saṃsāra*, the cycle of birth and death, means "passing through" or, by extension, undergoing rebirth. One undergoes continual rebirth in either good circumstances or bad, depending on one's deeds (*karma*). Regardless of one's circumstances, however, the samsaric world is marked by constant change or lack of permanence (*anitya*), suffering or unsatisfactoriness (*duḥkha*), and the lack of a permanent self (*anātman*). These three characteristics apply to all conditioned phenomena. Even the pleasures of a good rebirth are, in the end, fleeting, so in the Buddhist worldview, one should ultimately relinquish all attachments and seek to escape rebirth altogether. Escape from saṃsāra to an unconditioned state is called nirvāṇa, literally meaning "extinction" and usually understood as the eradication of delusion and suffering. Expressed in terms drawn from modern psychology, one might say that the benighted, impermanent ego that was the selfish and self-perpetuating subject of saṃsāra is finally destroyed when one achieves nirvāṇa. The attainment of nirvāṇa entails the absence of all unpleasant and impermanent characteristics, and it is often explained by the analogy of smothering a fire or starving it of fuel. During one's lifetime, in the explanation of later scholastics, nirvāṇa can be achieved "with remainder" because the effects of one's previous deeds have not been fully exhausted. At death, such a person is said to achieve "nirvāṇa without remainder," and for that individual, the cycle of rebirth is brought to an end.

This Buddhist worldview offered not only a map of the world but also a built-in value judgment about which regions of the world and their corresponding inhabitants at any given time are better, morally speaking, than others. Residents of the higher realms lead more pleasurable lives because in previous rebirths they cultivated good deeds. According to this worldview, the present world is composed of four continents surrounding a central mountain, Mount Sumeru. Animate beings occupy a finely graded vertical hierarchy. Early Buddhist thought recognizes five levels of existence, and by the time the *Lotus Sūtra* was composed, many scriptures speak of the "six destinies" (*ṣaḍgati*) or six paths of existence. At the top are the gods residing in the heavens on or above Mount Sumeru. The design of the heavenly realm and the ordering of its inhabitants were absorbed into early Buddhist mythology from early Indian religion. Throughout the history of Buddhism, the fluidity of Buddhist cosmology made it amenable to assimilating different kinds of deities and demons from local traditions. Whatever their origin or relative ranking, the gods are believed to live a very long and pleasurable existence, but they, too, are subject to impermanence, and once their stock of merit is exhausted, they are invariably reborn lower down the scale. Below the gods are humans and also *asuras*, a class of demigods or titans who sometimes battle the gods above them. *Asuras* are more powerful than humans, but their realm is marked by continual strife. The three lower destinies are animals, hungry ghosts, and inmates of the hells. Beings are reborn there as retribution for their bad deeds in previous lifetimes.

The law of cause and effect—the claim that every act (karma) has a result—not only determined one's realm of rebirth but was the foundation for Buddhist cultivation. Beings at all levels of the Buddhist universe could in principle achieve nirvāṇa in due time, but in general it was thought that one could reach that goal directly only from the human state, which itself was the consequence of many lifetimes spent performing good deeds and accumulating merit. Śākyamuni himself was able to reach his advanced spiritual status, according to early Indian Buddhism, only because he had been gradually perfecting himself through hundreds of lifetimes of self-sacrifice and compassion. These prior lives of the Buddha, reflected in paintings and literature known as *jātakas* ("birth stories"), suggested that the path to buddhahood required lifetimes of cultivation. The being-who-would-become-the-Buddha was known in his previous lifetimes as the "Bodhisattva," a being intent upon supreme enlightenment. Those disciples of the Buddha who, through mastery of his teachings or direct encounter with the Buddha, were considered to have achieved liberation, or nirvāṇa, were called *arhats* ("worthy ones" or "saints"). Such persons were thought to have put an end to further rebirth.

Not content with the goal of arhatship, Mahāyāna advocates resolved to follow the bodhisattva path, a heroic course demanding lifetimes of practice, as Śākyamuni himself had done. Some Mahāyāna apologists argued that the goal of nirvāṇa in earlier forms of Buddhism was premised on a selfish, philosophically misguided quest for purely personal liberation. The evidence from early Buddhist sources, however, shows that even before the development of the Mahāyāna critique, Buddhists entertained a wide range of interpretations of nirvāṇa that understood this achievement in broader, even communal terms.[7] Early Buddhists believed that the nirvāṇa of the historical Buddha was different from the death of ordinary human beings: having achieved insight into the nature of existence, Śākyamuni had been liberated from suffering and would not undergo further rebirth. That did not necessarily mean, however, that he was no longer accessible to followers; the postmortem availability of the Buddha is clearly presupposed by the veneration of Buddha relics. Early accounts of the Buddha's passing explain how Śākyamuni directed that his physical remains be treated after death: they were to be anointed, cremated, shared among all the kingdoms of the land, and enshrined in *stūpas* (reliquary mounds or structures). The underlying logic is consistent with the claim that the Buddha—or the principle of awakening—continued to be present in the Buddha's relics. Such tendencies in early Buddhism also suggest that nirvāṇa could entail an opening out to the broader Buddhist community rather than a turning inward toward a purely personal quest. As discussed under the heading "The Primordial Buddha," later in this chapter, a reinterpretation of the Buddha's nirvāṇa also lies at the heart of the *Lotus Sūtra*, and it is helpful to understand that such readings were not without precedent.

THE *LOTUS SŪTRA* AND MAHĀYĀNA MOVEMENTS

Contrary to the picture painted by *Lotus Sūtra* polemics, Mahāyāna Buddhism in India embraced many opinions about Buddhist ideals. Some groups, as we shall see, continued to endorse the arhat ideal as normative for the majority of practitioners. The *Lotus*, however, represents a later current within the Mahāyāna stream, according to which the bodhisattva rather than the arhat should be the sole model for religious practice. On the one hand, this concept of the bodhisattva was faithful to early Buddhism, which had used the word *bodhisattva* to refer to the previous incarnations of both Śākyamuni and the buddhas of prior ages while they were still practicing to achieve supreme enlightenment. On the other hand, the authors of some Mahāyāna texts, including the *Lotus Sūtra*, cast doubt on the path of the arhat and glorified the meaning of bodhisattvahood as a path that all should follow. Like some other sūtras, the *Lotus* divides preexisting Buddhist models of practice into two groups, or "vehicles," each defined by a separate ideal. One is the *śrāvaka* ("voice-hearer," "auditor," or "disciple"), one who aspires to the state of the arhat and to final nirvāṇa through hearing a buddha preach the dharma or otherwise receiving the Buddha's teachings. The other vehicle is the *pratyekabuddha* ("solitary buddha"), who achieves the same insight through his own efforts without the aid of a teacher.

Due to their own religious commitments or to an uncritical attitude toward Buddhist literature, some modern interpreters accept the claims of the *Lotus Sūtra* at face value and imagine that Mahāyāna in India was a unitary phenomenon. Specifically, where the *Lotus Sūtra* and certain other Mahāyāna scriptures portray arhats as misguided or inferior and proclaim that the bodhisattva path is intended for all, some readers tend to accept these claims unquestioningly, as if a polemical text objectively described different classes of practitioners. The *Lotus*, however, is a prescriptive and persuasive text rather than a dispassionate description of the world of its believers. Hence, recent scholarship has cast doubt on the claims that early Buddhism was founded on a narrow quest for personal liberation alone and that Mahāyāna Buddhism constituted an egalitarian path open to the broader lay community. This may have been how proponents of the *Lotus Sūtra* have viewed the world, but the key hermeneutical question is what the text was trying to accomplish by advancing its claims for the superiority of the bodhisattva path. Since the 1970s, Indian Mahāyāna has become one of the most exciting fields in the study of Buddhism, and the results of that new research have important implications for how one reads the *Lotus Sūtra*.[8]

One important trend in the study of Mahāyāna Buddhism has been to interpret early texts as attempts by authors in particular social settings to make rhetorical claims. Examined in this light, terms like "Mahāyāna" function more as powerful but largely indeterminate slogans than as widely accepted definitions. Mahāyāna authors meant different things in using the word *Mahāyāna* ("Great Vehicle"). The persuasive force of the term, however, covered up such disagreements and fostered the impression that Mahāyānists found common cause, if only in opposition to those whom they disparaged as followers of the Hīnayāna. Some recent work concludes that this vehemence, coupled with the lack of undisputed early evidence, means that in their Indian context Mahāyāna movements were marginal to mainstream Buddhism until at least the sixth century C.E; before then, proponents of the bodhisattva ideal were located geographically at the edges of Indian urban culture and subsisted as a tradition of forest monks who dissented from the majority of saṅghas in cities and towns. However, the rich scriptural literature beginning to be transmitted to China in the second century C.E. paints a different picture. While some Mahāyāna sūtras appear to have been composed by forest ascetics, others reflect a more urban environment.

Another important result of the close study of other Mahāyāna texts is a picture of multiple Mahāyānas. Consider, for example, the literature championing the perfection of wisdom (*prajñāpāramitā*), or nondual insight. Such texts advance a dialectical view of achieving transcendent wisdom. The bodhisattva practitioner is enjoined to view all the constituent elements of reality (*dharmas*) simultaneously as both empty (*śūnya*) of own-being or a permanent essence (*svabhāva*) and as provisionally existent, each dependent on and hence connected to other elements. Edward Conze writes of the entire prajñāpāramitā corpus, comprising early texts in verse, later sūtras such as the *Diamond* and the *Heart*, and still later elaborations: "The thousands of lines of the prajñāpāramitā can be summed up in the following two sentences. (1) One should become a bodhisattva (or buddha-to-be), i.e., one who is content with nothing less than all-knowledge attained through perfection of insight for the sake of all beings. (2) There is no such thing as a bodhisattva, or as all-knowledge, or as a 'being,' or as the perfection of insight, or as an attainment. To accept both these contradictory facts is to be perfect."[9]

The doctrine of the perfection of wisdom does seem to be taught in a dialectical manner here: the reader is encouraged to hold two seemingly contradictory positions at the same time, thus giving rise to a third position that either transcends or escapes the opposition between the two opposing tenets. Not all Mahāyāna sūtras, however, stress the perfection of wisdom. Attentive readers of the *Lotus Sūtra* will note that, although the text sometimes refers in formulaic terms to the six perfections and the perfection of wisdom, overt discussion of the doctrine of the emptiness of dharmas is minimal.[10] One could maintain that the doctrine of the perfection of wisdom is simply assumed in the *Lotus Sūtra*, but the fact remains that a focus on the positing of opposites and an interest in dialectical negation are not central to the mode of argumentation in the *Lotus*. The same could be said for other doctrines, such as nonduality and the joining of wisdom and compassion contained in other Mahāyāna texts: they are not ruled out nor are they thematized in the *Lotus Sūtra*.

Another new avenue of research draws attention to understandings of the path to liberation different from the position of the *Lotus Sūtra*. Recent work has focused on early Mahāyāna sūtras like *The Inquiry of Ugra*, *The Sūtra of the Samādhi of Direct Encounter with the Buddhas of the Present*, *The Inquiry of Rāṣṭrapāla*, and others.[11] The first of these texts, for example, asserts a number of positions at odds with the *Lotus Sūtra*. It does not disparage the career of the auditor (śrāvaka), who converts to the path toward nirvāṇa after hearing a buddha speak, nor does it use the term *Hīnayāna*. It does not depict the bodhisattva path as a possibility open to all people, and, although buddhas appear as supernatural, magnificent beings, they are not described as ever present, as the *Lotus Sūtra* speaks of Śākyamuni. The earliest version of *The Inquiry of Ugra* does not mention stūpas, nor does it prescribe devotion to the text itself. There are no references to pure lands as special fields purified and overseen by buddhas—a characteristic of some Mahāyāna sūtras—nor does the text mention the salvific actions of bodhisattvas or people worshipping bodhisattvas. Moreover, *The Inquiry of Ugra* insists that the bodhisattva path can be achieved best by becoming a monk: "For no bodhisattva who lives at home has ever attained supreme perfect enlightenment [*anuttarasamyaksaṃbodhi*]."[12] Some early ways of imagining the Mahāyāna, then, view it as a difficult career intended for a small elite who could devote themselves to the practice of renunciation in isolation from lay society.

Recent studies have also begun to investigate the origins of Mahāyāna sūtra literature and how it was legitimized as the Buddha's word, thus opening up new readings of the *Lotus Sūtra*. One approach has cast a systematically suspicious eye on the claim to orality in Mahāyāna literature.[13] Like most Buddhist sūtras, the *Lotus* begins with the words "Thus have I heard," thereby announcing that it is a text based on accurate oral transmission of words from the mouth of Śākyamuni, usually through his disciple Ānanda, to later generations. Yet, despite their conventional openings, Mahāyāna scriptures—like other Buddhist texts compiled well after the Buddha's lifetime—in effect advertise, rather than hide, their distance from the early teachings. Some scholars argue that Mahāyāna authors presumably knew that Ānanda, the unnamed and thus partially hidden narrator or reteller of all Buddhist sūtras, could not have heard directly from the historical Buddha the newly revealed dharma attributed in Mahāyāna texts to Śākyamuni. Nevertheless, Mahāyāna authors maintained the fiction that their sūtras faithfully transmitted the words preached by the Buddha, heard by Ānanda, and fixed into authoritative oral form in front of the entire Buddhist community after the historical Buddha died. To some extent the modern suspicion about claims about the origin of sūtras is not new, since how texts justify their authority has always been an important part of what has been called Buddhist hermeneutics, a systematic theory of how Buddhist texts should be interpreted.[14] By focusing on problems like textual authority and the literary devices by which sūtras assert their claims, research in this vein is developing new ways of understanding how Buddhist texts, the *Lotus* included, combine poetics, politics, and philosophy in complex literary creations.

Another body of scholarship focuses on possible connections between the origins of Mahāyāna sūtra literature and the complex visualizations undertaken by some Mahāyāna practitioners. In this form of meditation, one constructs according to set formulas a detailed mental image of a buddha, a bodhisattva, or a holy assembly. Mastery of such meditations was said to ensure future enlightenment or birth in a buddha's realm. Some scholars suggest that Mahāyāna sūtras depicting buddhas and their assemblies may have originated in adepts' meditative visions, in which they experienced themselves as being in a buddha's presence and hearing his teachings.[15] This approach shows how the *Lotus* and other Mahāyāna sūtras represent the Buddha's words as emerging from meditative practice. In this perspective, for their redactors, the Mahāyāna sūtras may indeed have been preaching heard directly from the Buddha.

CENTRAL CLAIMS OF THE *LOTUS SŪTRA*

As we have seen, the *Lotus Sūtra* was one of a number of scriptures that, although extolling the bodhisattva path and claiming to be "Mahāyāna," nonetheless differ from one another in significant ways. Let us consider some of the distinctive claims of the *Lotus Sūtra*.

The One Vehicle and Expedient Devices

As noted, many Indian Buddhist texts speak of their tradition as comprising "three vehicles" or modes of liberation from suffering. First is that of the śrāvaka, a disciple of the Buddha who, by hearing and practicing the Buddha's teachings, is able to eradicate craving and achieve the liberated state of the arhat; at life's end, such a person is said to enter final nirvāṇa. Śākyamuni's immediate disciples come within this category, and most Buddhist monastics of the later Indian tradition also appear to have understood themselves as following the śrāvaka path. Second is the vehicle of the pratyekabuddha, the "solitary buddha"—one who, without the aid of a teacher, intuits the principle that all things exist through causes and conditions and that nothing exists independently. Pratyekabuddhas are typically represented as practicing in reclusion and not teaching others. And third is the path of the bodhisattva, culminating in perfect buddhahood. Those who have, respectively, perfected these three paths—arhats, pratyekabuddhas, and buddhas—are said to share insight into the same truth, expressed in doctrinal terms as the law of conditioned origination or the four noble truths. Nevertheless, the three vehicles categorization clearly sets the buddha above the others. Unlike the arhat, the buddha gains awakening without the aid of a teacher, and unlike the pratyekabuddha, he teaches for the welfare of all.[16]

A chief characteristic of the Mahāyāna was its expansion of the bodhisattva path; no longer limited to the historical Buddha Śākyamuni or to the buddhas of the past and future in their quest for supreme enlightenment, the term *bodhisattva* was broadened to denote a path to which others might aspire as well. Embracing the bodhisattva path as a personal vocation brought Mahāyāna monks into conflict with the mainstream Buddhist tradition. How were they to account for the status of personal nirvāṇa, which the Buddha himself had set forth as the ultimate goal of practice? The great number of Mahāyāna sūtras deal with this problem in varying ways. For some, the personal nirvāṇa of the arhat remains a legitimate goal, just not one as worthy or exalted as the buddhahood to which bodhisattvas aspired. Other Mahāyāna sūtras are frankly hostile, in effect condemning the other two paths—so-called Hīnayāna—as spiritual dead ends.[17] The *Lotus Sūtra*, however, attempts to reconcile the earlier forms of Buddhism with the Mahāyāna by asserting that the threefold division of the Buddhist teaching into separate vehicles for śrāvakas, pratyekabuddhas, and bodhisattvas is simply the Buddha's "expedient device" or "skillful means" (Skt.: upāyakauśalya or upāya, Ch.: *fangbian,* Ja.: *hōben*); in reality, there is only "one buddha vehicle." That is, according to the *Lotus*, the Buddha taught these three separate vehicles as a pedagogical strategy, in accordance with his audience's varying capacities for understanding, but all three are designed to lead ultimately to the one buddha vehicle and thus spring from a unitary intent. Chapter 2 of the *Lotus* presents in general terms the concepts of the Buddha's teaching through skill in means and the ultimate resolution of the three disparate vehicles in the one vehicle. Subsequent chapters illustrate these two intertwined themes through the parables of the burning house (Chapter 3), the rich man and his poor son (Chapter 4), medicinal herbs (Chapter 5), the magically conjured city (Chapter 7), and the gem hidden in the robe (Chapter 8).

While the *Lotus Sūtra* repeatedly asserts the supremacy of the one vehicle as the Buddha's final intent, it never actually explains what the one vehicle is—a promised sermon that is never delivered, as one scholar has described it.[18] This has opened the way for radically divergent readings of the sūtra. Let us consider a few of the long-standing controversies surrounding the relationship between the one vehicle and expedient devices in the *Lotus Sūtra*'s history of interpretation.

One disputed question among Chinese commentators concerned whether the one vehicle or buddha vehicle is the same as, or different from, the bodhisattva vehicle. This question is sometimes known as the "three carts or four carts" debate. In Chapter 3 of the *Lotus Sūtra*, "Parable," as a device to lure his children out of a burning house where they are heedlessly at play, a father promises them three kinds of carts—drawn by sheep, goats, and oxen, respectively—that they have always desired. When he has succeeded in persuading them to exit to safety, he gives them equally not the three differing carts that he had promised but a magnificent white oxcart, far exceeding their expectations. Is this great white oxcart the same as, or different from, the oxcart that is one of the three originally promised? At stake in the reading of this allegory was the question, is the Mahāyāna the true, final teaching, and only the two other vehicles provisional, or is the Mahāyāna itself, like the two Hīnayāna vehicles, also ultimately an expedient device, leading to but transcended by a truth beyond expression?

One can in fact find passages in the sūtra that will support either reading.[19] Some scholars have reconciled the two perspectives by arguing that the discourse of three vehicles in the *Lotus Sūtra* operates on two levels. From a relative or conventional perspective, it makes unmistakable claims for the superiority of the Mahāyāna over the two lesser vehicles. For example, in Chapter 4, in the parable of the rich man and his poor son, in order to help his wayward son mature and gain confidence sufficient to assume his true station, the father assigns him the interim employment of sweeping up dung—a clear reference to the lower, provisional status of the two vehicles. From an absolute standpoint, however, all three vehicles, including the bodhisattva path, can be understood as skillful means leading to the one vehicle that transcends the three vehicles but has no independent existence apart from them. In other words, no doctrine or practice ("expedient device") can fully express what the Buddha has realized ("one vehicle"), because the one vehicle is ultimately beyond words or concepts—but for that very reason, it cannot be taught except through the skillful use of expedient devices. In this reading, the one vehicle is understood in terms of emptiness and the nonduality of ultimate and conventional truths: the one vehicle is not a separate path but the final intent underlying the three.[20]

The fact that the one vehicle is never explicitly defined has also raised the question of whether the *Lotus Sūtra* can be said to have any substantive philosophical content. This issue, too, has a long history, but here we will consider only some recent opinions. Some readers answer with an unqualified negative. For example: "The *Lotus Sūtra* is thus unique among texts. It is not merely subject to various interpretations, as all texts are, but is open or empty at its very center. It is a surrounding text, pure context, which invites not only interpretation of what is said but filling in of what is not said. It therefore lends itself more easily than do other scriptures to being shaped by users of the text."[21] For some commentators, this understanding of the sūtra as an empty text is reinforced by the self-referential character of the *Lotus*, which appears so often as an actor in its own script. For example, in Chapter 1, when the Buddha emits light from his forehead illuminating eighteen thousand worlds, the earth shakes and flowers fall from the sky, and Mañjuśrī Bodhisattva interprets these omens to mean that the Buddha will now preach the *Lotus Sūtra*, which all buddhas throughout time and space expound as their final teaching. In other words, the *Lotus Sūtra* describes the signs that foretell its own preaching. In Chapter 11, a magnificent jeweled stūpa containing a buddha called Many Jewels (Skt.: Prabhūtaratna) emerges from beneath the earth. This buddha has made a vow that, wherever it may be preached, he will come to bear witness to the truth of the *Lotus Sūtra*—the very sūtra in which he himself is now appearing. Thus, in the view of some readers, the point of the *Lotus Sūtra* is simply to glorify itself.

In contrast, scholars who approach the *Lotus Sūtra* as a literary text have tended to see the one vehicle's lack of explicit doctrinal content, along with the sūtra's self-referential character, as a distinctive literary technique that in fact performs or enacts the sūtra's meaning. Viewed in this light, the *Lotus Sūtra* dramatizes the message that, in light of the emptiness of all things, means and end cannot ultimately be divorced, and that buddhahood is inseparable from the practices undertaken to achieve it. From this perspective, Taigen Dan Leighton notes, "The *Lotus Sūtra* is not separate from, or talking *about*, a realm of transcendent spirit outside itself. . . . The self-referential or self-reflexive aspect of the sūtra demonstrates the non-separation of its liberative goals from the Buddha's skillful modes."[22] A similar argument has been made by William R. LaFleur in analyzing the sūtra's parables: "The narratives of the *Lotus* are not a means to an end beyond themselves. Their concrete mode of expression is not 'chaff' to be dispensed with in order to attain a more abstract, rational, or spiritual truth. The *Lotus* is unequivocal on this point: 'Seek as you will in all ten directions: / There is no other vehicle / Apart from the modes [upāyas] of the buddhas' [Hurvitz, 68–69]. This accounts for what seems to be an inordinate amount of praise directed by the sūtra toward itself. It also implies that within the sūtra there is an unmistakable philosophical move . . . to affirm the complete reality of the world of concrete phenomena in spite of the fact that they are impermanent."[23]

These literary readings assume that the one vehicle has no independent form of its own and that it cannot be separated from various modes, expressions, or expedient devices. This kind of interpretation is related to another controversy, also stemming from the fact that the one vehicle is never explicitly defined in the *Lotus Sūtra* text. That is, should the one vehicle be read inclusively or exclusively? From an inclusive standpoint, since the one vehicle is all encompassing, all practices and doctrinal formulations can be seen as expedient devices that, while different in themselves, nonetheless all lead ultimately to the same realization. From this perspective, any religious practice, properly understood, becomes the practice of the one vehicle. From an exclusive or hierarchical viewpoint, however, the one vehicle is equated with one specific teaching, which is thereby invested with absolute status, over and against all other teachings, which are then relegated to the lesser category of provisional. Inclusive readings of the *Lotus Sūtra* have proven attractive to those seeking to reconcile the great diversity of Buddhist teachings and practices. Others, however, have read the *Lotus*, in Carl Bielefeldt's words, "less as a call for a broad catholic acceptance of real religious pluralism than as a summons to a single higher vision that transcends and supersedes historical religious variety. . . . Here, then, in the guise of a universalistic teaching, lurks a logic for the exclusion of alternative forms of religion."[24]

Those favoring exclusive readings of the *Lotus Sūtra* have sometimes linked their interpretations to Buddhist theories of decline. The sūtra itself speaks repeatedly of "an evil age after the nirvāṇa of the Tathāgata," and several passages equate bodhisattva practice specifically with the job of spreading the *Lotus* in that inauspicious time, a task presented as immensely noble but fraught with danger and opposition. The three-stage model of decline in the transmission of Buddhism—through the ages of the True Dharma, Semblance Dharma, and Final Dharma—that developed in China was unknown to the *Lotus Sūtra*'s redactors.[25] Nonetheless, in East Asia, references in the *Lotus Sūtra* to an evil age were assimilated to the age of the "Final Dharma" or "End of the Dharma" (Ch.: *mofa*, Ja.: *mappō*), the era said to begin long after the Buddha's passing when human receptivity to his teaching deteriorates and liberation becomes harder to achieve. Bielefeldt has suggested that readings of the one vehicle as a call to a higher truth going beyond all earlier expressions may have inspired famous claims by some Buddhist teachers of Japan's Kamakura period (1185–1333), to the effect that there is one single practice uniquely suited to this troubled time period.[26] A salient example is Nichiren (1222–1282), who taught a message of devotion to the *Lotus Sūtra* alone. Nichiren's contemporaries maintained that the *Lotus Sūtra* is like a great ocean that gathers all rivers: once one understands that all the varied forms of Buddhist practice are like the rivers absorbed by the great sea of the *Lotus*, then it is perfectly acceptable to uphold various sūtras or engage in practices based upon them in accordance with one's inclination. In his counterargument, Nichiren reversed the interpretation of the metaphor of rivers and ocean. He pointed out that, once rivers flow into the sea, they assume the same salty flavor and lose their original names; similarly, once other practices merge into the ocean of the *Lotus Sūtra*, they no longer possess independent status and there is no meaning in upholding them.[27] In this particular dispute, both sides agreed that the *Lotus Sūtra* encompasses all truth and leads all beings to buddhahood. But where one side saw the one-vehicle teaching as legitimating a range of practices, the other thought that it mandates devotion to the *Lotus Sūtra* alone.

The controversy over whether to understand the one-vehicle teaching of the *Lotus Sūtra* in an inclusive or exclusive mode continues to this day, not only in *Lotus* practice communities but also among scholars and persons of religion eager to promote interfaith harmony. Could the one vehicle of the *Lotus* provide a key to resolving the problems of religious conflict that continue to divide humanity? Some have argued that the concept of expedient devices might apply not only to diverse forms of Buddhism but also to religious pluralism more broadly. In this view, a perspective that regards all teachings as each expressing some aspect of the same, ultimately inexpressible truth might work to reconcile the disparate messages of different religious traditions. Over and against this position, however, others have maintained that, far from mandating tolerance, the teaching of the one vehicle represents a strategy for conversion to a single path—a strategy that, in the name of oneness and cooperation, subsumes all other paths within its own frame of reference without critically engaging them.[28]

Universal Buddhahood

A corollary to the *Lotus Sūtra*'s claim that there is only one buddha vehicle is its assertion that buddhahood is the final goal of all. In the sūtra's words, "Of any who hear the dharma, / None shall fail to achieve buddhahood" (Hurvitz, 38). This point is illustrated by predictions of future buddhahood bestowed upon the Buddha's śrāvaka disciples as they come one by one to understand that the goal of personal nirvāṇa they had embraced was a skillful expedient and not a final destination. Chapter 12, "Devadatta," was widely interpreted as extending the promise of buddhahood to persons seen as having particular obstacles to liberation.[29] Although the chapter touches only on a past lifetime of Devadatta and makes no reference to his present identity as the Buddha's jealous cousin, Devadatta would have been well known to the sūtra's early devotees as the Buddhist archetype of an evildoer. Devadatta is said to have incited his friend, Prince Ajātaśatru, to kill his father, King Bimbisara, who was the Buddha's patron, and usurp the throne. Devadatta also fomented dissension within the saṅgha and even attempted to kill the Buddha. In the context of the *Lotus Sūtra*, with its teaching of the one vehicle and promise of buddhahood for everyone, this chapter became widely understood as illustrating the potential for enlightenment even in evil persons. The same chapter also describes the instantaneous realization of buddhahood by the daughter of the nāga, or dragon, king Sāgara, by virtue of the power of the *Lotus Sūtra*. Some commentators, notably Saichō (766 or 767–822), who established the Japanese Tendai school, focused on the immediate nature of her attainment and used it to argue that buddhahood did not necessarily require three incalculable *kalpas* (eons) of practice to achieve, as was commonly thought. In Saichō's view, the *Lotus Sūtra* offered a "direct path" (Ja.: *jikidō*) to awakening, and by its power, some individuals might "realize buddhahood with this very body" (*sokushin jōbutsu*).[30] The dragon girl's story has also been understood as guaranteeing the buddhahood of women. In keeping with traditional male/female hierarchy and the view that buddhahood must be achieved in a male body, the *Lotus* narrates how the dragon princess changes into a male in the moment before her enlightenment, a transformation whose significance is discussed in Jan Nattier's chapter in this volume. Modern readers seeking support in the Mahāyāna for a position of gender equality find this element in the story troubling. Traditional Buddhists, however, have not generally understood "equality" in the same way we do today. In addition, not all the *Lotus Sūtra*'s exegetes and devotees have necessarily read the text to mean that women must become men in order to achieve buddhahood.[31]

The *Lotus Sūtra*'s promise of universal buddhahood has also been extended to the natural world. The Noh drama and other forms of medieval Japanese literature interpreted Chapter 5, "Medicinal Herbs," as teaching the potential for buddhahood in grasses and trees (*sōmoku jōbutsu*), an issue mentioned in Jacqueline I. Stone's chapter in this volume. According to this doctrine, not only sentient beings but also inhabitants of the vegetable world can achieve full enlightenment. This is not in fact the purport of the parable of medicinal herbs, which rather illustrates that, just as a single rain nurtures various trees and plants, the Buddha's single dharma benefits all in accordance with their differing capacities. Nonetheless, in Japan the message of universal buddhahood—extended to nonsentient existence—was read into this chapter.

Nowhere does the *Lotus Sūtra* contain the words "buddha nature," an abstract technical term for the innate potential for enlightenment that appeared in somewhat later Mahāyāna literature, perhaps most famously in the statement of the *Sūtra on the Buddha's Final Nirvāṇa* (*Mahāparinirvāṇa sūtra*) that "all sentient beings have the buddha nature."[32] Buddha nature also formed an important category in the doctrinal developments of later Chinese schools. Because this term does not appear in the *Lotus Sūtra*, early Chinese Buddhist exegetes tended to rank the *Lotus* below the *Sūtra on the Buddha's Final Nirvāṇa* in their systematizing of the Buddhist scriptures. By the sixth century, however, commentators from a number of schools sought to establish that the *Lotus Sūtra* does in fact teach the principle of universal buddha nature. One of their arguments invoked the example of Bodhisattva Never Disparaging, who appears in Chapter 20 of the *Lotus Sūtra* and who carried out the practice of bowing to everyone he met, treating them as future buddhas. It is precisely because all beings have the potential for buddhahood, exegetes argued, that the bodhisattva revered people in this way.[33] Once this reading was offered, the *Lotus Sūtra* came to be widely understood as teaching the universality of the buddha nature.

The Primordial Buddha

Following the sūtra's declaration of the one buddha vehicle and Śākyamuni's subsequent predictions of future buddhahood for all his leading disciples, Chapters 11 through 22 of the *Lotus Sūtra* represent the so-called assembly in open space. In Chapter 11, the jeweled stūpa of Many Jewels Buddha emerges from beneath the earth and rises into the air; Many Jewels bears witness to the truth of the *Lotus Sūtra;* and Śākyamuni Buddha accepts Many Jewels's offer of a seat beside him in the stūpa, using his transcendent powers to lift the entire assembly into the air, on a level with the two buddhas. At this point, we recognize that Śākyamuni Buddha is now being presented as something more than a historical figure, however spiritually advanced. Before he opens the jeweled stūpa, Śākyamuni first "recalls his emanations," and the buddhas who then gather from throughout the ten directions are shown to be his manifestations, so many that he must magically conjure two hundred myriads of millions of *nayutas* (one hundred billions) of realms in each of the eight directions to make room for them. This episode in the *Lotus* stands in radical contrast to earlier Indian notions of buddhas, in which only one buddha appears in a given world sphere at a time. Śākyamuni, it suggests, is the source of countless buddhas.

Chapter 15 marks a further challenge to conventional understandings of the Buddha: vast throngs of bodhisattvas, incalculably numerous and noble in appearance, spring forth from beneath the earth, and Śākyamuni claims that they are his direct disciples, whom he has taught and converted ever since he himself achieved buddhahood. Bodhisattva Maitreya protests that only forty-some years have passed since Śākyamuni left his father's palace and reached awakening under the bodhi tree: since then, he has not had sufficient time to have instructed such a large group of fully realized bodhisattvas. Maitreya's question forces a redefining of Śākyamuni's buddhahood, which occurs in the next, sixteenth, chapter, considered by some exegetes to be the very heart of the *Lotus Sūtra*. Here Śākyamuni reveals that he first achieved enlightenment not under the bodhi tree in this lifetime, as people think, but billions of kalpas ago, in the inconceivably remote past—so long ago that the intervening time can be estimated only by reducing countless world systems to dust and allowing each particle to stand for one kalpa. The "life span" referred to in the chapter's title, "Life Span of the Thus Come One," means the "life" of Śākyamuni as the Buddha, beginning from his original attainment of the way. Ever since that inconceivably remote time, he says, he has been here in this world and also in others, preaching the dharma and converting living beings. Thus his birth, renunciation, practice, awakening, and entry into nirvāṇa are all revealed to be the expedient devices by which he constantly teaches and liberates others. In other words, the doctrine of skillful means expounded earlier in the sūtra as the Buddha's method of teaching is here transposed to the very events of his own biography. The revelation of Śākyamuni Buddha's original attainment in the far distant past in effect redefines him in Mahāyāna terms: no longer is he a buddha departed into nirvāṇa without remainder, but a fully realized bodhisattva, constantly active in the world for the sake of sentient beings.

Contemporary secondary literature sometimes uses the term "eternal buddha" to describe the concept of Śākyamuni's buddhahood put forth in Chapter 16. Although the term is easy to understand, it tends to flatten out a long and complex history of interpretation. Chinese exegetes disagreed over whether this buddha's life span was finite or infinite, or whether he was a buddha in the sense of the dharma body (*dharmakāya*), the universal ground of reality imagined as a "body"; the "reward body" (*sambhogakāya*), or resplendent subtle body, achieved through lifetimes of cultivation and visible to those of advanced faculties; or the "manifest body" (*nirmāṇakāya*), the flesh and blood person who appears in the world in order to teach sentient beings. In a dynamic synthesis, Zhiyi, whom later generations regarded as the founder of the Tiantai school, interpreted the original buddha of the *Lotus Sūtra* as embodying all three bodies in one. According to Zhiyi, the dharma body is the truth that is realized; the reward body is the wisdom that realizes it; and the manifest body, a compassionate expression of that wisdom as the human buddha who lived and taught in this world.[34] Interpretations of the primordial buddha of the *Lotus Sūtra* underwent further development in Japan, especially in the Tendai and Nichiren traditions.

TRANSLATIONS OF THE *LOTUS SŪTRA*

To understand Kumārajīva's early fifth-century Chinese version of the *Lotus Sūtra* and its place in Buddhist history, it is necessary to appreciate something of the history and broader problems involved in translating Indian Buddhist literature into Chinese and other languages. In the first place, translation from Sanskrit into Tibetan and Mongolian, and from Indic languages into Chinese and later Uighur and Tangut, was a function of the geographical spread of Buddhism out of the Indian homeland. Following the Buddha's directions that the dharma should be comprehensible in the local language, followers of the Mahāyāna created and transmitted new texts. The emergence of the Mahāyāna, a large set of disparate reform movements, coincided roughly with the expansion of interchange along the ancient Silk Road. The distances involved were great, and the terrain difficult. Moving largely from west to east, Buddhist art, Buddhist texts, and Buddhist devotion were subject to the same process of intercultural exchange as were material goods. The *Lotus Sūtra* joined the eastward flow of Buddhist ideas after emerging from India.

In trying to imagine how scriptures could be transported and translated over such vast stretches in the premodern world, the commonsense notion of a nation or country can be as misleading as it is helpful. Although "India" and "China" conveniently name the two poles between which the *Lotus Sūtra* was at first transmitted, one should also keep in mind that the realities designated by these binary terms were not the same then as they are now. The Indian subcontinent in the first centuries C.E. was ruled at any one time by a patchwork of small empires, and Buddhist saṅghas and large centers of learning depended on the patronage not of national rulers but of the kings of these small city-states and empires. In place of stereotypes like "Indian," "Chinese," and "Tibetan," more accurate units of analysis for this time period would be Kushan, Vākāṭakan, Gupta, Pallava, and so on. Similarly, China over the centuries was a relatively small, often fragmented empire, with non-Han groups from the north frequently occupying the Chinese imperial throne.

The labels "Indian" and "Chinese" can also be misleading from a linguistic point of view if one misconstrues the process of translation as moving simply from an Indian source text (such as the *Lotus Sūtra* in a Prakrit or Sanskrit form) to a classical Chinese target. Translations of the *Lotus* and other sūtras into Chinese were made not by one person who knew Sanskrit and Chinese thoroughly but rather by a committee in which no single individual had a thorough grasp of both source and target languages. (One of the few persons in premodern times who was effectively bilingual, the pilgrim-translator Xuanzang [596–664], never translated the *Lotus Sūtra*.) Given this method of translation, it is natural that in the process some errors and differences in emphasis crept in.

The translation of the *Lotus* in the year 286 by Dharmarakṣa (Chinese name: Zhu Fahu [ca. 265–313, or 239–316]), a Buddhist monk of Yuezhi ancestry who grew up in the western border town of Dunhuang, is a fitting example of the dynamics of translation. The earliest descriptions of Dharmarakṣa's method explain how he worked with his collaborators to produce a translation over a three-week period in the year 286. Dharmarakṣa held the original text in his hands and gave an oral translation. Three Chinese laymen wrote down his words, turning his vernacular speech into the literary medium of classical Chinese. Then an Indian monk and a Kuchean layman collated the different versions of the text, and after that the text was reedited by others.[35]

The process of group translation is important to analyze, since it has profound implications for the later interpretation of the *Lotus Sūtra* in the history of Buddhism, as well as for our interpretation, in turn, of those interpretations. The mechanism of rendering a foreign text into written Chinese made no provision for ensuring a word-to-word correspondence between the original text and the final product. Sanskrit and literary Chinese are notoriously dissimilar languages. The grammar, syntax, word formation, inflection and gendering of nouns, declension and tense of verbs, and use of articles all differ radically between the two languages, as do their writing systems: Sanskrit employs a syllabary, while Chinese is written in ideographs. But even if those involved in the translation had wanted to ensure that every important semantic unit of the original was reflected faithfully in the translation, they would have had a hard time doing so. No individual commanded a view of the whole process, and the chief translator was not fully literate in the two languages of source and target. It is true that over his thirty-five-plus years of working in central

China, Dharmarakṣa's spoken Chinese improved, which can be discerned in the texts he translated later in his life.[36] But even then, the language he commanded was the spoken language, which was, in effect, a different language from the literary Chinese in which the final text was written. Dharmarakṣa, like most foreign translators of Chinese Buddhist texts, did not devote the decades of study to literary Chinese that would have been required to judge accurately the Chinese texts to which his name was attached. A reasonable analogy would be to say that by the end of his life he had never studied Latin but was fluent in Italian, which provided him only fleeting, partial glimpses into the polished and allusive Latin language in which the texts were written. Thus, much of the enterprise on the receiving end of the process—the work of Dharmarakṣa's Chinese secretaries, collators, and polishers—was conducted without the oversight of a bilingual specialist who comprehended thoroughly the language in which they were writing.

Rendering the general rather than the word-by-word meaning and polishing the resulting literary creation were translation strategies also adopted by the most important translator of the *Lotus*, Kumārajīva.[37] Born in the city-state of Kucha along the Silk Road, as the bicultural offspring of a local Kuchean princess and a father from India, Kumārajīva entered the saṅgha at a young age and spent his youth in Kashmir (northern India and Pakistan). There he studied scores of Buddhist and non-Buddhist texts written in Sanskrit, following the standard practice of learning through recitation. He was especially adept in various Mahāyāna traditions, and when he finally moved to the Chinese capital (under pressure from the Chinese emperor) in 401, he immediately set to work translating philosophical treatises and sūtras. Installed in a villa by his imperial patron, Kumārajīva pursued his mission of translation, with hundreds of monks in attendance, employing the same kind of committee structure as in earlier translation efforts. Kumārajīva often read aloud from a Sanskrit text he held in his hands before offering a translation into vernacular Chinese. That spoken translation was then written down, reworked into a semiliterary, semivernacular form, and polished. Kumārajīva directed his team to compare the words of their draft translation to the efforts of earlier translators who had attempted the same text, but he believed that exactitude in translation was best achieved by accurately reflecting the central meaning of the phrase in question.

Kumārajīva's philosophy of translation resulted in a rendering of the *Lotus Sūtra* quite different from versions produced earlier. (It is also true, however, that the source text he possessed was different from that used earlier by Dharmarakṣa.) One of Kumārajīva's closest collaborators was a Chinese monk from the Hebei area, Sengrui (355–439). One of Sengrui's famous interventions is recounted in later sources: "Sengrui took part by reviewing and correcting the sūtras translated by Kumārajīva. In *The Lotus of the True Law* translated by Dharmarakṣa, the chapter 'Receipt of Prophecy [by the Five Hundred Disciples]' says that gods see humans and humans see gods. When Kumārajīva was translating the sūtra and reached here, he said, 'This wording [by Dharmarakṣa] has the same meaning as the Sanskrit text, but the words exceed the substance.' Sengrui responded, 'Why not render it, "Humans and gods will interact, and the two will gain sight of each other"?' Kumārajīva was delighted and said, 'That captures it fully.' "[38]

The story is important because it shows how different Chinese versions were produced. The passage in question is from Chapter 8 of the *Lotus Sūtra*. It praises the wondrous sights in a pure land that will be graced by the Buddha's disciple Pūrṇa after Pūrṇa achieves supreme, perfect enlightenment. As a buddha named Dharma Glow (Dharmaprabhāsa), he will transform his surroundings into a buddha realm lacking the lower three destinies. Dharmarakṣa's description of the way that humans and gods will interact in that realm takes up a full nineteen words in the original Chinese, which can be rendered literally as, "Those in heaven will see the human world, and those in the human world will gain sight of the heavens. Beings in heaven and beings in the human world will come and go and have interactions."[39] Our source suggests that upon reaching this passage in the original and thinking about how to render it into Chinese, Kumārajīva was particularly bothered by the prolixity of his predecessor's translation. The meaning of the earlier Chinese version was adequate to the original, in Kumārajīva's opinion, but the words were excessive. After Kumārajīva passed judgment on the meaning, his Chinese collaborator suggested a new, more economical and elegant way to express the original, using only eight Chinese words (rendered in English literally as, "Humans and gods will interact, and the two will gain sight of each other").

Dharmarakṣa and Kumārajīva carried out their work separated in time by about 120 years, and the originals they translated were almost certainly different from each other, but they also adopted quite different philosophies of translation. Kumārajīva believed in capturing the general meaning of the original and expressing the Chinese in a fluid and compact style, and he relied heavily on the literary sensibilities of his Chinese disciples in arriving at a finished translation. Nonetheless, both translators ended up producing texts that were similar in that they combined features of both the spoken and the literary languages. For example, both have frequent occurrences of two-syllable words (binomes), which characterizes spoken Chinese, in contrast to literary Chinese, which is largely monosyllabic. The translators also made use of demonstrative pronouns (this, that, and so forth) and the copula, or verb corresponding to English "is," again, features more characteristic of vernacular than literary Chinese.

In addition to Dharmarakṣa's and Kumārajīva's versions, one other complete Chinese translation of the *Lotus Sūtra* survives. Entitled *The Scripture of the Lotus Blossom of the Fine Dharma with Added Sections*, it was translated by Jñānagupta (Zhenajueduo [523–600]), a monk from Gandhāra (modern Pakistan), and Dharmagupta (Damojiduo [d. 619]), from central India, and completed in 601 or 602. These two translators were worried about the discrepancies among the translations of the *Lotus Sūtra* that existed in their day. They compared the Chinese versions and also consulted various Sanskrit manuscripts held in sūtra repositories in the capital. The resulting text largely reproduces Kumārajīva's version, adding some material not present in his original.

Modern readers would be mistaken if they were to assume that the three surviving Chinese translations of the *Lotus Sūtra* were the only versions circulating in premodern times. In the first place, other translators or editors in China claimed to have produced other versions of the *Lotus Sūtra*. Precisely how many distinct editions existed is hard to tell. Several texts translated into Chinese in the past do not survive. Furthermore, although Chinese authors wrote prefaces and epilogues to their translations discussing such issues, and Chinese Buddhist monks compiled catalogs detailing the contents of monastery libraries, they often disagreed over what criteria to use in judging scripture. Huixiang (ca. 639–706), a devotee of the *Lotus Sūtra* from Shanxi, compiled *Accounts of the Propagation of the Lotus Sūtra* in the middle of the seventh century. The second chapter of the book is devoted to translators of the *Lotus*. Out of fourteen different translations (of the whole text or of portions), he judges ten to be authentic and four to be spurious. Defining textual authenticity in narrower terms than did Huixiang, a monk cataloger writing in 730, Zhisheng (ca. 669–740), credited only six translations as reliable, only three of which survived in his day and could be properly entered into the official canon of Buddhist texts that he created.[40]

The *Lotus Sūtra* was also translated into several Asian languages other than literary Chinese. An Indian-Tibetan team rendered the Sanskrit version into Tibetan in the early ninth century. That translation was the source for a later rendering into Mongolian in the seventeenth century, which in turn was the basis for a translation into Manchu. Kumārajīva's Chinese translation became the basis for other translations throughout East Asia. The text was taken to Japan by pilgrims as early as the sixth or seventh century. Schooled in literary Chinese, many educated Japanese read the *Lotus Sūtra* in Chinese and wrote about it using the form of literary Chinese developed in Japan (*kanbun*); the text often was (and still is) recited in Sino-Japanese pronunciation, using the Chinese word order. At the same time, over the centuries, versions of the *Lotus Sūtra* have been produced wholly or partly in Japanese script. These renderings are of various kinds. Some reproduce the sūtra's Sino-Japanese pronunciation using the Japanese phonetic syllabary (*kana*) as an aid to pronunciation for those unfamiliar with Chinese characters. Others translate the text into Japanese syntax or provide Japanese glosses in order to convey the meaning of the text.[41] The Chinese *Lotus Sūtra* was also translated into Uighur (Old Turkish) around the tenth century, perhaps through an intermediary translation into Sogdian.[42] The *Lotus Sūtra* was also part of the Buddhist canon translated from Chinese into Tangut under the Western Xia dynasty (1038–1227). More recently the text has been rendered into colloquial Chinese, Vietnamese, and Korean. The *Lotus Sūtra* was also the first Mahāyāna text translated in its entirety into a Western language, in Eugène Burnouf's 1852 French translation, based on twelfth-century Sanskrit manuscripts discovered in Nepal. (Translations of the *Lotus Sūtra* into European languages are listed in the appendix.)

If the *Lotus Sūtra* existed in such a plethora of versions and in so many different languages, why does so much of Buddhist scholarship, religious and secular, adhere so closely to Kumārajīva's Chinese translation? First, independently of this particular sūtra, the language that Kumārajīva and his translation team adopted for rendering Buddhist texts soon became the new "church language" of medieval Chinese Buddhism. Kumārajīva and his associates translated a total of seventy-four works, numbering 384 scrolls. His translation work, including his version of the *Lotus Sūtra*, accorded best with the literary preferences of later centuries. Second, some centuries after Kumārajīva, schools of thought and religious sects centering on his version of the *Lotus Sūtra* grew up in China, Korea, and Japan. These traditions (introduced in the next section of this chapter) drew on the text of the *Lotus*, offered their own interpretations, and made the text a central part of their own programs of thought and practice. Third, we must consider the influence of modern Japanese religions devoted to the *Lotus Sūtra*, which also take Kumārajīva's version as standard. This influence is surely felt in the scholarly world as well as in the realm of Japanese

Buddhism. The only Chinese version of the *Lotus* translated into English is Kumārajīva's; to date it has been translated into English in its entirety at least seven times. In contrast to the perennial appeal of Kumārajīva's Chinese translation, other versions of the *Lotus* remain understudied. The only English translation of the full Sanskrit text, by Hendrik Kern, is already more than one hundred years old, and important new discoveries of early Sanskrit fragments from central Asia and elsewhere have yet to be collated in a complete critical edition.

This is not to say, however, that modern scholarly studies of the *Lotus Sūtra* are limited entirely by sectarian traditions. As the chapters in this book demonstrate, the *Lotus Sūtra* is best understood within its various historical contexts and from a variety of disciplinary perspectives. New interpretations of the *Lotus Sūtra* are produced in each generation—or, as some scholars would argue, in each individual reading of the text. Avenues that seem particularly promising for the study of Kumārajīva's version have to do with the close analysis of the language of the text. Modern scholars often analyze the Chinese (or earlier Sanskrit) text into different layers. They also compare the Sanskrit, Middle Indic, and Chinese manuscript versions of the text, using phonology to reconstruct the language of the original source texts. And recent attention to the prevalence of colloquial Chinese in Kumārajīva's translation may lead to a significantly different English translation.[43]

MOVEMENTS DEDICATED TO THE *LOTUS SŪTRA*

The influence of the *Lotus Sūtra* on the religious culture of East Asia can be broadly understood as moving simultaneously in two directions. On the one hand, *Lotus*-specific efforts aimed at promoting the sūtra. Such endeavors include writings about the *Lotus Sūtra*, such as commentaries interpreting its teachings and tales illustrating its powers and benefits, as well as sectarian movements centered on the *Lotus Sūtra*. Many of the so-called schools or sects (Ch.: *zong*, Ja.: *shū*) in Chinese Buddhism were created only after the time of their alleged founder or first patriarch, and in both China and Japan the nature and strength of sectarian identity often varied considerably. In some cases, being a follower of one school as opposed to another simply meant that monks concentrated their study on one textual tradition rather than another. In other cases, however, the lines of sectarian distinction were drawn more exclusively and schools competed for economic and political support, establishing separate monastic institutions. Regardless of whether the lines of sectarian affiliation were defined more or less clearly, *Lotus*-centered schools influenced the position of the *Lotus Sūtra* in its surrounding culture. But, as later sections of this chapter show, even as specific movements of practice and interpretation gave rise to *Lotus* groups, at the same time, symbolism, ideas, holy beings, and practices drawn from the text but not tied to any particular movement were appropriated in different contexts and became diffused into the broader East Asian cultural milieu.

Lotus Sūtra *Commentaries*

Buddhist scriptural commentary as practiced in China owed much to a long tradition of commentary on Confucian and Daoist classics already well established at the time of Buddhism's entry into China. Chinese commentaries on Buddhist sūtras were produced in especially great numbers from the fifth through tenth centuries, perhaps even surpassing the number of Confucian commentaries dating from this period.[44] It was within this Chinese interpretive context—and not in India, where it was compiled—that the *Lotus Sūtra* first drew sustained scholarly attention.[45] The Chinese Tiantai school of Buddhism (named after Mount Tiantai, where its putative founder, Zhiyi, lived) accords the *Lotus Sūtra* a central place. But even after Tiantai became well established, Chinese Buddhist teachers from a range of schools authored commentaries on the *Lotus*, which became central to debates over key doctrinal issues.[46] In Korean Buddhist scholarly circles, where, despite considerable Tiantai influence, ideas from other schools of Buddhism eventually predominated, *Lotus*-related doctrinal discussion figured less prominently. But in Japan, a number of *Lotus* commentaries were produced. The earliest surviving example is traditionally attributed to Prince Shōtoku (574–622), though it may have been composed in Korea or China; another early *Lotus* commentary was written by Saichō, the founder of the Japanese Tendai school (which follows the name of the Chinese Tiantai school). Even down to the present, commentaries still constitute an important medium for the sūtra's modern interpreters.[47]

Mention of sūtra commentary might initially suggest a rather dry exercise in which an author merely explains or elaborates on the meaning of a source text. In Buddhism, however, as in other religions, commentaries represent a major vehicle by which—in the form of explicating a canonical scripture—thinkers disseminated their original insights. From around the eighth century, especially famous commentaries became the focus of still further annotation and interpretation, and these subcommentaries, too, served to express the compilers' own ideas while invoking the authority of an established text. In the case of the *Lotus Sūtra*, some commentaries, such as those of Zhiyi and their subcommentaries by the later Tiantai patriarch Zhanran (711–782), became so authoritative that later generations found it almost impossible to discuss the *Lotus* apart from the categories and frames of reference that these two figures had established.

The oldest surviving Chinese commentary on the *Lotus Sūtra* was composed by Daosheng (ca. 355–434), a student of the sūtra's renowned translator Kumārajīva and famous in his own right for espousing the doctrine of sudden enlightenment and for his claim that even the *icchantika*—a person utterly without a store of merit—possesses the buddha nature and can achieve buddhahood.[48] Zhiyi, whose *Lotus* commentaries were later claimed as the doctrinal foundation for the Tiantai school, used earlier *Lotus* commentaries as a foil against which to develop his own readings.[49] Zhiyi is credited with two *Lotus Sūtra* commentaries: *Profound Meanings of the Lotus Sūtra* (*Fahua xuanyi*), an elucidation of the sūtra in terms of its major principles, and *Words and Phrases of the Lotus Sūtra* (*Fahua wenju*), a commentary on specific passages. These commentaries were not written personally by Zhiyi but are said to have been compiled by his disciple Guanding (561–632) from the latter's notes on Zhiyi's *Lotus Sūtra* lectures.[50] Other significant *Lotus Sūtra* commentaries were compiled from interpretive standpoints different from that of Zhiyi.[51]

Chinese sūtra commentaries often employed a technique known as "analytic division" (*fenke*) or parsing that purported to uncover categories of meaning implicit within a particular sūtra and thus to reveal the Buddha's intent.[52] Among the best known examples of such analysis is Zhiyi's division of the *Lotus Sūtra* into two sections. According to Zhiyi, the first fourteen chapters represent the "trace teaching" (Ch.: *jimen*, Ja.: *shakumon*), which presents Śākyamuni Buddha as a "trace" or manifestation, that is, the historical figure who lived and taught in this world, while the second fourteen chapters constitute the "origin teaching" (Ch.: *benmen*, Ja.: *honmon*), which presents Śākyamuni as the primordial buddha, awakened since the inconceivably remote past. The intent of the trace section, Zhiyi says, lies in opening the three vehicles to reveal the one vehicle, while the intent of the origin section is to reveal the Buddha's original awakening in the distant past. Zhiyi then proceeds to elucidate ten points of subtlety belonging to the trace teaching and another ten that distinguish the origin teaching, an example that may convey some small idea of the complex interpretive structures that conceptual parsing could produce.[53] This mode of analysis afforded exegetes great scope to develop their own innovations even while retaining the legitimizing format of commentary on an authoritative text. It also enabled them to move beyond elucidation of a single scripture and to produce elaborate schemas of the entire Buddhist system of doctrine and soteriology, a major development in medieval Chinese Buddhist thought.

The Emergence of Comprehensive Schemas

Buddhist texts were introduced to China in a more or less random, unsystematized fashion. As translation and study proceeded, it became obvious that not only the teachings but even the goals set forth in various Buddhist scriptures were sometimes at variance, or even contradictory. Yet for Chinese Buddhist exegetes of premodern times, all sūtras represented the Buddha's preaching. One of the interpreters' overriding concerns, informing the production of sūtra commentaries, was to develop some comprehensive order or principle that would harmonize the differing, often inconsistent ideas in the vast number of Buddhist texts. Such attempts led to the formation of rival schemes of "doctrinal classification" (*panjiao*; literally, "dividing the teaching"), attempts to systematize the entirety of the Buddhist teachings in a way that would make clear the underlying unity of diverse teachings and the place of individual sūtras within that unity. Two concepts proved crucial to these attempts: that the Buddha's teaching progresses from shallow to profound, or from "provisional" to "true," and that he leads different individuals by various means in accordance with their capacities. The *Lotus Sūtra*'s claim that the three vehicles all lead toward the one buddha vehicle played a foundational role in these huge classificatory projects.[54]

Early systems of doctrinal classification tended to adopt some version of a presumed chronological sequence for the Buddha's teachings, in increasing order of profundity. Exegetes disagreed as to whether the *Flower Garland* (*Avataṃsaka*) *Sūtra*, *Nirvāṇa Sūtra*, or *Lotus Sūtra* represented the highest teaching. Later thinkers, however, such as Zhiyi and Jizang (549–623), rejected the attempt to establish a fixed hierarchy among Mahāyāna sūtras, arguing that each text played an indispensable role in the Buddha's soteriological project of guiding beings of varying capacities to supreme enlightenment. Zhiyi's and Jizang's schemas focused less on the putative sequence in which particular teachings had been expounded than on the relationship between doctrines and their expression of the Buddha's underlying intent. Here in particular the *Lotus Sūtra*'s one-vehicle doctrine proved crucial. According to Zhiyi, sūtras other than the *Lotus* provided different messages to different audiences, depending on their particular mind-sets. The *Lotus Sūtra*, by contrast, is uniquely comprehensive, in that it draws together these various approaches to the dharma in light of the Buddha's underlying intent.[55]

Modern scholarship now accepts that even the early Buddhist canon was compiled over time, and that the Mahāyāna sūtras in particular were produced by many individuals active in widely separated parts of India and perhaps central Asia. Thus, doctrinal classification schemes that purport to organize the canon into a chronological sequence of the Buddha's preaching are not tenable from a historical perspective. Nonetheless, as attempts to systematize the whole of Buddhism and to articulate the interrelationship of individual doctrines and their place within an overall soteriological scheme, the Chinese systems of doctrinal classification stand as a monumental scholarly achievement. Central to this enterprise was the one-vehicle doctrine of the *Lotus* and its premise that the great diversity among the teachings represents an expedient device, ultimately reconciling all in a unitary salvific intent. These conceptualizations also hold historical value for the modern reader, since they demonstrate how the *Lotus* and other sūtras were interpreted in the past.

Miracle Tales

Another group of writings helping to disseminate faith in the *Lotus Sūtra* consisted of didactic tales illustrating the sūtra's powers and virtues. Tales of the *Lotus Sūtra* formed a subset of a larger genre of so-called Buddhist miracle tales. Although scholars often use this term, it represents something of a misnomer. "Miracle" in English implies a divine intervention that temporarily suspends the natural order. Stories of the kind referred to here, however, describe events that, while remarkable or even awe-inspiring, are nonetheless presented as instances of a universal—and therefore eminently natural—causal law.

Originating in medieval China, Buddhist miracle tales drew on two preexisting genres, biography and tales of the uncanny, as Daniel B. Stevenson explains in his chapter in this volume.[56] They recount in narrative form the wondrous effects brought about by the Buddhist practices of particular individuals. Encompassing both practical and transcendent benefits, these stories tell of healing illness, overcoming poverty, acquiring progeny, winning justice from officials, being protected from enemy attack, eradicating sins, acquiring meditative insight or other powers, receiving extraordinary signs, spreading the dharma, achieving birth in a pure land after death, and saving deceased relatives and associates from the hells. Tales of the horrific retribution incurred by those who slight or oppose the dharma also appear. One of the underlying principles informing these tales is that of "sympathetic resonance" (*ganying*), or in modern terms, "stimulus and response," which reflects ancient Chinese cosmological thinking about the unity of human beings, heaven, and earth and the consequent power of human moral and ritual conduct to elicit beneficial responses from the larger world.[57] Onto these older ideas of the integral relationship between human beings and the cosmos were mapped Buddhist notions of karmic causality and the nonduality of persons and their environments. Miracle tales recount how the Buddhist practices (stimuli) of specific individuals—monks, nuns, laymen, and laywomen—draw forth wondrous results (responses). Tales on this broad pattern composed in China, Korea, and Japan often stress the merits to be gained from devotion to specific bodhisattvas or sacred scriptures, including the *Lotus Sūtra*.

Examples of tales focused specifically on the *Lotus Sūtra* include Huixiang's *Accounts of the Propagation of the Lotus Sūtra*, compiled in the seventh century, and the eleventh-century *Miraculous Tales of the Lotus Sūtra from Japan* (*Dainihonkoku Hokekyō kenki*, or simply *Hokke genki*, written ca. 1044), by the monk Chingen (1007–1044?).[58] Both collections appear to have been drawn from local tradition and oral lore, and the stories they contain were adopted, transmitted, and reworked by later authors. These stories depict specific individuals, from villages and provinces in many cases known by name to their readers, who engaged in the practices described in the *Lotus*, such as copying, memorizing, and reciting the sūtra, revering and making offerings to it, and teaching it to others. Thus, these stories worked to indigenize the *Lotus Sūtra*, an Indian text, by placing both its practice and its resulting benefits within the context of local religious culture. It is tempting to assume that, unlike the highly technical *Lotus Sūtra* commentaries produced by scholar-monks, miracle tales must have been intended for the common people, but this would not be wholly accurate. It is true that miracle tales are entertaining and, when related orally or used as the basis of sermons, would have been accessible to auditors of varying social levels. However, we know that they were also, or perhaps even primarily, read and disseminated among literate elites.

Zhiyi and the Tiantai Tradition

As noted, the reception of the *Lotus Sūtra* in East Asia has transcended sectarian divisions. The *Lotus* has been studied by monks of all schools and revered by devotees, monastics, and laity with no particular sectarian affiliation; it is the common property, so to speak, of East Asian Buddhists. At the same time, however, it has also come to be particularly associated with two specific Buddhist denominations: the Tiantai school, which spread in China, Korea, and Japan, and also the Nichiren school, which emerged in thirteenth-century Japan and gave rise to a number of contemporary and modern movements. The *Lotus*-related practices of these schools were influenced by, and in turn helped to shape, broader traditions of *Lotus* religious practice more generally.

The Chinese Tiantai school traces its origins to the patriarch Zhiyi. While studying meditation with his teacher, Huisi (515–577), Zhiyi is said to have realized awakening on reading a passage from Chapter 23 of the *Lotus*, "The Former Affairs of Bodhisattva Medicine King."[59] Zhiyi is known for a grand and comprehensive reading of the *Lotus Sūtra*, integrating the entirety of Buddhist teachings and practice and envisioning the mind and the phenomenal world as an interdependent unity. While indebted to a number of sources, Zhiyi cited as the textual basis for his system a passage from Kumārajīva's Chinese translation of the *Lotus Sūtra* enumerating ten "suchnesses" as the "true aspect of the dharmas," or ultimate reality, mentioned in Chapter 2 of the *Lotus Sūtra*, which only buddhas can fully understand. By punctuating this passage in three different ways, Zhiyi derived the three truths (Ch.: *sandi*, Ja.: *santai*) of emptiness (Ch.: *kong*, Ja.: *kū*), conventional (or provisional) existence (Ch.: *jia*, Ja.: *ke*), and the middle (Ch.: *zhong*, Ja.: *chū*). Zhiyi used this tripartite structure to explain both doctrine and meditative practice.[60]

Emptiness means that all phenomena, arising through causes and conditions, are impermanent and lack self-essence or independent existence. From this perspective all categories, hierarchies, and boundaries are collapsed; emptiness is a discernment of absolute equality and nondifferentiation. Insight into all phenomena as empty of independent substance is said to free one from attachment to desires and intellectual constructs. Understanding of this first truth corresponds to the wisdom of arhats and those bodhisattvas at preliminary stages of practice. Nonetheless, while lacking substance or permanence, phenomena exist provisionally as elements of conventional reality. This second discernment reestablishes conceptual distinctions as elements of commonsense, empirical experience but without false essentializing or biased clinging; it frees one to be active in the world without being bound to it and thus corresponds to the wisdom of advanced bodhisattvas. Third, phenomena are neither one-sidedly empty nor conventionally existing but exhibit both aspects simultaneously. This insight, which encompasses both poles of understanding without dissolving the tension between them, corresponds to the buddha wisdom. Zhiyi organized his system of meditative practice around contemplation of the three truths, a threefold contemplation that might be cultivated in either a gradual and sequential fashion or by a more advanced "perfect and sudden method" that discerns the three insights simultaneously, or by a combination of the two approaches. Zhiyi also used the three truths to organize his classification of doctrines. In his view, while the various sūtras might stress one or another of these three perspectives, only the *Lotus Sūtra* represents the "pure and perfect teaching" that reveals the integrated threefold truth in its entirety.[61]

While the *Lotus Sūtra* is central to Zhiyi's unifying schema, he did not regard it in exclusivistic terms, because each sūtra, being suited to persons of a particular capacity, has its own role to play in the Buddha's grand soteriological design.[62] However, later Tiantai thinkers such as the sixth patriarch, Zhanran, who lived in a time of increased sectarian rivalry, organized the sūtras into a hierarchy with the *Lotus Sūtra* at its apex. Zhanran's classification, which was further refined by the Korean Tiantai scholar Chegwan (d. 971), became known as the "five periods and eight teachings" (Ch.: *wushi bajiao*, Ja.: *goji hakkyō*). Zhanran was instrumental in establishing the *Lotus Sūtra*'s reputation as supreme among the Buddha's teachings and in closely identifying it with the Tiantai school.[63]

The "true aspect of the dharmas" mentioned in Kumārajīva's *Lotus Sūtra* not only served Zhiyi as the basis for the threefold truth by which he integrated Buddhist doctrine and practice but also informs the concept of the "three thousand realms in a single thought-moment" (Ch.: *yinian sanqian*, Ja.: *ichinen sanzen*), his architectonic vision of the mind and the universe as an interpenetrating whole. The "single thought-moment" refers to the briefest possible instant in the thoughts of ordinary persons that arise from moment to moment, while the "three thousand realms" indicates the totality of existence. As set forth in his meditation treatise *Great Calming and Contemplation* (*Mohe zhiguan*), the "three thousand realms in a single thought-moment" denotes both an ontological vision of how reality exists and also a mode of contemplation. The basic idea of this intricate vision is that at each moment the mind and the whole of phenomenal reality—subject and object, internal and external, person and environment, matter and mind, delusion and enlightenment—contain one another and interpenetrate. While not treated extensively in Zhiyi's own works, this concept would be of great importance to later Chinese Tiantai thinkers and, in Japan, especially to Nichiren.[64]

The "three thousand realms in a single thought-moment" may be understood as part of a broader attempt on the part of medieval Chinese Buddhist commentators to make clear the relationship between concrete phenomena (*shi*) and ultimate truth or principle (*li*).[65] Many Chinese Buddhist thinkers equated principle with an originally undifferentiated pure mind that, observed through the filter of deluded perception, produces the distinctions of the phenomenal world. This perspective developed especially in the Huayan (Ja.: Kegon, "Flower Garland," named after the scripture on which it was focused, Skt.: *Avataṃsaka sūtra*) and Chan (Ja.: Zen; literally "meditation") traditions. For Zhiyi, however, phenomena do not arise from a pure, abstract, prior principle. "Principle" means that form and mind, subject and object, good and evil, delusion and enlightenment are always nondual and mutually inclusive; this is the true aspect of reality. Zhiyi's notion of principle establishes a firm soteriological equality. Each thought-moment of sentient beings in the nine deluded (or not fully awakened) dharma realms—that is, hell dwellers, hungry ghosts, animals, asuras, humans, gods, śrāvakas, pratyekabuddhas, and bodhisattvas—includes the buddha realm, and thus all beings have the capacity to manifest buddhahood. Similarly, even the Buddha retains within himself the potential of the nine deluded states and thus is able to exercise compassion toward all.[66] In its refusal to privilege an abstract mind over concrete realities, Zhiyi's perspective also revalorizes the phenomenal world, now seen not as the product of deluded discrimination but as the very locus of liberation.[67] In this way, beginning with Zhiyi's systematization, the Tiantai school interpreted the one vehicle of the *Lotus Sūtra* as a framework that encompassed and integrated all Buddhist teachings by showing their true purport: to lead all beings to the buddha wisdom.

Tendai in Japan

The Tendai school, the Japanese counterpart of the Chinese Tiantai tradition, was established by the monk Saichō, who journeyed to China for Buddhist study. Saichō founded the great Tendai monastery Enryakuji on Mount Hiei, north of the capital city of Heian (today's Kyoto). Following Saichō's death, Enryakuji became Japan's leading religious institution, a position it held for several centuries. Like Zhiyi before him, Saichō sought to encompass all forms of Buddhist practice within the umbrella of the one vehicle of the *Lotus Sūtra*.[68] However, new approaches to the *Lotus Sūtra* developed within Japanese Tendai that soon distinguished it from its continental parent.

One of the most important of these developments was the rise of esoteric approaches to the *Lotus Sūtra*. In Japan during Saichō's lifetime, esoteric Buddhism (*mikkyō*) placed Great Sun (Skt.: Mahāvairocana, Ja.: Dainichi) Buddha at the basis of all things and emphasized union with this buddha through performance of the "three mysteries": the forming of *mudrās*, or scripted bodily and hand gestures; the chanting of *mantras*, or incantations; and the contemplation of deities or symbols, whether represented in *maṇḍalas* (palaces of deities or diagrams of the cosmos) or visualized internally. Esoteric Buddhism took institutional form in the Shingon school, founded by Kūkai (774–835); at the same time, Saichō also brought esoteric teachings from China and incorporated them into Tendai. After Saichō's death, his disciples developed a distinctively *Lotus Sūtra*–oriented system of esoteric thought and practice, known as Taimitsu ("Tendai esotericism"). Where Kūkai had relegated the *Lotus Sūtra* to the inferior category of the "exoteric," Taimitsu theoreticians such as Ennin (794–864), Enchin (814–891), and Annen (841–?) reinterpreted the *Lotus Sūtra* as an esoteric scripture. They equated the primordially awakened Śākyamuni Buddha of the "origin teaching" (*honmon*)—the latter fourteen chapters of the *Lotus*—with Mahāvairocana, the cosmic buddha of the esoteric teachings. The *Lotus* was also incorporated into Taimitsu ritual, in, for example, the "*Lotus* rite" (*Hokke hō*), performed to eradicate sin, build merit, and realize awakening. The maṇḍala used in this ritual depicts the two buddhas Śākyamuni and Many Jewels seated together in its central court, as they appeared in the jeweled stūpa of the *Lotus Sūtra*.[69]

Esoteric teachings hold that the cosmic buddha or dharma body is without beginning or end and pervades everywhere. This buddha is not a person, whether historical or mythic, but universal principle conceived as a buddha body: all forms are this buddha's body, all sounds are his voice, and all thoughts are his mind. Thus the body, speech, and mind of ordinary persons are no different from those of the cosmic buddha, though the unawakened fail to realize this. Through practice of the esoteric three mysteries—mudrās, mantras, and contemplations—the adept is said to align his or her body, speech, and mind with those of the cosmic buddha and thus realize awakening. Esoteric Buddhism helped bring about a broad conceptual shift in which liberation came increasingly to be understood not in linear terms as a goal to be achieved after a long period of practice, but as innate from the outset and manifested in the very act of practice. Within the Tendai school, the *Lotus Sūtra* itself as well as traditional Tiantai/Tendai doctrinal categories were reinterpreted from this perspective. This development, known as the doctrine of original enlightenment (*hongaku*), dominated Tendai doctrinal studies from approximately the eleventh through seventeenth centuries.[70]

From the perspective of original enlightenment, all things, just as they are, manifest the true aspect or reality of the dharmas; there is no greater truth above, behind, or prior to the phenomenal world. Enlightenment is neither a goal to be achieved nor a potential to be realized but the true status of all things. Seen in their true light, all forms of daily conduct, just as they are—eating, sleeping, even one's deluded thoughts—are the expressions of original enlightenment. Modern scholars have hotly debated the ethical and soteriological implications of this doctrine. Some have criticized original enlightenment doctrine as an authoritarian discourse that, by claiming that all things are already enlightened, in effect legitimates social inequity by sacralizing the status quo. Others have seen it as a dangerous antinomianism that denies the need for both moral and religious cultivation: why practice, if one is already enlightened? In its medieval context, however, original enlightenment doctrine—and the esoteric assumptions that inform it—amounts not to a rejection of religious efforts but to their reconception. It reverses the causal sequence traditionally thought to obtain between practice (cause) and enlightenment (effect); practice is not a means to "attain" enlightenment but its paradigmatic vehicle of expression. Similarly, the need for ongoing effort is not abrogated but reframed; one continues in practice not in order to progress toward enlightenment as a future goal but to deepen the insight (or faith) that enlightenment is already one's true condition. While this general idea transcended denominational boundaries, Tendai scholars held that it represented the unique message of the "origin teaching," or latter fourteen chapters of the *Lotus Sūtra*, and they reinterpreted their tradition's classic texts and doctrines in its light.

Nichiren

Another Buddhist tradition based on the *Lotus Sūtra* is the Nichiren school (Nichirenshū), of which there are now several branches. First known as the "*Lotus* school" (Hokkeshū), it was later called by the name of its founder, Nichiren, to distinguish it from Tendai. Nichiren initiated one of the so-called new Buddhist movements of Japan's Kamakura period (1185–1333).[71] He began his religious career as a Tendai monk and was deeply versed in traditional Tendai *Lotus*-based doctrine as well as esoteric Buddhism, and his own teachings draw on both traditions. In Nichiren's time, a small but vocal trend was emerging, both within the Buddhist establishment and in newer movements, that stressed the absolute efficacy of a single form of practice, said to be accessible to all. The best known of these movements was that of the Pure Land teacher Hōnen (1133–1212), who held that invoking the *nenbutsu*—chanting the name of the buddha Amitābha or Amitāyus (Amida in Japanese)—was alone sufficient to achieve birth after death in Amida's pure land. In contrast, Nichiren taught his followers that buddhahood is to be achieved solely by embracing faith in the *Lotus* and chanting its title (*daimoku*) in the formula *Namu myōhō renge kyō* ("Devotion to the *Sūtra of the Lotus Blossom of the Wonderful [or Fine] Dharma*"). In advancing this claim, he drew on the commentaries of Zhiyi, who taught that the title of the *Lotus* contained the meaning of the entire sūtra. Nichiren did not himself invent the practice of chanting the title, but he was the first to accord it absolute status as a single practice and to provide it with a detailed doctrinal foundation.[72] For Nichiren, the daimoku contains all the practices that the primordially awakened Śākyamuni Buddha undertook over inconceivable kalpas and also their resulting virtues and merits; by chanting the title with faith in the *Lotus Sūtra*, he taught, one is able to receive the same merits as Śākyamuni Buddha and realize buddhahood.

Nichiren also devised a calligraphic maṇḍala as a focus of practice for his followers. Where many Buddhist maṇḍalas are artistic representations of the realms of Buddhist deities, Nichiren's "great maṇḍala" (*daimandara*), or "revered object of worship" (*gohonzon*), uses Chinese and Sanskrit characters to represent the world of the *Lotus Sūtra*. The words "*Namu myōhō renge kyō*" are inscribed vertically down the center and are flanked by the characters for the names of the two buddhas, Śākyamuni and Many Jewels, just as they sat together in the jeweled stūpa. They in turn are surrounded by the names of representatives of the *Lotus* assembly as they appeared in the air above Vulture Peak. As an ensemble, these figures together with the central inscription of the daimoku represent what Nichiren terms the "three thousand realms in a single thought-moment in actuality," or more specifically, the mutual inclusion of all ten dharma realms within the single realm of buddhahood. By chanting the title with faith in the *Lotus Sūtra*, Nichiren taught, one is able in effect to enter the assembly of the *Lotus* maṇḍala and participate in the enlightened reality that it depicts.[73]

Nichiren inherited the Tendai stance revering the *Lotus Sūtra* as the Buddha's ultimate teaching, understanding the *Lotus* as "true" (*jitsu*) and all other teachings as "provisional" (*gon*). This distinction was closely linked to his conviction, shared by many of his contemporaries, that the world had entered the benighted age of the Final Dharma, when the Buddha's teachings are filtered through an increasingly flawed understanding, and enlightenment is difficult to achieve. In this age, Nichiren held, only the *Lotus Sūtra* was profound and powerful enough to lead all people to enlightenment; lesser, provisional teachings, though efficacious in former times, were no longer of any avail. Accordingly, he stressed the practice of *shakubuku* (cutting off and subduing attachment), a severe method

FIGURE 1.1 Nichiren's calligraphic maṇḍala, depicting the assembly of the *Lotus Sūtra* in the air above Vulture Peak, with *Namu myōhō renge kyō* written vertically down the center. This particular example, inscribed by Nichiren in 1280, has been designated as the official object of worship of the Nichiren sect (Nichirenshū).

MYŌHONJI, KAMAKURA, JAPAN. COURTESY OF FUTABA PUBLISHING, TOKYO.

of instruction that involved directly rebuking attachment to provisional teachings. Nichiren believed that his work of spreading faith in the *Lotus* would prepare the way for Bodhisattva Superior Conduct (Skt.: Viśiṣṭacāritra, Ja.: Jōgyō), the leader of the bodhisattvas who emerge from beneath the earth as described in the fifteenth chapter of the *Lotus Sūtra*. These are Śākyamuni's original disciples, taught by him since his awakening in the inconceivably distant past, and to whom, in Chapter 21, he entrusts the practicing and preaching of the *Lotus Sūtra* after his nirvāṇa. (Many of Nichiren's later followers in fact identified him as an actual manifestation of Bodhisattva Superior Conduct.) Nichiren maintained that embracing the *Lotus Sūtra* would not only enable individual devotees to realize buddhahood but would also transform the present world into an ideal buddha land, a distinctive aspect of his thought that is further discussed in Jacqueline I. Stone's chapter in this volume. Nichiren's reading of the *Lotus Sūtra* thus reversed the conventional grim connotations of the final age: because the final age is the time when the *Lotus Sūtra*, the Buddha's highest teaching, is destined to spread, it is, soteriologically speaking, the best of all times to be alive.[74]

Nichiren's insistence on the exclusive validity of the *Lotus Sūtra* in the present era and his harsh criticisms of other Buddhist groups and practices (and of government officials for supporting them) led to persecution by the authorities. The *Lotus Sūtra* foretells grave trials that its devotees will face during an evil age after the Buddha's nirvāṇa. Historically, such passages may reflect opposition from the Indian Buddhist establishment experienced by the particular Mahāyāna community that compiled the sūtra. Nichiren, however, read them as prophecies and saw his encounters with persecution as demonstrating both the truth of the sūtra's words and the correctness of his own practice. Nichiren wrote that personally to encounter the very trials that the *Lotus Sūtra* predicts was "to read [the sūtra] with one's body" (*shikidoku*), that is, to live the sūtra through one's actions and not merely recite it with one's mouth or comprehend it intellectually. This "bodily reading" of the *Lotus*, explained further in Ruben Habito's chapter in this volume, represents a circular hermeneutic in which the words of the sūtra and conduct of the practitioner mirror and validate one another. Hard-pressed by two periods of exile, attempts on his life, and the imprisonment, banishment, and fines imposed on his followers, Nichiren developed what might be termed a "soteriology of meeting persecution," in which hardship encountered in the course of practicing the *Lotus Sūtra* serves to eradicate past misdeeds, repay one's debt to the Buddha and all living beings, and enable the realization of buddhahood.[75]

Modern Lotus-*Based Movements*

Both the Tendai and Nichiren traditions—indeed the whole of Japanese Buddhism—underwent profound changes in the shift from medieval to early modern times. Under the rule of the Tokugawa shoguns, or military leaders, during Japan's early modern period (1603–1867), as part of a broader policy of governmental social control, temples were organized by sect, and all families were required to become supporters of a local Buddhist temple. Thus sectarian boundaries solidified, and for the first time, the majority of lay Buddhists acquired exclusive sectarian affiliations. At the same time, in addition to membership in the hereditary system of family temple affiliation, lay Buddhists in the eighteenth and nineteenth centuries often participated in lay associations, usually connected with temples but sometimes led independently by laypeople. These groups organized pilgrimages to sacred sites, supported local temples in celebrating festivals and ceremonies, and promoted devotional practices. Although found across sectarian divisions, they were especially active in connection with Nichiren temples in urban areas.

Institutionalized forms of *Lotus* devotion in Japan today reflect this early modern heritage. Tendai and Nichiren number among the denominations of Japanese "temple Buddhism," or traditional Buddhist schools, in which people usually inherit affiliation from their families. Since the twentieth century, however, a number of lay movements based on the *Lotus Sūtra* or Nichiren's teachings have overshadowed traditional Tendai and Nichiren temples as the most prominent representatives of organized *Lotus Sūtra* practice. These newer movements have antecedents in the lay associations of the early modern period.

Among the most well known of today's *Lotus*-based lay groups are Reiyūkai, Risshō Kōseikai, and Sōka Gakkai; the latter two in particular claim several million members apiece and represent the largest of Japan's so-called new religions. They also have international followings, Sōka Gakkai's being by far the largest. These groups share a commitment to working for world peace and social betterment, and members engage in various local and international activities for peace, education, famine relief, aid to refugees, and the like. Ideologically conservative, they tend to work for social betterment within existing structures. In contrast, one can note the more radical Nipponzan Myōhōji, a small Nichiren Buddhist monastic order founded in 1918, which since the postwar period has espoused the antinuclear movement and an ethic of absolute pacifism, based on a fusion of the *Lotus Sūtra*, Nichiren's teachings, and the example of nonviolent resistance set by Mohandas Gandhi (1869–1946). Nipponzan Myōhōji monks and nuns embrace a strict ascetic discipline and also engage in acts of nonviolent civil disobedience such as protests against nuclear sites.[76] The social ideals and welfare projects of today's *Lotus*-based groups are shared by many contemporary present-day Japanese religions, both new and traditional, and are not limited to Buddhism, let alone to *Lotus Sūtra* devotion. In the case of the *Lotus*-based movements, however, both proselytizing and social action are often based on modern interpretations of Nichiren's teaching that faith in the *Lotus* will transform this world into a buddha realm.[77]

BROADER DISSEMINATION OF THE *LOTUS SŪTRA*

In addition to the specific *Lotus*-based schools and movements that have been introduced, devotion to the *Lotus Sūtra* also spread in a more diffuse fashion, merging with local religious culture in ways that did not entail sectarian identification. In a reciprocal fashion, indigenous practice throughout East Asia influenced the understanding and development of *Lotus Sūtra* culture. The most common forms of *Lotus* practice involved ritualized devotion to the text. In Buddhism, as in other religious traditions, scriptures were not only studied for their intellectual content but were also deemed to embody the very truth they set forth and were thus revered as objects sacred in and of themselves. In India, Mahāyāna movements in particular were often characterized by what scholars now call the "cult of the book"—reverence for the physical texts of sūtras—that grew up alongside the "stūpa cult," or organized veneration of buddha relics contained in reliquary structures (stūpas) or shrines (*caityas*).[78] The *Lotus Sūtra* provides several references to the cult of the book and explicitly equates its physical text with the person of the Buddha, stating, "If there is anyone who can hold it [the sūtra], / Then he holds the buddha body" (Hurvitz, 176).

Reverence for the *Lotus* book is also central to the so-called five practices, a template set forth in the sūtra. The five practices are (1) upholding the *Lotus* (which Hurvitz usually renders "accepting and keeping"); (2) reading the sūtra; (3) reciting it aloud; (4) explaining (or interpreting) it, and (5) copying it (Hurvitz, 159, 242, 263). Upholding the *Lotus Sūtra* generally involves an underlying attitude of faith in or commitment to the sūtra, expressed in some concrete regimen of practice. Such regimens were expanded to include Buddhist rituals not necessarily confined to *Lotus* devotion, such as repentance, fasting, and other ascetic disciplines; cultivation of specific mental states (*samādhis*); and rites for healing, for the transfer of merit, and for seeking a better rebirth. The development of the five modes of practice in China is discussed in detail in Daniel B. Stevenson's chapter in this volume.

Throughout East Asia, devotion to the *Lotus Sūtra* often revolved around reciting, copying, and preaching the text. Such acts were sometimes sponsored officially, by the court, and were also performed privately by both monastics and laypeople at all social levels, in accordance with their means. The merit believed to result from these acts was dedicated to a number of aims, both pragmatic and soteriological, including the realization of awakening; rebirth in a buddha's pure land or other ideal realm; eradication of sins; salvation of deceased relatives; and this-worldly benefits such as peace and stability in the country, healing, longevity, and protection from harm. These practices were deemed to benefit both the practitioner and others as well. Many miracle tales narrate how, because the power of the sūtra was thought to be embodied in the sound, reciting the *Lotus Sūtra* affected not only the reciter but also those who heard its recitation. The eleventh-century *Miraculous Tales of the Lotus Sūtra from Japan*, for example, says of the ascetic Eijitsu, a *Lotus* devotee: "The miraculous power of his recitation subjugated evil and cured the pains of the sick."[79] Other stories relate how evildoers were released from torture in the hell realms and how animals achieved human birth in their next life merely because of having heard the recitation of a portion of the *Lotus Sūtra*.

The *Lotus Sūtra* extols those who can explain even a single phrase of the sūtra to another person, and "explaining" or "interpreting" the *Lotus* was also taken seriously throughout East Asia as a meritorious practice. Lectures on the *Lotus Sūtra* were held at temples, shrines, and private residences for a variety of purposes, including the dedication of newly completed temples, Buddhist sculptures, or sūtra transcriptions; praying for longevity, health, and prosperity; and transferring merit to the deceased. The more elaborate *Lotus* lectures were often costly affairs, involving pageantry, processions, solemn chanting, and lavish offerings of incense, flowers, jeweled banners, and other sacred implements, as well as performances of music and dancing. In Japanese court circles, sequential lectures were often given on the sūtra's individual chapters, and on the day of the lecture on Chapter 12, "Devadatta," monks and nobles would carry out an elaborate "firewood procession" of ritual offerings, reenacting Śākyamuni Buddha's service to an ascetic in a prior lifetime, as that chapter describes.[80] *Lotus* lectures thus provided opportunities for entertainment as well as merit making and doctrinal edification. Preaching on the *Lotus Sūtra* ranged from court-sponsored monastic debates on the sūtra's meaning to sermons for nonelite audiences. The sūtra's imagery and parables especially suited it to popular preaching. Vernacular sermons, sometimes illustrated with paintings to which the preacher would point, made its message broadly accessible.

Copying the *Lotus Sūtra*, another of the five practices, was widely conducted in China, Korea, and Japan. Large-scale sūtra-copying projects requiring considerable resources were sponsored by Buddhist monasteries and government officials. Willa Jane Tanabe's chapter in this volume explains how in Japan, as early as the eighth century, state-sponsored scriptoria for sūtra copying were established at Tōdaiji and other leading Buddhist temples. These were staffed by the most skilled calligraphers available as well as by proofreaders, title writers, decorators, and those who polished characters written in gold.[81] Copying the *Lotus Sūtra* was also undertaken privately, by individual monks or lay devotees or by associations formed for that purpose. In either case, devotees might donate funds for copying by a professional calligrapher or write out the sūtra in their own hand, and copies ranged from the humble to the ornate.

Copying was not merely a pragmatic effort undertaken to increase availability of the text but a religious act thought to generate profound merit. Thus, copying procedures were sometimes highly ritualized. Brushes, paper, and copying materials had to be "pure," or free from sinful associations. Sometimes writing brushes were made from plant fibers rather than animal hairs, which might have been obtained by taking life, and water from sacred springs was often used for grinding the ink. Copyists might prepare for their task by refraining from meat eating and undertaking other forms of abstinence for a certain period. Some individuals, such as the famous Tendai pilgrim Ennin, combined writing the text with other forms of bodily devotion, bowing once or even three times after writing each character.[82] The idea that "each character of the *Lotus Sūtra* is a living buddha" was sometimes expressed by drawing each character of the text on a lotus pedestal or inside a small stūpa, as though it were a seated buddha. In Japan copies of the *Lotus Sūtra* and other texts were sometimes placed in bronze or ceramic cylinders and buried with the aim of preserving them through the darkness of the age of the Final Dharma until the advent of the next buddha, Maitreya.[83]

Like other text-centered practices, copying the *Lotus Sūtra* was thought to produce immense merit for oneself and for others, both in this life and the next. Thus the sūtra was frequently copied as a memorial offering for the deceased. A manuscript of the *Lotus* made in northwestern China in the late seventh century, for instance, contains the prayer of the donor, a local nun named Shanxin, for the salvation of her deceased mother. An epilogue attached to the surviving twelve-inch fragment of the text (from Chapter 13 of the *Lotus*) reads:

> The *bhikṣuṇī* [nun] Shanxin of Lingxiusi understands that the body does not have permanent existence and that shallow understanding is marked by suffering and emptiness. Therefore she economized on everything beyond the three required garments of the nun and reverently on behalf of her deceased mother had one copy made of the *Lotus Sūtra*. With this merit she prays that her mother ride on this fortunate karma and achieve rebirth in the highest of the superior grades, that she presently enjoy ease and bliss, and that [the benefits] be extended to include her realization along with that of all animate beings of the marvelous fruit [of enlightenment]. Copied on the twenty-ninth day of the third lunar month in the second year of the Tianshou era [May 2, 691].[84]

These few surviving lines suggest that, even within the strictures of her ascetic lifestyle, Shanxin lived frugally in order to collect enough money to pay the copyist, thus generating merit to ensure her mother's well-being in the afterlife, birth in a pure land, and eventual realization of enlightenment. It is probably not accidental that the thirteenth chapter of the *Lotus* predicts the future buddhahood of two women close to Śākyamuni Buddha, his maternal aunt and foster mother, Mahāprajāpatī, and his former wife, Yaśodharā. The theme of the chapter Shanxin selected for reproduction has a close connection to the person she prayed would benefit from the act of copying, her mother.

Although in East Asia text-centered practices were by no means confined to the *Lotus Sūtra*, the *Lotus* came to occupy a special status as the paradigmatic example of text-centered Buddhist practice. Another, more diffuse way in which the *Lotus Sūtra* spread into the broader religious culture was through the worship and emulation of holy beings represented in the text. A particularly striking case is devotion to the bodhisattva He Who Observes the Sounds of the World.[85] Chapter 25 of the *Lotus*, which also circulated as an independent text, explains how this bodhisattva will rescue all living beings who call upon him. He will, for example, save persons threatened by fire, drowning in a river, or in boats threatening to capsize; persons hunted by murderers or under attack by demons; prisoners seeking deliverance; and merchants pursued by robbers. He will relieve beings of lust, anger, and folly and grant sons and daughters to women wishing to bear children (Hurvitz, 287–89). He also manifests himself in thirty-three different forms—representing all possible modes of existence—in order to save living beings. Bodhisattva Sound Observer was well known in Buddhist circles all over Asia, and many sūtras aside from the *Lotus* depict him in various ways.[86] Pure Land texts, for example, sometimes portray Sound Observer as the right-hand attendant of the buddha Amitābha, who descends to guide dying devotees to that buddha's pure land. In Buddhist iconography, Sound Observer is sometimes pictured with eleven heads, showing that he heeds the cries of beings in all directions, and a thousand arms, illustrating his capacity to rescue people from all forms of torment. In Japan, multiple pilgrimage routes devoted to this bodhisattva developed, many of them marked out by thirty-three stations, each representing one of the forms that Sound Observer can assume.

Given the postulate in Mahāyāna Buddhism that bodhisattvas can assume countless forms in order to benefit living beings, it is not surprising that manifestations of Sound Observer would be widespread and divergent over the course of time. One particularly noteworthy shift from early to later understandings of the deity was a change in gender from male to female. Beginning in the eleventh century, some legends in central China recounted how Sound Observer was incarnated as a princess named Miaoshan (literally, "Wondrous Goodness"), who, in the course of the story, rejects the marriage arranged for her and gives up her limbs, eyes, and finally her life in order to cure her sick father. The story holds rich implications for Buddhist notions of filial piety, since it seems to reverse the usual family model in China in which sons provide for their fathers' posthumous salvation and daughters are married into other families. Another fascinating element is the mutilation and self-sacrifice of the daughter. Miaoshan's willingness to harm herself on behalf of her parents can be interpreted as devotion to her family, as an illustration of a self-abnegating feminine ideal, and as a demonstration of a bodhisattva's undiscriminating compassion. Sculpture and painting after the fourteenth century in China also attest to a transformation of Sound Observer from male to female. One particular iconographic form depicts Sound Observer as a female bodhisattva, descending from the clouds with a baby boy in her arms. In this form, she is believed to ensure the birth of sons to women seeking her blessing. Other developments in the culture of Sound Observer include a pilgrimage center on the island believed to be her realm, Putuoshan (Zhejiang province, China).[87]

Like the saints of other religious traditions, the bodhisattvas depicted in the *Lotus Sūtra* were revered both as agents of salvation and as models for emulation. Chapter 23 describes how Bodhisattva Medicine King (Bhaiṣajyarāja), known in a prior life as Seen with Joy by All Living Beings (Sarvasattvapriyadarśana), makes the highest offering by burning his body in offering to a buddha in a dramatic act of auto-cremation. As discussed in James Benn's chapter in this volume, in China this bodhisattva's example became a model for the controversial but nonetheless highly respected practice of ascetic suicide. Like Sound Observer, Medicine King also appears in texts other than the *Lotus Sūtra*, where he is represented, for example, as helping to cure sickness and prolong life.[88]

Symbols drawn from the *Lotus Sūtra* were also incorporated into local religion in East Asia and assumed a life of their own in the arts. Parables such as the burning house or the gem hidden in the robe were depicted in painting and also figure in poetry, narrative, and popular songs, thus entering the common religious vocabulary.[89] *Lotus Sūtra* imagery also inspired new iconographic forms, as in the case of the jeweled stūpa that appears in Chapter 11. Representations of the two buddhas, Śākyamuni and Many Jewels, seated together in the jeweled stūpa, were produced across East Asia and were used as maṇḍalas, objects of worship, and funerary art.[90]

Ideas from the *Lotus* also spread beyond specific devotion to the sūtra itself and influenced the larger religious culture. This process is especially evident in Japan, where the *Lotus Sūtra* became the best known and most popular of Buddhist scriptures. Although many Mahāyāna scriptures teach that buddhahood is accessible to all, it was the *Lotus* that was most strongly identified with universal liberation, especially with the salvation of those deemed hard to save. These included women, who were often thought to bear heavier karmic burdens than men, and also "evil men"—persons such as hunters and warriors, whose hereditary professions forced them to violate Buddhist ethical norms.[91] The *Lotus Sūtra* was also associated with discourses of the enlightenment of grasses and trees—the buddhahood of the insentient world—a favorite theme in poetry and Noh drama. Many of medieval Japan's most noted poets were monks and nuns, and the question arose as to whether poetry was a proper activity for those who had renounced the world. Was not poetic composition an ultimately frivolous pursuit that ensnared one in the realm of the senses and the worldly quest for literary fame? Over and against this critique, by invoking the argument that various skillful means all lead to the one vehicle—especially as interpreted through Tendai teachings about the nonduality of conventional reality and ultimate truth—poetry, literature, and the performing arts were redefined as "paths" or "ways" (*michi*) of spiritual attainment. From this perspective, far from being a worldly distraction, the arts (or indeed all activities) can, when practiced with the proper attitude, become vehicles by which religious truth is realized. Similarly, in a famous passage from the early eleventh-century novel *The Tale of Genji*, the protagonist, Prince Genji, likens the creation of fictional tales to the Buddha's teaching of expedient devices in the *Lotus Sūtra*.[92] The influence of such thinking can still be seen today in the orientation espoused by members of present-day *Lotus* movements that faith finds expression in the activities of daily life.

It is impossible, in a single volume, to present a thorough picture of the *Lotus Sūtra*'s impact on the East Asian Buddhist world. In this introductory chapter and in the essays that follow we have sought to outline some of the major themes in the history of the *Lotus Sūtra*'s reception and to provide interested readers with signposts for further study.

NOTES

1. General treatments of the transmission of texts and the formation of canons in early Buddhism include Steven Collins, "On the Very Idea of the Pāli Canon," *Journal of the Pāli Text Society* 15 (1990): 89–126; Ronald M. Davidson, "Appendix: An Introduction to the Standards of Scriptural Authenticity in Indian Buddhism," in *Chinese Buddhist Apocrypha*, ed. Robert E. Buswell Jr., 291–325 (Honolulu: University of Hawai'i Press, 1990); K.R. Norman, *Pāli Literature: Including the Canonical Literature in Prakrit and Sanskrit of All the Hīnayāna Schools of Buddhism* (Wiesbaden, Ger.: Harrassowitz, 1983); and Oskar von Hinüber, *A Handbook of Pāli Literature* (Berlin: de Gruyter, 1996).
2. The most important scholarship on the early history of the *Lotus Sūtra* is by Japanese scholars such as Fuse Kōgaku, Seishi Karashima, Ōchō Enichi, and Suguro Shinjō. A list of major studies in Japanese can be found in the bibliography of Seishi Karashima, *The Textual Study of the Chinese Versions of the Saddharmapuṇḍarīkasūtra in the Light of the Sanskrit and Tibetan Versions*, Bibliotheca Indologica et Buddhologica 3 (Tokyo: Sankibō Press, 1992). For studies in European languages, see Akira Yuyama, *A Bibliography of the Sanskrit Texts of the Saddharmapuṇḍarīkasūtra*, Australian National University, Faculty of Asian Studies, Oriental Monograph Series 5 (Canberra: Australian National University Press, 1970); Gérard Fussman, "Histoire du monde indien," in *Annuaire du Collège de France 1995–1996, Résumé des cours et travaux*, 779–86 (Paris: Collège de France, 1996); Leon Hurvitz, "The Lotus Sūtra in East Asia: A Review of *Hokke shisō*," *Monumenta Serica* 29 (1970–71): 697–762; Karashima, *Textual Study*; Seishi Karashima, "Who Composed the Lotus Sutra? Antagonism between Wilderness and Village Monks," in *Annual Report of the International Research Institute for Advanced Buddhology at Soka University for the Academic Year 2000*, 143–79 (Tokyo: The International Research Institute for Advanced Buddhology, Soka University, 2001); Michael Pye, *Skilful Means: A Concept in Mahayana Buddhism*, 2nd ed. (London: Routledge, 2003), 168–82; and Ryōdō Shiori, "The Meaning of the Formation and Structure of the *Lotus Sutra*," trans. George J. Tanabe Jr., in *The Lotus Sutra in Japanese Culture*, ed. George J. Tanabe Jr. and Willa Jane Tanabe, 15–36 (Honolulu: University of Hawai'i Press, 1989).

3. Fuse Kōgaku, *Hokekyō seiritsushi* (Tokyo: Daitō shuppansha, 1934).
4. Chapter 12 did not appear in Kumārajīva's original translation completed in the year 406, but around 490 the chapter was translated into Chinese and subsequently inserted into his translation. Several other brief passages were added to this expanded version after the completion of a new translation of the entire *Lotus* in the year 601. Thus, the current version attributed to Kumārajīva in the *Taishō* canon (the standard Sino-Japanese Buddhist canon used by modern scholars) contains these two sets of interpolations; see Shiori, "Meaning of the Formation and Structure," 25–27; Paul Groner, "The *Lotus Sutra* and Saichō's Interpretation of the Realization of Buddhahood with This Very Body," in Tanabe and Tanabe, *Lotus Sutra in Japanese Culture*, 58–61.
5. Modern scholars avoid the use of pejorative terms like *Hīnayāna* ("Small Vehicle" or "Lesser Vehicle") to refer to Buddhism before or other than the Mahāyāna. The Pāli term *Theravāda* (or its Sanskrit equivalent *Sthaviravāda*, meaning "Teaching of the Elders") is limited in range, since it applies to only one of the schools of early Buddhism or to present-day South and Southeast Asian Buddhism. Instead, many scholars prefer locutions like "mainstream Buddhism" to refer to Indian Buddhism prior to or outside Mahāyāna movements. On terminological questions, see Jonathan A. Silk, "What, If Anything, Is Mahāyāna Buddhism? Problems of Definitions and Classifications," *Numen* 49 (2002): 76–109.
6. For general studies of mainstream Buddhism and Buddhist cosmology, see André Bareau, *Les sectes bouddhiques du Petit Véhicule*, Publications de l'École française d'Extrême-Orient 38 (Paris: École française d'Extrême-Orient, 1955); Collett Cox, *Disputed Dharmas: Early Buddhist Theories on Existence* (Tokyo: International Institute for Buddhist Studies, 1995); Randy Kloetzli, *Buddhist Cosmology: From Single World System to Pure Land* (Delhi: Motilal Banarsidass, 1983); Étienne Lamotte, *History of Indian Buddhism: From the Origins to the Śaka Era*, trans. Sara Webb-Boin (Louvain, Belg.: Peeters Press, 1988); and Akira Sadakata, *Buddhist Cosmology: Philosophy and Origin*, trans. Gaynor Sekimori (Tokyo: Kosei, 1997).
7. Steven Collins, *Nirvana and Other Buddhist Felicities: Utopias of the Pali Imaginaire*, Cambridge Studies in Religious Traditions 12 (Cambridge: Cambridge University Press, 1998); Luis O. Gómez, "Nirvāṇa," in *Encyclopedia of Buddhism*, ed. Robert E. Buswell Jr., 600a–605b (New York: Macmillan Reference, 2004); Trevor O. Ling, *The Buddha: Buddhist Civilization in India and Ceylon* (Harmondsworth, UK: Penguin, 1976); and John S. Strong, *Relics of the Buddha*, Buddhisms (Princeton, N.J.: Princeton University Press, 2004).
8. Two classic studies of Mahāyāna, now questioned because of their uncritical acceptance of the tradition's claims, are Har Dayal, *The Bodhisattva Doctrine in Buddhist Sanskrit Literature* (London: Paul, Trench, Trubner, 1932); and Akira Hirakawa, "The Rise of Mahāyāna Buddhism and Its Relationship to the Worship of Stūpas," trans. Taitetsu Unno, *Memoirs of the Research Department of the Tōyō Bunkō*, no. 22 (1963): 57–106. Examples of more recent scholarship include Paul M. Harrison, "Searching for the Origins of the Mahāyāna: What Are We Looking for?" *Eastern Buddhist*, n.s. 28, no. 1 (1995): 48–69; Harrison, "Who Gets to Ride in the Great Vehicle? Self-Image and Identity among the Followers of the Early Mahāyāna," *Journal of the International Association of Buddhist Studies* 10, no. 1 (1987): 67–89; Karashima, "Who Composed the Lotus Sutra?"; Jan Nattier, *A Few Good Men: The Bodhisattva Path according to "The Inquiry of Ugra (Ugraparipṛcchā),"* Studies in the Buddhist Traditions (Honolulu: University of Hawai'i Press, 2003);

Reginald A. Ray, *Buddhist Saints in India: A Study in Buddhist Values and Orientations* (New York: Oxford University Press, 1994), 251–92; Gregory Schopen, *Figments and Fragments of Mahāyāna Buddhism in India: More Collected Papers*, Studies in the Buddhist Traditions (Honolulu: University of Hawai'i Press, 2005); and Silk, "What, If Anything, Is Mahāyāna Buddhism?"

9. Edward Conze, *The Prajñāpāramitā Literature* (The Hague: Mouton, 1960), 15, with minor changes in capitalization and hyphenation.
10. According to Karashima, the relevant technical meaning of "emptiness" occurs only four times in Kumārajīva's *Lotus Sūtra*, at Hurvitz, 51, 96, 148, and 158, corresponding to *Miaofa lianhua jing* (*Saddharmapuṇḍarīka*), trans. Kumārajīva (Jiumoluoshi, 344–413, or 350–409), *Taishō shinshū daizōkyō*, 100 vols., ed. Takakusu Junjirō, Watanabe Kaigyoku, and Ono Gemmyō (1924–1934; repr., Taibei: Xinwenfeng chuban gongsi, 1974) (hereafter abbreviated as *T*), no. 262, 9:11a, 18c, 25c, 27c; see Seishi Karashima, *A Glossary of Kumārajīva's Translation of the Lotus Sutra*, Bibliotheca Philologica et Philosophica Buddhica 4 (Tokyo: The International Research Institute for Advanced Buddhology, Soka University, 2001), s.v. *kong fa*, "the teaching of emptiness," 154.
11. Daniel Boucher, "The Textual History of the Rāṣṭrapālaparipṛcchā: Notes on Its Third-Century Chinese Translation," in *Annual Report of the International Research Institute for Advanced Buddhology at Soka University for the Academic Year 2000*, 93–116 (Tokyo: International Research Institute for Advanced Buddhology, Soka University, 2001); Paul M. Harrison, *The Samādhi of Direct Encounter with the Buddhas of the Present: An Annotated English Translation of the Tibetan Version of the "Pratyutpanna-Buddha-Saṃmukhāvasthita-Samādhi-Sūtra" with Several Appendices Relating to the History of the Text*, Studia Philologica Buddhica 5 (Tokyo: The International Institute for Buddhist Studies, 1990); Harrison, *The Pratyutpanna Samādhi Sutra Translated by Lokakṣema*, BDK English Tripiṭaka 25-2 (Berkeley: Numata Center for Buddhist Translation and Research, 1998); and Nattier, *A Few Good Men*.
12. Cited in Nattier, *A Few Good Men*, 265.
13. Alan Cole, *Text as Father: Paternal Seductions in Early Mahāyāna Buddhist Literature*, Buddhisms (Berkeley: University of California Press, 2005); Richard Gombrich, "How the Mahāyāna Began," *The Buddhist Forum* 1 (1990): 21–30; and Donald S. Lopez Jr., "Authority and Orality in the Mahāyāna," *Numen* 42 (1995): 21–47.
14. Donald S. Lopez Jr., ed., *Buddhist Hermeneutics*, Kuroda Institute, Studies in East Asian Buddhism 6 (Honolulu: University of Hawai'i Press, 1988); John Powers, *Hermeneutics and Tradition in the Saṃdhinirmocana-sūtra* (Leiden: Brill, 1993).
15. Paul M. Harrison, "*Buddhānusmṛti* in the *Pratyutpanna-buddha-saṃmukhāvasthita-samādhi-sūtra*," *Journal of Indian Philosophy* 6 (1978): 35–57, especially 52–54; Harrison, "Mediums and Messages: Reflections on the Production of Mahāyāna Sūtras," *Eastern Buddhist* 35, nos. 1–2 (2003): 115–47; and E. Gil Fronsdal, "The Dawn of the Bodhisattva Path: Studies in a Religious Ideal of Ancient Indian Buddhists with a Particular Emphasis on the Earliest Extant Perfection of Wisdom Sutra" (Ph.D. diss., Stanford University, 1998), chap. 6.
16. For an overview of the three vehicles in Indian Buddhist literature, see Kōtatsu Fujita, "One Vehicle or Three?" trans. Leon Hurvitz, *Journal of Indian Philosophy* 3 (1975): 79–166.
17. A well-known example of overt rejection of the two vehicles is the *Vimalakīrti Sūtra*; see Burton Watson, trans., *The Vimalakirti Sutra* (New York: Columbia University

Press, 1996); and Robert A. F. Thurman, trans., *The Holy Teaching of Vimalakīrti: A Mahāyāna Scripture* (University Park: Pennsylvania State University Press, 1976).

18. George J. Tanabe Jr. and Willa Jane Tanabe, "Introduction," in Tanabe and Tanabe, *Lotus Sutra in Japanese Culture*, 2–3.
19. Fujita, "One Vehicle or Three?" 109–17.
20. Fujita, "One Vehicle or Three?"; Pye, *Skilful Means*.
21. Tanabe and Tanabe, "Introduction," 2. Similarly, Kazuhiko Yoshida argues that the *Lotus Sūtra* is a "tautological text" that "does not attempt to do more than assert the self-aggrandizing proposition of its own preeminent teaching." See Kazuhiko Yoshida, "The Enlightenment of the Dragon King's Daughter in *The Lotus Sutra*," translated and adapted by Margaret H. Childs, in *Engendering Faith: Women and Buddhism in Premodern Japan*, ed. Barbara Ruch (Ann Arbor: Center for Japanese Studies, University of Michigan, 2002), 302.
22. Taigen Dan Leighton, *Visions of Awakening Space and Time: Dōgen and the Lotus Sutra* (New York: Oxford University Press, 2007), 29.
23. William R. LaFleur, *The Karma of Words: Buddhism and the Literary Arts in Medieval Japan* (Los Angeles: University of California Press, 1983), 87. LaFleur's translation of the *Lotus Sūtra* passage has been modified here to accord more fully with the rendering by Leon Hurvitz, *Scripture of the Lotus Blossom of the Fine Dharma (The Lotus Sūtra), Translated from the Chinese of Kumārajīva*, Records of Civilization: Sources and Studies, no. 94, Translations from the Asian Classics, rev. ed. (1976; New York: Columbia University Press, 2009), which we have used as the standard for this volume. However, we have retained LaFleur's preference for the word "modes" here over "expedient devices" or "skillful means" precisely because it avoids reifying a duality of means and end.
24. Carl Bielefeldt, "The One Vehicle and the Three Jewels: On Japanese Sectarianism and Some Ecumenical Alternatives," *Buddhist-Christian Studies* 10 (1990): 9. See also Jacqueline Stone, "Inclusive and Exclusive Perspectives on the One Vehicle," *Dharma World* 26 (1999): 20–25.
25. On Buddhist theories of decline that arose in East Asia, see Jan Nattier, *Once upon a Future Time: Studies in a Buddhist Prophecy of Decline*, Nanzan Studies in Asian Religions 1 (Berkeley: Asian Humanities Press, 1991), 65–118.
26. Bielefeldt, "The One Vehicle and the Three Jewels."
27. *Shoshū mondō shō*, Nichiren (1222–1282), in *Shōwa teihon Nichiren Shōnin ibun*, ed. Risshō daigaku Nichiren kyōgaku kenkyūjo, 4 vols. (Minobu-chō, Yamanashi, Japan: Minobusan Kuonji, 1952–1959; rev. 1988), 1:25.
28. Jamie Hubbard, "Buddhist-Buddhist Dialogue? The *Lotus Sutra* and the Polemic of Accommodation," *Buddhist-Christian Studies* 15 (2005): 118–36.
29. As pointed out (n. 4), Chapter 12, "Devadatta," originally circulated independently and was later inserted into the *Lotus Sūtra*. Not all Chinese translations contain it.
30. Groner, "*Lotus Sutra* "; Groner, "Shortening the Path: Early Tendai Interpretations of the Realization of Buddhahood with This Very Body (Sokushin Jōbutsu)," in *Paths to Liberation: The Mārga and Its Transformations in Buddhist Thought*, ed. Robert E. Buswell Jr. and Robert M. Gimello, Kuroda Institute, Studies in East Asian Buddhism 7, 439–74 (Honolulu: University of Hawai'i Press, 1992).
31. On later readings of the Devadatta chapter and the question of women's attaining enlightenment as women, see Groner, "*Lotus Sutra*," 61–62; Edward Kamens, "Dragon-Girl, Maidenflower, Buddha: The Transformation of a Waka Topos, 'The Five Obstructions,'" *Monumenta Nipponica* 53, no. 2 (winter 1993): 389–442;

Miriam L. Levering, "The Dragon Girl and the Abbess of Mo-Shan: Gender and Status in the Ch'an Buddhist Tradition," *Journal of the International Association of Buddhist Studies* 5, no. 1 (1982): 19–35; Reiko Ohnuma, "The Story of Rūpāvatī: A Female Past Birth of the Buddha," *Journal of the International Association of Buddhist Studies* 23, no. 1 (2007): 103–45, especially 124–34; Lucinda Joy Peach, "Social Responsibility, Sex Change, and Salvation: Gender Justice in the Lotus Sutra," in *A Buddhist Kaleidoscope: Essays on the Lotus Sutra*, ed. Gene Reeves, 437–67 (Tokyo: Kōsei, 2002); and Yoshida, "Enlightenment of the Dragon King's Daughter," 313–17. For issues concerning women's attainment of enlightenment in Buddhism more broadly, see Alan Sponberg, "Attitudes toward Women and the Feminine in Early Buddhism," in *Buddhism, Sexuality, and Gender*, ed. José Ignacio Cabezón, 3–36 (Albany: SUNY Press, 1992); and Bernard Faure, *The Power of Denial: Buddhism, Purity, and Gender*, Buddhisms (Princeton, N.J.: Princeton University Press, 2003).

32. *Da banniepan jing* (*Mahāparinirvāṇa sūtra*), Dharmakṣema (Tanwuchan, 385–433), *T* no. 374, 12:522b24; *Da banniepan jing* (*Mahāparinirvāṇa sūtra*), Huiyuan (363–443) and Xie Lingyun (385–433), *T* no. 375, 12:770b12, 772b27. The phrase occurs in other sūtras as well.
33. Hiroshi Kanno, "The Practice of Bodhisattva Never Disparaging in the *Lotus Sūtra* and Its Reception in China and Japan," *Journal of Oriental Studies* 12, no. 12 (2002): 111–15. On Zhiyi's concept of buddha nature, see also Yu-kwan Ng, *T'ien-t'ai Buddhism and Early Mādhyamika* (Honolulu: Tendai Institute of Hawaii, Buddhist Studies Program, University of Hawai'i, 1993); and the critique of Ng's argument by Paul L. Swanson, "Understanding Chih-i: Through a Glass, Darkly?" *Journal of the International Association of Buddhist Studies* 17, no. 2 (1994): 337–60.
34. Lucia Dolce, "Between Duration and Eternity: Hermeneutics of the 'Ancient Buddha' of the Lotus Sutra in Chih-i and Nichiren," in Reeves, *Buddhist Kaleidoscope*, 223–39.
35. *Chu sanzang ji ji*, Sengyou (445–518), *T* no. 2145, 55:56c; translated in Daniel Boucher, "Buddhist Translation Procedures in Third-Century China: A Study of Dharmarakṣa and His Translation Idiom" (Ph.D. diss., University of Pennsylvania, 1996), 71.
36. Boucher, "Buddhist Translation Procedures in Third-Century China," 251–52.
37. On Kumārajīva, see Yang Lu, "Narrative and Historicity in the Buddhist Biographies of Early Medieval China: The Case of Kumārajīva," *Asia Major*, 3rd ser., 17, no. 2 (2004): 1–43; Richard H. Robinson, *Early Mādhyamika in India and China* (Madison: University of Wisconsin Press, 1967), 71–77; and Robert Shih, trans., *Biographies des moines éminents de Houei-Kiao: Kao seng tchouan, traduites et annotées par Robert Shih*, Bibliothèque du Muséon 54 (Louvain, Belg.: Institut orientaliste, Bibliothèque de l'Université, 1968), 60–81.
38. Translation from *Kaiyuan shijiao lu*, Zhisheng (ca. 669–740), *T* no. 2154, 55:515a. Earlier versions of the same account read "western regions" (*xiyu*) in place of "Sanskrit text" (*fanben*). See, for instance, *Gaoseng zhuan*, Huijiao (497–554), *T* no. 2059, 50:364a. The passage in the *Lotus Sūtra* occurs at *T* 9:27c; for other English translations, see Hurvitz, 146; and Burton Watson, trans., *The Lotus Sūtra*, Translations from the Asian Classics (New York: Columbia University Press, 1993), 145.
39. Translation from Dharmarakṣa's Chinese translation of the *Lotus Sūtra*, *Zheng fahua jing* (*Saddharmapuṇḍarīka*), Dharmarakṣa (Zhu Fahu [ca. 265–313, or 239–316]), *T* no. 263, 9:95c.

40. *Hongzan Fahua zhuan*, Huixiang (ca. 639–706), *T* no. 2067, 51:14b–17c. On Huixiang and his work, see Daniel B. Stevenson, "Tales of the Lotus Sūtra," in *Buddhism in Practice*, ed. Donald S. Lopez Jr., 427–51 (Princeton, N.J.: Princeton University Press, 1995); and Stevenson's contribution in this volume (chapter 5). For Zhisheng's estimation, see *Kaiyuan shijiao lu*, *T* no. 2154, 55:591b–c.
41. Kabutogi Shōkō, *Hokke hangyō no kenkyū* (Tokyo: Daitō shuppansha, 1982), 139, 174–77, 478–91.
42. Johan Elverskog, *Uygur Buddhist Literature*, Silk Road Studies 1 (Turnhout, Belg.: Brepols, 1997), 59–61.
43. See the groundbreaking essay by Erik Zürcher, "Late Han Vernacular Elements in the Earliest Buddhist Translations," *Journal of the Chinese Language Teachers Association* 13, no. 3 (1977): 177–203. See also Zürcher, "A New Look at the Earliest Chinese Buddhist Texts," in *From Benares to Beijing: Essays on Buddhism and Chinese Religion in Honour of Prof. Jan Yün-hua*, ed. Koichi Shinohara and Gregory Schopen, 277–304 (Oakville, Ont.: Mosaic Press, 1991); Daniel Boucher, "Gāndhārī and the Early Chinese Buddhist Translations Reconsidered: The Case of the *Saddharmapuṇḍarīkasūtra*," *Journal of the American Oriental Society* 118, no. 4 (1998): 471–506; Seishi Karashima, *A Glossary of Dharmarakṣa's Translation of the Lotus Sutra*, Bibliotheca Philologica et Philosophica Buddhica 1 (Tokyo: The International Research Institute for Advanced Buddhology, Soka University, 1998); Karashima, *Glossary of Kumārajīva's Translation of the Lotus Sutra*; and Victor H. Mair, "Buddhism and the Rise of the Written Vernacular: The Making of National Languages," *Journal of Asian Studies* 53, no. 3 (1994): 707–51.
44. Hiroshi Kanno, "A General Survey of Research Concerning Chinese Commentaries on the *Lotus Sūtra*," in *Annual Report of the International Research Institute for Advanced Buddhology at Soka University for the Academic Year 2006* (Tokyo: The International Research Institute for Advanced Buddhology, Soka University, 2007), 417.
45. Only one surviving full-length *Lotus* commentary, a work attributed to Vasubandhu (ca. fourth to fifth centuries), seems to have been composed in India. The text does not survive in Sanskrit but was apparently translated twice into Chinese; see Terry Rae Abbot, "Vasubandhu's Commentary to the *Saddharmapuṇḍarīka-sūtra*: A Study of Its History and Significance" (Ph.D. diss., University of California, Berkeley, 1985).
46. For summaries of the major Chinese commentaries on the *Lotus*, see Leon Hurvitz, *Chih-i (538–597): An Introduction to the Life and Ideas of a Chinese Buddhist Monk*, *Mélanges chinois et bouddhiques* 12 (Brussels: Institut Belge des Hautes Études Chinoises, 1962), part 3; Hiroshi Kanno, "The Reception of *Lotus Sūtra* Thought in China," *Journal of Oriental Studies* 11 (2001): 106–22; and Kanno, "General Survey." For translations of Chinese *Lotus* commentaries, see Paul L. Swanson, *Foundations of T'ien-t'ai Philosophy: The Flowering of the Two Truths Theory in Chinese Buddhism*, Nanzan Studies in Religion and Culture 9 (Berkeley: Asian Humanities Press, 1989); and Young-ho Kim, *Tao-sheng's Commentary on the Lotus Sūtra: A Study and Translation*, SUNY Series in Buddhist Studies (Albany: SUNY Press, 1990).
47. For examples of modern Japanese commentaries on the *Lotus* in English translation, see Niwano Nikkyō, *Buddhism for Today: A Modern Interpretation of The Threefold Lotus Sutra*, trans. Kōjirō Miyasaka (Tokyo: Kōsei, 1976); Niwano, *A Buddhist Approach to Peace*, trans. Masuo Nezu (Tokyo: Kōsei, 1977); and Shinjo

Suguro, *Introduction to the Lotus Sutra*, trans. Nichiren Buddhist International Center (Fremont, Calif.: Jain Publishing, 1998).

48. Kim, *Tao-sheng's Commentary on the Lotus Suūtra.*
49. Zhiyi responded in particular to the *Lotus* commentary of Fayun (467–529); see Swanson, *Foundations of T'ien-t'ai Philosophy*, 125–28, 170–71.
50. Recent scholarship, especially that of Hirai Shun'ei, suggests that the *Profound Meanings of the Lotus Sūtra* (*Fahua wenju*) in particular may owe a great deal to Guanding, who in turn relied heavily on the *Lotus* commentaries of Jizang (549–623); see Kanno, "General Survey," 424–29.
51. Three *Lotus* commentaries were authored by Zhiyi's near contemporary, the influential Sanlun (Mādhyamika) scholar Jizang, and a later one by Kuiji (632–682), written from the perspective of the Faxiang school. On Jizang's view of the *Lotus Sūtra*, see Hiroshi Kanno, "The Three Dharma Wheels of Jizang," in *Buddhist and Indian Studies in Honour of Professor Dr. Sodo Mori* , ed. Publication Committee for Buddhist and Indian Studies in Honour of Professor Dr. Sodo Mori, 399–412 (Hamamatsu, Japan: International Buddhist Association, 2002).
52. Hiroshi Kanno, "Chinese Buddhist Sutra Commentaries of the Early Period," in *Annual Report of the International Research Institute for Advanced Buddhology at Soka University for the Academic Year 2002* (Tokyo: The International Research Institute for Advanced Buddhology, Soka University, 2003), 302–3.
53. The ten subtleties of the trace and origin teachings represent Zhiyi's elucidation of the word *miao* (Ja.: *myō*), meaning "wondrous," "fine," or "subtle," the first of the five characters composing the title of the *Lotus Sūtra* in Kumārajīva's translation (Ch.: *Miaofa lianhua jing*, Ja.: *Myōhō renge kyō*). See Swanson, *Foundations of T'ien-t'ai Philosophy*, 136–37, 206–11.
54. On "division of the teachings" and the centrality of the one-vehicle concept in these schemas, see Enichi Ōchō, "The Beginnings of Buddhist Tenet Classification in China," *Eastern Buddhist*, n.s., 14, no. 2 (1981): 7–94; and Kanno, "Reception of *Lotus Sūtra* Thought in China," 110–12.
55. See, for example, *Miaofa lianhua jing xuanyi*, Zhiyi (538–597), *T* no. 1716, 33:800b 12–13.
56. On miracle tales as a genre, see Robert F. Campany, *Strange Writing: Anomaly Accounts in Early Medieval China* (Albany: SUNY Press, 1996); Campany, "Notes on the Devotional Uses and Symbolic Functions of Sūtra Texts as Depicted in Early Chinese Buddhist Miracle Tales and Hagiographies," *Journal of the International Association of Buddhist Studies* 14, no. 1 (1991): 28–72; John Kieschnick, *The Eminent Monk: Buddhist Ideals in Medieval Chinese Hagiography*, Kuroda Institute, Studies in East Asian Buddhism 10 (Honolulu: University of Hawai'i Press, 1997); and Franciscus Verellen, "'Evidential Miracles in Support of Taoism': The Inversion of a Buddhist Apologetic Tradition in Late Tang China," *T'oung Pao* 78 (1992): 218–63.
57. For a discussion of "stimulus and response," see Robert H. Sharf, *Coming to Terms with Chinese Buddhism: A Reading of the "Treasure Store Treatise,"* Kuroda Institute, Studies in East Asian Buddhism 14 (Honolulu: University of Hawai'i Press, 2002), 77–133.
58. Excerpts from *Accounts of the Propagation of the Lotus Sūtra* (*Hongzan Fahua zhuan*) have been translated by Daniel B. Stevenson as "Tales of the Lotus Sūtra," in *Buddhism in Practice*, ed. Donald S. Lopez Jr., 427–51 (Princeton, N.J.: Princeton University Press, 1995); see also chapter 5 in this volume. Chingen's Japanese col-

lection has been translated by Yoshiko K. Dykstra as *Miraculous Tales of the Lotus Sutra from Ancient Japan: The Dainihonkoku Hokekyōkenki of Priest Chingen* (Honolulu: University of Hawai'i Press, 1983); see also William E. Deal, "The *Lotus Sūtra* and the Rhetoric of Legitimation in Eleventh-Century Japan," *Japanese Journal of Religious Studies* 20, no. 4 (1993): 261–96.

59. *Xu gaoseng zhuan*, Daoxuan (596–667), *T* no. 2060, 50:564b18–19; and Hurvitz, *Chih-i*, 109.

60. The "true aspect of the dharmas" (Ch.: *zhufa shixiang*, Ja.: *shohō jissō*) indicates the true "face" of reality and is another term for ultimate truth. Hurvitz renders it "reality [of the dharmas]." In Kumārajīva's *Lotus* translation, this reality is elaborated as ten "suchnesses" of the dharmas: their marks, nature, substance, powers, functions, causes, effects, retributions, and absolute identity of beginning and end (Hurvitz, 22–23). Since this passage is found only in Kumārajīva's translation, one can assume either that it is his interpolation or that he worked from an unknown Sanskrit version of the text. For Zhiyi's reading of the passage, see *Miaofa lianhua jing xuanyi*, *T* no. 1716, 33:693b9–26; and Hurvitz, *Chih-i*, 290–92.

61. On the three truths in relation to Zhiyi's system of contemplative practice and doctrinal classification, see Swanson, *Foundations of T'ien-t'ai Philosophy*, 114–56; and Neal Donner and Daniel B. Stevenson, *The Great Calming and Contemplation: A Study and Annotated Translation of the First Chapter of Chih-i's Mo-ho chih-kuan*, Kuroda Institute, Classics in East Asian Buddhism (Honolulu: University of Hawai'i Press, 1993), 9–17.

62. Hiroshi Kanno, "A Comparison of Zhiyi's and Jizang's Views of the *Lotus Sūtra*: Did Zhiyi, after All, Advocate a 'Lotus Absolutism'?" in *Annual Report of the International Research Institute for Advanced Buddhology at Soka University for the Academic Year 1999*, 125–47 (Tokyo: The International Research Institute for Advanced Buddhology, Soka University, 2000).

63. Contrary to Hurvitz's claim (*Chih-i*, 229–71), the system of "five periods and eight teachings" developed only in the later Tiantai tradition under the influence of growing sectarian consciousness; see David Chappell, ed., *T'ien-t'ai Buddhism: An Outline of the Fourfold Teachings* (Tokyo: Daiichi shobō, 1983), 36–40. On the development of the Tiantai *Lotus*-centered stance, see Linda L. Penkower, "T'ien-t'ai during the T'ang Dynasty: Chan-jan and the Sinification of Buddhism" (Ph.D. diss., Columbia University, 1993), 225–80; and Penkower, "Making and Remaking Tradition: Chan-Jan's Strategies toward a T'ang T'ien-t'ai Agenda," in *Tendai Daishi kenkyū: Tendai Daishi sen yonhyakunen go-onki kinen shuppan*, ed. Tendai Daishi kenkyū henshū iinkai (Kyoto: Tendai gakkai, 1997), 1338–1289 (reverse pagination).

64. Hurvitz, *Chih-i*, 271–318; Jacqueline I. Stone, *Original Enlightenment and the Transformation of Medieval Japanese Buddhism* (Honolulu: University of Hawai'i Press, 1999), 178–81; and Kanno Hiroshi, *Ichinen sanzen to wa nani ka* (Tokyo: Daisan bunmeisha, 1992).

65. For an illuminating discussion of this issue with regard to the Huayan school, see Robert M. Gimello, "Apophatic and Kataphatic Discourse in Mahāyāna: A Chinese View," *Philosophy East and West* 26, no. 2 (1976): 117–36.

66. In the eleventh century, this understanding led to the controversial Tiantai doctrine that "inherent evil is not extirpated" even in the mind of the Buddha; see Brook Ziporyn, *Evil and/or/as the Good: Omnicentrism, Intersubjectivity, and Value*

Paradox in Tiantai Buddhist Thought (Cambridge, Mass.: Harvard University Asia Center, 2000).

67. Zhiyi held that, in theory, even the person living in depraved circumstances can achieve liberation by making evil the object of contemplation; see Neal Donner, "Chih-i's Meditation on Evil," in *Buddhist and Taoist Practice in Medieval Chinese Society*, ed. David W. Chappell, Buddhist and Taoist Studies 2, 49–64 (Honolulu: University of Hawai'i Press, 1987).
68. On Saichō and early Tendai, see Paul Groner, *Saichō: The Establishment of the Japanese Tendai School*, Berkeley Buddhist Studies Series 7 (Berkeley: Center for South and Southeast Asian Studies, 1984; repr., Honolulu: University of Hawai'i Press, 2000); and Jikō Hazama, "The Characteristics of Japanese Tendai," *Japanese Journal of Religious Studies* 14, nos. 2–3 (1987): 101–11.
69. On Taimitsu, see Fumihiko Sueki, "Annen: The Philosopher Who Japanized Buddhism," *Acta Asiatica* 66 (1994): 69–86; Stone, *Original Enlightenment*, 21–33; Lucia Dolce, "Esoteric Patterns in Nichiren's Interpretation of the Lotus Sutra" (Ph. D. diss., University of Leiden, 2002), especially 29–53, 215–78; and Dolce, "Reconsidering the Taxonomy of the Esoteric: Hermeneutical and Ritual Practices of the Lotus Sutra," in *The Culture of Secrecy in Japanese Religion*, ed. Bernhard Scheid and Mark Teeuwen, 130–71 (London: Routledge, 2006).
70. Stone, *Original Enlightenment*.
71. On Nichiren, see Ruben L. F. Habito and Jacqueline I. Stone, eds., "Revisiting Nichiren," special issue, *Japanese Journal of Religious Studies* 26, nos. 3–4 (1999), which includes a bibliography of Western-language studies on Nichiren through 1999; Stone, *Original Enlightenment*, chap. 6; and Dolce, "Esoteric Patterns in Nichiren's Interpretation of the Lotus Sutra."
72. *Myōhō renge kyō* is the title in Japanese pronunciation of Kumārajīva's Chinese translation of the *Lotus Sūtra*. *Namu*, from Sanskrit *namo-* or *namas*, indicates devotion, praise, and the taking of refuge. *Namu myōhō renge kyō* represents proper scholarly romanization; in actual recitation, minor variations in pronunciation occur among practice groups. On Nichiren's *daimoku* practice and its antecedents, see Jacqueline I. Stone, "Chanting the August Title of the *Lotus Sūtra: Daimoku* Practices in Classical and Medieval Japan," in *Re-Visioning "Kamakura" Buddhism*, ed. Richard K. Payne, Kuroda Institute, Studies in East Asian Buddhism 11, 116–66 (Honolulu: University of Hawai'i Press, 1998); and Dolce, "Esoteric Patterns in Nichiren's Interpretation of the Lotus Sutra," 294–315.
73. Stone, *Original Enlightenment*, 263–95.
74. Lucia Dolce, "Awareness of *Mappō*: Soteriological Interpretations of Time in Nichiren," *Transactions of the Asiatic Society of Japan*, 4th ser., 7 (1992): 81–106.
75. Ruben L. F. Habito, "Bodily Reading of the *Lotus Sūtra*: Understanding Nichiren's Buddhism," *Japanese Journal of Religious Studies* 26, nos. 3–4 (1999): 281–306; Jacqueline I. Stone, "Giving One's Life for the *Lotus Sūtra* in Nichiren's Thought" (unpublished ms.).
76. On Nipponzan Myōhōji, see Ha Poong Kim, "Fujii Nichidatsu's *Tangyō-Raihai*: Bodhisattva Practice for the Nuclear Age," *Cross Currents*, summer 1986, 193–203; and Robert Kisala, *Prophets of Peace: Pacifism and Cultural Identity in Japan's New Religions* (Honolulu: University of Hawai'i Press, 1999), 45–57, 159–62. Works by Nipponzan Myōhōji's founder, Nichidatsu Fujii (1885–1985), have been translated into English. See, for example Fujii, *Buddhism for World Peace*, trans. Yumiko

Miyazaki (Tokyo: Japan-Bharat Sarvodaya Mitrata Sangha, 1980); and Nichidatsu Fujii, *Tranquil Is This Realm of Mine: Dharma Talks and Writings of the Most Venerable Nichidatsu Fujii*, trans. Yumiko Miyazaki (Atlanta: Nipponzan Myōhōji, 2007).

77. Jacqueline I. Stone, "Nichiren's Activist Heirs: Sōka Gakkai, Risshō Kōseikai, Nipponzan Myōhōji," in *Action Dharma: New Studies in Engaged Buddhism*, ed. Christopher Queen, Charles Prebish, and Damien Keown, 63–94 (New York: RoutledgeCurzon, 2003).
78. Gregory Schopen, "The Phrase *sa pṛthivīpradeśaś caityabhūto bhavet* in the *Vajracchedikā*: Notes on the Cult of the Book in Mahāyāna" (1975), reprinted in Schopen, *Figments and Fragments of Mahāyāna Buddhism*, 25–62.
79. Dykstra, *Miraculous Tales of the Lotus Sutra from Ancient Japan*, 2:66, 88.
80. William H. McCullough and Helen Craig McCullough, trans., *A Tale of Flowering Fortunes: Annals of Japanese Aristocratic Life in the Heian Period*, 2 vols. (Stanford, Calif.: Stanford University Press, 1980), 1:267–69; 1:267, n. 47; 2:720.
81. Willa Jane Tanabe, *Paintings of the Lotus Sutra* (New York: Weatherhill, 1988), 7, 33.
82. Ibid., 44–46.
83. Tanabe, *Paintings of the Lotus Sutra*, 42–45; D. Max Moerman, "The Archaeology of Anxiety: An Underground History of Heian Religion," in *Heian Japan: Centers and Peripheries*, ed. Mikael Adolphson, Edward Kamens, and Stacie Yamamoto, 245–71 (Honolulu: University of Hawai'i Press, 2007).
84. The manuscript is Stein no. 2157 in the British Library. The colophon is transcribed and translated in Lionel Giles, *Descriptive Catalogue of the Chinese Manuscripts from Tunhuang in the British Museum* (London: The British Museum, 1957), Giles no. 2771, p. 76, slightly modified. "Shallow consciousness" is our translation of *qianshi*. We follow the term's pre-Buddhist meaning, as noted in Luo Zhufeng et al., eds., *Hanyu dacidian*, 13 vols. (Hong Kong: Sanlian shudian / Shanghai: Shanghai cishu chubanshe, 1987–1995), 5:1367a. The same word occurs in the *Lotus Sūtra* (*T* 9:15b; Hurvitz, 71, "those of shallow perception"), where it means "an ignorant man"; see Karashima, *Glossary of Kumārajīva's Translation of the Lotus Sutra*, s.v. *anfu*. We thank Daniel B. Stevenson for help in interpreting the colophon.
85. The name of this bodhisattva is a complicated problem. Some early Sanskrit manuscripts read "Avalokitasvara," meaning "He Who Observes the Sounds of the World." The corresponding Chinese (in Kumārajīva's rendering) is Guanshiyin (Ja.: Kanzeon) or Guanyin (Ja.: Kannon). Other Chinese renderings (Guanzizai) instead construe the Sanskrit original as Avalokiteśvara, "The Lord Who Looks Down on the World [with Compassion]" or "Perceiving Master."
86. Marie-Thérèse de Mallmann, *Introduction à l'étude d'Avalokiteśvara*, Annales du Musée Guimet, Bibliothèque d'études 57 (Paris: Presses Universitaires de France, 1967); John Clifford Holt, *Buddha in the Crown: Avalokiteśvara in the Buddhist Tradition of Sri Lanka* (New York: Oxford University Press, 1991); and Chün-fang Yü, *Kuan-yin: The Chinese Transformation of Avalokiteśvara* (New York: Columbia University Press, 2001).
87. On the later history of Sound Observer in China, see Glen Dudbridge, *The Legend of Miao-shan*, Oxford Oriental Monographs 1 (London: Ithaca Press for the Board of the Faculty of Oriental Studies, Oxford University, 1978); Dudbridge, "Miao-shan on Stone: Two Early Inscriptions," *Harvard Journal of Asiatic Studies* 42, no. 2 (1982): 589–614; Rolf A. Stein, "Avalokiteśvara/Kouan-yin, un exemple de transformation d'un dieu en déesse," *Cahiers d'Extrême-Asie* 2 (1986): 17–77; P. Steven

Sangren, "Female Gender in Chinese Religious Symbols: Kuan Yin, Ma Tsu, and the 'Eternal Mother,'" *Signs* 9, no. 1 (1983): 4–25; and Yü, *Kuan-yin*. For worship of Sound Observer in Japan, see Yoshiko K. Dykstra, "Tales of the Compassionate Kannon: The *Hasedera Kannon Genki*," *Monumenta Nipponica* 31, no. 2 (1976): 113–43.

88. Raul Birnbaum, *The Healing Buddha* (Boston: Shambhala, 1979), 54–55.
89. On Japanese art of the *Lotus Sūtra*, see Bunsaku Kurata and Yoshirō Tamura, *Art of the Lotus Sutra: Japanese Masterpieces*, trans. Edna B. Crawford (Tokyo: Kōsei, 1987); Tsugio Miya, "Pictorial Art of the *Lotus Sutra* in Japan," in Tanabe and Tanabe, *Lotus Sutra in Japanese Culture*, 75–94; Tanabe, *Paintings of the Lotus Sutra*; and Tanabe's contribution to this volume (chap. 6). On the *Lotus Sūtra* in poetry and songs, see Shōzen Yamada, "Poetry and Meaning: Medieval Poets and the *Lotus Sutra*," in Tanabe and Tanabe, *Lotus Sutra in Japanese Culture*, 95–11; and Yung-Hee Kim, *Songs to Make the Dust Dance: The Ryōjin hishō of Twelfth-Century Japan* (Los Angeles: University of California Press, 1994), especially 75–89.
90. Kawakatsu Kenryō, *Tahōtō to Hokke shisō* (Tokyo: Tōkyōdō shuppan, 1984).
91. On the connections between the *Lotus Sūtra* and women's enlightenment in Japan, see Groner, "The *Lotus Sūtra* and Saichō's Interpretation," 61–62; Kamens, "Dragon-Girl"; and Yoshida, "Enlightenment of the Dragon King's Daughter," 313–17.
92. On poetry, see LaFleur, *Karma of Words*, 80–106; and Stone, *Original Enlightenment*, 43–46. More broadly, see Rajyashree Pandey, *Writing and Renunciation in Medieval Japan: The Works of the Poet-Priest Kamo no Chōmei* (Ann Arbor, Mich.: Center for Japanese Studies, 1998), 9–55. For Genji, see *The Tale of Genji*, trans. Royall Tyler, 2 vols. (New York: Viking, 2001), 1:461.

[2]

EXPEDIENT DEVICES, THE ONE VEHICLE, AND THE LIFE SPAN OF THE BUDDHA

Carl Bielefeldt

EXPEDIENT DEVICES

THE *LOTUS SŪTRA* begins on an odd note. Before an enormous crowd, both human and nonhuman, the Buddha Śākyamuni enters into a deep state of concentration; emitting a beam of light from his brow, he illumines myriad world systems in all directions. The bodhisattva Maitreya naturally wonders what is going on; the bodhisattva Mañjuśrī explains to him that, in his experience from previous lives, this sort of thing happens when a buddha is about to preach the *Scripture of the Lotus Blossom of the Fine Dharma*. Thereupon, the Buddha emerges from his trance and starts talking to his disciple Śāriputra: "The buddhas' wisdom is profound and incalculable. The gateways of their wisdom are hard to understand and hard to enter, so that no voice-hearer [*śrāvaka*] or *pratyekabuddha* can know them. . . . What he preaches accords with what is appropriate, but the end point of its meaning is hard to understand. Śāriputra, since achieving buddhahood I have, by a variety of means and by resort to a variety of parables, broadly set forth the spoken doctrine, by countless devices leading the living beings and enabling them to abandon their encumbrances" (Hurvitz, 22).

The śrāvakas in the audience are troubled: "Why has the World-Honored One made this speech earnestly praising expedient devices?" Why does he tell us that what he knows is so hard to understand that śrāvakas and pratyekabuddhas cannot get it? Śāriputra asks the Buddha to explain. The Buddha replies that he would rather not talk about it, since everyone would get upset (Hurvitz, 25–27).

What troubles the audience, what the Buddha is reluctant to discuss, is the fact that he may not have been entirely frank with his followers. He may not have been telling them what is really on his mind; in fact, what is really on his mind is so difficult that he may not be able to tell them. Instead, he has been resorting to various expedient devices, simply to help them get free from their spiritual "encumbrances." The disciples are troubled because they assume that the Buddha means what he says and says what he thinks, and that, by following what he has been telling them, they can master his teaching. Indeed, we are told, among the disciples in the audience are no less than twelve hundred who have already mastered his teachings, have already become "worthies" (*arhats*) and attained the goal of *nirvāṇa* by following what the Buddha has been telling them (Hurvitz, 25).

This opening passage of the *Lotus Sūtra*, occurring in the first two chapters, is one of the most famous and influential in the text; and the Buddha's revelation in this passage that his teachings are "expedient devices" for guiding his followers introduces one of the most popular and powerful notions of the Mahāyāna tradition. The authors of the *Lotus Sūtra* did not invent this notion, and the history of the notion takes it to places well beyond what the authors may have had in mind. Still, especially in East Asian Mahāyāna, where the *Lotus Sūtra* was particularly popular, this passage and its elaboration in the chapters immediately following it become something like the locus classicus for the term "expedient device" and the chief source of much thinking about the nature of the Buddha's teachings. In this chapter, I want simply to describe the context and use of the term in the sūtra; at the end I shall briefly try to say just a bit about its impact on East Asian Buddhism. First, however, a word or two on the word itself.[1]

What Leon Hurvitz likes to translate in English as "devices" or "expedient devices" is the Chinese word *fangbian*, chosen by the translator Kumārajīva (Jiumoluoshi [344–413, or 350–409]) to render what appears in the Sanskrit text here as *upāyakauśalya*, the title of the famous second chapter of the *Lotus Sūtra*. Kumārajīva seems to have had a habit of using fangbian for both the compound upāyakauśalya and the single word *upāya*; and writers in English have been similarly casual in their treatment of these two terms, such that we have an array of expressions for them. The Chinese fangbian suggests a "convenience" or "convenient method." The Sanskrit upāya connotes an "approach" to a goal, a "strategy" for accomplishing something, a "method," or "technique"; kauśalya indicates "expertise" or "skill." Hence, a likely sense of the Sanskrit compound is probably something like "expertise in method(s)." From this, the Chinese and the Sanskrit (both the compound and the single term *upāya*) get rendered variously in English, not only as Hurvitz's preferred "device" or "expedient device" but also simply as "expedient," "means," and "skillfulness," as well as, perhaps most commonly, "skill in means" and "skillful means."

While the word *upāya* occurs here and there in the early Buddhist texts, it is only in the Mahāyāna that it flourishes as a term of art and takes on a rich life of its own. There, in soteriological literature, it becomes one of the prime virtues of the bodhisattva, often associated with compassion and paired with wisdom; it gets listed as one of the ten "perfections" (*pāramitās*) of the bodhisattva, said to be cultivated especially on the seventh stage of his path. In exegetical material, it becomes a tool for the interpretation of texts and teachings, used especially to distinguish what is merely a provisional formulation from the final word on a topic. In metaphysical and cosmological writing, it becomes a way of talking about the bodies of a buddha and sometimes even about the status of things in general.

Historically speaking, the *Lotus Sūtra* comes, if not quite at the beginning, quite early in the semantic life of the word upāya. Subsequent readers of the sūtra could, of course, see the text through lenses developed in that later life, but without those lenses, the uses of upāya in the sūtra appear fairly limited, even while their exact implications remain ambiguous and, as the Buddha warns us, difficult to understand. We are dealing here primarily with a sense of upāya as what we might loosely call "spiritual technique." In this sense, the term is sometimes used by Buddhist authors in reference to the techniques employed by a practitioner to "approach" the goal—that is, in reference to the methods of Buddhist spiritual practice. More often, and more famously, it indicates, as in the passage of the *Lotus Sūtra*, techniques used to guide others toward the goal. The Buddha, after all, has by definition already achieved the goal; his techniques are designed to help the rest of us. In the opening passage and early chapters, the Buddha's techniques are treated largely as his strategic ways of talking; but, as we shall see in the sūtra's later chapters, he also has other, more dramatic methods, of a sort suggested by that spotlight on his forehead.

THE ONE VEHICLE

The *Lotus Sūtra* has no explicit definition or theoretical account of the Buddha's expedient devices. Rather, it simply uses the notion primarily to explain and justify the fact that what the Buddha says in the sūtra seems so different from what he has previously taught. Hence, to see how the sūtra treats the notion, we have no choice but to look at what the Buddha has to say in the sūtra, how it differs from what he has previously said, and how he explains the apparent conflicts in his teachings. This is what the Buddha says he would rather not talk about.

The reader may well have wondered why the Buddha would begin a sermon with a topic that he does not want to discuss. In fact, of course, his reluctance is another of his rhetorical devices. Once Śāriputra asks him the requisite three times, he consents to address the matter. He was right, it seems, to worry that his talk would make people upset: immediately, five thousand members of the audience rise and withdraw. These are the arrogant ones, who think that they have "attained . . . what in fact they have not"—that is, who think they have mastered the Buddha's teachings and do not want now to hear that there is more to the dharma than they thought. The Buddha lets them go with good riddance and launches into his sermon (Hurvitz, 28).

First, he informs Śāriputra that what he is about to say is said by buddhas only very rarely, like the rare blossoming of the *udumbara* (cluster fig) flower. He repeats his warning that, while his words are "not vain," he preaches "appropriately," using countless "expedient devices." His dharma, he says in one of the most quoted lines of the text, is "not a thing that discursive or discriminatory reasoning can understand. Only buddhas can know it" (Hurvitz, 28–29).[2] Then, Śākyamuni reveals "the one great cause" of his mission as a buddha: "The buddhas, the World-Honored Ones, for one great cause alone appear in the world. . . . [They] appear in the world because they wish to cause the beings to enter into the path of the Buddha's knowledge and insight. . . . Śāriputra, the Thus Come One [Tathāgata] by resort to the one buddha vehicle alone preaches the dharma to the beings. There are no other vehicles, whether two or three" (Hurvitz, 29).

As noted in chapter 1 of this volume, present-day readers of the *Lotus Sūtra* sometimes speak of it as what we might call a medium without a message—that is, a work that has no message apart from the celebration of its own importance. It is certainly true that, like many Mahāyāna scriptures, the *Lotus* is highly self-referential: it explains its own origins and predicts its own future; it lavishes praise on its own significance and admonishes its audience (or the reader) to accept, revere, memorize, recite, copy, and teach the sūtra; it offers great rewards to the believer and threatens dire consequences for those who reject and slander the sūtra. In the midst of what sometimes seems an almost paranoid self-preoccupation, the reader may indeed begin to wonder if there is a self apart from the preoccupation.

This granted, it seems fairly obvious that, for the people who put together at least the first several chapters of the *Lotus*, and certainly for generations of Buddhist readers of those chapters, the prime message of the sūtra is the one conveyed in the lines from Chapter 2 that I have just quoted:

whatever else the Buddha may have said, in the end the sole purpose of his ministry is to establish beings on the path to buddhahood; everything he teaches is based on what he calls here "the one buddha vehicle." This message is repeated throughout the chapter and then reinforced in a series of parables and predictions in the following seven chapters.

For modern-day readers familiar with later Mahāyāna traditions, in which the ideal of the bodhisattva career and the goal of buddhahood are often taken largely for granted, it may seem oddly anticlimactic that the *Lotus Sūtra* would present its message with such fanfare as a rare and shocking revelation. It is, of course, a universal assumption of the Mahāyāna literature that the bodhisattva has the attainment of buddhahood as her goal. What is rare and shocking, then, is not that the Buddha would want to lead bodhisattvas to the enlightenment of a buddha but that he would want to turn everyone into a bodhisattva seeking the enlightenment of a buddha. There is, he says, only this one vehicle, not two or three.

Exactly what the Buddha means by two vehicles here is not entirely clear. One might think first of the common distinction, invoked in the subsequent verse section of Chapter 2, between the vehicles called "lesser" (*hīnayāna*) and "greater" (mahāyāna); but here the Buddha may well have in mind the vehicles of the śrāvaka (*śrāvakayāna*) and pratyekabuddha (*pratyekabuddhayāna*), the two types of followers, we may recall, that the Buddha declared in his opening remarks could not understand his wisdom. His reference to three vehicles, then, adds to these the vehicle of the bodhisattva (*bodhisattvayāna*), typically identified with the greater vehicle. In any case, the point remains that, whatever other vehicles the Buddha may have mentioned, they are not real alternatives to his one buddha vehicle (*ekabuddhayāna*).[3]

Here, the *Lotus Sūtra* stands out from the texts associated with the early Mahāyāna movement, which typically recognize the śrāvaka, pratyekabuddha, and bodhisattva as three distinct and legitimate types of followers, each with its own vehicle. The second of these, the pratyekabuddha, remains a rather mysterious type, its odd name often taken to mean "solitary buddha," interpreted as one who has acquired (some sort of) *bodhi* (enlightenment) without assuming the teaching mission of a buddha.[4] In contrast, the śrāvaka, a term Hurvitz translates as "voice hearer," is what we might call the standard follower of the Buddha, for whom he teaches the four noble truths and establishes the vehicle leading to the cessation of suffering and rebirth in *saṃsāra*. The successful śrāvaka is an arhat, like the twelve hundred worthies said to be in the audience at the time the *Lotus Sūtra* is taught.

The bodhisattvas, of course, aim higher. For them, the Buddha teaches the six perfections (pāramitās), the practice of which will ultimately lead to the "supreme perfect enlightenment" (*anuttarasamyaksaṃbodhi*) of a buddha. In current writing on Buddhism, we seem often to use the English word "enlightenment" as if it were simply some sort of liberating spiritual insight, sought by Buddhists of every persuasion as the goal of their religion. In fact, however, as we see in the *Lotus Sūtra*, the "supreme perfect enlightenment" attributed to a buddha in the Mahāyāna sūtras is an extraordinary state, quite different from anything dreamed of by the arhat (or the modern Zen master). It is a state of omniscience, what the *Lotus Sūtra* sometimes refers to by the technical term "knowledge of all modes" (*sarvākārajñatā*). It is not only complete knowledge but truly awesome power—not just the powers of a teacher with his countless heuristic devices; not just such meteorological tricks as making flowers rain from the sky or causing the earth to shake in six ways; not just the standard supernormal powers of a yogi to manifest multiple bodies, fly through the sky, read minds, predict the future, and so on; but powers of a cosmic reach, to stop time, alter the world, and even design a world, or buddha "field" (*kṣetra*), of one's own. A buddha in Mahāyāna sūtras, like Śākyamuni in the *Lotus Sūtra*, is no mere wise man and kindly teacher; he is more like a supernatural ruler, a lord of hosts.

The production of such a supernatural being is the purpose of the bodhisattva vehicle. Given this purpose, it is hardly surprising that accounts of the vehicle take on truly mythological proportions. In the literature of the Mahāyāna, the bodhisattva path is said to take three incalculable eons to complete. It begins with producing the aspiration for supreme perfect enlightenment (*bodhicittotpāda*) and making a formal vow (*praṇidhāna*) to attain it. It proceeds through life after life of practicing the perfections, as a follower of many buddhas. At some point, the bodhisattva will receive a prediction (*vyākaraṇa*) of his eventual buddhahood from one of these buddhas; and then, in his penultimate life, he will ascend to the Tuṣita Heaven, whence he will finally descend through an immaculate birth into the realm over which he is destined to preside as a buddha.[5]

This fantastic vision of the buddhas and bodhisattvas was surely developed less as practical prescription for Buddhist religious life than as mythic description intended to exalt the supernatural status of the objects of Buddhist devotion. When the Mahāyāna sūtras begin to talk of the vision as a real religious option, they do not advertise it for everyone; on the contrary, they emphasize the elite nature of this option, reserved for the truly heroic type, the "great being" (*mahāsattva*) willing to take on the enormous, impossible task of saving the world. For the rest of us, the vehicle of the śrāvaka remains the norm, and the purpose of a buddha's mission remains the teaching of this vehicle and the guidance of beings to nirvāṇa. No wonder, then, that the audience of the *Lotus Sūtra* is shocked to hear that, in fact, the one great cause of the Buddha's appearance in the world is to make everyone a buddha. No wonder the Buddha of the *Lotus Sūtra* feels the need to explain and justify his new revelation.

After revealing the true purpose of his mission, the Buddha goes on to claim that not only he but all the buddhas of the past, present, and future teach this same message. He then sharply disowns as disciples any among his followers who do not acknowledge the message, who think of themselves as arhats or pratyekabuddhas and do not seek supreme perfect enlightenment. Softening a bit, he does excuse those who live at a time after his nirvāṇa, when it may be difficult to find this sūtra (Hurvitz, 30). The text then turns to the verse restatement of the prose section we have been looking at. Here, the Buddha assures his audience that attaining the path of the buddha is not so daunting as it may seem: those who make offerings to the relics of past buddhas, those who build *stūpas* ("reliquaries") to buddhas or make images of buddhas (even children drawing with their fingers in the dirt), those who offer music or hymns to the Buddha, those who worship at the Buddha's sacred sites and speak his name but once—all these have attained the buddha path (Hurvitz, 36–38). Then, Śākyamuni recounts the story of his own enlightenment and teaching career—how he realized the difficulty of teaching the buddha vehicle and thus followed the practice of all past buddhas in using expedient devices to teach the three vehicles; how, after seeing that there are myriads of beings who seek the buddha path, he has decided that now is the time to reveal it:

> Now, I, joyfully and fearlessly,
> In the midst of the bodhisattvas
> Frankly casting aside my expedient devices,
> Merely preach the unexcelled path.
>
> (HURVITZ, 42)

The chapters following "Expedient Devices" are taken up with parables, designed to clarify the Buddha's message, and predictions of buddhahood for members of the audience, intended to verify the truth of the message. Chapter 3 opens with the interesting confession by Śāriputra that, although he had always wished he, too, might become a buddha, when he heard the

Buddha talking of this possibility, he could not help but wonder if this was really the Buddha speaking or the great obstructor of Buddhists, Māra, "The Evil One," masquerading as the Buddha. To put to rest any lingering doubts, the Buddha reveals to him that, though Śāriputra may now think of himself as an arhat, in fact he has been training as a bodhisattva for many lifetimes; and that, after incalculable, limitless, inconceivable eons to come, he will become a buddha named Flower Glow (Padmaprabha), established in a lovely realm called Free of Defilements (Viraja; Hurvitz, 47–53). Śāriputra is, of course, delighted by the prediction but notes that others in the audience may still need convincing. Hence, the Buddha consents to use the expedient device of a parable and proceeds to tell the famous story of the burning house.

Of the several parables in the *Lotus Sūtra*, the burning house has been the source of choice for interpretations of the implications of the teaching of the one vehicle. Unfortunately, although a relatively simple tale on the surface, on key points, the parable is notoriously problematic and subject to readings that take the one vehicle in sharply different directions. In brief, the story goes that the house of a wealthy man catches fire, trapping his sons within. The children, however, absorbed in their play, are oblivious to the danger. The father, therefore, knowing that the children like carriages of various sorts, lures them from the house with offers of carriages pulled by goats, deer, and oxen, respectively. When the ruse succeeds and the children are safely out of the house, the father presents them all with a great jeweled carriage pulled by a handsome, swift white ox (Hurvitz, 55–57). The story told, the Buddha asks Śāriputra if the father lied to his children. "No," says Śāriputra, for his intention was good, his words saved their lives, and in the end he delivered more than he offered. The Buddha approves and goes on to draw out the obvious correlations: the burning house is saṃsāra, the father is the Buddha, the children are his followers, the three carriages are the three vehicles of the śrāvaka, pratyekabuddha, and bodhisattva taught as an expedient device, and the jeweled carriage the father gives the children is the one great vehicle the Buddha now offers to all (Hurvitz, 57–60).

Like all parables, this one has its limits. For those trying to understand the actual status of the three vehicles and their relationship to the one buddha vehicle, it may raise more questions than it answers. If, for example, the children's escape from the house represents the freedom from suffering in saṃsāra, are we to understand all three vehicles as leading to nirvāṇa? If the great ox carriage is available to the children only once they are out of the house, does this mean that mastery of one of the three vehicles is a prior condition for riding in the one buddha vehicle? If all three vehicles have the equal effect of escape from the burning house, why privilege the bodhisattva vehicle as somehow more exalted than the other two? As generations of interpreters have realized, the answers to such questions and more may turn to a large degree on the issue of the relationship between the ox carriage promised by the father and the great ox carriage he actually delivers: if the carriage he delivers is what he promised, then the one great vehicle is the same as the bodhisattva vehicle; if the two carriages are different, then the one great vehicle is something else again. The possibility that it is something else again, and the search for what that might be, eventually becomes one of the driving forces of East Asian Buddhist thought and practice.

The authors of the *Lotus Sūtra* seem drawn to the father-son relationship; and whatever its problems as theology, their story of the burning house gives a reading of the Buddha's expedient devices familiar to any parent (and to many children): the father sees a bigger picture that the children do not grasp; rather than trying to explain this picture, he talks to them in their own terms, manipulating them, so to speak, to do what he knows is best for them. His decision to offer them three different kinds of carriage seems to be rather ad hoc, based simply on his sense of what will appeal to the children's varied tastes. In the chapter following this story, we encounter another father using expedient devices to help a son, but this time, his choices seem driven by a larger strategic program.

In Chapter 4, three of the Buddha's most famous disciples, Subhūti, Kātyāyana, and Maudgalyāyana, decide to offer their own parable to explain how the one vehicle fits with Śākyamuni's previous teachings. A rich man had an only son who ran away as a youth and eventually became a poor beggar. After many years, the son wandered unknowingly back to his father's residence. The father, recognizing him and delighting that he had found the heir to his fortune, sought to detain him, but the son, unaware of his parentage and terrified of the man's wealth and power, ran away. Therefore, the father devised a plan to hire the son as a menial and pay him to work at cleaning dung. After twenty years of this arrangement, gladly accepted, the son had grown into a confident, responsible worker; the father then elevated him to manager of the estate and, as the old man approached his end, finally announced to the son his true identity and turned over to him his inheritance (Hurvitz, 79–82). Again, of course, the rich man is the Buddha; the son represents his followers, who, unaware of their true status and in awe of the Buddha's majesty, have accepted the lowly task of dealing with the dung of lesser teachings, seeking only nirvāṇa as their wages. Now the Buddha has revealed their true station as legitimate heirs to his spiritual fortune of supreme, perfect enlightenment.

This story, sometimes dubbed the Buddhist parable of "the prodigal son," has been popular with readers perhaps especially because of its depiction of the Buddhist life as a return to one's original lot, a recovery of one's birthright. The Mahāyāna literature likes to talk of the bodhisattva as belonging to the buddha "clan" (*gotra*), and later Mahāyāna thought often extends this notion into a metaphysical claim that all beings share the nature of a buddha. In this view, like the son in the story, we have simply forgotten who we really are and need only to be reminded. While some who favor this view take the recognition of our birthright as a religious starting point, in the story, it comes at the very end of a long and difficult path. And in this we see what seems a rather different rationale for the Buddha's expedient devices than that suggested by the burning-house story. Here, the Buddha's teaching of the three vehicles is not simply a set of convenient white lies for different types of followers but a program intended to raise followers through stages of spiritual maturation. In this sense, mastery of the "dung" of the lesser teachings seems somehow to be a necessary condition for getting the greater truth.

At the beginning of the next chapter, Śākyamuni approves his disciples' efforts at a parable but then offers his own comment that seems at odds with it. This chapter is called "Medicinal Herbs," after the famous simile of plants and rain. Imagine, the Buddha says, a great cloud that rains everywhere equally, yet the plants receiving this moisture grow and blossom each according to its own nature. So, too, the Buddha rains down a single dharma, and beings who hear it flourish each in his or her own way (Hurvitz, 95–97). The verse section that follows expands on this vegetative metaphor: ordinary humans and gods represent lesser plants; arhats and pratyekabuddhas are intermediate plants; bodhisattvas are superior plants. Or, in a second formulation, arhats and pratyekabuddhas are medicinal herbs; beginning bodhisattvas are small trees; advanced bodhisattvas are great trees (Hurvitz, 100–2).

At this point, Kumārajīva's translation breaks off, but Sanskrit versions of the *Lotus Sūtra* continue the discussion with two additional similes: that of the light of the Buddha's wisdom shining equally on the whole world, just as the light of sun and moon illumines everything without distinction; and that of the one vehicle that becomes distinguished as many, just as the potter's clay becomes differentiated in its uses for different pots (Hurvitz, 103). What is striking about these three similes as explanations for the variety of the Buddha's teachings is that, if taken at face value, all seem to dismiss his use of expedient devices: the Buddha does not adapt his teaching to his audience; he has only a single teaching, which looks different or functions differently depending on how it is received and used.

The Sanskrit texts continue with yet another parable offering what seems yet another view of the three vehicles. There is a congenitally blind man who denies that there is any such thing as vision. A physician cures him of his blindness with medicinal herbs, and the man is quite proud that he can see everything. Then, mystic seers (*ṛṣis*) point out that what he can see with his normal vision is in fact quite limited, and they teach him the five "superknowledges" (*abhijñās*), or supernormal powers: the divine eye and divine ear, knowledge of others' thoughts, recollection of past lives, and magical powers. After practicing meditation and attaining the five, he realizes that his previous vision was like blindness. The Buddha explains that the blind man represents the ignorant beings in saṃsāra; normal vision indicates the śrāvaka and pratyekabuddha, who know only nirvāṇa; the superknowledges stand for the supreme, perfect enlightenment of a buddha (Hurvitz, 103–7). Here, the three vehicles are ranged in an explicit hierarchy of religious knowledge, a treatment of expedient devices quite common among later exegetes. The Buddha's earlier claim that there is only one vehicle, not two or three, seems here to have been almost forgotten.

Following the parable on plants, Chapters 6, 8, and 9 are taken with up with a series of increasingly generous prophecies of buddhahood. After the famous disciple Mahākāśyapa gets named as a future buddha, it seems almost everyone in the audience wants the same. Subhūti, Kātyāyana, and Maudgalyāyana come first (Chapter 6); next Purṇa and five hundred arhats (Chapter 8); then Śākyamuni's cousin, Ānanda, and son, Rāhula, plus two thousand other disciples (Chapter 9). This extraordinary display of prophetic liberality by the Buddha is climaxed at the start of Chapter 10, when he announces that he is hereby conferring a prophecy of supreme, perfect enlightenment on anyone who, even after his nirvāṇa, so much as hears with gladness a single verse or phrase of the *Lotus Sūtra* (Hurvitz, 159).

Nestled within this series of prophecies is yet another well-known parable, in Chapter 8, which is both similar to and different from the earlier story of the prodigal son. Here, the five hundred arhats receiving prophecy liken their situation to the following case. A drunken man falls asleep at his friend's house. The friend has to leave on a trip but, before going, kindly sews a priceless gem into the lining of the sleeping man's garment. Unaware of this gift, the man subsequently struggles to eke out a living. Only when he again encounters his friend and learns of the gem does he realize that he could have been rich all along (Hurvitz, 151). In this story, the gem is the bodhisattva vehicle, taught by the Buddha to the arhats in previous lives but subsequently forgotten; the man's life as a pauper is the śrāvaka vehicle, with its meager reward of nirvāṇa. In later uses of this popular story, the gem often becomes a metaphor for the buddha nature, the discovery of which reveals to us an inherent wealth we have ignored. Notice that, while the theme of forgetting our true status is shared with the parable of the prodigal son, here the practice and mastery of the śrāvaka vehicle play no religious role: the śrāvaka vehicle is just an expression of ignorance.

There is one other famous parable of the one vehicle in the *Lotus Sūtra*, the story of the conjured city in Chapter 7. Most of this chapter is taken up with an elaborate account of an otherwise obscure buddha from countless eons ago named Victorious Through Great Penetrating Knowledge (Mahābhijñājñānābhibhū), who also preached the *Lotus Sūtra* and who produced from among his disciples sixteen who went on to become buddhas now teaching in buddha fields throughout the ten directions. Among these is none other than Śākyamuni. In what seems an odd bit of editing, at its very end the chapter turns suddenly to a parable of the one vehicle. A caravan sets out to reach a cache of jewels. The road is very difficult, and the travelers want to turn back. The caravan leader uses his power of expedient devices to conjure up a city at which the caravan can rest. Then, rested and refreshed, they continue to their destination. The conjured city, the Buddha explains, is the nirvāṇa of the śrāvaka and pratyekabuddha vehicles. It is not real but only taught by the Buddha to encourage followers who think the path of the buddha is too difficult for them (Hurvitz, 136–37).

Here we have an account of the one vehicle that draws on the common image of a pilgrim's progress along the path to buddhahood. In the image of a progress, there is something of the spiritual development seen in the prodigal son story but nothing of the latter's model of a return home or of a discovery of one's true status. Unlike the other parables, in this one it seems that everyone is from the outset intentionally pursuing the buddha path. The alternative, easier teaching of the śrāvaka's nirvāṇa, is just a rest stop on the road for those weary of the journey. It is a mirage, an illusion, but apparently such a powerful illusion that it actually functions to refresh the travelers. In this sense, then, the parable works something like the burning-house story, where a false promise produces a desired effect. Perhaps most interesting, the parable introduces a use of expedient devices not just as heuristic method but as magical display. This use points us toward an image of the Buddha that is the focus of later chapters of the text.

THE LIFE SPAN OF THE BUDDHA

The early chapters of the *Lotus Sūtra* are devoted, as we have seen, to the theme of the one vehicle, and the meaning of upāyakauśalya here revolves around interpretation of the nature of Śākyamuni's teachings. In subsequent chapters, the focus of the text shifts to the nature of Śākyamuni himself, and here his skill in expedient devices takes on a new, more mysterious sense that significantly complicates an already difficult picture. Despite the mythical accounts of his prior career as a bodhisattva and the hyperbolic praise of his myriad virtues, the Buddha of the early chapters remains largely an expositor of the dharma, the latest in a long series of buddhas who preach the *Lotus*. In later chapters, this function as supreme teacher is eclipsed by his images as master illusionist and what might almost be called the ringmaster of a cosmic performance. In effect, these chapters do for the Buddha what the earlier did for his teaching: just as the true dharma is much greater than people think, so the true Buddha is much grander than people imagine.

The revelation of the Buddha's true nature unfolds in a narrative developed over Chapters 11 through 16. A hint of what is to come occurs at the end of Chapter 10. There, in the context of encouraging his followers to preach the *Lotus Sūtra* "after the extinction of the Thus Come One," the Buddha offers to help: "I will send magically conjured men as multitudes gathered to listen to dharma. I will also send magically conjured *bhikṣus* [monks], *bhikṣuṇīs* [nuns], *upāsakas* [laymen], and *upāsikās* [laywomen], who shall listen to the preaching of dharma. . . . I will send large numbers of gods and dragons, ghosts and demons, *gandharvas* [mythical birds] and *asuras* [demigods] to hear him preach the dharma. . . . From time to time I will enable the preacher of dharma to see my body. If he forgets or otherwise loses a single period of this scripture, I will simply tell it to him" (Hurvitz, 164).

The reader may well wonder how the Buddha can do all this after his extinction in nirvāṇa. The answer comes in the following chapters.

The opening of Chapter 11 is the most dramatic scene in the sūtra. A gigantic jeweled stūpa emerges from the earth and rises high into the air above the Buddha and his assembly. From within the towering edifice comes a voice praising Śākyamuni's preaching of the *Lotus Sūtra*. The Buddha explains that this is the reliquary of the ancient buddha Many Jewels (Prabhūtaratna), who made a vow to bring his stūpa wherever the *Lotus* is taught. Śākyamuni uses the beam on his forehead to reveal countless buddhas in all directions preaching the dharma in their own buddha realms. He then transforms his own realm into a magnificent land in which all these buddhas can gather. Once they have all arrived, Śākyamuni flies into the air, opens the stūpa of Many Jewels, and joins him inside. Śākyamuni then uses his powers to lift the entire assembly into the air, announces to them that he will soon enter nirvāṇa, and calls for volunteers to whom he can entrust the *Lotus Sūtra*.

Needless to say, this scene is heavy with symbolism, and students of the Mahāyāna will see in it a vivid representation of the Buddhist cults of book and stūpa that are often said to have informed the early literature of the great vehicle. The *Lotus* has previously recommended the construction of stūpas in honor of the book and has even claimed that, like the stūpa reliquary, the book itself contains the body of the Buddha (Hurvitz, 163). Here, however, the complex interrelation of the two is particularly well done: the stūpa of Many Jewels, witness of the *Lotus*, comes to validate the preaching of the book; the preacher of the book enters into the stūpa, identifying himself with the witness, and announces, in effect, his transformation into everlasting relic; the book remains his enduring legacy, kept alive by those to whom it is entrusted. As a literary device, this fantastic scene can be read as a direct revelation of the universal significance of the *Lotus Sūtra* as well as a demonstration of the cosmic dominion of Śākyamuni as its revealer. It is hardly surprising that the scene is one of the most popular depictions of the sūtra in Buddhist art.

At this dramatic point in the story (beginning with Chapter 12 in Kumārajīva's version), there is something of an interlude, as the Buddha tells the interesting tale of his service in a previous life to the evil Devadatta, and Mañjuśrī introduces the famous dragon girl who shocks everyone by becoming a buddha on the spot. In Chapter 13, the Buddha gives prophecies of buddhahood to his aunt and his former wife; and in the next chapter, he sets out a fourfold set of guidelines for those who would teach the *Lotus*.[6] Finally, in Chapter 15, the tale of the giant stūpa picks up again: the Buddha announces that, despite his call for teachers of the *Lotus*, he does not really need more than he already has, for he has among his disciples "bodhisattva-mahāsattvas equal in number to the sands of sixty thousand Ganges rivers." Immediately the earth splits open, and incalculable thousands of myriads of millions of bodhisattvas emerge, rise into the air, take their places by the suspended stūpa, and begin praising the Buddha. The praise, we are told, takes fifty minor eons, but the Buddha uses his supernormal powers to make it appear to happen in half a day (Hurvitz, 206–7).

When Śākyamuni declares that all these bodhisattvas dwelling under the earth were trained by him, his audience is dubious. As it has been only some forty years since he achieved buddhahood and started teaching, they point out, how could he possibly have trained this vast multitude? The Buddha responds, in effect, "Just believe it." When asked three times, he consents to explain. What he says forms the content of Chapter 16, "The Life Span of the Thus Come One," long considered by readers of the *Lotus* to rival or surpass Chapter 2, "Expedient Devices," in importance: "In all the worlds, gods, men, and asuras all say that the present Śākyamunibuddha left the palace of the Śakya clan and at a place not far removed from the city of Gayā, seated on the platform of the path, attained anuttarasamyaksaṃbodhi. And yet, O good men, since in fact I achieved buddhahood it has been incalculable, limitless hundreds of thousands of myriads of millions of *nayutas* [hundred billions] of *kalpas* [eons]" (Hurvitz, 219).

The Buddha goes on to explain that it is only as an expedient device that he pretends to come into this life, achieve enlightenment, and pass into nirvāṇa; in fact, he has been dwelling here, and also in countless other realms, from time immemorial, and he will continue to endure for twice that time in the future (Hurvitz, 220–21).[7] He then provides one of his parables to justify his show of nirvāṇa.

A doctor has many sons who become ill from drinking poison. The father prepares medicine for them. Some of the sons take the medicine and are cured, but some are so crazed by the poison that they refuse the medicine. So the doctor devises a strategy to shock them: he tells them he is dying and is leaving the medicine for them to take after his death. He departs and has word sent back that he has died. The crazed sons then take the medicine and are restored to health, whereupon the father returns (Hurvitz, 221–23). The point of the parable would seem to be that, in the presence of the Buddha, we may focus on him and fail to take the medicine of his dharma, but surprisingly the Buddha does not himself make this point. Instead, he says that he makes a show of passing into nirvāṇa lest his followers take his presence for granted and fail to plant the "wholesome roots" (*kuśalamūla*) of humble reverence for him (Hurvitz, 221). On this reading, we are supposed to focus on the Buddha, and his expedient device is intended precisely to encourage us in this.

The *Lotus Sūtra* is not only about itself; it is also about the Buddha Śākyamuni. And the treatment of the Buddha's expedient devices in the sūtra is not only a justification for the sūtra itself; it is also a glorification of the powers of Śākyamuni. The Buddha's skill in adapting his teachings to his audience is just one—indeed, one of the less impressive—powers of the Buddha celebrated throughout the sūtra, from his initial illumination of countless world systems in the opening chapter, through his manipulation of these world systems in the Many Jewels stūpa cycle, to the remarkable display in Chapter 21, "The Supernatural Powers of the Thus Come One," in which he lights up the worlds of the ten directions with multicolored rays from his pores and extends his tongue up to the heaven of the god Brahmā for a period of one hundred thousand years (Hurvitz, 263).[8] The Buddha here is a master of space and time, playing with them as he likes. His revelation from the stūpa of Many Jewels tells us why: he is a being of almost infinite extent and duration who appears in particular times and places through the expedient device of self-conjuring. He conjures himself, and then he conjures other buddhas, whom he sometimes describes as "emanations of his own body" (*ātmabhāvavigrahas* [for example, Hurvitz, 169–71]).

The revelation of the full extent of the Buddha's life span is, of course, happy news for his devotees. It addresses the issue of why, having spent three incalculable eons in preparation as a bodhisattva, he serves a scant forty-five years in his role as a buddha; why, unlike buddhas in other realms—such as the popular buddha Amitābha in Sukhāvatī (his land of "Perfect Bliss")—who seem to have an indefinite teaching career, Śākyamuni appears but briefly in his Sahā World before vanishing into nirvāṇa. In fact, he only appears to vanish. Presumably, then, he remains somehow hidden in the Sahā World, though the *Lotus Sūtra* does not explain how this works. Perhaps he is still accessible to those with the eyes of faith to see him; perhaps he is still inspiring the Mahāyāna sūtras composed in his name; perhaps he may even reappear, like the good doctor, after his crazy children have taken the medicine of the sūtras.

All this may be fine for Śākyamuni and his devotees, and it is really for them that the *Lotus Sūtra* is written; but for those looking to the sūtra for Buddhist doctrine, the question will arise whether and what one can extrapolate from Śākyamuni's case to general statements about buddhahood. Do all buddhas, for example, have hidden lives beyond their appearance in particular times and places? What is the relationship between a buddha as he really is and the limited public life he manifests as an expedient device? And, perhaps most pressingly for readers of the *Lotus*, there is the question of the connection, if any, between the extraordinary hidden life of the Buddha revealed in the later chapters and the revelation of the one buddha vehicle for all that dominates the early chapters—a theme the sūtra's authors (likely a different set of authors) seem almost to have abandoned in their celebration of Śākyamuni. These are the sorts of issues that later interpreters of the sūtra would need to address, and, in closing, I offer a few general remarks about how they addressed them.

INTERPRETIVE TRADITIONS

The extraordinary popularity of the *Lotus Sūtra* in East Asia made it imperative that interpreters there come up with explanations of how the text coheres as a doctrine and how that doctrine is related to other Mahāyāna teachings. This process began in China soon after the appearance of Kumārajīva's translation and continues in Japan right up to our day. Almost the first step in the process was to "section the text"—to recognize that the sūtra has little continuous narrative but is rather broken into at least two distinct parts, devoted separately to the one vehicle and the Buddha. These two parts were sometimes called the "cause" (*yin*) and "effect" (*guo*) sections, respectively. The first is a presentation regarding, or from the perspective of, the practitioner on the Buddhist path, and the second is the view from the end of the path. Most famously the two sections were known, in nomenclature favored by the great sixth-century expositor Zhiyi (538–597), as what might loosely be translated the "trace teaching" (*jimen*) and the "origin teaching" (*benmen*). We see here already that the interpretations assume not just two separate themes but shallower and deeper levels of discourse.

The distinction between levels of discourse becomes one of the chief means through which the Buddha's expedient devices get developed into a major tool for talking about Buddhist topics. Expositors of the dharma had long recognized the need to distinguish statements in scripture that were definitive from those subject to interpretation. In the former, the meaning was said to be explicit (*nitārtha*); in the latter, it was still implicit (*neyārtha*). The referents of the first type were held to be "ultimate truths" (*paramārthasatya*); those of the second were "conventional truths" (*saṃvṛtisatya*) that concealed the ultimate. Chinese authors often made the analogous distinction between what they called the "provisional" (*quan*) and the "real" (*shi*). It was not much of a leap for readers of the *Lotus Sūtra* to fit the notion of the Buddha's expedient devices into such distinctions, aligning the three vehicles with implicit discourse and the one vehicle with the explicit, taking the true life span of the Tathāgata as an ultimate truth and the comings and goings of his manifest body as conventional. The question remained, of course, how to read the explicit statements and understand the ultimate truths.

On the question of the ultimate truth of the one vehicle, the major commentators on the *Lotus* took three basic positions. At once the most conservative and, to believers in the sūtra, the most radical was to treat the teaching of the three vehicles as definitive and the revelation of the one vehicle as, in effect, itself a form of expedient device, intended merely to convert the Buddha's followers. This position, favored by the Faxiang (Ja.: Hossō) school, held that, contrary to what the sūtra seemed to claim, in fact, people came in five distinct types ("five natures," *wuxing*): three groups consisting of followers of the three vehicles; a fourth group composed of people with "indeterminate" identities, who might eventually be converted to the Mahāyāna; and finally those without the possibility of ever mastering Buddhism. A less extreme view—indeed the one most likely in the minds of the *Lotus* authors themselves—held that the one buddha vehicle was the third vehicle, the Mahāyāna teaching of the bodhisattva path to buddhahood. This position understood the Buddha's denial that there were three vehicles to refer only to the view that the three were distinct and that the careers of the śrāvakas and pratyekabuddhas would end in nirvāṇa, without continuing on to supreme, perfect enlightenment.

By far the most influential view was that of the Tiantai thinker Zhiyi, who adopted an interpretive tradition of the burning-house parable that saw not three but four carriages in the story. In this view, all three carriages offered by the father are merely expedient devices; the true teaching of Buddhism is represented only by the great ox carriage actually given to the children. This "four cart" reading of the sūtra story potentially has profound consequences for doctrine, since it raises the question of what the one buddha vehicle actually is if it is not the traditional bodhisattva path taught by the Mahāyāna. The Tiantai literature on this topic is exceedingly rich, Zhiyi himself famously offering no less than ten different perspectives on the relationship between the one and the three. In sum, the school tends to take a binocular view, at once asserting a distinctive buddha vehicle beyond the bodhisattva path while at the same time subsuming all the expedient devices of the Buddha into this vehicle. In this way, Tiantai interpreters were able to develop what was called a "sudden" (*dun*) theory of the buddha vehicle while retaining a more traditional "gradual" (*jian*) approach to its practice.[9]

The interpretive rubrics of sudden and gradual are Chinese inventions, not drawn directly from the *Lotus Sūtra* or, indeed, from any Sanskrit literature. But the use of these rubrics is closely tied both to the sūtra's teaching of expedient devices and to doctrinal developments in India. The term "sudden" in Buddhism is most familiar in the Chan (Ja.: Zen) claim to a "sudden awakening" (*dunwu*), but this is only one—and probably one of the less significant—uses of the word. More important for us is the notion of a "sudden teaching" (*dunjiao*)—that is, a teaching that offers the whole truth all at once rather than revealing it gradually. With this, of course, we are back in the neighborhood of the early chapters of the *Lotus* and the Buddha's claim there that he is "frankly casting aside [his] expedient devices" to teach only the ultimate truth about the vehicles. The content of a sudden teaching is almost by definition an ultimate truth. For the content of their sudden theory of the buddha vehicle, the Tiantai authors turned to the fundamental teachings of the later chapters of the sūtra, read now in the light of Mahāyāna speculations on the body of a buddha.[10]

From very early on, Buddhist authors made a distinction between the physical body of a buddha—what they often called his "form body" (*rūpakāya*)—and the corpus of his teachings—known as his "dharma body" (*dharmakāya*). As Mahāyāna followers developed their philosophical systems and devotional practices, two further steps were taken in thinking about a buddha's bodies. In the first step, the dharma body became increasingly metaphysical, until it came to stand for the whole of reality itself, coextensive with a buddha's omniscient consciousness. In the second step, a third option, sometimes styled the "reward body" (*saṃbhogakāya*), was added "between" the physical and metaphysical, to represent a buddha's supernatural form perfected through his eons of practice as a bodhisattva. With these buddhological theories in place, then, readers of the later chapters of the *Lotus Sūtra* could choose to take its revelation of the life span of the Tathāgata either as a description of the Buddha's supernatural spirit body or as a metaphor for a more abstract, all-pervasive spiritual reality. The latter option, what we might call "the buddha of the philosophers," became the basis for defining a sudden buddha vehicle beyond the old bodhisattva path.

Once the Buddha is defined as everything, it becomes obvious that he (it?) has only one real body; hence, it is easy to understand why Śākyamuni would say in the *Lotus* that other buddhas were merely the "emanations of his own body." Not only other buddhas but everything else must belong to this dharma body. Consequently, in some (much debated) sense, the Buddha's followers are already somehow participating in his supreme, perfect enlightenment, already somehow enlightened by the very nature of their existence. This is the true jewel sewn in the robe, the true home to which the prodigal son returns; this is the great oxcart given to all. The various vehicles taught by the Buddha, including the one carrying the bodhisattva to buddhahood, are merely provisional, expedient devices accommodated to the followers' misguided sense of themselves as unenlightened beings. The real buddha vehicle goes nowhere; it is sudden because, like the Buddha himself, it has already arrived at the end of the path.

The ambiguous consequences, both theoretical and practical, of positing a form of Buddhism for people who think they are already somehow buddhas inevitably generated a rich literature of theoretical innovation and religious experimentation ranging well beyond interpretations of the *Lotus Sūtra* itself—a literature far too vast and complex to pursue here. Broadly speaking, more conservative styles sought to fend off the most radical conclusions and find ways to accommodate the traditional theories and practices of Mahāyāna within inclusive versions of the one vehicle. But others, what we might call "buddha vehicle fundamentalists," were less shy about claiming to represent only the unadulterated form of the final truth—what some called the "supreme vehicle" (*zuishang sheng*)—in which expedient devices have been left behind.[11] In the tension between these inclusive and exclusive styles of interpretation, we can see later readers struggling with what is in the end perhaps the prime paradox of the *Lotus Sūtra*: that it claims to reveal an ultimate truth by its nature expressible only through expedient devices.

NOTES

1. The classic work on the topic of *upāya* in English is Michael Pye, *Skilful Means: A Concept in Mahayana Buddhism*, 2nd ed. (London: Duckworth, 1978; 2nd ed., London: Routledge, 2003). A broader, less academic treatment can be found in John W. Schroeder, *Skillful Means: The Heart of Buddhist Compassion* (Honolulu: University of Hawai'i Press, 2001).
2. The reader may note here what might be called a soft version of the liar's paradox: that the Buddha is about to reveal to us something he warns in advance we will not understand (unless we are buddhas).
3. On the reference to the Hīnayāna and Mahāyāna, see Hurvitz, 32–33, where the Buddha says it would be greedy of him to teach the former (and, presumably, not share the opportunity for buddhahood with others).
4. Hurvitz sometimes uses "condition perceiver" to translate pratyekabuddha, based on the tradition that the content of his bodhi is the Buddha's teaching of the twelvefold chain of conditions (*pratyāya*); see Hurvitz, xxii.
5. The classic study of the bodhisattva is Har Dayal, *The Bodhisattva Doctrine in Buddhist Sanskrit Literature* (London: Paul, Trench, Trubner, 1932; repr., Delhi: Motilal Banarsidass, 1999). For a study of the properties of a buddha, see Paul Griffiths, *On Being Buddha: The Classical Doctrine of Buddhahood* (Albany: SUNY Press, 1994).
6. The verse section at the end of Chapter 13 is particularly interesting for the sharp contrast it creates between the glorious scene of the universal veneration of the *Lotus* and the kind of reception from the Buddhist community the authors predict for later preachers of the sūtra: the monks and forest dwellers will call us "non-

Buddhists" (*tīrthika*), banish us from the stūpas and monasteries, malign us, disgrace us, and mock us, saying, "You fellows are all buddhas" (Hurvitz, 189).

7. The degree to which Śākyamuni is here describing himself as something like an ur-buddha is unclear, but it is worth noting that he seems to be claiming in this passage that he invented Buddha Torch-Burner (Dīpaṃkara), the buddha who is supposed to have given him his prediction of buddhahood when he who would become Śākyamuni was still a bodhisattva.
8. Following this display, the Buddha remarks that, even with such supernormal powers, he could never say enough about the *Lotus Sūtra* to exhaust its merits. In what may have been an earlier version of the sūtra, Chapter 21 seems to represent a summary statement, placed just before what may have been the final chapter, entitled "Entrustment" (Chapter 22 in Kumārajīva's version).
9. For a study of Zhiyi's thought on such topics, see Paul L. Swanson, *Foundations of T'ien-t'ai Thought: The Flowering of the Two Truths Theory in Chinese Buddhism*, Nanzan Studies in Religion and Culture 9 (Berkeley: Asian Humanities Press, 1989).
10. For studies on the uses of the "sudden" and "gradual" rubrics, see Peter N. Gregory, ed., *Sudden and Gradual: Approaches to Enlightenment in Chinese Thought*, Kuroda Institute, Studies in East Asian Buddhism 5 (Honolulu: University of Hawai'i Press, 1991).
11. As some Chan masters liked to say, we do not engage in "second-rate truths" (*di'erdi*); we practice the Buddhism of the buddhas, not the Buddhism of sentient beings. See, for example, the famous *Platform Sutra of the Sixth Patriarch*, trans. Philip B. Yampolsky (New York: Columbia University Press, 1967), 165–69.

[3]

GENDER AND HIERARCHY IN THE *LOTUS SŪTRA*

Jan Nattier

LIKE VIRTUALLY all Mahāyāna sūtras, the *Lotus Sūtra* is a work of uncertain origins. Produced by an unknown author—or rather authors, for scholars today agree that the sūtra is a pastiche containing layers produced by different hands—the time(s) and place(s) of its composition are unknown.[1] Thus its precise cultural background cannot be reconstructed with confidence. For establishing the date of the text our only firm evidence comes from China, where the earliest translation of the text was produced in the late third century C.E.; from this we can infer that one or more versions of the sūtra were circulating in India prior to this date. As to the place where the scripture was written, we have even less to go on: there is some evidence that the text was transmitted in one of the dialects of northwest India at some point in its history, but this does not constitute proof that the text was originally composed in this region. All that we can say for sure is that the *Lotus* appears to have been produced somewhere within what we might call "greater India," a region that, in the early centuries of the Common Era, stretched from modern Afghanistan in the north to the island of Sri Lanka in the south.

Given this dearth of concrete historical information, the best way to understand what is distinctive about the *Lotus Sūtra* is to view it against the backdrop of its "ancestors," that is, to read it in the light of what is found in Buddhist scriptures known to have been produced at an earlier date in greater India. Like any family tree, this group includes close relatives as well as distant relations, and we cannot assume that the authors of the *Lotus* were familiar with anything resembling any of the Buddhist canons that are in circulation today.

Nonetheless, if we want to understand how issues of gender and hierarchy were understood by the *Lotus*'s authors, our best chance for success is through beginning with its family background—that is, by examining how these issues were treated in texts composed by Buddhists in earlier times. Having done so, we can then turn to the *Lotus* itself to see what was genuinely innovative in its message and what its authors simply inherited from earlier times.

HIERARCHY IN EARLY BUDDHISM

Modern Buddhists in the West (and, indeed, an increasing number of Buddhists in urbanized regions of Asia) often present Buddhism as an egalitarian tradition, portraying the Buddha as a social reformer who criticized the caste-based society of his time and formed an "equal-opportunity" religious community in which the goal of *nirvāṇa* was open to all.[2] The idea that entrance into the Buddha's religious community was open to everyone has a solid basis in fact: an ancient tradition holds that after the Buddha's death, when an assembly was held to collect his remembered teachings, the monk called upon to recite teachings concerning the rules for monastic conduct (the *vinaya*) was Upāli, a man who, before his ordination, had been a barber, an occupation quite low on the Indian social scale. The Buddha is also portrayed as teaching that a real Brahman is not one who was born into a Brahman family but one whose deeds are deserving of the term.[3]

On the other hand, caste does play a visible role in some contexts. It is assumed, for example, that birth into a high-caste family is the result of good deeds performed in past lives and, conversely, that birth into a low-caste community reveals a less admirable karmic past. In accounts of the lives of the buddhas who preceded Śākyamuni in the distant past, and of the advent of the future buddha, Maitreya, we can also see an awareness of the importance of caste, for Buddhist scriptures routinely describe them as being born into one of the two highest castes: that of the rulers (*kṣatriyas*, sometimes translated "warriors") or that of the priests (*brāhmaṇas*).

Another hierarchical system, one based on seniority, can also be discerned in early Buddhist scriptures. Respect for one's elders was viewed as part of the natural order of things, though a slight variation on this theme is found in Buddhist sources. In the case of ordained monks and nuns, levels of seniority were based not on biological age but on their respective dates of ordination. Thus a forty-year-old man who had been a monk for twenty years would be viewed as senior to, and thus higher in status than, a sixty-year-old man who had only recently been ordained.

The widespread practice in ancient India of leaving home to become a religious renunciant itself contributed another hierarchical scale to the mix, for such renunciants—of whom those who were followers of the Buddha were referred to as "monks" (or, more literally, "beggars" [*bhikṣus*]) and "nuns" (*bhikṣuṇīs*)—were viewed as superior to lay devotees, being worthy of formal expressions of respect as well as of offerings of food and other necessities. Exceptions were made, of course, if a renunciant had violated the socially accepted standards of behavior (for example, by indulging in sexual activity). In such cases he or she would lose the respect of the laity and would no longer be considered a worthy recipient of alms.

Within the Buddhist community we also find what might be called a spiritual hierarchy, based on levels of advancement on the path to nirvāṇa. A widely used traditional list begins with the status of the ordinary unawakened person and proceeds through four levels of noble beings (*ārya*): the stream enterer, who will attain nirvāṇa after seven more lifetimes at most; the once returner, who will be reborn in this world just once before attaining nirvāṇa in that lifetime; the nonreturner, who will not return to this world but will instead be reborn in a heavenly realm, where he or she will complete the final prerequisites for nirvāṇa; and the worthy one (*arhat*), who has attained nirvāṇa; in this life and will never be born again. However exalted these four levels of spiritual development were considered to be, they were all overshadowed by the status of the Buddha himself, who—without the help of a fully awakened teacher—had discovered the path to nirvāṇa by himself and then passed on that knowledge to his followers.

Finally, we should take note of what might be called a hierarchy of species, for according to early Buddhist teachings there is no guarantee that someone who is a human being in this life will necessarily come back as a human. On the contrary, early Buddhism posited five realms of beings—including gods, humans, animals, hungry ghosts (*pretas*), and the denizens of hell—into which one could, according to the quality of his or her actions, be reborn.[4] While Buddhists (as well as non-Buddhists) in India commonly aspired to be reborn in heaven, Buddhist scriptures contend that it is the human realm and not heaven (that is, the realm of the gods) that is the most desirable. Life in heaven may well be extremely pleasurable, but the ultimate goal of life is to attain liberation from the cycle of rebirth, and—with the exception of the nonreturner—this can ordinarily be accomplished only in human form.

GENDER IN EARLY BUDDHISM

All these hierarchical systems were viewed, in early Buddhist literature as well as in Indian society more broadly, as applying to both women and men. But an additional—and pervasive—hierarchical distinction was based on gender itself. Buddhists shared in the views of what constitutes maleness and femaleness that were current in India at the time, which portrayed women as passionate by nature, having a stronger sex drive (as well as other sensual desires) than men. While men were of course subject to desire as well, they were viewed as more easily able to curb their passions and to embark on a life of renunciation. Buddhists also accepted the widespread Indian belief that birth as a woman was lower than birth as a male, and that being female, like being a member of a low-caste family, was evidence of a less than stellar karmic past. Accordingly, it was assumed that women were less capable than men of reaching a high level of spiritual development.[5]

Nonetheless, early scriptural sources demonstrate that both women and men were admitted to monastic ordination. This decision—which early canonical sources attribute to the Buddha himself[6]—clearly encountered resistance in some quarters. One ancient account of the foundation of the order of nuns (probably composed around a century after the death of the Buddha) describes the Buddha's closest disciple, his cousin Ānanda, as interceding on behalf of Mahāprajāpatī, the Buddha's foster mother, who, with a number of her attendants, wanted to renounce the worldly life and become a nun. Ānanda is said to have pleaded repeatedly with the Buddha for the establishment of an order of female renunciants parallel to that available to men before the Buddha finally relented and agreed. The tale represents the Buddha as doing so with great reluctance, however, for he is said to have described the effect of the presence of women on the monastic community as like "mildew on a field of rice, or rust on the sugar cane plant," adding that allowing women to become nuns would shorten the life span of the Buddhist religion by half.[7]

Other early sources provide clear evidence of the importance of gender as a hierarchical category for early Buddhists. As we have seen, within the Buddhist monastic community relative status was determined by ordination date. But what if a woman who had been ordained for twenty years needed to communicate with a man ordained for only a year? Which hierarchical system should take priority—that of seniority, in which case the woman would be considered as senior, or that of gender, in which case higher status would be accorded to the man?

That a decision on how to adjudicate this issue was made early in Buddhist history is clear, for in every surviving list of monastic rules for men and women, there is a set of extra rules for the nuns. Here the conflict between the systems of seniority and gender is addressed directly in a list of eight special rules (*gurudharma*; literally, "heavy items"), which are binding only upon the nuns. According to these rules, a nun, regardless of the level of her seniority, is considered inferior to a monk. The specifics of these eight rules differ slightly in the vinaya rules belonging to different Buddhist schools, but in all cases they are clearly intended to subordinate the nuns' order to that of the monks. The first of the eight rules makes their overall intent clear: "When a nun, even though she has been ordained for a hundred years, meets a monk who has newly entered the order, she ought to rise, venerate, and pay obeisance to him."[8] Other rules on the list state that nuns are also forbidden to criticize monks even when the latter are actually at fault, and that they must submit to instruction by the monks—but not vice versa—at frequent intervals.

Despite this clear evidence of the subordination of women to men on an institutional level, early Buddhist scriptures also make clear that women were viewed as capable of attaining the highest goal set forth by the Buddha, the experience of nirvāṇa, which was understood to result in bringing the eons-long process of birth and death to an end. An early canonical collection of poems known as the *Songs of the Women Elders* (*Therīgāthā*), for example, contains dozens of accounts of women who are said to have attained this goal.[9] Thus, becoming a worthy one (arhat), a title given to those who had attained nirvāṇa, was open to women as well as men. To be sure, it was considered to be more difficult for women, and far fewer female than male arhats are named in Buddhist scriptures. Nonetheless, the idea that women could attain nirvāṇa as women—that is, without first being reborn as men—was a remarkable statement for its time.

In sum, early Buddhist sources portray a religious community that was inclusive—in the sense of allowing women to become renunciants like their male counterparts, and even admitting that some women were capable of attaining the final goal—but that can hardly be described as egalitarian. Thus, in many ways the treatment of gender parallels that of caste in early Buddhist scriptures: birth as a female and birth into a low-caste family were both considered genuine signs of negative karma, but with extraordinary effort in this lifetime even women and low-caste men could succeed in pursuing the path to its end.

HIERARCHY IN MAHĀYĀNA SCRIPTURES

The authors of those texts said to belong to the Mahāyāna ("great vehicle") inherited these various hierarchical systems from earlier Buddhism—and from Indian culture more broadly. In most cases, there was relatively little change in how they were understood and used. Men are still viewed as superior to women, and distinctions of caste (and of course species) still remain. Likewise, monastics—provided they live up to the high standards of their calling—are still viewed as worthy of respect.

In one area, however—that of degrees of spiritual development—Mahāyāna thinkers introduced a dramatically new hierarchy of their own. While maintaining the fourfold system of degrees of awakening, from stream enterer at the bottom to the arhat at the top, Mahāyāna writers introduced a new and even higher goal. As the name Mahāyāna implies, these thinkers introduced a new spiritual destination: the attainment of full buddhahood, equal in every way to the accomplishment of Śākyamuni.

Based on the assumption that Buddhism—like all conditioned things—will eventually disappear, the idea became current that the teachings, practices, and religious community established by Śākyamuni Buddha would someday die out.[10] Accordingly, it would be necessary for a uniquely qualified individual to replicate Śākyamuni's achievement by rediscovering the basic truths of Buddhism in the distant future, when they have long been forgotten. Such a figure, it was believed, was the future buddha Maitreya, now a bodhisattva living in the Tuṣita Heaven and awaiting the right time to be born into this world, some five and a half billion years from now.[11]

But Maitreya's Buddhist community, like that of Śākyamuni, was believed to have a finite life span, and thus the need for others to follow in the footsteps of these exemplary sages was an ongoing concern. Those who volunteered for this mission, however, were embarking on an extremely difficult spiritual path. Such people (known as bodhisattvas) were required not simply to attain nirvāṇa but to emulate in every detail all that Śākyamuni Buddha had done in both his final and former lives. Only by carrying out all these activities, it was believed—and they included dramatic acts of self-sacrifice, as when the future Śākyamuni, while still a bodhisattva, threw himself before a hungry tigress to feed her and her cubs—could the practitioner become the sort of being who could rediscover on his own the truths of Buddhism in the distant future. The Mahāyāna thus originated as a particularly demanding vocation within the Buddhist community, requiring countless additional lifetimes to accumulate the merit and knowledge required to become a buddha.

In those circles in which what we might call the bodhisattva option was accepted as legitimate—and it is clear that this included some, but not all, Buddhist communities in India—those Buddhists who volunteered for this extraordinarily grueling path to awakening were accorded particular respect. Thus, with the advent of the Mahāyāna we find yet another hierarchical system in Buddhist thinking: the distinction between the candidate for arhatship (known as the *śrāvaka* ["disciple"]) and the bodhisattva who was striving for full buddhahood.

Early Mahāyāna scriptures contain hints that this new option created some tension in Buddhist communities, where the distinction between śrāvakas and bodhisattvas introduced yet another hierarchical system into the mix. Bracketing the issue of gender , the question once again arises as to how these various hierarchical systems can be integrated. How, for example, should a monk ordained five years ago, who considers himself a bodhisattva, relate to a much more senior monk who is on the śrāvaka path? Does seniority dictate that the younger monk bow to the older one, or does the bodhisattva's exalted status as a candidate for buddhahood trump the śrāvaka's position as a candidate for "mere" arhatship?

Judging from comments made in early Mahāyāna texts, this was a real issue in those Buddhist monasteries that included such pioneering bodhisattvas, and it was a source of potential conflict. In *The Inquiry of Ugra* (*Ugraparipṛcchā*), for example, bodhisattvas are warned not to look down on their śrāvaka counterparts—a warning that suggests that some bodhisattvas, at least, were subject to spiritual pride.[12] Other Mahāyāna sūtras took a different position; no longer trying to keep the peace, the authors of the *Discourse to Kāśyapa* (*Kāśyapaparivarta*), for example, proclaim that all bodhisattvas, from the first moment they resolve to attain buddhahood, are superior not just to śrāvakas but also to arhats.[13] These differences in stance toward practitioners striving for arhatship suggest that, while in some communities bodhisattvas and śrāvakas coexisted peacefully, if perhaps uneasily, in other groups bodhisattvas—no longer attempting to maintain harmony within the monastic community—were beginning to form separate communities.

The introduction of the bodhisattva path as a new option for spiritual practice, while offering an admirable new goal for some, clearly exacerbated already existing possibilities for conflict between various hierarchical systems. The *Lotus Sūtra* offers a new and highly innovative response to this problem.

GENDER IN MAHĀYĀNA SCRIPTURES

Relatively few men, let alone women, seem to have expected to attain nirvāṇa (that is, arhatship) during the Buddha's lifetime, and in subsequent centuries—when the Buddha's inspiring presence was no longer directly accessible—the expectation of attaining liberation in one's present lifetime seems to have declined even further. With the rise of the Mahāyāna, however, the equation changed dramatically. Because a buddha was defined as someone who discovered the path to awakening in a world that had no knowledge of Buddhism, only the traditional goal of arhatship—and not the new ideal of buddhahood—was available in the present. For those who chose the vocation of the bodhisattva, the experience of full awakening was automatically deferred to the distant future, at which time the teachings of Śākyamuni would have been forgotten and another buddha could appear in the world to rediscover them.

In the earliest extant Mahāyāna scriptures, the bodhisattva path seems to have been envisioned as appropriate only for men.[14] To some degree this may be simply a reflection of the fact that the so-called historical Buddha, Śākyamuni, was a male, and it was assumed that those who followed in his footsteps to become buddhas would thus become male as well. The particulars of the bodhisattva path, however, may also have contributed to this perception, for the acts of extreme heroism that it required—remaining calm and not arousing anger while being cut to pieces by an evil king, for example, or plucking out one's own eyes in response to a blind Brahman's request—were culturally scripted, in Indian society at the time, as male.[15]

Before long, however, other scriptures appeared that described the path as open (at least in the beginning stages) to women as well. Yet for a female practitioner aspiring to buddhahood, a new obstacle stood in the way. Arhatship could, as we have seen, be attained by both men and women, but buddhahood was universally said to be reserved exclusively for males.[16] Consequently, a woman who embarked on the bodhisattva path had, in addition to the acts of renunciation expected of all bodhisattvas, to give up her female identity as well.

HIERARCHY IN THE *LOTUS SŪTRA*

Read against this background, it becomes clear that the *Lotus Sūtra* is in many ways a revolutionary text. Most dramatic is its overriding of what had been a clear distinction, in earlier Buddhist scriptures, between the status of the śrāvaka and that of the bodhisattva. In earlier Mahāyāna texts (and in many later ones, too) both the śrāvaka vehicle and the vehicle of the bodhisattva were viewed as viable paths to awakening, though the vocation of the bodhisattva was considered by far the more worthy of the two. With its new doctrine of "one vehicle" (*ekayāna*), however, the *Lotus* wiped out this dichotomy in a single stroke. No longer was the śrāvaka viewed as destined for a more immediate (albeit lower-level) experience of nirvāṇa than the bodhisattva; on the contrary, all Buddhists were now said to be on the path to buddhahood, whether they were aware of it or not. Those who believe that they have attained arhatship, according to the *Lotus*, are simply mistaken: their supposed experience of nirvāṇa is only an illusion—a rest stop, as it were, on the path to full buddhahood.

That its authors viewed arhatship as unreal is made vividly apparent in the section of the text where hundreds of Buddhists, including a number of those considered by the earlier tradition to have already attained arhatship, receive prophecies of their future buddhahood. Having declared, in Chapter 2, that "there is only one vehicle, not two" (Hurvitz, 35), the Buddha confers on Śāriputra—well known as one of the leading arhats in the early Buddhist community—a prediction of his own attainment of buddhahood in the future: "Śāriputra, you, in an age to come, beyond incalculable, limitless, inconceivable *kalpas* [eons], having made offerings to several thousands of myriads of millions of buddhas, having upheld the true dharma and having acquired to perfection the path trodden by bodhisattvas, shall be able to become a buddha named Flower Glow [Padmaprabha]" (Hurvitz, 51).

Thus Śāriputra—who, as an arhat, would be expected to be finished with the round of birth and death and never to appear in *saṃsāra* again—is told that he still has many millions of lifetimes to live, during which he will serve "myriads of millions of buddhas," gradually acquiring all the qualities of a buddha. In subsequent sections of the text (especially Chapters 6–9), the Buddha confers similar prophecies on a wide range of other characters who were known in earlier Buddhist scriptures as arhats. Thus the *Lotus* succeeds in eliminating the hierarchical relationship between bodhisattvas and śrāvakas, but it does so by making the reality of the śrāvaka's attainments disappear.

Given this sweeping inclusion of supposed śrāvakas within the bodhisattva vehicle, it is small wonder that the *Lotus* has often been interpreted as a thoroughly egalitarian text. Yet a close reading shows that not all hierarchies have been eliminated. Though there is no explicit discussion of the caste system in the *Lotus*, those at the very bottom of the Indian social scale (known in many English-language sources as "outcastes") are mentioned among those kinds of people with whom a bodhisattva who is a devotee of the *Lotus* should not interact: "He also does not approach with familiarity *caṇḍālas* [outcastes] or those who raise pigs, sheep, chickens, and dogs; nor those who hunt, or fish, or cultivate other evil practices. If such persons on some chance occasion come to him, then he preaches dharma to them but hopes for nothing" (Hurvitz, 192).

By encouraging the bodhisattva to avoid contact with caṇḍālas and other low-caste individuals, the *Lotus* makes it clear that social status—that is, one's place in the Indian hierarchy of caste—was still relevant to its authors.

An asymmetrical relationship between lay and monastic practitioners also seems still to be in force; at any rate, all those in the long list of recipients of prophecies of future buddhahood in Chapters 3–9 appear to be monks and nuns. Yet other passages in the text (quite possibly composed in a different time or place) present a different picture. In Chapter 10, "Preachers of the Dharma," the Buddha suggests that laypeople and even nonhuman beings can obtain a prophecy of buddhahood if they merely hear the *Lotus* itself. After describing an audience that includes gods, dragons (*nāgas*), *yakṣas*, *gandharvas* (divine musicians), *asuras* (jealous demigods), *garuḍas* (mythical birds), *kinnaras* (half-man, half-horse figures), and *mahoragas* (great serpents), as well as human beings, both lay and monastic, the Buddha proclaims: "If any like these in the Buddha's presence hears a single *gāthā* [verse] or a single phrase of the *Scripture of the Blossom of the Fine Dharma*, or devotes to it a single moment of rejoicing, I hereby confer on him a prophecy that he shall attain *anuttarasamyaksaṃbodhi* [buddhahood]" (Hurvitz, 159).

We will return to the importance of such passages, but, for now, we may simply note that they appear to contain a seed of radical egalitarianism with respect to the ultimate attainment of buddhahood that was sometimes—but by no means always—actualized by the adherents of later *Lotus*-centered communities.

GENDER IN THE *LOTUS SŪTRA*

Continuity with the Past

Readers of the *Lotus Sūtra* who are familiar with other Mahāyāna sūtras will notice many features that can also be found in other texts. The scripture opens with a long list of names of members of the Buddha's audience, beginning with a group of twelve thousand (in some versions, twelve hundred) monks (bhikṣus), all of them arhats (Hurvitz, 3).[17] Of these, a select group is named (numbering twenty-one in the version of the text by Kumārajīva [Jiumoluoshi, 344–413, or 350–409]). All are well known from earlier scriptures, and—as is usual in the opening lines of Mahāyāna sūtras—all of them are male. After mentioning "another two thousand persons," some still on the path to arhatship and others who have already arrived there (Hurvitz, 3), there follows a group of eighty thousand bodhisattvas, all said to be at an advanced stage ("all nonbacksliders in anuttarasamyaksaṃbodhi"). Again, a subset of these are named individually, and again all the names are male (Hurvitz, 3–4).[18] The same is true even when the sūtra turns to a list of representatives of various heavens, and even nonhuman beings such as nāgas, kinnaras, and garuḍas. Despite the great diversity of the audience, all those mentioned by name are male.

Interspersed among these lists, however—at least in the version of the sūtra translated by Kumārajīva—is a brief mention of two female characters: Mahāprajāpatī, the Buddha's foster mother, and Yaśodharā, his former wife and the mother of his son, Rāhula. Both are said to be nuns (bhikṣuṇīs), but in their cases no special attainment is mentioned. In the oldest version of the sūtra, however (the Chinese translation produced by Dharmarakṣa [Zhu Fahu, ca. 265–313, or 239–316] in the late third century C.E.), even the brief mention of these two women is absent. Thus, when the *Lotus* was first composed, we may infer, the entire list of named members of the audience was male.

This is typical of what is found in Mahāyāna sūtras; indeed, this writer is not aware of any case in which a female arhat or a female bodhisattva is named in such an audience list. This does not imply, of course, that the authors considered it impossible for a woman to be an arhat or a bodhisattva, but the male-centered frame of reference is clear.

The same traditionalist stance is maintained in later chapters of the *Lotus* (Chapters 23–28 in the traditional version of Kumārajīva). In these sections—thought to have circulated originally as independent sūtras—the extraordinary abilities of various powerful bodhisattvas are related in detail. Once again, all these figures are male.[19]

The Role of Female Characters

Reading more widely in the sūtra, we can observe that virtually all the characters who play active roles are male. Indeed, it is difficult to find any named human female character anywhere in the text. (An unnamed and nonhuman female character, the daughter of a nāga king, is discussed in a following section, "Gender, Species, and Seniority.") Only in one brief passage is there an exception: after dozens of other characters (all of them men) have received prophecies of their future attainment of buddhahood, Mahāprajāpatī and Yaśodharā rise in turn to ask if they might receive the same. The Buddha obliges, predicting buddhahood for each of them, and they respond with delight (Hurvitz, 186–88). It is worth noting, however, that these two women are the last to receive prophecies in this very long series; indeed, before receiving hers, Yaśodharā muses that "in the course of his prophecies the World-Honored One failed to mention only my name" (Hurvitz, 187).

One other female character—Vimaladattā, the mother of two boys who in a former life asked permission to visit the Buddha—appears in one of the latter (and later) chapters of the text, and we are told that she has now become a distinguished bodhisattva.[20] But otherwise, all the other speakers—from the various disciples of the Buddha (Śāriputra, Maudgalyāyana, and others) to the great bodhisattvas (Avalokiteśvara, Mañjuśrī, and so on) to, of course, Śākyamuni Buddha himself—are men. It is therefore difficult to avoid drawing the conclusion that the authors of the *Lotus* viewed the ideal religious practitioner as male.[21]

That this androcentric frame of reference is not due just to accident or oversight is confirmed by other mentions of women in the text. In two cases, descriptions of an ideal realm—the future world of Śākyamuni Buddha's disciple Pūrṇa, on the one hand, and that of the past buddha Pure and Bright Excellence of Sun and Moon (Candrasūryavimalaprabhāśrī) on the other—we are told that, among the admirable features of these lands, they lack any of the "evil destinies" (that is, the lower realms inhabited by hell beings, hungry ghosts, and animals) and that no women are present there (Hurvitz, 146, 269). In another case it is said that if a woman hears, accepts, and remembers the chapter on Bodhisattva Medicine King, she will never again be born as a woman (Hurvitz, 275). Yet another passage urges the bodhisattva who goes to a private home to preach not to talk with girls, maidens, or widows, as well as to avoid association with the "five types of unmanly men"—advice that is obviously based on the assumption that the dharma preacher is male (Hurvitz, 192).[22] Finally, in the closing chapter of the sūtra, the bodhisattva Samantabhadra offers his devotees a magic spell (*dhāraṇī*) that is guaranteed to protect those who uphold it against being killed by nonhumans or being "led astray or confused by women" (Hurvitz, 307).

In sum, the *Lotus* echoes themes found in many other Buddhist (especially Mahāyāna) texts: that rebirth as a woman is lower than that as a male, that an ideal world is characterized by the absence of women, and that the paradigmatic arhats, and all the great bodhisattvas, are men. In this respect, the *Lotus* appears as a typical Mahāyāna sūtra—not denying women entry to the bodhisattva path, perhaps, but reminding them that, if they wish to progress in their practice, they must strive to be reborn as men.[23]

General Exhortations to Women

Female characters, as we have seen, are extremely rare in the *Lotus Sūtra*. If, however, we turn to theoretical, rather than actual, attainment by women, we find that statements about women's spiritual potentialities abound. In virtually all these cases, women are mentioned together with men, above all in the phrase "a good man or a good woman."[24] Dozens of such statements occur in the *Lotus*, of which a typical example occurs in Chapter 10: "If a good man or a good woman shall receive and keep, read and recite, explain, or copy in writing a single phrase of the *Scripture of the Dharma Blossom* [that is, of the *Lotus Sūtra* itself], or otherwise and in a variety of ways make offerings to the scriptural roll with flower perfume, necklaces, powdered incense, perfumed paste . . . or join palms in reverent worship, that person is to be looked up to and exalted by all the worlds, showered with offerings fit for a Thus Come One [a buddha]. Let it be known that that person is a great bodhisattva" (Hurvitz, 160).

A similarly dramatic promise of benefits to the practitioner occurs in Chapter 17, and again women are explicitly included. Speaking to the bodhisattva Maitreya (here called Ajita ["The Invincible One"]), the Buddha makes the following declaration: "O Ajita! Whatever living beings, hearing that the Buddha's life span is as long as this, can produce as much as a single moment of faith and understanding shall gain merit that shall have no limit, no measure. . . . That a good man or good woman having this sort of merit should recede from anuttarasamyaksaṃbodhi [should fail to attain buddhahood] is simply not possible" (Hurvitz, 229).

What is noteworthy about these promises of benefits, however, is that they are far from evenly distributed throughout the text. On the contrary, they are concentrated in only a few places: those chapters that take for granted the existence of a text called the *Lotus Sūtra* and that deal with the proper relationship of the practitioner to that text.[25] In every case the content of the discussion is an exhortation to accept, remember, recite, and make offerings to the sūtra. In short, these are passages in which women are treated not as heroines whose spiritual accomplishments should be celebrated but as potential customers—that is, as believers being recruited to become devotees of the *Lotus* itself.

GENDER, SPECIES, AND SENIORITY: THE STORY OF THE DRAGON KING'S DAUGHTER

In one exceptional case, however, a female character—the unnamed daughter of Sāgara, the king of the nāgas (a category of beings regularly equated with the dragons of Chinese mythology)—is presented as a remarkably accomplished and admirable bodhisattva. In this story, the bodhisattva Mañjuśrī is asked whether he found a worthy audience when he went to the underwater realm of the nāgas to preach the dharma. He replies that indeed he did, for he found that the nāga king's daughter, who was present when he preached the *Lotus Sūtra* there, was capable of attaining buddhahood despite her tender age of only eight years. This pronouncement is greeted with predictable skepticism by the bodhisattva Wisdom Accumulation (Prajñākūṭa), a member of Mañjuśrī's audience, and, as if on cue, the nāga girl herself appears in the assembly. When she does so, she is confronted by the Buddha's well-known disciple Śāriputra, who questions her not about her species (for, as a nāga, she is, after all, not human) or her age, but about her gender: "You say that in no long time you shall attain the unexcelled way [that is, buddhahood]. This is hard to believe. What is the reason? A woman's body is filthy, it is not a dharma-receptacle. How can you attain unexcelled bodhi? The path of the Buddha is remote and cavernous.... How can the body of a woman speedily achieve buddhahood?" (Hurvitz, 184).

The nāga girl, in response, offers a jewel to the Buddha, which he immediately accepts. "Was that quick?" she asks, and both Wisdom Accumulation and Śāriputra reply that it was. "You shall see me achieve buddhahood even more quickly than that!" she tells them (Hurvitz, 184). And indeed she does, but the specifics of her accomplishment are worthy of note: "At that time, the assembled multitude all saw the dragon girl in the space of an instant turn into a man, perfect bodhisattva conduct, straightway go southward to the world sphere Spotless, sit on a jeweled lotus blossom, and achieve undifferentiating, right, enlightened intuition [that is, buddhahood], with thirty-two marks and eighty beautiful features setting forth the fine dharma for all living beings in all ten directions" (Hurvitz, 184).

As presented here, the nāga girl does indeed attain buddhahood, but she does not do so as a woman (nor as a nāga). Instead, she changes into a man (as required by the standard script of how to attain buddhahood), carries out all the practices of a bodhisattva (albeit on fast-forward), and attains complete and full awakening. Even the location of her accomplishment conforms to canonical specifications, for, rather than becoming a buddha in the presence of the audience—which would violate the principle of "one buddha per world-system," widely held in both Mahāyāna and pre-Mahāyāna texts—she migrates at inconceivable speed to another realm, "the world sphere Spotless," in the south.

The story of the nāga girl thus conveys several messages simultaneously: first, that age, gender, and species are not in and of themselves indicators of the spiritual level of a human or nonhuman being; second, that certain practices are required of a bodhisattva prior to attaining buddhahood, even if in the present narrative they are performed at extremely high speed; and third, that however spiritually advanced a female character may be, it is essential that she become a male prior to the final attainment of buddhahood. Thus, the nāga girl's story is not at all unique but is best understood in the light of the substantial body of stories of instantaneous sexual transformation of female bodhisattvas found in other Mahāyāna sūtras.[26]

It should be noted, however, that even this story of rapid spiritual accomplishment by a female character (despite its ambivalent message that women cannot become buddhas without first becoming men) does not appear to have been present in all the recensions of the *Lotus* that were circulating in India. Though it is found in the late third-century Chinese translation produced by Dharmarakṣa, it was not included in the translation produced by Kumārajīva at the beginning of the fifth century. Its inclusion in Hurvitz's English translation of the text is a reflection of the fact that this portion of the text was added to Kumārajīva's translation (as Chapter 12) some decades after Kumārajīva's time.[27]

"SONS OF THE BUDDHA": THE HIERARCHY OF FAMILY ROLES

One of the best-known features of the *Lotus Sūtra* is its liberal use of parables, that is, explanatory stories that teach, by analogy, how the main messages of the sūtra are to be understood. And in many of these stories, the Buddha is portrayed as a father.[28] In the story of the burning house, in Chapter 3, for example, the father induces his foolish sons to escape from the fire by promising them three kinds of marvelous carts. In the parable sometimes referred to in English by the biblical title "the prodigal son," in Chapter 4, the wise father waits for his rebellious son to pass through various stages of devoted servitude before revealing to him his birthright as heir apparent.[29] And in the parable of the physician, in Chapter 16, the Buddha is represented as a doctor whose sons have drunk poison in his absence and become so crazed that many of them cannot even heed his prescription of an antidote. What is noteworthy about these stories is not only that they focus on a father-son (and not mother-daughter, mother-son, or father-daughter) relationship but also that, in every case, the children are portrayed as profoundly foolish and immature. It is only the father who can persuade the heedless boys to leave the burning house by luring them with toys, restore the wandering son to his rightful inheritance, and prescribe the antidote for the poison his boys have taken. In short, the father-son association is portrayed in highly asymmetrical fashion, with wisdom belonging to the father alone.

Yet, the authors of the *Lotus* clearly considered the realization of one's status as a "son of the Buddha" to be a cause for rejoicing. After hearing the Buddha proclaim the accessibility of buddhahood to all—even to those who, like Śākyamuni's great disciples, were thought to have already attained arhatship[30]—Śāriputra exults: "This day, at long last, I know that I am truly the Buddha's son, born of the Buddha's mouth, born of dharma transformation" (Hurvitz, 47). And after relating the story of the prodigal son, a group of the Buddha's leading disciples (all of them again previously considered to be arhats) explicitly compare the characters in the story to themselves: "The great rich man is the Thus Come One. We are all alike the Buddha's sons. . . . We did not know that we are truly the Buddha's children. Now, at last, we know" (Hurvitz, 82–83).

Before gaining this great realization, they state, they used to teach about the bodhisattva path to others, without ever dreaming of embarking on it themselves:

> Although we, for the sake of
> The Buddha's sons,
> Preached the bodhisattvadharma,
> Wherewith the buddha path was to be sought,
> Yet with respect to this dharma,
> We never had any hopes [of attaining it ourselves].
>
> (HURVITZ, 89)[31]

Now, however, they realize that they, too, are on the bodhisattva path—something they had not sought but that "has come into our possession of its own accord" (Hurvitz, 90).

The idea that bodhisattvas (and only bodhisattvas) are true "Buddha-sons" was not, however, introduced by the authors of the *Lotus*; on the contrary, it appears in many other Mahāyāna texts, a number of which surely preceded the *Lotus*. Like the *Lotus*, they reserve the epithet "son of the Buddha" for bodhisattvas, yet there is a noteworthy difference in how it is used. Whereas in the *Lotus* it designates a child who is clearly inferior to his father in wisdom and realization, other Mahāyāna texts use the idea of sonship to assert the near or even total equality of bodhisattvas with the Buddha himself. It is not at all unusual to find the statement that even a beginning bodhisattva "who has just brought forth the thought of awakening" should be viewed as equal in status to the Buddha.[32] In some cases these texts go even farther, proclaiming that the bodhisattvas, and not the Buddha, should be accorded the highest rank.[33]

Thus, while other Mahāyāna sūtras use the term "son of the Buddha" to indicate the bodhisattva's likeness (or, in some cases, even superiority) to the figure whom he strives to emulate, in the *Lotus* the term "son" is fraught with images of dependence. In light of this observation, it is noteworthy that the text (in both its Sanskrit and Chinese versions) teems with transitive and causative verbs, verbs portraying the Buddha as directly causing (and not merely inspiring) others to progress on the bodhisattva path.

BRIDGING THE GAP: DEVOTION TO THE *LOTUS* AS A "LEAP OF FAITH"

It is difficult, at first glance, to reconcile one of the overriding messages of the *Lotus*—that all Buddhists, whether they know it or not, are en route to the attainment of buddhahood—with the overwhelmingly powerful image of the Buddha as father presented in the text. Given the sūtra's claim that the Buddha's wisdom is incomprehensible by anyone except another buddha, that he was awakened many eons ago but is now manifesting himself in the world in order to teach, and that his death was not real but only an expedient device designed to persuade beings to take his message seriously, how can we understand the claims of the same text that "Even children who in play / Gather sand and make it into buddha stūpas" have all achieved buddhahood (Hurvitz, 36)? If the Buddha's glory is so far beyond that of ordinary human beings, how can it be that anyone who "hears a single gāthā or a single phrase of the *Scripture of the Blossom of the Fine Dharma*" will receive a prophecy of his or her own attainment of buddhahood (Hurvitz, 159)?

It is on this point, perhaps, that the message of the *Lotus* was most startling in its time, and that it remains so for many Buddhists today.[34] For in place of the step-by-step practice of self-cultivation posited by early Buddhism (and by most of forms of Mahāyāna), the *Lotus* recommends a leap of faith: what is ultimately required of its practitioners is not the gradual accumulation of virtue and insight but the willing acceptance of the message of the sūtra itself. Here, at last, the potential for sweeping egalitarianism inherent in the idea of one vehicle is realized, because all those who accept and revere the message of the *Lotus* are certain to attain buddhahood. In making this claim, the authors of the *Lotus* took the idea of "nonretrogression" found in earlier Mahāyāna texts and subjected it to a sweeping act of democratization. No longer is the certainty of future buddhahood reserved for bodhisattvas at an extremely advanced stage of spiritual progress; on the contrary, all men, women, and children who perform even the smallest act of devotion based on faith can now share in this exalted state.

In making faith the center of its message—and not "works," to borrow a contrast from Christian theology—the *Lotus* departs from the model of gradual progress on the path that was seemingly universal in earlier Buddhism and that continues to characterize a majority of Buddhist communities today.[35] In place of gradual self-cultivation, the *Lotus* proposes a model of sudden progress (what Karl Potter has called a "leap philosophy"),[36] in which the definitive turning point is the realization that there is just one vehicle and that we are all destined for buddhahood. The proper response, then, is one of joy, gratitude, and acceptance. As the Buddha tells his audience at the end of the chapter on "Expedient Devices":

> All of you, knowing now
> That the buddhas, the teachers of the ages,
> In accord with what is peculiarly appropriate have recourse to expedient devices,
> Need have no more doubts or uncertainties.
> Your hearts shall give rise to great joy,
> Since you know that you yourselves shall become buddhas.
>
> (HURVITZ, 43–44)

There is no distinction between old and young, male and female, laity and monastics, or Brahmans and members of low-caste groups, for all are equally included in the Buddha's promise.

Such equality for all who have faith still leaves standing, of course, one last hierarchical relationship: the distinction between those who believe and those who do not. And the sūtra makes it quite clear where its authors stand on the status of those who reject the idea of the one vehicle. In a famous scene in the second chapter of the sūtra, five thousand members of the audience get up—just when Śākyamuni is about to declare this new teaching—and walk out. They are then subjected to harsh criticism by the narrator: "This group had deep and grave roots of sin and overweening pride, imagining themselves to have attained and to have borne witness to what in fact they had not. Having such faults as these, therefore they did not stay. The World-Honored One, silent, did not restrain them" (Hurvitz, 28).

Though it may be true (at least theoretically) that such people are themselves destined for buddhahood, it is also clear that those who reject the

Lotus's message are not being portrayed from a perspective of compassion but on the contrary are stigmatized as obstinate and proud. "It is just as well," Śākyamuni remarks to Śāriputra, "that such arrogant ones as these have withdrawn" (Hurvitz, 28).

Such passages point to an inherent contradiction in the *Lotus*'s seemingly all-inclusive message. On the one hand, it makes the universalizing claim that all Buddhists (not just an elite few, as many earlier Mahāyāna scriptures had held)[37] are included in the bodhisattva vehicle and thus are ultimately certain to become buddhas. On the other hand, those who reject this new message of the one vehicle are subjected to harsh criticism. If they not only hold a different opinion but also actually dare to criticize the *Lotus* and its devotees, the sūtra threatens them with rebirth in the lowest hell, even suggesting that, by these actions, such persons may completely destroy their own potential to achieve buddhahood (Hurvitz, 71–72).

Such scathing critiques are surely related to the fact that not all Buddhists in India (and, it should be emphasized, not even all Mahāyāna Buddhists) accepted the *Lotus*'s startling new teachings. Yet, for those who did, its message opened vast new spiritual horizons, enabling ordinary practitioners to see themselves as future buddhas while diminishing the power of a long list of hierarchical systems that had kept this glorious self-image out of view.

These hierarchies of age, caste, gender, and so on that were taken for granted in Indian society at the time were not fully eliminated, of course, by the authors of the sūtra. As the story of the dragon king's daughter makes clear, for example, it was still seen as necessary for a woman to become a (human) male before attaining buddhahood. Nonetheless, the significance of these hierarchies was profoundly weakened when placed in the context of the believer's certainty of eventually attaining this glorious goal. Indeed, for the authors of the *Lotus*, the sole hierarchy that fully retains its power is one related to its own message: the distinction between those who accept the *Lotus*'s vision of an egalitarian community of faith and those stubborn and misguided Buddhists—whether śrāvakas or bodhisattvas—who do not.

NOTES

1. For a recent discussion of this issue, see Seishi Karashima, "Who Composed the Lotus Sutra? Antagonism between Wilderness and Village Monks," in *Annual Report of the International Research Institute for Advanced Buddhology at Soka University for the Academic Year 2000*, 143–79 (Tokyo: The International Research Institute for Advanced Buddhology, Soka University, 2001), especially 171.

2. The well-known list of four castes, consisting (in order from highest to lowest) of the priests (*brāhmaṇas*), warriors (*kṣatriyas*), merchants (*vaiśyas*), and menial workers or cultivators (*śudras*), rarely appears in early Buddhist scriptures, which instead mention only three groups: first, the kṣatriyas (here generally understood as rulers); second, the priests or brāhmaṇas; and third, the house lords (*gṛhapatis*), a term used to refer to men who held positions of significant financial and social standing but did not belong to the two highest social levels. The regular mention of just three castes in early Buddhist sources, with people of lower status generally referred to simply by their names or occupations, suggests that the four-level system generally associated with Hinduism in India had not yet solidified and, in particular, that the preeminence of the Brahmans had not yet been secured.
3. See, for example, the *Suttanipāta*, v. 136: "Not by birth does one become an outcaste, / Not by birth does one become a Brahman; / By (one's) action one becomes an outcaste, / By (one's) action one becomes a Brahman" (K. R. Norman, trans., *The Group of Discourses* [*Sutta-nipāta*] [London: Pali Text Society, 1995], 2:16).
4. Later a sixth realm—that of the jealous gods, or *asuras*—was added to the list by some (but not all) Buddhist schools. (The Sarvāstivādin school, for example, did not accept the inclusion of the asuras as a separate group.) The *Lotus* mentions five realms in some sections and six realms in others; this is one of many ways in which we can tell that the scripture as we have it includes material written by more than one author.
5. For a sophisticated study of negative images of women in early Buddhist literature (especially pertaining to women's bodies as posing a threat to male monastic celibacy), see Liz Wilson, *Charming Cadavers: Horrific Figurations of the Feminine in Indian Buddhist Hagiographic Literature* (Chicago: University of Chicago Press, 1996). A good balance to this work is Kathryn Blackstone's study of the *Therīgāthā*, which focuses on the positive portrayal of women's spiritual achievements (*Women in the Footsteps of the Buddha: Struggle for Liberation in the Therīgāthā* [Richmond, UK: Curzon, 1998]). A nuanced treatment of both positive and negative images of women and their contexts can be found in Alan Sponberg, "Attitudes toward Women and the Feminine in Early Buddhism," in *Buddhism, Sexuality, and Gender*, ed. José Ignacio Cabezón, 3–36 (Albany: SUNY Press, 1992).
6. This has been questioned in a recent study by Oskar von Hinüber, who marshals evidence that the controversial decision to ordain women was not implemented until after the Buddha's death ("The Foundation of the Bhikkhunīsaṃgha: A Contribution of the Earliest History of Buddhism," in *Annual Report of the International Research Institute for Advanced Buddhology at Soka University for the Academic Year 2007*, 3–29 [Tokyo: The International Research Institute for Advanced Buddhology, Soka University, 2008]).
7. *Cullavagga*, X, 1, 6; see T. W. Rhys Davids and Hermann Oldenberg, trans., *Vinaya Texts, Part III: The Cullavagga, IV-XII* (London: Oxford University Press, 1884), 325–26. For discussions of this account, see Sponberg, "Attitudes toward Women and the Feminine"; and Jan Nattier, *Once upon a Future Time: Studies in a Buddhist Prophecy of Decline*, Nanzan Studies in Asian Religions 1 (Berkeley: Asian Humanities Press, 1991), 27–33.
8. Akira Hirakawa, trans., *Monastic Discipline for the Buddhist Nuns: An English Translation of the Chinese Text of the Mahāsāṃghika-Bhikṣuṇī-Vinaya*, Tibetan Sanskrit Works Series 21 (Patna, India: Kashi Prasad Jayaswal Research Institute, 1982), 49.

9. For a reliable scholarly translation, see K. R. Norman, trans., *Elders' Verses*, 2 vols. (London: Luzac, 1969–1971). An insightful scholarly study of the text (comparing the *Therīgāthā* with the *Theragāthā*, which contains accounts of male disciples of the Buddha) can be found in Blackstone, *Women in the Footsteps of the Buddha*. The discussion of the *Therīgāthā* by Susan Murcott, while highly readable, must be used with caution, as it is based on paraphrases of existing English translations rather than directly on the Pāli-language original; the author also treats later legends concerning various figures dealt with in the *Therīgāthā* as historical fact (Murcott, *The First Buddhist Women: Translations and Commentaries on the Therigatha* [Berkeley: Parallax Press, 1991]).
10. For a study of various traditions concerning the duration and eventual death of the dharma, see Nattier, *Once upon a Future Time*.
11. On traditions concerning Maitreya, see Alan Sponberg and Helen Hardacre, eds., *Maitreya, the Future Buddha* (Cambridge: Cambridge University Press, 1988).
12. Nattier, *A Few Good Men: The Bodhisattva Path according to "The Inquiry of Ugra (Ugraparipṛcchā),"* Studies in the Buddhist Traditions (Honolulu: University of Hawai'i Press, 2003), especially 84–89.
13. Garma C. C. Chang et al., trans., *A Treasury of Mahāyāna Sūtras: Selections from the Mahāratnakūṭa Sūtra* (University Park: Pennsylvania State University Press, 1983), 398; for references to similar statements in other sūtras not yet translated into English, see Nattier, *A Few Good Men*, 87, n. 22.
14. Paul Harrison, "Who Gets to Ride in the Great Vehicle? Self-Image and Identity among the Followers of the Early Mahāyāna," *Journal of the International Association of Buddhist Studies* 10, no. 1 (1987): 67–89.
15. For these stories, see the Pāli jātaka collection, nos. 313 (*Khantivādijātaka*) and 499 (*Śibijātaka*), respectively. For an English translation of the entire collection, see E. B. Cowell et al., eds. and trans., *The Jātaka; or, Stories of the Buddha's Former Births*, 6 vols. (Cambridge: Cambridge University Press, 1895–1907).
16. The only exceptions seem to be in tantric texts dating from the closing years of Buddhist history in India, most of which are now preserved only in Tibetan or Chinese translations.
17. Something has gone wrong in Kumārajīva's version, for Ānanda is included in the list of arhats, though he is universally held to have attained nirvāṇa only after the Buddha's death; see *Miaofa lianhua jing*, trans. Kumārajīva (Jiumoluoshi, 344–413, or 350–409), *Taishō shinshū daizōkyō*, 100 vols., ed. Takakusu Junjirō, Watanabe Kaigyoku, and Ono Gemmyō (1924–1934; repr., Taibei: Xinwenfeng chuban gongsi, 1974) (hereafter abbreviated as *T*) no. 262, 9:1c27–28; Hurvitz, 3. In the Sanskrit text, by contrast, Ānanda is (as expected) classified not as an arhat but instead as one who still "has more to learn" (*śaikṣa*, translated as "still under training" in [Jan] H[endrik] Kern, trans., *Saddharma-Puṇḍarīka or The Lotus of the True Law*, The Sacred Books of the East 21 [Oxford: Clarendon Press, 1884; repr., New York: Dover, 1963], 3).
18. In the Chinese text it is not always possible to discern whether the names refer to a male or a female character, but in the Indian languages (Sanskrit and Prakrit) from which the Chinese scriptures were translated, gender is clearly indicated.
19. The bodhisattva Avalokiteśvara does, however, come to be viewed as female in China (under the name Guanyin), but this is a much later development. On the variety of representations of Guanyin in Chinese thought and practice, see Chün-fang Yü, *Kuan-yin: The Chinese Transformation of Avalokiteśvara* (New York: Columbia University Press, 2001).

20. The story is related in Chapter 27 of Kumārajīva's version. In Hurvitz's translation, the bodhisattva who was formerly Vimaladattā is referred to simply as Marks of Adornment (Hurvitz, 304); in the Sanskrit text, however, the masculine form of the name, Vairocanaraśmipratimaṇḍitarāja, makes clear that the former queen has now become a male; see Kern, *Saddharma-Puṇḍarīka*, 429.
21. In one other place in the sūtra female characters appear to be mentioned by name: in a reference to members of the audience in Chapter 20, "Bodhisattva Never Disparaging," there is a mention of Lion Moon, heading a group of five hundred nuns, and Thoughtful of the Buddha, heading a group of five hundred laywomen. Once again, however, if we look at the oldest version of the sūtra, the picture changes, for here Lion Moon heads a group of five hundred monks *and* nuns (and is therefore presumably male), while the character Thoughtful of the Buddha does not appear at all; see *Zhengfahua jing* (*Saddharmapuṇḍarīka*), Dharmarakṣa (Zhu Fahu , ca. 265–313, or 239–316), *T* no. 263, 9:123b22–24.
22. Hurvitz's explanation of the word *paṇḍaka* (which he translates as "impotent" [Hurvitz, 192, note]) is based on only one (rather unrepresentative) source; for a far richer discussion of various types of paṇḍakas and of Buddhist attitudes toward homosexuality in general, see Leonard Zwilling, "Homosexuality as Seen in Indian Buddhist Texts," in *Buddhism, Sexuality, and Gender*, ed José Ignacio Cabezón, 203–14 (Albany: SUNY Press, 1992).
23. For a detailed discussion of treatments of this theme in Mahāyāna scriptures, see Jan Nattier, "Gender and Awakening: Sexual Transformation in Mahāyāna Sūtras" (unpublished ms.).
24. In Sanskrit the terms in question are *kulaputra* and *kuladuhitṛ*, which might best be translated as "gentleman" and "lady." In Kumārajīva's Chinese version, the corresponding terms are *shan nanzi* and *shan nüren*, meaning simply "good man" and "good woman," respectively.
25. These sections include Chapters 10, 17, 18, and 19; other exhortations to women occur in the chapters concerning the "great bodhisattvas" appended at the end of the text (Chapters 25–28).
26. For discussion of the story of the nāga girl's transformation (with special attention to the reception of the story in Japan), see Kazuhiko Yoshida, "The Enlightenment of the Dragon King's Daughter in *The Lotus Sutra*," translated and adapted by Margaret H. Childs, in *Engendering Faith: Women and Buddhism in Premodern Japan*, ed. Barbara Ruch, 297–324 (Ann Arbor: Center for Japanese Studies, University of Michigan, 2002). For further studies, see, in the present volume, chap. 1, n. 31. Several Buddhist scriptures illustrating the necessity of women's transformation into men prior to the attainment of buddhahood are discussed in Nattier, "Gender and Awakening."
27. On the late addition of the Devadatta chapter to the sūtra, see n. 4 in chap. 1 of this volume.
28. Alan Cole makes much of this father imagery in *Text as Father: Paternal Seductions in Early Mahāyāna Literature*, Buddhisms (Berkeley: University of California Press, 2005), though for him it is the sūtra itself, and not the Buddha, that effectively plays this parental role. Cole's study is provocative and raises interesting issues concerning the *Lotus*, but his analysis is marred by the fact that it views Chapters 1 to 4 as the work of a single individual, despite the rich body of scholarship identifying at least three distinct chronological layers within this material. For a brief summary

of the results of these studies, see Karashima, "Who Composed the Lotus Sutra?" 171. Cole's claims about the *Lotus* and other sūtras cannot be applied directly to India, since he does not deal with the Indian (that is, Sanskrit) text itself but only with its Chinese translations. As a result, Cole sometimes generates arguments based on ideas not found in the Sanskrit version—for example, the frequently repeated assertion that the bodhisattva Mañjuśrī is being portrayed as the "son of a dharma king," which Cole understands to mean "the son of a Buddha" (Cole, *Text as Father*, 56, 73, and passim), whereas in the Sanskrit *Lotus Sūtra* (as in other Sanskrit Buddhist texts), Mañjuśrī's epithet is simply *kumārabhūta* ("young man" or "prince").

29. This parable is actually taught by a group of the Buddha's most senior disciples and not by the Buddha himself (Hurvitz, 78–79).

30. Earlier Mahāyāna scriptures held that once one had become an arhat—or, indeed, once one had becoming a stream enterer (and thus had a maximum of seven lives left to live)—it was no longer possible to "change lanes," as it were, and become a bodhisattva instead. Thus for an arhat to receive a prediction of his or her future buddhahood would have been shocking to audiences at the time.

31. This conforms to what is actually found in some Mahāyāna sūtras, for example, in the *Perfection of Wisdom in Eight Thousand Lines*, in which Subhūti and Śāriputra—both considered to be arhats by the early Buddhist tradition—hold an extensive discussion of the practices of the bodhisattva; see Edward Conze, trans., *The Perfection of Wisdom in Eight Thousand Lines and Its Verse Summary*, Wheel Series 1 (Bolinas, Calif.: Four Seasons Foundation, 1973), 83–102 and passim.

32. See, for example, the *Discourse to Kāśyapa*, which states that "if a Tathāgata is surrounded by hundreds of thousands of millions of śrāvakas, but no bodhisattvas, he will not consider any of them as his true son" (Chang et al., *Treasury of Mahāyāna Sūtras*, 397), and that "a bodhisattva, even when he first brings forth *bodhicitta* [the thought of awakening], surpasses all śrāvakas and pratyekabuddhas combined" (ibid., 398).

33. Quoting again from the same text, the *Discourse to Kāśyapa* suggests that "just as people adore a new moon more than a full moon," a bodhisattva should be adored even more than a Buddha himself, the reasoning being that bodhisattvas will help the world by becoming buddhas in the future (Chang et al., *Treasury of Mahāyāna Sūtras*, 398).

34. On the stark contrast between the message of the *Lotus* and that of much of the rest of the Mahāyāna tradition (including present-day Tibetan Buddhism), see Jan Nattier, "A Greater Awakening," *Tricycle: The Buddhist Review* 15, no. 3 (2006): 65–69.

35. On the range of interpretations of the structure of the path found in traditional Buddhist sources, see Robert E. Buswell Jr. and Robert M. Gimello, eds., *Paths to Liberation: The Mārga and Its Transformations in Buddhist Thought*, Kuroda Institute, Studies in East Asian Buddhism 7 (Honolulu: University of Hawai'i Press, 1992); on the emergence of the idea of "sudden awakening" in East Asian Buddhism, see Peter N. Gregory, ed., *Sudden and Gradual: Approaches to Enlightenment in Chinese Thought*, Kuroda Institute, Studies in East Asian Buddhism 5 (Honolulu: University of Hawai'i Press, 1987).

36. Karl H. Potter, *Presuppositions of India's Philosophies* (Westport, Conn.: Greenwood Press, 1963).

37. For a convenient and reliable discussion of the Mahāyāna idea of three vehicles—that is, that there are three different paths, leading to three distinct goals, that are appropriate to different persons based on their temperament and spiritual capacity—see Richard H. Robinson, Willard L. Johnson, and Thanissaro Bhikkhu, *Buddhist Religions: A Historical Introduction*, 5th ed. (Belmont, Calif.: Wadsworth, 2005), 84–91. The view that only some people (and not all) are suited for the rigors of the bodhisattva path was standard in early Mahāyāna and remained a fundamental assumption in many Mahāyāna circles long after the authors of the *Lotus* set forth their arguments for a single vehicle; see Nattier, *A Few Good Men*, 174–76.

[4]

THE *LOTUS SŪTRA* AND SELF-IMMOLATION

James A. Benn

BEGINNING AROUND the end of the fourth century of the Common Era, and continuing sporadically into modern times, some Chinese Buddhists have drawn inspiration from the *Lotus Sūtra* for a particular style of religious practice involving burning a finger or the whole body in homage to the scripture. Chinese sources usually refer to the incineration of the body as "auto-cremation" (*zifen* or *shaoshen*); it is one manifestation of a broader range of Buddhist practices that involve making a gift of the body (for example, feeding oneself to hungry animals or humans, jumping from cliffs or trees, or drowning oneself) that are termed "self-immolation" (*sheshen, wangshen,* or *yishen*).[1] The best-known example of Buddhist self-immolation in recent times is that of the Vietnamese monk Thích Quang Đuc (1897–1963), whose public auto-cremation in downtown Saigon in 1963 was captured in a series of dramatic photographs that have been widely reproduced.[2]

We know that Chinese Buddhists particularly associated burning the body with the *Lotus Sūtra* because this connection is stressed in many surviving records beyond the sūtra itself, such as biographies of outstanding monks and nuns, popular tales about miracles associated with the sūtra, and epitaphs for self-immolators inscribed on stone. These accounts tell of men and women who chanted the text as they burned, or who deliberately imitated the model of the bodhisattva Medicine King (Bhaiṣajyarāja), who is depicted in the scripture as burning himself in a selfless and heroic manner. These Chinese sources make frequent allusions to the way in which Medicine King—then known by his earlier name of Seen with Joy by All Living Beings (Sarvasattvapriyadarśana)—carefully prepared his body to be burned. They also draw parallels between their subjects and the story of the bodhisattva, with particular attention to his devotion to the *Lotus Sūtra* and the relics of his teacher, the miraculous response of the universe to his extreme act of devotion, and the joyous approval of those who witnessed it. So well known was Medicine King's self-immolation that, from the fourth century on, many East Asian Buddhist authors would point to the *Lotus Sūtra* as the locus classicus for auto-cremation.

Although the practice of burning the body was criticized on occasion by both secular authorities and Buddhist monks, it has been an accepted feature of Buddhist devotionalism in East Asia until recent times. The offering of fingers and burning of incense on the skin (another symbolic act of self-immolation) still occur in China, Taiwan, and Korea. The tradition of making small burn marks on the crown of the head as part of the ordination ceremony for Chinese monks and nuns ultimately derives from the example of Medicine King.[3] In Japan, such practices have tended to be less common, although by no means unknown.

The *Lotus Sūtra* provided not only a template for auto-cremation, by showing readers how and why it might be performed, but also the liturgy: self-immolators chanted the chapter on the Medicine King as they enacted it, thus making the scripture into a kind of performative speech. But, although immolators drew on the sūtra for inspiration, the biographies of self-immolators are by no means formulaic and repetitive; rather, in their variety, they make explicit some aspects of self-immolation that are only suggested by the scripture, such as the power of the act to convert people to Buddhism and to save sentient beings.

THE STORY IN THE *LOTUS SŪTRA*

In order to understand what kind of literary blueprint the *Lotus Sūtra* offered for Chinese Buddhist auto-cremators, we need to examine the account given of the spectacular offering made by one advanced bodhisattva, in Chapter 23, "The Former Affairs of the Bodhisattva Medicine King." The chapter is introduced by the bodhisattva Beflowered by the King of Constellations (Nakṣatrarājasaṃkusumitābhijña), who asks Śākyamuni Buddha to explain the "difficult deeds and austerities" (*nanxing kuxing*) of the bodhisattva Medicine King. The Buddha relates that, in the past, innumerable eons ago, there was a buddha called Pure and Bright Excellence of Sun and Moon (Candrasūryavimalaprabhāsaśrī). This buddha is described as having been accompanied by a vast retinue of advanced practitioners and as living in a world that was considerably more impressive than our own. He had an entourage of eighty million bodhisattva-mahāsattvas, all of whom had a life span of forty-two thousand eons. His realm was perfectly flat and adorned with jeweled trees, banners, and terraces; there were no women, hell dwellers, hungry ghosts, or *asuras* (demigods) there. It was, in other words, a pure land, a place in which only favorable states of rebirth were possible.

At that time in the far distant past, in a buddha realm very different from our own, the buddha Pure and Bright Excellence of Sun and Moon taught the *Lotus Sūtra* to the bodhisattva Seen with Joy by All Living Beings. This bodhisattva was so inspired by the teaching that he wished to attain buddhahood himself, which he aimed to do by cultivating austerities. He then practiced diligently for twelve thousand years (the sūtra does not tell us exactly what his practices were) and thus attained a level of meditational skill called the "*samādhi* [absorption] that displays all manner of physical bodies" (*yiqie seshen sanmei*). He was delighted with this result, which he attributed not to his own practice alone but to his having heard the *Lotus Sūtra*.

Bodhisattva Seen with Joy thereupon resolved to make offerings (Skt.: *pūja*, Ch.: *gongyang*) to the buddha Pure and Bright Excellence of Sun and Moon and to the *Lotus Sūtra*. First, the bodhisattva entered samādhi and magically produced a rain of flowers and incense. But he considered that this offering was inferior to the donation of his own body. The *Lotus Sūtra* then describes his preparations in a way that was to echo through later accounts of auto-cremation in China: "Straightway then he applied [to his body] various scents, *candana* [sandalwood], *kunduruka*, *turuṣka* [two kinds of frankincense], *pṛkkā* [*Trigonella*], the scent that sinks in water, and the scent of pine-tar; and he also drank the fragrant oils of *campaka*-flowers. When a thousand two hundred years had been fulfilled, he painted his body with fragrant oil and, in the presence of the buddha Pure and Bright Excellence of Sun and Moon, wrapped his body in a garment adorned with divine jewels, anointed himself with fragrant oils, with the force of supernatural penetration took a vow, and then burned his own body" (Hurvitz, 270).

The bodhisattva thus doused himself in fragrance, drank scented oil, and wrapped his anointed body in an oil-soaked cloth. These details seem to be borrowed from descriptions of similar preparations that were made for Śākyamuni's cremation and may reflect a practical concern with making the human body (which is notoriously difficult to reduce to ashes) more readily flammable.[4] The bodhisattva made a vow (presumably stating his intention and identifying the recipients of his donation) and then ignited himself. The light of his burning body reached innumerable other world systems. The buddhas of these realms were much impressed and compared his auto-cremation favorably with other types of donation: "Good man, this is true perseverance in vigor! This is called a true dharma offering to the Thus Come One. If with floral scent, necklaces, burnt incense, powdered scent, paint-scent, divine cloth, banners, parasols, the scent of the candana of the near seashore, and a variety of such things one were to make offerings, still they could not exceed this former [act of yours]. Even if one were to give realms and walled cities, wives and children, they would still be no match for it. Good man, this is called the prime gift. Among the various gifts, it is the most honorable, the supreme. For it constitutes an offering of dharma to the Thus Come Ones" (Hurvitz, 271).

In this passage, the giving of "inner wealth" (that is to say, the body) is described as far surpassing the most extravagant offerings of external wealth and even the donation of one's own wife and children—an allusion to a well-known story about one of Śākyamuni's former lives.[5] The enthusiasm of the buddhas for the offering of the body as exemplified in this passage was an element of the chapter that caught the attention of Medicine King's Chinese imitators, who took it as an unequivocal endorsement of self-immolation.

The bodhisattva's body burned for twelve hundred years before it was fully consumed. Because he had made such a great offering, he was immediately reborn in the realm of the buddha Pure and Bright Excellence of Sun and Moon. He was born not in the normal manner but by transformation, and he materialized sitting cross-legged in the household of King Pure Virtue (Vimaladatta). There he introduced himself in verse, explaining how he had come to be reborn there:

> O great king! Now be it known that
> I, going about in that place,
> Straightway attained the All-
> Body-Displaying Samādhi,
> Whereby, striving and greatly persevering in vigor,
> I cast off the body to which I had been so attached
> And offered it to the World Honored One,
> In order to seek the unexcelled wisdom.
>
> (HURVITZ, 271)[6]

These lines tell us three important things about the bodhisattva's self-immolation. First, he made the offering as a consequence of attaining the samādhi, with the implication, perhaps, that his self-immolation was an advanced practice accessible to him because of his highly developed skills in meditation and the supernatural powers that come with it. Second, his self-immolation was primarily a practice of one of the other perfections (*pāramitās*) of the bodhisattva path, that of vigor (*vīrya*), and not the perfection of charity (*dāna*), as we might have expected in light of other Buddhist tales of bodily donation. The heroic, energetic mode of vigor contrasts somewhat with the humility required of selfless devotion. The association of self-immolation with vigor as well as charity may help to explain why Chinese self-immolators often made a show of the strenuous effort required for public auto-cremation. Third, it was an offering to the buddha, made by the bodhisattva in the hopes of his attaining the full awakening of buddhahood. This last aspect is important for understanding the ultimate goal of self-immolation and why it could be said to benefit others—by becoming a buddha rapidly the self-immolator would soon find himself in a position to rescue sentient beings from suffering by means of a buddha's salvific powers.

Having explained himself in verse, the bodhisattva announced to his new father, Pure Virtue, that he intended to make further offerings to the buddha Pure and Bright Excellence of Sun and Moon. But when he presented himself, the buddha informed him that he, the buddha, was about to pass from the world and enter *parinirvāṇa* that very night. He entrusted Seen with Joy with his teaching, the bodhisattvas of his retinue, the world systems that made up his realm, and finally his precious bodily relics (*śarīras*), instructing him on how they should be venerated. In the last hours of that night, the buddha entered extinction.

The bodhisattva cremated the deceased buddha and collected the relics, which he placed in eighty-four thousand reliquaries (*stūpas*). He made the usual kinds of offering appropriate for venerating relics—draping the stūpas with banners, covering them with parasols, and adorning them with jeweled bells—but again it occurred to him that he should make a further oblation. He announced to the assembled bodhisattvas, their disciples, gods, *nāgas*, *yakṣas*, and others, "You are all to attend single-mindedly. For I will now make an offering to the śarīras of the buddha Pure and Bright Excellence of Sun and Moon" (Hurvitz, 272). The bodhisattva then burned his forearms for seventy-two thousand years, causing many beings to aspire to complete, perfect enlightenment (*anuttarasamyaksaṃbodhi*) and enabling them also to acquire the "samādhi that displays all manner of physical bodies." Despite this result, the assembled witnesses remained somewhat upset that he had no arms. The bodhisattva then vowed, "I have thrown away both arms. May I now without fail gain the buddha's golden-colored body! If this oath is reality and not vanity, then may both arms be restored as before!" (Hurvitz, 273). Because of the sincerity of this vow, his arms were immediately restored, the universe responded by shaking "in six ways," and all men and gods "gained something they had never had before" (Hurvitz, 273).

At this point in the chapter, the story of the former acts of the bodhisattva Medicine King concludes and we return to the narrative frame. Śākyamuni Buddha now reveals to the bodhisattva Beflowered by the King of Constellations that the bodhisattva Seen with Joy by All Living Beings, who made such remarkable offerings in the distant past, is none other than the present-day bodhisattva Medicine King. The Buddha extols this bodhisattva's practices, and then makes a recommendation to ordinary practitioners: "Gifts of his own body, such as this one, number in the incalculable hundreds of thousands of myriads of millions of *nayutas* [hundred billions]. O Beflowered by the King of Constellations! If there is one who, opening up his thought, wishes to attain anuttarasamyaksaṃbodhi, if he can burn a finger or even a toe as an offering to a buddhastūpa, he shall exceed one who uses realm or walled city, wife or children, or even all the lands, mountains, forests, rivers, ponds, and sundry precious objects in the whole thousand-millionfold world as offerings" (Hurvitz, 273).

In this speech—which was often quoted or alluded to by Chinese Buddhist authors—Śākyamuni states that burning the body is not restricted to advanced bodhisattvas but may be practiced by anyone who wishes to attain buddhahood. However, in the typical fashion of the *Lotus Sūtra*, this claim for the powers of auto-cremation is immediately undercut by a further declaration that the merit accrued by one who memorizes even a single verse of the sūtra exceeds that gained by one who gives away a universe full of jewels. The purpose of this sentence is probably not to devalue self-immolation but rather to reiterate the awesome power of the *Lotus Sūtra*, which, it seems, must never be allowed to be overshadowed by any other text or practice described in the sūtra itself. The chapter on the prior lifetime of Medicine King concludes with the customary hymns of praise to the miraculous powers of the *Lotus Sūtra*. Finally, Śākyamuni entrusts the chapter to the care of Bodhisattva Beflowered by the King of Constellations.

READINGS OF THE STORY

The Chinese commentarial literature on the *Lotus Sūtra* is extensive, but it is not always that helpful for understanding how practitioners made sense of Medicine King's self-immolation.[7] This is because Buddhist commentators often do not explain sūtras word by word, nor do they usually summarize the teachings or narrative. Instead, they concentrate on dividing up the text according to a predetermined structural scheme, resulting in a work that reads as an extended list or outline, with many subsections.[8] Commentators aim to reveal the deep structure of the sūtra as a complex and comprehensive teaching of the Buddha, and so are usually less interested in expounding on the meaning of individual episodes such as Medicine King's self-immolation. For this reason, we must also look to other materials, such as the biographies of Chinese self-immolators, in order to appreciate how this chapter of the *Lotus Sūtra* was read and understood.

Despite their emphasis on structure, the commentators did not leave Medicine King's self-immolation entirely without exegesis. Sometimes they tried to place it within a coherent doctrinal scheme, as, for example, in the earliest extant Chinese commentary on the *Lotus Sūtra*, by Daosheng (360–434). Daosheng studied under the translator Kumārajīva (Jiumoluoshi [344–413, or 350–409]) and had a sophisticated understanding of Mahāyāna doctrine in general and of the sūtra in particular. He uses the duality of "principle" (*li*, the underlying nature of reality experienced by the awakened mind) and "phenomena" (*shi*, the transient, insubstantial world experienced by ordinary beings) to comment on the auto-cremation of the bodhisattva.[9] He argues that the validity and efficacy of making a donation of the body are dependent on the mental attitude of the practitioner. He claims that if the practitioner is able to perceive the true nature of the gift of the body from an enlightened perspective—from the point of view of principle, in Daosheng's terms—then such a mental state would be as good as continually burning the body. Conversely, a perspective that is tainted by worldly views—a concern for fame and reputation, for example—would not be able to generate a true (that is, selfless) gift of the body. Later writers expanded upon this theme of the attitude with which self-immolation was, or should be, undertaken. In Buddhist terms, the intention behind the act is understood to determine the nature of the resulting karmic effect. Thus, those who burned themselves without focusing on the loftiest goals were likely to suffer the painful consequences in their subsequent rebirths.

The story of Medicine King was not just edifying or awe-inspiring; his auto-cremation could also offer an opportunity for the awakening of those who heard it. Zhiyi (538–597), one of the most influential Buddhist figures of the sixth century and later recognized as a Tiantai patriarch, was said to have become enlightened upon reading this chapter of the *Lotus Sūtra*.[10] A commentary attributed to him says of the Medicine King chapter, "This text explains how Seen with Joy by All Sentient Beings spontaneously discarded his body and later burned his two arms, considering his own life less important than the dharma, and letting his life end so that the way [that is, Buddhism] should prosper."[11] He also says that the bodhisattva exemplifies a manner of riding in the "great vehicle" through the cultivation of austerities (*nanxing*)—in other words, that he represents a distinct bodily or somatic path toward buddhahood.[12] Kuiji (632–682), a disciple of the famous Buddhist pilgrim and translator Xuanzang (600–664), also sees Medicine King as a representative of the ascetic mode of Buddhism: "Through his own cultivation of austerities he propagates the true dharma."[13] Jizang (549–623), another major Buddhist thinker, emphasizes the multiple effects of self-immolation when he says that the bodhisattva uses his own life "to repay the kindness [of the Buddha] and pay homage to him, thus propagating the sūtra, creating merit for humans, teaching and converting myriad beings."[14] Thus, commentators emphasized the altruistic nature of surrendering the body.

The later Tiantai patriarch Zhanran (711–782) offers a somewhat more sophisticated attempt at making sense of the bodhisattva's self-immolation from the perspective of the nonduality of body and flames.[15] In his commentary, he also takes up the most vexing problem for Chinese Buddhist monks—to wit, the fact that the *vinaya* (the corpus of texts regulating monastic behavior) forbade monks to kill themselves, yet Medicine King was praised by the buddhas for doing just that.[16] I discuss this crucial problem and some of the ways in which it was resolved in more detail in a subsequent section, "Apocryphal Practices and Their Significance."

BIOGRAPHIES OF SELF-IMMOLATORS: THE *LOTUS SŪTRA* IN PRACTICE

To obtain a clearer picture of how the story of Medicine King was read, we need to examine the records of Chinese Buddhist auto-cremators. By burning their bodies as prescribed by this chapter of the *Lotus Sūtra*, Chinese monks and nuns took on the role of the devoted bodhisattva. Some were careful to mimic his consumption of incense and oil and the wrapping of the body in oil-impregnated cloth that preceded his auto-cremation; some burned themselves in front of stūpas or before large audiences. Evidence of their success in emulating his example was manifested if not by the "world system shaking in six ways" then at least by lights and signs in the sky, by miraculous trees growing in practitioners' cells or at the site of the act, by dreams and portents, and, perhaps most important of all, by the production of relics from their auto-cremation. The homage paid by the bodhisattva to the relics of the Buddha in the *Lotus Sūtra* thus provided the inspiration for the production of additional Buddhist relics in our own world system. It may be useful to consider here one such biographical account—a somewhat rare surviving record of female auto-cremation in medieval China. The seventh-century biography states:

> At the beginning of the Zhenguan reign period (627–649), in Jingzhou, there were two sisters who were nuns [*bhikṣuṇīs*].[17] Together they recited the *Lotus Sūtra* and they had a deep loathing for their physical form. Both wished to abandon their bodies. They restricted their food and clothing and admired the practice of austerities. They consumed incense and oil and gradually cut out grain from their diet. Later they completely abstained from grain and ate only incense and honey. They were filled with strength of essence; their spiritual determination was bright and vigorous.
>
> They widely advertised, to both religious and laity, that on the appointed day they would burn their bodies. On the eighth day of the second month of the third year of the Zhenguan reign period [March 8, 629], they set up two high seats on the main road of Jingzhou. Then they wrapped their bodies in waxed cloth right up to the crown of the head, so that only their faces and eyes were visible. The crowds massed like mountains, their songs and eulogies like gathering clouds.
>
> They recited [the *Lotus Sūtra*] up until the point where [the bodhisattva] burns. The older sister first applied a flaming wick to her younger sister's head, then she asked the younger sister to apply a burning wick to her head. In the peace of the night the two torches blazed away together simultaneously. The fire burned down to their eyes, but the sound of their recitation became louder. [The flames] gradually reached their noses and mouths and then [the recitation] came to an end.
>
> This was just at daybreak, and they were still sitting together and intact. Then, simultaneously the fires flared up, and their bones were smashed and broken, but the two tongues remained intact. The assembled crowd sighed admiringly and raised a high pagoda for them.[18]

This account emphasizes the preparation for auto-cremation and is concerned with locating the action in time and space, constructing a dramatic narrative of a public performance. Aside from the mention of their "deep loathing" for their own bodies (which no doubt reflects the negative connotations of a female rebirth in medieval Chinese Buddhism), there is little in this account that appears to mark out any gendered vision of auto-cremation. The sisters' preparatory fast and their abstention from grain were common to both male and female auto-cremators. The fact that the sisters imitated Medicine King, who was a male hero of the *Lotus Sūtra*, does not seem to have caused any concern to the onlookers or to whoever recorded their story. But, significantly, the *Lotus Sūtra* also contains the famous story of the dragon girl who changes her body from female to male and becomes a buddha (Hurvitz, 183–85).[19] This message about the ultimately empty nature of gender may have encouraged women to take up such "advanced" practices as self-immolation. The sisters burned themselves in public, just as monks did, and the onlookers witnessed the same kinds of miraculous signs as manifested by their male counterparts. Their auto-cremation was celebrated with a pagoda (another word for stūpa), just as monks' remains were similarly commemorated.

One of the most notable features of this account is the appearance of the unburned tongue. This particular miracle offers a good example of how elements taken from the chapter on Medicine King were creatively combined with beliefs that can be traced to other parts of the sūtra. There are about twenty cases in the medieval Chinese biographical sources in which the tongue either does not rot or remains intact, pink and moist, after the cremation of the body.[20] Where did this belief in the indestructibility of the tongue come from? In Chapter 10 of the *Lotus Sūtra*, "Preachers of Dharma," we discover that reading, reciting, interpreting, and copying the sūtra bring physical rewards to the body and sense organs (eyes, ears, nose, tongue) of the practitioner. Later in the text, the Buddha, in addressing the bodhisattva Ever Persevering (Satatasamitābhiyukta), promises that the tongue in particular will have twelve hundred virtues: "Further, O Ever Persevering, if a good man or good woman accepts and keeps this scripture, whether reading it, reciting it, interpreting it, or copying it, he shall attain a thousand two hundred virtues of the tongue. All things whether good or ugly, whether delicious or foul-tasting, or even bitter and astringent, shall all change for his lingual faculty into things of superior flavor, like the sweet dew of the gods, none failing to be delicious. If in the midst of a great multitude he has anything to expound, then, producing a profound and subtle sound, with his lingual faculty he shall be able to penetrate their hearts, causing them all to rejoice and be cheerful" (Hurvitz, 250).

The text goes on to list all the deities, nāgas, yakṣas, *garuḍas*, monks, nuns, kings, and so on who will come to listen to the preacher. It is true that preservation of the tongue after death is not mentioned explicitly, but the scripture does promise definite changes in the power of that particular organ. This passage, together with others from the *Lotus Sūtra*, evidently supplied the imaginary world of medieval Buddhists with the idea that the sense organs could be made literally incorruptible by chanting the sūtra.

Not only sages but also quite ordinary men and women were able to produce the miraculous relic of the indestructible tongue, and this prodigy must, I think, be understood to imply that virtually anyone could be a "preacher of the dharma" if they were determined enough. The power of the sūtra itself was what encouraged some people to go even further than just preaching and to enact the role of the bodhisattva by burning themselves. The biographies of the auto-cremators offer interesting examples of the creative conflation of different episodes from the sūtra to produce a single bodily mode of devotion.

Another biography shows how baroque the miracles associated with auto-cremation could become. Sengming (ca. 502–519) built a temple to the buddha of the future and installed an image of Maitreya within it. He constantly recited the *Lotus Sūtra*, and as he did so, he always heard the sound of fingers snapping in approval and someone saying, "Excellent!" Several times he wrote to Emperor Wu, of the Liang dynasty (r. 502–549), asking permission to burn his body. This emperor was a generous patron of Buddhism who sponsored large-scale ceremonies involving thousands of clerics, and who occasionally ransomed himself in order to swell the coffers of the *saṅgha*—his courtiers had to pay the monastic community a hefty fee in order to get him back. Emperor Wu finally approved his request and Sengming burned himself on a rock in front of his Maitreya shrine. Sengming's auto-cremation was followed by a remarkable series of miracles at the site, including healing, spontaneously blooming flowers, and a moving statue: "His body was completely reduced to ashes, and all that remained was one fingernail. When the burning was over, the ground surrounding the rock to a radius of four or five yards sank, thus forming a pond. Two or three days later, flowers bloomed there; bright and luxuriant, they were unmatched in beauty. All those who drank from this pond were cured of their illnesses. Later, people gathered up the ashes and made an image of him with them. They also made a small wooden image. They burned the nail again, took the ashes, and made a paste. When people smeared it on, the image moved away. In all the places where it went, flowers bloomed. They were as big as pear and jujube trees, and there were more than 100,000 of them."[21]

Clearly, the miracles associated with Sengming's auto-cremation (the fingernail relic, apparitions of flowers, magical water, and mobile images) do not map precisely onto any episodes recounted in the *Lotus Sūtra* chapter. Rather, they emerged out of a larger world of the medieval Chinese imagination in which the *Lotus Sūtra* was but another element alongside others with antecedents both Buddhist and indigenous. We can see that the merit of Sengming's self-immolation was shared rather tangibly with others, in the form of the magic water from the pond. His ability to heal also hints at his identification with the bodhisattva Medicine King. Thus we observe a tendency to extrapolate from the *Lotus Sūtra* and to make explicit in practice themes and ideas that are only hinted at in the text.

Attached to Sengming's biography is another account of an image produced by auto-cremation.[22] A layman chanted the *Lotus Sūtra* and aspired to follow the example of Medicine King. After he burned himself, the earth swelled up in the shape of a human body. His father dug up the mound and within it found a life-size golden statue. When he had excavated the image, he wanted to set it upright, but suddenly it disappeared.

This miracle tale combines the idea of the bodhisattva revealing his true form in the shape of a golden image, echoing both Medicine King's vow ("May I now without fail gain the buddha's golden-colored body!") and the idea of bodhisattvas "welling up out of the earth," as described in the eponymous chapter of the *Lotus Sūtra*. These bodhisattvas, depicted as golden in color, dwell beneath our world sphere and appear out of cracks in the earth as the Buddha is preaching. This brief tale of auto-cremation hints at the kind of imaginative associations that Buddhists in medieval China made between text and practice.

One final example will serve to show how Buddhists dealt with the issue of pain associated with auto-cremation. Tanyou (d. 666) was a devout reciter of the *Lotus Sūtra* but would only begin to chant the text after he had set up a purified altar and decorated it with banners.[23] He vowed to burn himself in front of a buddha image that was said to have been made by the great Indian king Aśoka (r. 268–232 B.C.E.) himself and that had miraculously flown to China.[24] Tanyou wrapped himself in waxed cloth and set fire to his hands and the crown of his head. He kept his eyes on the image and vowed to see Buddha Pure and Bright Excellence of Sun and Moon, to whom Medicine King had offered himself. When people asked him how he felt, he replied that his mind was like a diamond and that he felt no pain. As the flames finally flared up and consumed him, he could still be heard preaching. Tanyou's biography reveals the kinds of concerns that often came to the fore in the practice of self-immolation: reverence and devotion for the text as word and object (the so-called cult of the book), connections with India as the home of Buddhism (here symbolized by the

Aśokan image), and pious imitation of the selfless heroes of Mahāyāna literature (the stress on the technique of auto-cremation and the lack of pain).

The biographies of Chinese self-immolators show a considerable variety of ways in which the story of Medicine King could be imitated and interpreted. It is clear that many Buddhists took the *Lotus Sūtra* at its word, adopted the "difficult deeds" of Medicine King as a viable path to complete awakening, and considered that their actions could liberate others from saṃsāra.

SCRIPTURAL AND COMMENTARIAL ELABORATIONS

The offering of the body as a worthy practice is a theme not unique to the *Lotus Sūtra* but found all through Buddhist literature, especially in *jātaka* tales (accounts of the former lives and deeds of the Buddha Śākyamuni) and scattered throughout the scriptures of the Mahāyāna.[25] In these texts, self-immolation is usually presented as a way of cultivating the perfection of generosity or giving (*dānapāramitā*), considered fundamental to the bodhisattva path by which buddhahood was to be attained. For example, one of the most influential Mahāyāna texts known to the medieval Chinese, *The Treatise on the Great Perfection of Wisdom (Da zhidu lun)*, which was translated by Kumārajīva and attributed to the great Indian thinker Nāgārjuna (ca. 150–250), explains: "What is to be understood by the fulfillment of the perfection of generosity appertaining to the body which is born from the bonds and karma? Without gaining the dharma body [*dharmakāya*] and without destroying the fetters, the bodhisattva is able to give away without reservation all his precious possessions, his head, his eyes, his marrow, his skin, his kingdom, his wealth, his wife, his children and his possessions both inner and outer. But his mind remains unmoved."[26]

This passage addresses the donations that are possible for one on the bodhisattva path who is still subject to the fetters of karma. It suggests that, even though he has not yet attained awakening and the powers of a buddha (expressed here in terms of acquiring a new body), he is nonetheless capable of making extraordinary gifts. It is worth noting that in order to give away such "precious possessions," one must possess them in the first place—the bodhisattva's status is not therefore one characterized by simplicity and austerity, but by wealth and fecundity. There is an emphasis here on the impassive mental state of the bodhisattva that matches the kind of attitude that Daosheng and others saw as characterizing true self-immolation. The biographies of self-immolators also often note the calmness and tranquillity of their heroes as they offer their bodies.

The Treatise on the Great Perfection of Wisdom continues by recounting the jātaka stories of Prince Viśvantara (Pāli: Vessantara), who famously gave away his wife and children; King Sarvada, who lost his kingdom to a usurper and then surrendered himself to a poor Brahman so that he could collect a reward from the new king; and Prince Candraprabha, who donated his blood and marrow in order to cure a leper.[27] Elsewhere in *The Treatise on the Great Perfection of Wisdom*, the story of Medicine King is recounted with approval as an example of the immense benefits of worshipping the Buddha (*buddhapūja*).[28] The *Lotus Sūtra*'s lengthy account of a bodhisattva who gives away his own body as an act of homage (to a text, to a buddha, or to his relics) thus fits into an established pattern of the heroic behavior expected of such advanced beings.

The *King of Samādhi (Samādhirāja) Sūtra*, a text that was quite well known in China and elsewhere in East Asia, also contains a dramatic and extended description of a similar kind of offering. However, this particular sūtra is hardly ever referred to in Chinese accounts of self-immolation, and we must assume that the auto-cremation of Medicine King in the *Lotus Sūtra* took such a powerful hold on the Chinese imagination that it could not be usurped by other scriptural accounts.

The auto-cremation episode in the *King of Samādhi Sūtra*, like that in the *Lotus Sūtra*, centers on a junior bodhisattva who offers his body to relics.[29] But it is different from the *Lotus Sūtra* account in several important respects. During the period after the passing away of a buddha called Virtue of Voice (Ghoṣadatta), King Virtuous Sound (Śrīghoṣa) had erected eighty-four thousand tens of millions of stūpas containing relics, which were worshipped with innumerable lamps, music, flowers, incense, and so forth. A bodhisattva-mahāsattva called Virtue of Calm Tranquillity (Kṣemadatta) was a young monk (*bhikṣu*) at that time. Observing all the millions of lamps that blazed in front of the stūpas and the vast assembly of gods, courtiers, and commoners assembled in devotion, he vowed to make an act of homage before the relic stūpas. This act, he said, should cause all gods, humans, and asuras to marvel and to be joyous. He wanted his offering to surpass that of King Virtuous Sound and thus cause the king and his courtiers in particular to wonder at his act and to be happy.

That night, when Virtue of Calm Tranquillity saw the great assembly in front of the stūpas listening to the dharma, he wrapped his right arm in cloth and soaked it with oil before burning it as an offering to the buddha. At that moment, he aspired to perfect and total enlightenment, and thinking of nothing else, he did not move while his arm was burning. There was a great earthquake, and the radiance from his flaming limb spread in all directions. Bodhisattva Virtue of Calm Tranquillity attained the "samādhi in which the fundamental identity of all *dharmas* [constituents of existence] is made manifest," and with beautiful and melodious speech, he preached to the assembly. Gods and heavenly nymphs (*apsaras*) offered him homage and sang his praises. King Virtuous Sound, who was then observing the scene from the top of a pavilion along with his harem, saw Virtue of Calm Tranquillity act and realized that he must have attained great spiritual powers. He was so delighted that, accompanied by his entire harem, he flung himself off the pavilion. But, even though it was thousands of feet high, the deities all protected the king and his entourage and did not allow them to hit the ground. Seeing the pitiful state of the bodhisattva's arm, the king and the rest of the crowd wept. When Virtue of Calm Tranquillity asked the reason for their tears, the king sang his praises in verse. Meanwhile, Virtue of Calm Tranquillity raised his arm, and it was restored to its former state.

It is interesting to note that Virtue of Calm Tranquillity, a bodhisattva, is explicitly and repeatedly described in the *King of Samādhi Sūtra* as a fully ordained monk (bhikṣu) and not a layman. As we shall see, there were serious disputes in China over the issue of whether monastics in particular were permitted to burn themselves, since some thought that the vinaya prohibited this kind of self-harm. It is surprising, then, that none of the defenders of monastic self-immolation seems to have brought up this scriptural example. The text also stresses that Virtue of Calm Tranquillity felt no pain but only joy and euphoria, the same emotions the participants experienced. We can note that the sūtra's emphasis on the happiness of the self-immolator and his audience echoes the former name of Medicine King: Seen with Joy by All Sentient Beings.

As noted above, self-immolation is a practice that is often enthusiastically described in the literature of the Mahāyāna. The collection of short texts called *The Lotus of Compassion* (*Karuṇāpuṇḍarīka*) contains numerous tales of the extreme violence the Buddha had inflicted on his own body in his previous lives, most of them narrated with meticulous attention to the goriest detail.[30] It seems to have been quite popular in China, and episodes from it are frequently alluded to in the biographies of self-immolators. In this scripture, for example, as part of a cycle of stories about King Pradīpapradyota, a former life of Śākyamuni, the bodhisattva wraps his arm in oiled cloth and sets fire to it in order to light the way for five hundred merchants lost at sea. His arm burns for seven days.[31]

Another story, from a popular collection of *avadānas* (stories of past lifetimes), tells of a disciple of a Brahman who soaks his turban in oil and sets fire to it in order to act as a lamp for the Buddha.[32] As a result of this, he becomes Buddha Dīpaṃkara (literally, "He Who Acts as a Lamp"). While this lamp is burning, the young man shows no sign of pain but continues to read the holy texts.

The trope of self-immolation was popular not just in medieval China but also elsewhere in the Buddhist world. *Knowledge of the World* (*Lokapaññatti*), a Pāli text compiled in Burma in the eleventh or twelfth century, relates a story about King Aśoka in which he wrapped his body in cotton and had his body soaked in oil before burning himself before a stūpa containing relics of Śākyamuni. He burned for seven days, but so great was his spiritual power that "the flames did not burn his body in the slightest, and he remained cool as if he had been smeared with sandalwood paste."[33]

Evidently, auto-cremation in front of relics as recounted in the *Lotus Sūtra* and the *King of Samādhi Sūtra* was such a powerful trope that it could be applied even to historical figures such as King Aśoka and not just to mahāsattvas in other, far-off universes. The Burmese text appears to adopt features from the *Lotus Sūtra*, such as wrapping the body in oil-soaked cotton, but circumvents the issue of death and rebirth by having the king's body remain cool and untouched by the flames even after seven days of auto-cremation.

Birth Stories of the Ten Bodhisattvas (*Dasabodhisattuppattikathā*), a late Pāli text of Mahāyāna inspiration, contains many stories featuring the classic themes of the offering of children, the head, the eyes, and so on. The story told of the buddha Rāmarāja relates that, in a former life, he saw the buddha Kassapa (Skt.: Kāśyapa) and thought, "A perfect buddha is very rare; what is the use to me of this disgusting life; it is worthwhile sacrificing one's life for the Buddha."[34] He wrapped himself in oil-soaked cloth and burned himself before Kassapa. Kassapa made a prediction of his future buddhahood, and at the site of his offering a lotus bud bloomed. Śākyamuni Buddha, who is narrating this story to his disciple Sāriputta (Skt.: Śāriputra), explains: "Thus, Sāriputta, by reason of the offering of life and limbs, in the future he will be the perfect buddha named Rāma. By the merit of offering the body, he will be eighty cubits in height; on account of sacrificing his life, his span of life will be ninety thousand years; from the merit accruing by burning the body as an offering throughout one night, buddha-rays will radiate continuously night and day all over the world, overpowering the light of the moon and sun."[35]

This example offers some ways of understanding what role auto-cremation could play on the path to buddhahood. Like the Burmese text, the scripture on the ten bodhisattvas repeats the detail about wrapping the body in oil-soaked cloth and emphasizes the bodhisattva's calm state of mind as he burns. It explains that, after his auto-cremation, he was reborn in the Tusita (Skt.: Tuṣita) Heaven—the abode in which a bodhisattva enjoys his last rebirth before descending to earth and attaining awakening beneath the bodhi tree. The witnesses to his auto-cremation are rewarded with a blossoming lotus on the site of his offering—a trope that echoes the kinds of miracles found in the Chinese biographies, such as the auspicious appearance of tongues, relics, or statues. Finally, the Buddha spells out in detail the karmic effects of the bodhisattva's self-immolation—that, when he becomes a buddha, he will be extremely large, very long-lived, and possessed of a marvelously radiant body.

These post–*Lotus Sūtra* materials—biographies, commentaries, scriptures—show that Buddhists continued to reflect on the nature of Medicine King's actions and how they could be understood as part of a cause-and-effect process leading to buddhahood just as surely as practices such as meditation or the cultivation of wisdom. It is clear that self-immolation could be (and was) construed as a legitimate bodily path to complete awakening.

APOCRYPHAL PRACTICES AND THEIR SIGNIFICANCE

As I noted in the discussion of Chinese commentaries, Buddhist writers on the *Lotus Sūtra* were obliged to consider how the scripture could seemingly demand offerings of fingers or the whole body while the texts that regulated the conduct of monks (the vinaya) appeared to prohibit such practices.[36] Some Buddhist authors were convinced that monks and nuns should not burn their bodies because killing oneself was included under the category of killing a human being, which was the first of the four "offenses entailing defeat" (*pārājikas*), the most serious rules in the vinaya. Another reason given for not burning the body was that auto-cremation entailed killing the various types of parasites that dwell on or in the body. Objections to auto-cremation from within the tradition found their fullest expression in a lengthy diatribe written by the pilgrim Yijing (635–713) as part of an account of Buddhist practice that he sent back to China from India.[37] He argued that monastic auto-cremators were overzealous practitioners who were unfamiliar with the range of Buddhist literature. Thus, they did not realize that the *Lotus Sūtra's* exhortation to offer a finger or toe was intended only for laypeople. The monk's first duty, in his opinion, was to follow the vinaya, which prohibits such actions. Although Yijing was apparently content to allow laypeople to burn their bodies, there was no shortage of objections to lay auto-cremation from both Buddhist authors and secular authorities. For example, the eminent Ming cleric Zhuhong (1535–1615) wrote an extremely critical piece on the practice of burning the body that endeavors to move the discussion away from the question of precepts and authority toward more basic "buddhological" issues. He criticizes those who attempt to imitate such an advanced bodhisattva as Medicine King and attributes their ability to withstand temporarily the pain of auto-cremation not to the impassive, awakened mind but to the archenemy of awakening, Māra.[38] An edict promulgated in 955 by Emperor Shizong (r. 954–959) explicitly condemned auto-cremation by both monks and laity and appealed to the vinaya as the authority on whether such actions were permitted.[39] No doubt secular authorities in traditional China objected to self-immolation on other grounds, too, but they often chose to frame their criticisms in terms of Buddhist rather than secular law.

Despite Yijing's lengthy and strident objections, most auto-cremators in China, both before and after his time, were monastics. How, then, did they find textual support for their actions? Scholars commonly refer to texts in the Chinese Buddhist tradition that purported to be translations of teachings of the Buddha in Indian languages but were in fact composed outside India as "apocryphal sūtras."[40] Two such apocryphal sūtras that were well known and extremely influential in the Chinese Buddhist tradition—the *Sūtra of Brahmā's Net* (*Fanwang jing*) and the *Sūtra of the Heroic March* (*Shoulengyan jing*, Skt.: *Śūraṃgama sūtra*)—strongly recommend auto-cremation. Buddhist writers drew on them to justify not only the burning of fingers but also the kind of minor burning of the body at ordination that is common today. In these two texts, burning the body is, crucially, defined and endorsed as a practice for ordinary Buddhist monks and nuns and not restricted to advanced (lay) bodhisattvas.

Burning the body can be seen as an "apocryphal practice" in Chinese Buddhism in a number of different senses. Analogous traditions existed in China long before the translation of the *Lotus Śūtra* or the composition of the *Brahmā's Net* and *Heroic March* sūtras. These traditions included igniting mugwort on the skin for medicinal purposes and ritual auto-cremation as a means of praying for rain. Thus, body-burning practices can be considered apocryphal in the sense of being indigenous (non-Buddhist) techniques.

But passages in the two apocryphal sūtras were also specifically created in order to endorse auto-cremation as it developed in a Buddhist context beginning in the late fourth century. The *Sūtra of Brahmā's Net* and the *Sūtra of the Heroic March* were in turn productive of further modes of body burning, including burning at ordination. These practices are thus apocryphal in the sense of being inspired and justified by apocryphal texts.

Just as some apocryphal sūtras were composed in order to validate doctrinal innovation in China, passages in these two texts were created to justify practices that were at times the subject of controversy within the tradition and the subject of censure from without. Although critics of self-immolation within the Buddhist tradition such as Zhuhong were never entirely won over by these texts, burning at ordination at least emerged as a conventional practice.

The *Sūtra of Brahmā's Net* offers Mahāyāna precepts designed for bodhisattvas (that is to say, ordinary practitioners, both clergy and laypeople, who aspired to advance along the long path to buddhahood). Here is the relevant precept in its entirety:

> If a son of the Buddha is to practice with a good mind, he should start by studying the proper decorum, the scriptures and the regulations of the Mahāyāna, so that he thoroughly understands their meaning and sense. Later, he will meet bodhisattvas who are new to this study and who have come a hundred or a thousand miles in search of the scriptures and regulations of the Mahāyāna. In accordance with the dharma, he should explain to them all the ascetic practices, such as setting fire to the body, setting fire to the arm, or setting fire to the finger. If one does not set fire to the body, the arm, or the finger as an offering to the buddhas, one is not a renunciant bodhisattva. Moreover, one should sacrifice the feet, hands, and flesh of the body as offerings to hungry tigers, wolves, and lions and to all hungry ghosts. Afterwards to each and every one of them one should preach the true dharma, so that one causes the thought of liberation to appear in their minds. If one does not behave in this way, then this is a lesser wrongdoing.[41]

Although it is somewhat difficult to relate the content of the precept to what exactly constitutes a "lesser wrongdoing," it is clear that the precept was composed as a way of pinning down some of the elements of the somatic path to buddhahood. Body burners and monks who defended their actions in writing were able to point to this passage and claim that as "renunciant bodhisattvas" they were merely doing as the Buddha had told them, "setting fire to the body, setting fire to the arm, or setting fire to the finger."

The *Sūtra of the Heroic March* is a more complex scripture than the *Sūtra of Brahmā's Net,* but the following passage appears in a section of the text focused on the monastic regulations. The Buddha speaks to Ānanda about the vinaya and explains to him the prohibitions against lust, stealing, lying, and killing. In the middle of the discussion of the prohibition against stealing, we read:

> The Buddha said to Ānanda, "After my nirvāṇa, if there is a monk [bhikṣu] who gives rise to a mental state wherein he is determined to cultivate samādhi, and he is able to burn his body as a torch or to set fire to a finger joint before an image of the Thus Come One, or even to burn a stick of incense on his body, then in a single instant he will have repaid the debts of his previous existences since the beginningless past. He will always avoid [being reborn] in the world and he will be eternally free of all outflows. Even if he has not yet understood the supreme path of awakening, such a person has already focused his mind on the dharma. But if he does not have this secret underlying cause for sacrificing the body, then even if he attains the unconditioned he must be reborn again as a human in order to repay the debts from his previous lives."[42]

Again, this text makes explicit the concept that a fully ordained monk could or should burn his body or a finger, or burn his skin with incense. The Buddha explains that doing so will eradicate previously accumulated karma and lead to nothing less than full awakening (being free from rebirth and the outflows of karma). If, however, his mind were not focused on awakening, he would have to be reborn so as to work off any residual karma.

Burning incense on the body is a nice example of an apocryphal practice. It is justified by an apocryphal sūtra that takes the rhetoric of the *Lotus Sūtra,* which urges its readers to offer "even a finger or a toe," and pushes it a stage further—"even to burn a stick of incense on his body." The *Sūtra of the Heroic March* takes the rewards promised by the *Lotus Sūtra,* makes them more specific, and applies them unambiguously to monks.

As for the question of whether self-immolation violates the precept against killing, some Chinese Buddhist authors were unequivocal in claiming that the attitude or intention of the bodhisattva trumped any concerns about suicide. The vinaya authority Daoshi (596–683), for example, claims that, since the bodhisattva is intent on leaving saṃsāra in order to worship the buddhas and has developed compassion toward all beings, he has no intention of harming others, and so his giving up of the body only generates merit. Thus, there is no offense against the precept.[43] The most sustained and fully developed endorsement of self-immolation as a valid path of practice for both monks and laypeople was written by Yanshou (904–975), a monk who was as well known for his expertise in the vinaya as he was for his skill in meditation.[44] He considers the gift of the body at length from the perspective of both principle and phenomena and identifies the mind and intention of the practitioner as the most significant factors in determining the validity of the act.

The *Lotus Sūtra* may be a unique scripture, but the auto-cremation of Medicine King within it is by no means sui generis. The analogous cases of gifts of the body in many forms of Buddhist literature must have convinced Chinese Buddhists that his was a perfectly orthodox form of offering and that, furthermore, auto-cremation was an option open to the ordinary practitioner. The major problem that remained was whether monks and nuns were such "ordinary practitioners" or if they were bound by statements made by the Buddha elsewhere in the canon. Ultimately this dichotomy could be resolved only by the creation of new texts that explicitly permitted monastics to burn their bodies.

The *Lotus Sūtra* provided much material for the repertoire of imagination upon which auto-cremators, their audiences, and biographers drew. Auto-cremators declared their devotion to the text even as they acted out key elements from it. The biographers' descriptions of enthusiastic donations of lavish material goods (jewels, clothing, banners, and flags) echoed the sūtra's own fascination with wealth and commerce. The logic behind these donations—that they actually facilitated the rapid journey to buddhahood—was also drawn from the scripture. While the *Lotus Sūtra* was but part of the repertoire of self-immolation, it was an essential element that provided both legitimation and script for medieval auto-cremators.

The biographies of auto-cremators offer important evidence that devotion to the *Lotus Sūtra* was a significant mode of belief and behavior within Chinese Buddhism that spanned apparent divisions between monastic and lay practice. Details in the biographies such as the revelation of a golden body or the miraculously unburned tongue did not have to be explicitly traced back to the text; it was enough to allude to the parallels between our world and the miraculous universe of the *Lotus Sūtra*. An appreciation of the complex interplay between text and practice in Chinese Buddhism shows that auto-cremation was far from the extreme or deviant practice that it might first appear to be, and that it possessed a logic and aesthetic that could be appreciated by the larger Buddhist community.

NOTES

1. For studies of self-immolation in Buddhism, see James A. Benn, *Burning for the Buddha: Self-Immolation in Chinese Buddhism*, Kuroda Institute, Studies in East Asian Buddhism 19 (Honolulu: University of Hawai'i Press, 2007); Benn, "Fire and the Sword: Some Connections between Self-Immolation and Religious Persecution in the History of Chinese Buddhism," in *The Buddhist Dead: Practices, Discourses, Representations*, ed. Bryan J. Cuevas and Jacqueline I. Stone, Kuroda Institute, Studies in East Asian Buddhism 20, 234–65 (Honolulu: University of Hawai'i Press, 2007); Benn, "Spontaneous Human Combustion: Some Remarks on a Phenomenon in Chinese Buddhism," in *Heroes and Saints: The Moment of Death in Cross-cultural Perspectives*, ed. Phyllis Granoff and Koichi Shinohara, 101–33 (Newcastle, UK: Cambridge Scholars Press, 2007); Jean Filliozat, "La mort volontaire par le feu et la tradition bouddhique indienne," *Journal Asiatique* 251, no. 1 (1963): 21–51; Jacques Gernet, "Les suicides par le feu chez les bouddhistes chinois de Ve au Xe siècle," in *Mélanges publiés par l'Institut des Hautes Études Chinoises*, 2:527–58 (Paris: Presses Universitaires de France, 1960); Jan Yün-hua, "Buddhist Self-Immolation in Medieval China," *History of Religions* 4, no. 2 (1965): 243–65; D. Max Moerman, "Passage to Fudaraku: Suicide and Salvation in Premodern Japanese Buddhism," in Cuevas and Stone, *The Buddhist Dead*, 266–96; and Liz Wilson, "Human Torches of Enlightenment: Autocremation and Spontaneous Combustion as Marks of Sanctity in South Asian Buddhism," in *The Living and the Dead: Social Dimensions of Death in South Asian Religions*, ed. Liz Wilson, 29–50 (Albany: SUNY Press, 2003).
2. For an account of Quang Đuc's auto-cremation and surrounding events seen from the perspective of American war correspondents in Vietnam, see William W. Prochnau, *Once Upon a Distant War* (New York: Vintage, 1995), 300–31.
3. James A. Benn, "Where Text Meets Flesh: Burning the Body as an 'Apocryphal Practice' in Chinese Buddhism," *History of Religions* 37, no. 4 (1998): 295–322. For Chinese ordination ceremonies, see Johannes Prip-Møller, *Chinese Buddhist Monasteries: Their Plan and Its Function as a Setting for Buddhist Monastic Life* (Hong Kong: Hong Kong University Press, 1982), 318–20; and Holmes Welch, *The Practice of Chinese Buddhism* (Cambridge, Mass.: Harvard University Press, 1967), 285–96.
4. John Strong, *Relics of the Buddha*, Buddhisms (Princeton, N.J.: Princeton University Press, 2004), 101–5; Strong, "The Buddha's Funeral," in Cuevas and Stone, *The Buddhist Dead*, 32–59.
5. Hubert Durt, "The Offering of the Children of Prince Viśvantara/Sudāna in the Chinese Tradition," *Journal of the International College for Advanced Buddhist Studies* (*Kokusai bukkyōgaku daigakuin daigaku kenkyū kiyō*) 2 (1999): 147–82. For a translation of the *jātaka*, see Margaret Cone and Richard F. Gombrich, *The Perfect Generosity of Prince Vessantara: A Buddhist Epic* (Oxford: Clarendon Press, 1977).
6. The last two lines of this verse do not appear in Hurvitz's translation or in some editions of the original.

7. For an overview of some of the major Chinese commentaries, see Hiroshi Kanno, "An Overview of Research on Chinese Commentaries of the *Lotus Sūtra*," *Acta Asiatica, Bulletin of the Institute of Eastern Culture* 66 (1994): 87–103.
8. The commentary by Fayun (467–529) offers an excellent example of this architectonic style; see *Fahua jing yiji*, Fayun, *Taishō shinshū daizōkyō*, 100 vols., ed. Takakusu Junjirō, Watanabe Kaigyoku, and Ono Gemmyō (1924–1934; repr., Taibei: Xinwenfeng chuban gongsi, 1974) (hereafter abbreviated as *T*) no. 1715, 33:676a–677b. For a study in English of a Chinese sūtra commentary, see Julian F. Pas, *Visions of Sukhāvatī: Shan-tao's Commentary on the Kuan Wu-liang shou-fo ching*, SUNY Series in Buddhist Studies (Albany: SUNY Press, 1995).
9. *Miaofa lianhua jing shu*, Daosheng (360–434), *Dainihon zoku zōkyō*, ed. Maeda Eun and Nakano Tatsue, 150 vols. (Kyoto: Zōkyō shoin, 1905–1912) (hereafter abbreviated as *Z*) 2b, 23:411v.b. Translated in Young-ho Kim, *Tao-sheng's Commentary on the Lotus Sūtra: A Study and Translation*, SUNY Series in Buddhist Studies (Albany: SUNY Press, 1990), 324.
10. Leon Hurvitz, *Chih-i (538–597): An Introduction to the Life and Ideas of a Chinese Buddhist Monk*, Mélanges chinois et bouddhiques 12 (Brussels: Institut Belge des Hautes Études Chinoises, 1962), 108–9.
11. *Miaofa lianhua jing wenju*, attributed to Zhiyi (538–597), *T* no. 1718, 34:143a 14–15.
12. *Miaofa lianhua jing wenju*, *T* 34:143b3.
13. *Miaofa lianhua jing xuanzan*, Kuiji (632–682), *T* no. 1723, 34:843b24–25.
14. *Fahua yishu*, Jizang (549–623), *T* no. 1721, 34:620a20–22.
15. *Fahua wenju ji*, Zhanran (711–782), *T* no. 1719, 34:354a–55b.
16. Ibid., *T* 34:354c11–28.
17. Jingzhou is present-day Jiangling county, in Hubei.
18. *Xu gaoseng zhuan*, Daoxuan (596–667), *T* no. 2060, 50:683c26–84a7. See Valentina Georgieva, "Representation of Buddhist Nuns in Chinese Edifying Miracle Tales During the Six Dynasties and the Tang," *Journal of Chinese Religions* 24 (1996): 47–76, especially 57–58.
19. This episode is discussed in chapter 3 of this volume, by Jan Nattier.
20. Suwa Gijun, *Chūgoku nanchō bukkyōshi no kenkyū* (Kyoto: Hōzōkan, 1997), 303–48.
21. *Hongzan Fahua zhuan* (ca. 706), Huixiang (ca. 639–706), *T* no. 2067, 51:24c3–9
22. Ibid., *T* 51:24c10–13.
23. Ibid., *T* 51:26b; Daniel B. Stevenson, "Tales of the Lotus Sūtra," in *Buddhism in Practice*, ed. Donald S. Lopez Jr. (Princeton, N.J.: Princeton University Press, 1995), 435–36; Koichi Shinohara, "Guanding's Biography of Zhiyi, the Fourth Chinese Patriarch of the Tiantai Tradition," in *Speaking of Monks*, ed. Phyllis Granoff and Koichi Shinohara (Oakville, Ont.: Mosaic Press, 1992), 169.
24. On the Aśokan image, see Koichi Shinohara, "The Maitreya Image in Shicheng and Guanding's Biography of Zhiyi," in *From Benares to Beijing: Essays on Buddhism and Chinese Religion in Honour of Prof. Jan Yün-hua*, ed. Koichi Shinohara and Gregory Schopen (Oakville Ont.: Mosaic Press, 1991), 213–15.
25. Reiko Ohnuma, "Dehadāna: The 'Gift of the Body' in Indian Buddhist Narrative Literature" (Ph.D. diss., University of Michigan, 1997); Ohnuma, "The Gift of the Body and the Gift of the Dharma," *History of Religions* 37, no. 4 (1998): 323–59; Ohnuma, "Gift," in *Critical Terms for the Study of Buddhism*, ed. Donald S. Lopez Jr., 103–23 (Chicago: University of Chicago Press, 2005); and Ohnuma, *Head, Eyes,*

Flesh, and Blood: Giving Away the Body in Indian Buddhist Literature (New York: Columbia University Press, 2007).

26. *Da zhidu lun*, trans. Kumārajīva (Jiumoluoshi, 344–413, or 350–409), *T* no. 1509, 25:146b; translated by Étienne Lamotte, *Le traité de la grande vertu de sagesse de Nāgārjuna (Mahāprajñāpāramitāśāstra)*, 5 vols., Publications de l'Institut orientaliste de Louvain 25–26 (Louvain, Belg.: Université de Louvain, Institut orientaliste, 1944–1980), 712–13.
27. See the translations of these stories, as well as references to their sources in various canonical languages, iconography, and secondary scholarship, in Lamotte, *Traité*, 713–23. Jātakas relating to King Sarvada are translated in Édouard Chavannes, *Cinq cents contes et apologues extrait du Tripiṭaka chinois*, 4 vols. (Paris: Leroux, 1910–1934), 1:38–49, 2:59–61.
28. *Da zhidu lun*, *T* 25:130c9–19; Lamotte, *Traité*, 579–80.
29. I summarize the Chinese version of this episode from *Yuedeng sanmei jing* (*Samādhirāja sūtra*), Narendrayaśas (Naliantiyeshe, 517–589), *T* no. 639, 15:598a–99c. See also Filliozat's translation from the Sanskrit and Tibetan ("La mort volontaire," 23–27).
30. Isshi Yamada, *Karuṇāpuṇḍarīka: The White Lotus of Compassion* (1968; repr, New Delhi: Heritage, 1989). A Chinese translation, *Dabeijing*, *T* no. 380, was made by Narendrayaśas (Naliantiyeshe, 517–589) in 552.
31. Yamada, *Karuṇāpuṇḍarīka*, 110.
32. *Liudu ji jing*, Kang Senghui (d. 280), *T* no. 152, 3:14c–15a; translated in Chavannes, *Cinq cents contes*, 1:85–86.
33. Translated and discussed in John Strong, *The Legend and Cult of Upagupta: Sanskrit Buddhism in North India and Southeast Asia* (Princeton, N.J.: Princeton University Press, 1992), 207–8. Strong notes a similar version of this account starring the monk Upagupta rather than King Aśoka.
34. H. Saddhatissa, *The Birth-Stories of the Ten Bodhisattas and the Dasabodhisattuppattikathā: Being a Translation and Edition of the Dasabodhisattuppattikathā* (London: Pali Text Society, 1975), 63.
35. Ibid., 63.
36. Christoph Kleine, "'The Epitome of the Ascetic Life': The Controversy over Self-Mortification and Ritual Suicide as Ascetic Practices in East Asian Buddhism," in *Asceticism and Its Critics: Historical Accounts and Comparative Perspectives*, ed. Oliver Freiberger, 153–77 (Oxford: Oxford University Press, 2006).
37. *Nanhai jigui neifa zhuan*, Yijing (635–713), *T* no. 2125, 54:231a–34a, translated in Junjirō Takakusu, *Record of the Buddhist Religion as Practised in India and the Malay Archipelago* (A.D. *671–695) by I-tsing* (London: Clarendon Press, 1896), 195–215; see also the discussion in Benn, "Where Text Meets Flesh," 312–16.
38. I translate Zhuhong's piece in Benn, *Burning for the Buddha*, 197–98.
39. Ibid., 116–17.
40. Robert E. Buswell Jr., ed., *Chinese Buddhist Apocrypha* (Honolulu: University of Hawai'i Press, 1990).
41. *Fanwang jing*, translation attributed to Kumārajīva, *T* no. 1484, 24:1006a; see also Jan J. M. de Groot, *Le code du Mahâyâna en Chine: Son influence sur la vie monacale et sur le monde laïque* (Amsterdam: Müller, 1893), 50–51. For a discussion of the sūtra and its importance in East Asian Buddhism, see Paul Groner, "The Fanwang ching and Monastic Discipline in Japanese Tendai: A Study of Annen's Futsū jubosatsukai kōshaku," in Buswell, *Chinese Buddhist Apocrypha*, 251–90.

42. *Da foding rulai miyin xiuzheng liaoyi zhupusa wanxing shoulengyan jing* (*Śūraṃgama sūtra*), translation attributed to Pāramiti (Banlamidi [ca. 705]), *T* no. 945, 19:132b; see also Charles Luk (Lu Kuan Yü), trans., *The Śuraṅgama Sūtra (Leng Yen Ching)* (London: Rider, 1966), 155.
43. Benn, *Burning for the Buddha*, 106–7.
44. There is a longer discussion in ibid., 104–31.

[5]

BUDDHIST PRACTICE AND THE *LOTUS SŪTRA* IN CHINA

Daniel B. Stevenson

IN HIS RUMINATIONS on the concept of "sacred text" in the academic study of religion, William Graham observes that there is nothing about the formal appearance of holy scripture that preannounces a given text as "sacred." That is to say, no specific characteristic—written script, material composition, literary or phonetic form—accounts intrinsically for the ways in which particular texts are assigned the sort of privileged status over other literatures and utterances that we might call sacred. "The sacrality or holiness of a book," Graham states, "is not an a priori attribute of a text but one that is realized historically in the life of communities who respond to it as something sacred or holy. A text becomes 'scripture' in active, subjective relationship to persons, and as part of a cumulative communal tradition."[1]

This notion that the textualities of sacred scripture arise at the intersection of the believer's active relationship with the text bespeaks the presence of complex cultural practice, or what Graham calls "ritualization." As learned behavior, these ritualizations are at once reiterable, socially sanctioned, and reinforced by the institutions of ongoing community practice. At the same time they are cognitively and somatically diverse, taking shape through mediations of the body and sense no less than the mind. Precisely because these ritual mediations are formed within the immediate context of community practice, often with no precedent in pages of the text itself, they tend to be historically shifting and diverse. Thus it becomes exceedingly difficult to predict how scripture in a given tradition will operate from one time or place to the next, let alone between one religious tradition and another.

Different interpretations of the contents of the *Lotus Sūtra* are discussed in other chapters of this volume. This chapter examines representative ways in which the *Lotus Sūtra* has been objectified and engaged as sacred text within Chinese Buddhist communities, premodern as well as contemporary. I focus in particular on practices that center on the physical text as a repository of sacred power and object of ritual devotion.

CONSTRUCTION OF THE *LOTUS SŪTRA* AS AN OBJECT OF DEVOTIONAL PRACTICE

As noted in the introductory chapter of this book, many passages in the *Lotus Sūtra* propound worship of the text. Śākyamuni at one point declares to Bodhisattva Medicine King (Bhaiṣajyarāja):

> Wherever it [the *Lotus Sūtra*] may be preached, or read, or recited, or written, or whatever place a roll of this scripture may occupy, in all those places one is to erect a *stūpa* [reliquary mound] of the seven jewels, building it high and wide and with impressive decoration. There is no need even to lodge *śarīras* [relics] in it. What is the reason? Within it there is already a whole body of the Thus Come One. This stūpa is to be showered with offerings, humbly venerated, held in solemn esteem, and praised with all manner of flowers, scents, necklaces, silk banners and canopies, music skillfully sung and played. If there are persons who can see this stūpa and worship and make offerings to it, be it known that these persons are all close to *anuttarasamyaksaṃbodhi*.
>
> (HURVITZ, 163)

Similar passages can be found throughout the *Lotus Sūtra*. They set up basic parameters of *Lotus Sūtra* practice and convey the range of boons to be expected from worship of the text: speedy realization of buddhahood, enlightening visions of Śākyamuni Buddha and great bodhisattvas such as Universally Worthy (Samantabhadra), protection from demonic influence and worldly misfortune, and rebirth in favorable abodes.

A quick read through almost any Mahāyāna sūtra reveals that this sort of sacralization of the sūtra text as object of worship is by no means unique to the *Lotus Sūtra*. Appropriating the imagery of the stūpa cult and its worship of the Buddha's relics (śarīras), the Mahāyāna sūtras routinely transpose this apparatus from its traditional ritual focus on the figure of the Buddha to the physical text of the sūtra itself, marking what Gregory Schopen has described as a distinctively Mahāyānist "cult of the book."[2] The text of the *Lotus* could thus be considered the equivalent of the Buddha. Chinese Buddhist exegetes themselves took due note of this feature more than a millennium and a half ago, when the Mahāyāna sūtras began to gain ground in China. By the middle of the fifth century it became standard practice to refer to these passages commending cult worship of the sūtra text as the "sections enjoining dissemination [or circulation] of the sūtra" (*liutong fen*), thereby distinguishing them categorically from those portions of the text otherwise known as the "main discourse [or exposition]" (*zhengshuo fen*) and opening "preface" (*xu fen*).

At first encounter, the choice of the term "dissemination" seems a touch dismissive, as though Chinese exegetes regarded these self-lauding injunctions to cherish, worship, and reproduce the text to be little more than a ploy to ensure survival of the Mahāyāna sūtras—intended, perhaps, for minds less capable of appreciating the doctrinal subtleties of the main discourse. This interpretation also may appear similar to views expressed by various present-day Western scholars, many of whom work from the modern, Protestant assumption that scripture should be read only in private, with the goal of personal understanding. Ironically, however, the situation seems to have been quite the opposite in China. Chinese commentaries to the Mahāyāna sūtras often lay great store by these dissemination passages, attaching to them extraordinary claims of efficacy and illustrative tales of miraculous response. Indigenous understandings provide no indication that somatic devotion to the sūtra text is any less authentic than poring over its doctrinal contents.

In fact, Buddhists believed the appearance of the *Lotus Sūtra* in China was driven by the sacred power and predestined fate of the sūtra text itself. By the end of the eighth century, the event of the translation of the *Lotus Sūtra* by Kumārajīva (Jiumoluoshi [344–413, or 350–409]) was itself considered an elaborate spectacle of divine power, pregnant with implications for China's spiritual fortune. A later source relates how Yao Xing (r. 394–416), king of the Later Qin dynasty, resolved to test the sanctity of the scripture. He had Kumārajīva's new translation of the *Lotus* copied in gold pigment and ceremoniously escorted by golden cart to the Great Monastery for ritual veneration. Extraordinary signs ensued, the likes of which the king and his subjects had never before encountered. When the miracles were related to Kumārajīva, the latter attributed the phenomena to the ruler's devotion: "The great teaching of the *Lotus Sūtra* has a divine affinity with this land. In the era after the Buddha's extinction, this kind of manifestation is rare to behold."[3]

The tale itself is apocryphal, composed several centuries after the time of Kumārajīva. But it underscores the importance that Buddhists in China have traditionally placed on the Mahāyāna sūtra as a repository of sacred power. In the Chinese Buddhist lexicon, the operative dynamic behind this cult of the sūtra text is known as "sympathetic resonance" or "stimulus and response" (*ganying*). The concept of stimulus and response was traditionally used to refer to all manner of spiritual anomalies, from transformative encounters with an enlightened teacher or celestial bodhisattva to miraculous cures and meditative breakthroughs. Applied to the worship of sūtra texts, the sūtra as embodiment of the eternally abiding dharma was deemed capable of producing the full range of benefits associated with, say, devotion to a given buddha or bodhisattva. By using the same ritual gestures through which one might invoke a deity, devotees were said to forge an "opportune connection" or "nexus" (*jiyuan*) with the text that stimulated (*gan*) the scripture's resident power, causing it to manifest a response (*ying*) to their piety and salvific needs.

The elaborate self-constructions found in the *Lotus*, as well as China's sophisticated indigenous religious culture, earned the sūtra a prodigious following in China. Although some people chose to make the *Lotus Sūtra* the exclusive focus of religious endeavor, Buddhists in China never generated the sustained, organized traditions of exclusive reliance on the *Lotus* that occurred in medieval Japan. Very few of the actual gestures of day-to-day ritual practice can be identified as belonging solely to the *Lotus*. Thus, study of the *Lotus Sūtra* provides an especially valuable window onto broader patterns of Buddhist scriptural practice in China.

MIRACLE TALES AND HAGIOGRAPHIES

Different sources show how Chinese devotees actually deployed the *Lotus Sūtra* in their daily lives. Manuals and hymns composed for worship of the *Lotus* provide insight into the protocols of ritual devotion. Sūtra commentaries and transcripts of sūtra lectures illumine the intricacies of imparting religious knowledge. Iconography, architecture, and hand-copied scrolls of the *Lotus Sūtra*—many of them bearing personalized votive inscriptions—give us access to the visual and material practice of the *Lotus Sūtra*. Among the most revealing sources are tales of miraculous response and their close relative, epitaphs and hagiographies concerning persons of exemplary piety.

The miracle tale and hagiographical notice are closely related as literary genres. Hagiographies often recount episodes of miraculous response as proof of an individual's sanctity, while miracle tales might abstract these very same episodes from epitaphs and hagiographies to serve as independent testimonials to the efficacy of a given practice or object of devotion. Where the epitaph or hagiography tends to foreground the person, the miracle tale gravitates to the event. The ground on which they converge is the shared idiom of sympathetic resonance, in which the miraculous response is understood to arise from the resonances that are established between the individual's religious piety and the given locus of sacred power.

Tales of exemplary piety and miraculous response became an integral feature of *Lotus* devotional culture from the time the *Lotus Sūtra* first made its way to China. The stories were variously passed by word of mouth, written up as independent testimonials, incorporated into epitaphs, and reproduced in biographical collections. The two earliest known examples of anthologies dedicated specifically to the *Lotus Sūtra* are Huixiang's (ca. 639–706) *Accounts of the Propagation of the Lotus Sūtra* (*Hongzan Fahua zhuan*), completed around 706, and *Accounts and Notices on [the Transmission of] the Lotus Sūtra* (*Fahua jing zhuanji*), attributed to Sengxiang (dates unknown), compiled some decades later, around 754.[4]

At first glance these compendia and their tales look to be incidental to religious practice—a second-order representation of commitment rather than a religious act in its own right. In fact, tale-telling of this sort was integral to *Lotus Sūtra* devotion. On the one hand it served as a key medium by which devotees shaped their collective norms of *Lotus* practice and made sense of their actions to themselves and to others. But by the same token, broadcasting the wonders of the *Lotus Sūtra* itself constituted an act of great merit and piety, its efficacy no different from that of other, more familiar forms of ritual devotion. Indeed, from at least the seventh century, tales of miraculous response were appended directly to copies of sūtras produced for circulation among prospective devotees, while anthologies often express the prayer that their testimonials will cause the *Lotus Sūtra* to spread widely, bringing joy and future buddhahood to all who encounter it.

Thus, while their representations may be stereotypical, and the historical sweep and homogeneity of their entries something of a fiction, the circulation of *Lotus* compendia may have helped to create the very sense of tradition that they idealized. Properly situated in their specific economies of social practice, they have much to tell us not only about what *Lotus* devotees of a given time and place were actually doing but also, and more important, the significations that informed their actions.[5]

THE FIVE PRACTICES OF THE DHARMA PREACHER

The individual chapters of the *Lotus Sūtra* are rich in exemplary feats of devotion and accounts of bodhisattvas who have pledged to protect the sūtra and its faithful. Most were well known to devotees of the *Lotus*, and not a few of them generated subsidiary, even independent, cultic interest. For example, Bodhisattva Never Disparaging's habit of paying homage to every person he encountered enjoyed considerable vogue in early medieval China, ultimately serving as a model for the practice of "universal veneration" promulgated by Xinxing (540–594) and his controversial Three Stages movement.[6] As discussed by James A. Benn in chapter 4 of this volume, Bodhisattva Medicine King's self-immolation inspired a vibrant, if episodic, tradition of auto-cremation in China that has continued down to the present day. Accounts of this controversial practice appear in virtually every *Lotus* collection, where they are typically grouped into chapters dedicated to the offering up of the body. Chapter 25 of the *Lotus Sūtra*, dealing with Bodhisattva Sound Observer, circulated independently as part of a strong, varied tradition involving worship of the bodhisattva. With the exception of that chapter, however, most of these practices remained largely within the cultic orbit of the *Lotus Sūtra*.

Many, if not most, *Lotus* devotees were drawn to less dramatic forms of devotion, their efforts centering on the physical text of the *Lotus Sūtra* itself. These practices were most commonly described as the five practices of upholding (or, following Hurvitz's translation, "receiving and keeping"), reading, reciting, explaining, and copying the text of the *Lotus Sūtra*. They are a special focus of Chapter 19, "Merits of the Dharma Preacher." Although variant representations appear in other chapters of Kumārajīva's translation of the *Lotus*, on the whole his five-member listing in Chapter 19, which most commentators followed, became the principal norm.[7]

Upholding the Lotus Sūtra

The first practice is called in Chinese *shouchi*, a compound word meaning "upholding" but that can also be understood as the two activities of "accepting" (*shou*) and "keeping" (*chi*). Kumārajīva employed the compound to translate declensions of the single Sanskrit root √*dhṛ*, meaning "to retain" or "to keep." In the literature on *Lotus* devotion, "keeping the *Lotus Sūtra*" (*chi Fahua jing*) does not connote a specific regimen of practice but functions as a generic designation for *Lotus Sūtra* devotion in all its guises, above all devotion that is focused and sustained. Hence, anyone who enthusiastically embraces the text, whether reading it aloud, reciting, explicating, or copying it, is deemed to be a "keeper" or "upholder" of the *Lotus Sūtra*.

Upholding the text of the *Lotus Sūtra* assumed different shades of meaning, depending on how the Chinese word *shouchi* and its underlying Sanskrit root (√*dhṛ*) were interpreted. At the more rarefied end of the spectrum were connotations associated with the technical term *dhāraṇī*, sometimes translated as "spells" or "incantations." Dhāraṇī, in its simplest sense (rendered by the Chinese expression *zongchi*), means "total retention" or "apprehension" of a given teaching, as in committing the *Lotus Sūtra* and its meaning to memory. Total retention can also refer to instantaneous apprehension of all the teachings expounded by the buddhas in all times and places, an event that is equated with attainment of profound states of meditative absorption (*samādhi*) and enlightened insight (*prajñā*) into the true character of existence.[8] Thus one "apprehends" the *Lotus Sūtra* by awakening directly to the true aspect of the *dharmas* and the "secret treasure-store of all the buddhas" that is the sūtra's essence.

While resonances with the term *dhāraṇī* can thereby push the notion of upholding the *Lotus Sūtra* to extraordinary levels of abstraction, at the more commonplace end of the spectrum its meaning is grounded in the concrete gestures and paraphernalia of ritual practice. To uphold the *Lotus Sūtra* is to store the text in specially crafted cases, to enshrine it in consecrated altar spaces, and to handle it according to strict codes of purity. A story in *Accounts of the Propagation of the Lotus Sūtra* tells of an eminent layman named Xiao Yu (575–648) who commissioned one thousand copies of the *Lotus* with the intention of distributing them to local devotees. Whenever people approached him with the desire to receive and keep a copy of the sūtra, he first required them to ritually purify themselves by bathing and donning a set of clean robes. After kneeling down and formally requesting the sūtra three times, they were permitted to ascend the stone platform where the sūtras were enshrined. Only then were they allowed to uphold the sūtra text by reverently touching its jeweled case to the crown of their heads.[9]

Hence, to uphold the sūtra was not simply to possess it—or even to read it, recite it, and explicate it, strictly speaking—but to do so by the dictates of ritual cleanliness and decorum. Persons seasoned in these disciplines were accordingly regarded as deeply pious.

Reading and Reciting the Lotus Sūtra

As we have seen, one of the cardinal meanings associated with upholding the *Lotus Sūtra* was the notion of committing the text to memory. Once retained in this manner, the mnemonic text could be used for daily recitation. Tales of *Lotus* devotees refer often to such feats, describing how people "recite [the text] with perfect fluency," "not suffering lapses of memory," the words "flowing from their mouth like a stream of water from a vase."[10]

The chapters dedicated to recitation from memory are among the largest in compendia of *Lotus* miracle tales. The attention given to recitation from memory and reading—or more precisely, chanting aloud—from the written text of the *Lotus Sūtra* far exceeds the attention given to other forms of devotion. Such an emphasis may in part reflect trends in monastic education. Candidates for ordination routinely memorized large quantities of scripture in preparation for receiving the novitiate ordination. At various points in Chinese history, prospective ordinands were required by law to memorize (and demonstrate their accomplishment by reciting aloud) anywhere from four to eight scrolls of Buddhist sūtras. The *Lotus Sūtra,* which in the popular Kumārajīva translation comprised twenty-eight chapters in seven or eight scrolls, was the chief text of choice.[11]

The techniques by which sūtra texts were actually committed to memory are not altogether clear. For persons who were already literate, the process may simply have entailed repeated perusal or recitation of the written text, with the less educated requiring instruction in pronunciation and punctuation. By the same token, we also find instances where slaves or menials with no knowledge of the written language learned the text wholly from aural repetition. Ultimately, internalization of text as memory—a prerequisite for exegetical competence—meant that the text itself became a part of the practitioner's being, an imprint of mind that traveled with the individual from place to place and, in the indigenous perspective, from lifetime to lifetime. It is inevitable that, coupled with the Buddhist idea of cyclic rebirth and karmic predispositions from past lives, signs of unusual affinity for the *Lotus*—or, for that matter, any outstanding act of piety—would be linked to encounters with the text in past lives.

The Tiantai patriarch Zhiyi (538–597) is said to have repeated Chapter 25, "The Gateway of the Bodhisattva Sound Observer," from memory at the tender age of six, after hearing it recited once by local monks, while, in his late teens, he succeeded in memorizing the entire *Lotus Sūtra*, *The Sūtra of Innumerable Meanings*, and *The Sūtra on the Visualization of the Bodhisattva Universally Worthy* within a mere twenty days. Both feats are characterized by hagiographers as a "manifestation of predispositions from past lives." Echoing the prior-birth narratives recounted in the *Lotus Sūtra* itself, Zhiyi's followers ultimately push this connection as far back as to Gṛdhrakūṭa (Vulture Peak) by claiming that Zhiyi and his teacher, Huisi (515–577), were present in the Gṛdhrakūṭa assembly when Śākyamuni Buddha preached the *Lotus Sūtra*.[12]

Both reading and reciting generally involved intoning the text out loud (*fengsong*) as opposed to rehearsing its words in silence. Typically great emphasis was also placed on the enunciation, tone, and pace of the voice. As performed today, sūtras are chanted to the rhythmic, "tok-tok" tapping of a percussion instrument known as the "wooden fish" (*muyu*), each word or character falling evenly on the downbeat. Although this is by far the more common method, more exotic forms of recitation have also been practiced. Zongxiao (1151–1214) mentions a procedure, popular in his day, of making one prostration (or, for some devotees, three) every time a word of the text was chanted. A practitioner could thereby prostrate his or her way through the entire *Lotus Sūtra* one character at a time.[13] In the tenth century the monastic historian Zanning (919–1001) described how his contemporaries, viewing each character of sacred scripture as a buddha, accorded the words of the text the same treatment as that due a deity. He writes, "There are persons who, in imitation of the ancients, venerate the texts of the *Lotus* and *Flower Garland* sūtras [by prostrating themselves to] each character, one at a time. They regard this to be veneration of the undefiled treasure-store of the dharma itself. Thus we find members of the fourfold saṅgha who actually insert the words 'homage to' [*namo*] before each word and '-buddha' [*fo*] after each word [of the sūtra]."[14] Although the practice was, for some, controversial—Zanning himself dismissed it as excessive—it has continued to thrive to the present day, as I learned from a monastic acquaintance who once prostrated his way through the *Lotus Sūtra* during an extended period of retreat in the mountains of Taiwan.

The reading and reciting of the sūtra were framed by preparatory purifications. As with the procedures for receiving and keeping the text, recitations were reserved for a dedicated chapel, a smaller, purified chamber, or simply an altar space, their confines carefully demarcated from the surrounding environs by ritual sweeping and sprinkling with perfumed water and strict rules of access. A copy of the *Lotus Sūtra* was typically enshrined on the central altar, accompanied by a censer, banners and flowers, purified water, lamps, and a special dais or chair that the practitioner would ascend during the course of recitation. Purified garments were to be worn in the sanctuary proper, with bathing and a change of clothes required upon entering and exiting. Wine, meat, and the five types of pungent or onionlike herbs being noxious to the buddhas, bodhisattvas, and dharma-protecting spirits, these foods were also avoided as ritually polluting. Thus the Tang-dynasty (618–907) monk Huijin is said to have begun his daily round of devotions to the *Lotus Sūtra* with the following regimen: "He would first purify [the altar space] by sweeping and sprinkling, gather whatever flowers were in season, and do his utmost to decorate [the sanctuary] resplendently. In the center [of the sanctuary], a space of some five or six feet in width, he hung banners and offered incense [before a central altar]. At a spot set apart [from the altar] he placed a single chair [for seated recitation]. After donning a new, clean robe and ritually venerating the buddhas of the ten directions, he would join his palms [in adoration] and assume the formal posture [for seated meditation]. Only then did he begin to recite [the sūtra]."[15]

From start to finish, the act of chanting the text was governed by a well-defined series of ritual phases and gestures, each performed in proper sequence. In Chinese communities today, copies of the *Lotus* that have been printed for devotional distribution often contain litanies and instructions for ritual performance appended to the beginning and end of the sūtra text. Such is the case with a recent edition of Kumārajīva's *Lotus Sūtra* published by the temple Guoqingsi on Mount Tiantai (one of the traditional centers of the Tiantai school), used widely for recitation in monasteries and lay societies across Zhejiang and Jiangsu provinces.[16] The edition opens with two short manuals providing instructions on ritual procedure and various litanies that are intoned at the outset and conclusion of the sūtra recitation. The first tract is entitled "Rite for Recitation of the *Lotus Sūtra*." The second, entitled "Rite for Veneration of the *Lotus Sūtra*," serves as a formulary for word-by-word prostration to the text (or just the title) of the sūtra.[17]

The procedures sketched in the two manuals are similar in structure, even to the point of sharing the same verse and prose invocations. In each case the central act of recitation or veneration is circumscribed by a series of well-defined introductory and concluding phases, their sequence organized into such discrete modules as the offering of incense to the three jewels, homage to Śākyamuni Buddha and various deities of the *Lotus Sūtra* assembly, confession of sins, transfer of merits, prayers for the well-being of others, and a concluding profession of the three refuges. Current practice of the rituals includes a component not mentioned in the two texts. When lay patrons formally commission monks to recite the *Lotus* on behalf of the sick or the deceased, special announcements and benedictory prayers are inscribed on red or yellow paper and installed on a side altar. The officiating priest reads them out loud during the course of performance, and at the conclusion of the rite they are transported to a courtyard, where they are ceremoniously burned in charcoal braziers.

A third tract contained in the Guoqingsi edition of the *Lotus Sūtra*, entitled "Procedures for Performing Meditative Visualization Prior to Veneration and Recitation," provides instruction for visualizations intended to accompany ritual invocation and recitation. For example, practitioners are instructed to construct a mental image of themselves standing in the presence of the Buddha, garbed in the robe of a Buddhist monastic. As the incense is lighted, the devotees imagine that the smoke rises up and forms a canopy of clouds around the Buddha, turning into symmetrical rows of lotus-blossom lamps that bathe the setting in resplendent beams of light. Visualizing themselves to be surrounded by ancestors and parents, eminent monastics, and a train of beings gathered from all reaches of existence, together they pay obeisance to the Buddha, after which they take their seats and begin to recite or venerate the sūtra as the assembly looks on with loving approval.[18]

It is difficult to say precisely when this habit of appending a liturgical apparatus to the text of a sūtra came into vogue, or how widespread it was in the production of scriptures. Interestingly, the world's earliest surviving dated printed book—the celebrated *Diamond Sūtra* from Dunhuang that was produced for distribution by the layman Wang Jie in 868—bears clear evidence of this arrangement.[19] One might surmise thereby that the formula has long been characteristic of sūtras printed independently for meritorious circulation, in which case the modern Guoqingsi *Lotus* becomes a fitting example of just how deeply ritual protocol and scriptural text were intertwined in the Chinese devotional *imaginaire*.

This pairing of printed ritual apparatus and sūtra text brings us back to several observations about the ritualization of *Lotus Sūtra* practice in China raised earlier in this chapter. First, as addenda that, literally, encase but do not intrude upon the sūtra text itself, the ritual tracts in the Guoqingsi text are extrinsic to the content of the sūtra proper. Second, since their protocols are significantly more elaborate than the cultic injunctions found in the dissemination passages of the sūtra, it is clear that these ritual forms look to conventions external to the text itself. The modern ritual appendices to the *Lotus Sūtra* contain the same litanies as do ritual addenda to other popular sūtras, their contents emended slightly to match the sūtra at hand.

The most important liturgy for reading and reciting the *Lotus Sūtra* was written by the Tiantai patriarch Zhiyi in the sixth century. Zhiyi's *Rite of Repentance for the Lotus Samādhi* is a prompt text for a ritual program inspired jointly by Chapter 28 of the *Lotus* and *The Sūtra of Visualizing the Bodhisattva Universally Worthy*.[20] Since the end of the sixth century, the *Lotus* repentance, as set forth in Zhiyi's manual, has constituted one of the mainstays of practice in the Tiantai school, and its ritual forms continue to govern practice in the modern world. Undertaken in halls of retreat, the *Lotus* repentance (the duration ranging from twenty-one days to three years) served as a vehicle for individual cultivation of mindfulness and pursuit of the deepest truths of Tiantai teaching. When performed with or for laity (usually in abbreviated form), the rite was also used to avert calamity, eliminate obstacles, and generate merit for many different ends.

Lotus repentance (*Fahua chanfa*) or *Lotus* samādhi (*Fahua sanmei*) rituals were already well attested in Zhiyi's own day. Zhiyi selectively codified these traditions into a ten-part sequence, which he transcribed in his ritual manual. The first two phases of the ten-part formulary entail (1) purification of the altar site and (2) purification of the practitioner. The next phases include (3) initial incense offering, (4)–(6) veneration of assembled deities, and (7) confession of sins, with transfer of merits and prayers (more elaborate but resembling the structure found in the modern ritual tracts of the Guoqingsi *Lotus Sūtra*). Phase (8), chanting of the *Lotus Sūtra* proper, enters the picture only toward the end of the sequence, where it is performed concurrently with (9) circumambulation of the altar. Formal chanting and circumambulation conclude with profession of the three refuges, after which the participants retire to a separate location (10) to perform seated meditation or individual recitation of the *Lotus Sūtra* in preparation for the next cycle of ritual veneration. As in the modern ritual, mental visualizations accompany each phase of the performance.

Zhiyi crafted his formulary by drawing on contemporary Chinese Buddhist liturgical culture and on prototypes found in Indian sūtras and treatises. As the most detailed of his ritual manuals, Zhiyi's *Rite of Repentance for the Lotus Samādhi* became, in time, something of a classic in China, its contents consulted both within and outside the Tiantai school as a model for the production of new ritual programs unrelated to the *Lotus Sūtra*. At the same time, Zhiyi's liturgy exerted a formative influence on other forms of *Lotus Sūtra* practice, including public sūtra lectures and ritual copying of the sūtra text.

Explaining the Lotus Sūtra

Practices such as lecturing on the *Lotus Sūtra* were complex ritual activities. Though different in character from reading and reciting the *Lotus*, such procedures were framed by protocols similar to those described in connection with its reading and recitation.

Whether performed for monastery residents or the community at large, lectures on the *Lotus Sūtra* were very much public affairs, their performance often scheduled to key nodes of the annual monastic and festival calendars. While traveling in China during the lunar New Year of 839, the Japanese monk Ennin (794–864) witnessed a lecture series on the *Lotus Sūtra* that stretched over a period of some two months. Consisting of clergy, laity, and donors from the local community—male as well as female—the audience listened to formal lectures during the daylight hours and, at night, took part in rites of veneration and confession. As an early and relatively detailed record of sūtra-lecture protocol, Ennin's description offers a useful point of reference.

The audience having assembled in the hall, the principal lecturer and assistant lecturer were escorted to their high seats as monks intoned litanies of praise and invocations to various buddhas. Incense was then formally presented to the three jewels, after which the principal lecturer solemnly chanted the sūtra's title, summarized the sūtra passage selected for the lecture at hand, and read out the documents of benediction prepared on behalf of the rite's sponsors. The lecture then commenced, the exposition punctuated by questions and answers between the principal and assistant lecturers. At the end of the session, the assembly intoned verses of praise and dedication of merits. The two celebrants thereupon descended from their seats to accompanying hymns and joined the audience for a concluding profession of the three refuges.[21]

Although the cloister visited by Ennin belonged to expatriate monks from Silla (modern Korea), his description corresponds reasonably well to records of Chinese practice dating to the same period, including transcripts of sūtra lectures conducted in northwestern China.[22] Although the northwestern transcripts limit the role of the assistant lecturer, and later formularies dispense with the assistant lecturer altogether, they all nonetheless follow a format similar to that described by the Japanese pilgrim. Thus, in medieval times, the basic syntax of the rite was consistent: formal exposition of the sūtra's content is accompanied by chanting of the given sūtra passage, and the cycles of exposition (with verse rehearsal) are in turn framed by the familiar sequences for the offering of incense, homage to the three jewels, formal presentation of benedictory announcements, and a concluding sequence for dedication of merits. Beyond its doctrinal edification of the audience, the lecture became a ritually empowering event in its own right, aspiring to the same range of miraculous benefits that typify other forms of *Lotus* devotion: blessing of crops, protection of person and property, averting of calamity, alleviation of illness, salvation of the dead, and so forth. And indeed, the miracle-tale literature speaks frequently of divine manifestations accompanying the lectures of masters renowned for their learning and piety.[23]

Copying the Lotus Sūtra

Upholding the *Lotus* has always entailed a distinctly material dimension, whether it be use of the physical text as an object of devotion, the creation of consecrated altar spaces, or the accoutrements of ritual offering. The fifth form of practice, copying the sūtra, not only partakes of this corporal dimension but also moves the focus of ritual action directly into the field of textual production itself. Willa Jane Tanabe discusses the same coalescence of ritual activity, bodily performance, and textual creation in works of art in chapter 6 of this book; I confine myself here to ritual and devotional aspects of textual replication.

With the spread of wood-block printing beginning in the tenth century, reproduction of the *Lotus Sūtra* came to involve print runs numbering in the hundreds and thousands. Often done under private auspices, such an act of charitable distribution of the dharma was considered to bring extraordinary karmic rewards, much as it still is today. As a reminder of this fact, modern editions of sūtras printed for devotional distribution frequently attach a list of eight boons that come from the charitable printing of scriptures; the eight forms of merit are no different from the blessings acquired from reciting sūtras aloud or reproducing them by hand.

Yet, even with the rise of print technology, the execution of elegant handcrafted manuscripts of the sūtra continued to attract *Lotus* devotees. Records dating from the fifth and sixth centuries speak frequently of this practice. By the middle of the eighth century, handwritten copies of the *Lotus* were being executed on media ranging from paper to stone, with some of the most magnificent examples rendered in gold and silver ink on indigo paper. Even the practice of copying the sūtra with blood—in which the copyist used blood drawn from pricking a finger or, in more radical cases, the tongue to prepare the ink for the text—became popular.[24]

The practice of ritually copying the sūtra was not limited to reproducing the words alone. The preparation of decorated cases to contain the text, altar spaces for its enshrinement and public display, even the fashioning of the paper and ink itself, could all become part of the process, their fabrication governed by dictates of ritual protocol no different from those witnessed in other modes of *Lotus* practice. The tale of the seventh-century nun Miaozhi, as recounted in Huixiang's *Accounts of the Propagation of the Lotus Sūtra*, provides a vivid example of the effort that might go into such an endeavor.

To produce the pulp used in making the paper for her sūtra, Miaozhi planted saplings in the nearby hills, which she nurtured daily with perfumed water. Once the trees had matured, she constructed a hut from mud mixed with fragrant water, where she had a craftsman boil and press the bark into paper, ensuring all the while that he observed the proper protocols to purify both himself and the materials. With the paper in hand, she built yet another chamber for copying the sūtra, again with utmost attention to ritual purity. Having finally located a skilled calligrapher who was willing to uphold her ritual specifications, Miaozhi first had the man fast for a period of forty-nine days, after which he finally began to inscribe the text. Each time he entered the sanctuary to copy the sūtra, he was required to bathe and don a purified robe. Miaozhi knelt in adoration beside him as he wrote, incense burner in hand and right knee to the ground. When the scribe withdrew at the end of the day, she remained in the chamber to offer incense and ritually circumambulate the work in progress. The task finally completed, Miaozhi created splendid accoutrements for the manuscript, including ten sets of specially constructed robes that were to be worn (after bathing) by persons who came to pay obeisance to the sūtra.[25]

Though Miaozhi's actions verge on the extreme—and the tale itself is highly ramified—they nonetheless convey an ideal of practice that came to be widely recognized in medieval China and Japan, sufficiently so to earn the special designation "[copying] sūtras according to proper methods" and, by extension, "sūtras produced by proper ritual procedure" (*rufajing*, Ja.: *nyohōgyō*). One might rightly argue, of course, that if the power of a sūtra resides in the word as a repository of the eternally abiding dharma, then the form of reproduction should have little bearing on the sanctity of the text. And yet, in a manner that recalls the Buddhist cult of relics, it was precisely the subjective care and piety—above all, the ritual piety—that went into the creation of the manuscript that gave the "sūtra copied by proper ritual procedure" a valence beyond that of other reproductions.[26] When it comes to blood-written sūtras, for example, it is not unusual to hear Buddhist monks today measure the relative sanctity of the text according to the hue of the copyist's blood, texts that glow a lustrous yellow or orange and fail to fade over the years being the sign of particular potency. Such opinions are confirmation of Graham's insistence that the sacrality of scripture is built into the text not abstractly or solely according to content but rather through the bodily and emotional contributions of believers.

One principal theme in our *tour d'horizon* of *Lotus Sūtra* practice in China has been the promotion of the text of the *Lotus Sūtra* as a repository of religious power and as an object of worship. The sacred power of the text, as we have seen, was usually articulated in the idiom of stimulus and response. This interactive piety was grounded in concrete conventions of ritual gesture and devotion, the vocabularies of which were shared across a diversity of cultic venues—including worship of different sūtras, buddhas, and bodhisattvas—and hence not unique to *Lotus* devotion proper.

Although Buddhists developed a vibrant tradition of scriptural exegesis in China, the text of the *Lotus Sūtra* (like other important Mahāyāna sūtras) was never regarded merely as a repository of second-order statements *about* the nature of ultimate reality, their meaning to be decoded through analysis of the sūtra's doctrines. As we have seen, the sūtra was also thought to embody the very reality that it describes, and through veneration of the physical text this resident power could be brought to bear on all manner of needs, from the curing of illness to the realization of enlightenment itself. Some of the boons championed in the literatures of *Lotus* devotion are explicitly prefigured in the *Lotus* itself, such as the promise of visitations from Bodhisattva Universally Worthy and Śākyamuni Buddha (Hurvitz, 164, 306), visions of the divine Vulture Peak (Hurvitz, 223–25, 232), miraculous powers of sense perception (Chapter 19), and manifestation of bodily forms (Chapter 24). The *Lotus* faithful may also ascend to birth in the Trāyastriṃśa Heaven (Hurvitz, 307), Maitreya Bodhisattva's palace in Tuṣita Heaven (Hurvitz, 307), or the buddha Amitāyus's western pure land (Hurvitz, 275).

Other forms of miraculous response—ascent to Vulture Peak, manifestations of rarefied fragrances and radiant light, divine healings, deliverance from crisis, pacification of demons and beasts, and nondecay of the tongue—are promised only in other literature and find no precedent in the sūtra itself. All these manifestations, however, come by way of devotion to the text of the *Lotus Sūtra*. The devotional literature of the *Lotus Sūtra* presents them all as signs that verify successful cultivation; all such results are believed to tap the power of the *Lotus Sūtra* through correct religious practice. In terms of stimulus and response, these divine manifestations are understood to arise through the interaction of two discrete factors: the sūtra text as a reservoir of divine potency and the piety of the devotee. While miracles can be interpreted as testimony to either factor, efficacy per se is not strictly reducible to either pole. Neither an act of pure worship on the part of the devotee nor the intrusion of a wholly autonomous textual power, miraculous response is largely a relational phenomenon—the product of organic negotiations *between* devotee and text. Its operations are regular, predictable, and grounded in fixed principles of action. Moreover, those principles find actualization in a complex network of expectations, including everything from basic moral postures to regimens of diet, purity, and ritual protocol.

Beyond the most basic cultic injunctions, the *Lotus Sūtra* itself has little to offer by way of specifics on ritual procedure. As we have seen, in Chinese religious culture, the recitation, exposition, and reproduction of the *Lotus*

Sūtra were articulated through a strikingly consistent grammar and vocabulary. On the one hand, this language was transposed freely from one devotional format to another, from the act of copying the text to complex stories about the miracles accompanying its recitation. On the other hand, these same ritual gestures were applied to the veneration of sūtra texts and devotional activities not connected to the *Lotus*. Thus, while the *Lotus Sūtra* could become a focus of exclusive devotion, the concrete forms through which devotees carried out their venerations and displays of piety were, with rare exception, neither drawn sui generis from the pages of the *Lotus Sūtra* nor construed as unique expressions of *Lotus* devotion. They were informed by a larger, shared culture of liturgical and scriptural practice. To understand the patterns of *Lotus Sūtra* practice in China, it is therefore essential that we bear in mind this extended field within which the sacrality of the *Lotus Sūtra* was created.

NOTES

1. William Graham, *Beyond the Written Word: Oral Aspects of Scripture in the History of Religion* (Cambridge: Cambridge University Press, 1987), 5.
2. Gregory Schopen, "The Phrase *'sa pṛthivīpradeśas caityabhūto bhavet'* in the *Vajracchedika*: Notes on the Cult of the Book in Mahāyāna" (1975), reprinted in Schopen, *Figments and Fragments of Mahāyāna Buddhism in India: More Collected Papers*, Studies in the Buddhist Traditions, 25–62 (Honolulu: University of Hawai'i Press, 2005).
3. *Fahua jing zhuanji* (ca. 754), Sengxiang (dates unknown), *Taishō shinshū daizōkyō*, 100 vols., ed. Takakusu Junjirō, Watanabe Kaigyoku, and Ono Gemmyō (1924–1934; repr., Taibei: Xinwenfeng chuban gongsi, 1974) (hereafter abbreviated as *T*) no. 2068, 51:95a28–b1.
4. Ibuki Atsushi, "Tōsō Eshō ni tsuite," *Waseda daigaku daigakuin bungaku kenkyū kiyō, bessatsu: Tetsugaku-shigaku hen* 14 (January 1987): 33–45. Other extant compendia include *Fahua jing xianying lu* (1198), Zongxiao (1151–1214), *Dainihon zoku zōkyō*, ed. Maeda Eun and Nakano Tatsue, 150 vols. (Kyoto: Zōkyō shoin, 1905–1912) (hereafter abbreviated as *Z*) 2b, 7; *Fahua jing chiyan ji*, Zhou Kefu (Qing dynasty), *Z* 2b, 7; *Pŏphwakyŏng jiphŏmki*, Uijŏk (ca. 681–705), in *Tōkyō daigaku toshokan zō: Hokekyō shūkenki* (Tokyo: Kichō kotenseki kankōkai, 1981); and *Pŏhwa yŏnghŏm chŏn*, Yowŏn (ca. 1300), *Z* 2b, 7.
5. Robert F. Campany, "The Real Presence," *History of Religions* 32, no. 3 (February 1993): 256–68; Campany, "Notes on the Devotional Uses and Symbolic Functions of Sūtra Texts as Depicted in Early Chinese Buddhist Miracle Tales and Hagiographies," *Journal of the International Association of Buddhist Studies* 14, no. 1 (1991): 44.
6. *Lidai sanbao ji* (597), Fei Changfang (Sui dynasty), *T* no. 2034, 49:105b22–24; Jamie Hubbard, *Absolute Delusion, Perfect Buddhahood: The Rise and Fall of a Chinese Heresy*, Nanzan Library of Asian Culture and Religion (Honolulu: University of Hawai'i Press, 2001), 25, 27–30, 117–18; and Nishimoto Teruma, *Sangaikyō no kenkyū* (Tokyo: Shunjūsha, 1998), 46–50.

7. For alternative configurations of the so-called "five practices" in the *Lotus Sūtra*, see Hurvitz, 159–61, 162–63 ("Preachers of Dharma"), 188 ("Fortitude"), 233 ("Discrimination of Merits"), 242–43, 245, 250, 251–53 ("Merits of the Dharma Preacher"), and 264–65 ("Supernatural Powers"). Some exegetes divided "receiving" and "keeping" into two separate practices, resulting in a total of six practices; see *Miaofa lianhua jing wenju*, Zhiyi (538–597) and Guanding (561–632), *T* no. 1718, 34:107c26–108a2; *Fahua yishu*, Jizang (549–623), *T* no. 1721, 34:584a23–26. Sanskrit manuscripts of the *Lotus* are less consistent than Kumārajīva's Chinese text in their identification in Chapter 19 of the five practices, which suggests that Kumārajīva may have chosen to regularize the text in the course of translation.
8. Étienne Lamotte, *Le traité de la grande vertu de sagesse de Nāgārjuna (Mahāprajñāpāramitāśāstra)*, 5 vols., Publications de l'Institut orientaliste de Louvain (Louvain, Belg.: Université de Louvain, Institut orientaliste, 1976), 4:1854–64, especially 1860.
9. *Hongzan Fahua zhuan* (ca. 706), Huixiang (ca. 639–706), *T* no. 2067, 51:46a2–6. See also Campany, "Notes on Devotional Uses," 38–40.
10. *Fahua jing zhuanji*, *T* 51:79c4–5; *Hongzan Fahua zhuan*, *T* 51:28c20–23, 29a29–b2, and 32c19–21.
11. *Fozu tongji*, Zhipan (ca. 1258), *T* no. 2035, 49:430a23–27.
12. *Sui Tiantai Zhizhe dashi biezhuan*, Guanding (561–632), *T* no. 2050, 50:191b9–10, 191c9–10, and 191c21–92a9.
13. *Fahua jing xianying lu*, Zongxiao (1151–1214), *Z* 2b, 7:436r.a.14–15 and 437v.a.10–12.
14. *Song gaoseng zhuan*, Zanning (919–1001), *T* no. 2061, 50:888b13–16.
15. *Hongzan Fahua zhuan*, *T* 51:38b25–29.
16. *Miaofa lianhua jing*, trans. Kumārajīva (Jiumoluoshi, 344–413, or 350–409) (Tiantaishan: Tiantaishan Guoqing jiangsi fawu liutong chu, n.d.).
17. "Chisong *Fahua jing* yi" and "Li *Fahua jing* yi," respectively, in ibid., 4–5, 6–10. The latter tract is based on the *Li Fahua jing yishi*, a short manual attributed to Zhili (960–1028), *T* no. 1944.
18. "Lisong qian guanxiang fa," in *Miaofa lianhua jing*, 11–12. The visualization tract distantly resembles the *Guanxin songjing faji* (*Procedures for Contemplation While Reciting Sūtras*), attributed to Zhiyi and Zhanran (711–782), *Z* 2a, 4:56r.a.1-v.b.4.
19. The *Diamond Sūtra* in question is in the Stein Collection at the British Library (Or. 8210/P. 2, entitled *Jingang bore boluomi jing*). For a photographic reproduction of the text, see the British Library Web site, http://idp.bl.uk/database/oo_scroll_h.a4d?uid = 23815833137;recnum = 18824;index = 1.
20. *Fahua sanmei chanyi*, Zhiyi, *T* no. 1941. See Daniel B. Stevenson, "Zhiyi: The Lotus Samādhi Rite of Repentance," in *Sources of Chinese Tradition*, 2nd ed., ed. Wm. Theodore de Bary and Irene Bloom, 1:462–67 (New York: Columbia University Press, 1999); and Stevenson, "Where Meditative Theory Meets Practice: Requirements for Entering the 'Halls of Contemplation/Penance' in Tiantai Monasteries of the Song," *Tendai gakuhō, tokubetsugō: Kokusai Tendai gakkai ronshū* (October 2007): 71–142.
21. *Nittō guhō junrei gōki*, Ennin (794–864), in *Dainihon bukkyō zensho*, 151 vols. (Tokyo: Bussho kankōkai, 1912–1922), 113:207a9–208a8; Edwin O. Reischauer, trans., *Ennin's Diary: The Record of a Pilgrimage to China in Search of the Law* (New York: Ronald Press, 1955), 152–55.
22. Victor Mair, "Written Aspects of Chinese Sūtra Lectures (chiang-ching-wen),"

Hanxue yanjiu 4, no. 2 (December 1988): 311–34; Fukui Fumimasa, "Kōkyō gishiki no soshiki naiyō," in *Tonkō to Chūgoku bukkyō*, ed. Makita Tairyō and Fukui Fumimasa, Kōza tonkō 7, 359–82 (Tokyo: Daitō shuppansha, 1984).

23. See Sengxiang's chapter on "Stimulus and Response [Associated with] Lecture and Exegesis," *Fahua jing zhuanji*, *T* 51:57b5–62a4.
24. John Kieschnick, "Blood Writing in Chinese Buddhism," *Journal of the International Association of Buddhist Studies* 23, no. 2 (2000): 177–94.
25. *Hongzan Fahua zhuan*, *T* 51:45b20–c6; Daniel B. Stevenson, "Tales of the Lotus Sūtra," In *Buddhism in Practice*, ed. Donald S. Lopez Jr. (Princeton, N.J.: Princeton University Press, 1995), 449–50.
26. *Sanbao gantong lu*, Daoxuan (596–667), *T* no. 2106, 52:429a9; *Hongzan Fahua zhuan*, *T* 51:46c14; *Fahua jing zhuanji*, *T* 51:83c12; Mochizuki Shinkō, *Bukkyō daijiten*, rev. ed., 10 vols. (Kyoto: Seikai seiten kankō kyōkai, 1954–1963), 4140a–4141a.

[6]

ART OF THE *LOTUS SŪTRA*

Willa Jane Tanabe

THE *LOTUS SŪTRA* was first translated into Chinese shortly after the introduction of Buddhism in the first few centuries of the Common Era. But it was the popular translation supervised by Kumārajīva in 406 that spurred both faith in and art related to the *Lotus Sūtra*.[1] Indeed, both faith and art were closely connected. Transcriptions of the *Lotus* text and images in stone and pigment began appearing in significant numbers in the fifth century, reaching their apogee in the Tang dynasty (618–907), continuing strongly through the thirteenth century and sporadically after that. In Korea, too, transcriptions and images appeared shortly after the introduction of Buddhism in the fourth century, achieving great decorative beauty in the Koryŏ period (918–1392).

In Japan, the sūtra's popularity and significance reached unprecedented heights, particularly in the latter half of the Heian period (794–1185) and the Kamakura period (1185–1333). The popularity of the *Lotus Sūtra* in Japan is reflected in its link with important political and religious figures. Prince Shōtoku (574–622), a pivotal supporter of early Buddhism, is said to have written a commentary on the scripture. The leading courtier Fujiwara Michinaga (966–1027), whose actions were emulated by many aristocrats, sponsored one thousand printed and innumerable hand-copied *Lotus Sūtras*, as well as paintings, sculptures, and *Lotus* halls. After his rise to power, Michinaga arranged for the perpetual recitation of the sūtra.[2] Moreover, the rise of Tendai and later Nichiren Buddhism assured the continuation of *Lotus Sūtra* rituals and practice to this day.

The quantity and wide range of extant art related to the *Lotus Sūtra* in East Asia can be studied in various ways: chronologically; by place of production, from China through Korea to Japan; by artistic medium, covering painting, sculpture, architecture, the applied arts, and calligraphy; or by the functions and purposes for which the art was produced. The overview presented here organizes *Lotus* art according to its relationship to the written text of the scripture. I focus, therefore, on the art of (1) the copied text; (2) frontispiece illustrations that supplement the transcribed text; (3) jeweled stūpa maṇḍalas, which give equal importance to text and pictures by transforming the text into pictures and the pictures into text; (4) transformation pictures or tableaux, in which illustrations are primary and the text is abbreviated or omitted; and (5) art that is referential to or symbolic of the *Lotus*.

COPYING THE *LOTUS SŪTRA*

In China, sūtras were hand copied in ink onto paper hand scrolls for dissemination in the monastic community. By the sixth century, the lines of characters were standardized to seventeen characters per line (thirty-two if it was a miniaturized text), and scribes usually employed the clerical script that is easily read even today. The government and temples established scriptoria, and their locations, along with the names of the monks and nuns who copied the text, were often included in a colophon at the end of the scrolls. The scale of the copying can be seen in projects carried out by Emperor Wen (r. 581–605), who sponsored forty-six copies of the complete Buddhist canon, totaling 132,086 scrolls or fascicles; and by Emperor Yang (r. 605–616), who ordered 612 copies of the canon, amounting to 903,580 scrolls. While the usual scripture scrolls were copied in ink on plain paper, by the end of the sixth century, more beautiful copies were being written in gold or silver characters on paper dyed deep blue. An extant *Heart Sūtra* dated 607 is written in gold characters, and the Japanese priest Ennin (794–864), traveling in China in 840, reported seeing a complete canon in six thousand scrolls copied out in gold and silver characters.[3]

Other East Asian countries also supported scriptoria. Koryŏ monarchs established a royal scriptorium (Sagyŏng'wŏn). As in China, the Koreans copied sūtras in gold or silver characters, and in 1191, King Myŏngjong (r. 1170–1197) commissioned a copy of the canon written in silver characters on indigo paper. During the reign of King Ch'ungnyŏl (r. 1274–1308), the Scriptorium of Silver Letters (Ŭnjawŏn) and the Scriptorium of Gold Letters (Kŭmjawŏn) were established.[4] Japan, too, had set up a government-sponsored scriptorium, probably by 728, at Tōdaiji, followed, in 743, by another government-sponsored transcription office just for commentaries. The court established a third bureau in 762 for copied sūtras ordered by imperial request, and some years after that, created a scriptorium for copying sūtras in gold characters. As in China and Korea, copying scriptures was also carried out under private auspices.

In this tradition of copying scriptures, the *Lotus Sūtra* was one of the most popular. Perhaps no other scripture emphasizes so adamantly and repeatedly the benefits to those who uphold, read, recite, explain, or copy the sūtra, as noted by Daniel B. Stevenson in chapter 5 of this volume. Not only will devotees acquire the eight hundred virtues of the body (Hurvitz, 251), or be able to see Śākyamuni Buddha and the buddha Many Jewels (Prabhūtaratna [Hurvitz, 265–66]), but, most important, they will achieve perfect enlightenment (Hurvitz, 161). Moreover, the *Lotus Sūtra* encourages tangible ways to demonstrate one's devotion to the sūtra by copying it, making images, and building *stūpas* (reliquary mounds). Indeed, the *Lotus* notes that those who will achieve the buddha path include anyone who helps create an image, carving, or colored design, "even children in play, / [Who] with grass, sticks, and brushes / Or with their fingernails, / Draw buddha images" (Hurvitz, 37). Thus, copying the scripture and making art based on the *Lotus Sūtra* were acts of devotion resulting in significant religious consequence.

The promise of benefits to all who preserve and copy the text was a primary motivation leading to copying the sūtra in great numbers. In south China, for example, a center was established in the late sixth century just for the transcription of the *Lotus Sūtra*.[5] In the 670s, Empress Wu Zetian ordered three thousand copies in commemoration of her parents.[6] Even today the British Library alone houses at least 1,048 scrolls of the *Lotus Sūtra* originating in a repository of manuscripts from Dunhuang (Gansu province), in northwest China.[7] In Japan in the Nara period (710–794), the *Lotus Sūtra* was the third most-copied scripture, and it was the foundation for state-established nunneries, which were called "temples for eradicating sins by the *Lotus Sūtra*" (*Hokke metsuzaiji*). Not only were individual copies of the *Lotus Sūtra* made, but multiple sets as well. Prominent figures such as Emperor Shōmu, in 748, Saichō, in 814, Fujiwara Michitaka, in 992, and Fujiwara Motohira, in 1137, all sponsored sets of a thousand copies. Indeed, the *Lotus Sūtra* accounts for ninety percent of all extant sūtra scrolls dating from the Heian period.[8]

The *Lotus Sūtra* was copied for specific benefits and on particular occasions. The postscripts at the end of the scrolls often reveal the desired outcomes and include petitions for the peace and prosperity of the nation and its rulers, felicity in the next world, transfer of merit to parents and ancestors for seven generations, safe travel, and health and prosperity for both the sponsors and their families. These sūtras were offered at the time of the dedication of temples and sculpture, at memorial services, and on the occasion of longevity celebrations. They were also dedicated at the popular lectures on the *Lotus* that likely originated in China and were established in Japan by the priest Gonzō in 796. These lectures developed into a standard set of eight lectures based on the eight fascicles of the scripture, ten lectures on the eight fascicles and the opening and closing sūtras, or thirty lectures, which presented a lecture on each of the twenty-eight chapters and on the opening and closing sūtras.[9]

Japanese who feared that the dawn of the degenerate age of the Final Dharma (Ja.: *mappō*) would begin in 1052 took up the practice of copying sūtras and burying them in order to preserve the teachings until the future buddha (Maitreya Bodhisattva, who will become Maitreya Buddha) would be reborn on earth.[10] One of the earliest sūtra burials took place on Mount Kinpu in 1007 and included a number of scriptures, one of which was a *Lotus* copied in 998 by Fujiwara Michinaga in gold script on indigo paper. Between the eleventh and sixteenth centuries, many *Lotus Sūtra* copies were produced, placed in bronze or ceramic containers, buried underground, and marked with small wooden or stone stūpas. The Japanese even inscribed the *Lotus Sūtra* onto stone pebbles and ceramic tiles that were also buried in these sūtra mounds to ensure the preservation of the text.[11]

Copying the *Lotus* as an act of devotion led to a great emphasis on the adornment of the sūtra scroll. After all, the scripture itself draws a parallel between the text and the body of the Buddha, noting that "whatever place a roll of this scripture may occupy, in all those places one is to erect a stūpa. . . . There is no need even to lodge *śarīras* [relics of the Buddha] in it. What is the reason? Within it there is already a whole body of the Thus Come One [the Buddha]" (Hurvitz, 163). In other words, the sūtra declares itself to be the body of the Buddha. Dōgen (1200–1253), founder of Sōtō Zen in Japan, echoed this idea when he proclaimed that "the *Lotus Sūtra* . . . contains the entire body of the Tathāgata [Thus Come One] . . . and making a prostration before that sūtra is exactly like making a prostration to the Tathāgata."[12] This idea was carried out in a concrete way by copyists who made obeisance after completing each character, line, or fascicle. Even a Japanese emperor, Goreizei (950–1011), was

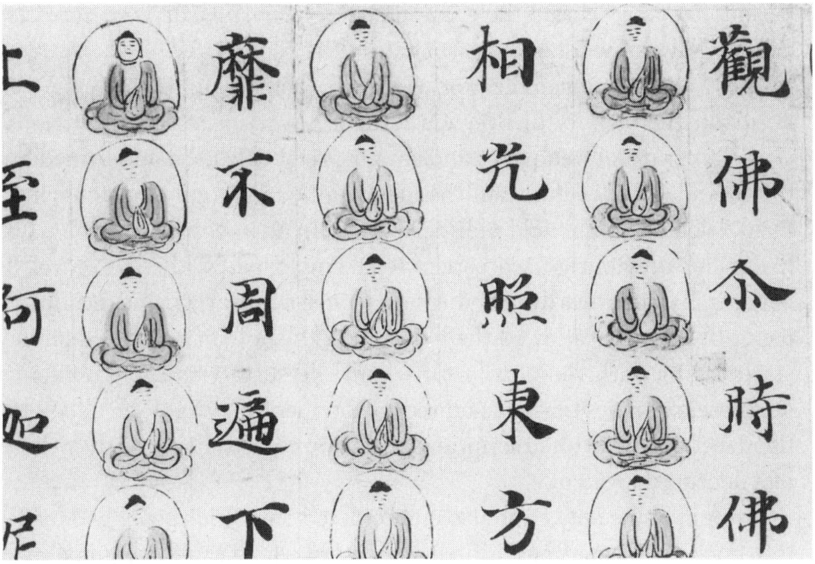

FIGURE 6.1 *Lotus Sūtra*: detail of hand scroll alternating lines of text and images of the Buddha. Ink and colors on paper, 29.4 x 2,124 cm. Twelfth century (Heian period).

ZENTSŪJI, KAGAWA PREFECTURE, JAPAN.

said to have bowed to each character he wrote. There are examples of *Lotus Sūtra* copies in which the scribe drew a lotus dais under each character, or a pagoda around each character, as if each character were a buddha. There is also a well-known *Lotus Sūtra* copy in which a buddha was drawn alongside each character to emphasize the integration of the Buddha and the text (fig. 6.1).

More commonly, however, the text was aesthetically enhanced by upgrading the paper and ink, demonstrating the reverence of the sponsor and evoking awe in the beholder. As mentioned above, by the seventh century, the *Lotus* began to be copied on dyed papers, especially papers dyed deep blue. The scripture was also copied onto paper that had decorative designs printed in mica, embedded with silver and gold dust and foil, or adorned with hand-drawn and printed-under drawings. Copyists replaced the ink characters with gold and silver script. Even the ruled lines between rows of text were drawn in gold and silver. If the sponsor wanted to demonstrate a more fervent sincerity in his votive offering, he could replace the ink with his own blood, or a mixture of ink and blood. Cases of blood writing were recorded in China and Japan, especially in the Kamakura period. To demonstrate their physical devotion, sponsors and copyists occasionally embedded their own hair in the paper.[13]

These acts of personalization were also heightened by copying the *Lotus* on the back of or over old letters, poem sheets, miscellaneous writings, or decorated paper and scrolls previously used and owned by the intended beneficiaries of the merit gained through pious copying. Even a dead person could indirectly participate in copying the *Lotus* if his or her previously used papers were employed. While the recycled paper was sometimes dyed or disguised, most scriptures using reclaimed paper deliberately allowed the old writing to show in order to demonstrate a link with the person for whom the sūtra was copied. Extant Japanese examples of sūtras on recycled paper (*hogu kyō*) include both handwritten and printed scriptures that were copied chiefly on the behalf of a deceased loved one.

The text of the *Lotus* was also embroidered onto thick paper and made into booklets. Sometimes printed characters, which acted as a guide, can be seen beneath the embroidery, and it is likely that both skilled amateurs and professionals created these works. Each character or line of characters was embroidered in different colors in columns separated by lines created by stitching or painting with gold dust. Interestingly, some Japanese examples were dedicated to Shintō deities and kept in shrines.

Buddhists transformed the transcription of the *Lotus Sūtra* into an act of petition and devotion, whose efficacy was amplified by making the external beauty of the scrolls as elegant as their internal message. Whether the text was written in black, gold, or silver inks, with colored threads, or on dyed, recycled, or decorated paper, the sponsors of these acts of beauty and faith treated their creations as precious talismans for inviting blessings and warding off misfortunes. They did not stop, however, at upgrading and beautifying the text and paper; just as Europeans added magnificent paintings to illuminate sacred texts, so too did East Asian Buddhists expound on the meaning of the text through frontispiece paintings, thus enabling even the illiterate to see something of the content of the *Lotus Sūtra*.

FRONTISPIECE PAINTINGS: ILLUSTRATIONS AS SUPPLEMENTS TO THE TRANSCRIBED TEXT

Frontispiece paintings (Ja.: *mikaeshi e*), placed at the opening section of the hand scrolls on which the text was copied, summarily expressed the ideas or stories of the scripture. Chinese and Korean artists tended to divide the *Lotus* into seven subdivisions or fascicles, placing one fascicle on each hand scroll, while the Japanese generally used an eight-fascicle division. Thus, sets of the transcribed text had seven or eight frontispieces. The Japanese also copied the text in a one-chapter-per-scroll format and often included in their sets the opening and closing sūtras. Some *Lotus* sets had, therefore, thirty scrolls and frontispieces. As opposed to this large set, East Asian Buddhists also produced miniature versions, with the complete scripture copied on a single scroll with thirty-two characters per line and a single frontispiece for the entire scripture. Obviously, the sets that allotted a single frontispiece for each chapter could include more detailed illustrations than those that devoted a frontispiece to a fascicle or to the entire scripture.

The largest number of *Lotus* frontispiece paintings are executed in gold and silver on indigo paper accompanying texts written in gold or silver, one fascicle per scroll. These frontispieces were painted essentially in Chinese styles that were also used in Korea and Japan. Many of the extant versions are Japanese productions. The frontispieces in gold and silver form a kind of standard body of *Lotus* illustrations that, regardless of their location of production, share characteristics of composition, content, and style common throughout East Asia. This is not to deny, of course, that they underwent change depending upon whether they were based on Tang-, Song-, or Yuan-dynasty models.

In general, there were three compositional arrangements. The first, and most likely the earliest style, placed a preaching scene in the center of the frontispiece (fig. 6.2). Śākyamuni, in frontal view and flanked by bodhisattvas, *arhats*, and an audience of laypeople, nuns, and priests, preaches the *Lotus*. The Buddha and bodhisattvas usually sit on lotus daises beneath canopies or jeweled trees. Above the Buddha are beribboned musical instruments (symbols of paradise) and Vulture Peak, often shaped theriomorphically into the head of a vulture (fig. 6.3). Around this central assembly (above, below, and at the sides) are illustrations of the parables, similes, and stories from the fascicle.

The second kind of composition placed the Buddha and his assembly to the right side in a three-quarter view, such that they face the illustrations drawn to the left. This compositional scheme appeared around the ninth century but was particularly popular in later productions. This style created a sense of horizontal as opposed to circular movement.

The third composition clearly divided the frontispiece into three registers, with Vulture Peak, hills, and clouds at the top; the Buddha assembly (often with a reduced number of figures) in the middle register; and the illustrations from the fascicles in the bottom register. The illustrations became conventionalized and easy to recognize. In late Heian Japan, the third compositional style became commonly used for frontis-

FIGURE 6.2 *Lotus Sūtra*: frontispiece to fascicle 2. Manuscript, gold on dark-blue paper, 26.3 x 22 cm. Twelfth century (Heian period).

HYAKUSAIJI, SHIGA PREFECTURE, JAPAN.

FIGURE 6.3 *Lotus Sūtra*: frontispiece to fascicle 4. Manuscript, gold on dark-blue paper, 26.3 x 22 cm. Twelfth century (Heian period).

HYAKUSAIJI, SHIGA PREFECTURE, JAPAN.

pieces decorating the canon, whose sheer number of scrolls necessitated such simplification.

Despite these compositional differences, the scrolls tended to repeat the same choice of vignettes for illustration. Frontispieces typically depicted two or three scenes from each fascicle. The accompanying list presents the most commonly illustrated scenes in Japanese sets of eight scrolls; similar selections are seen in Korean and Chinese sets.

FASCICLE	CHAPTER	EPISODES
1	1	*Lotus* assembly of the Buddha and attendants and audience
	2	Boys building stūpas of sand
2	3	Burning house with three carts
	4	Prodigal son
3	5	Farmers with rain and thunder god
	6	King's feast for the famished
	7	Occasionally includes travelers and conjured city
4	8	Occasionally includes drunken man with jewel hidden in garment
	10	Digging for water on a high plain
	11	Appearance of the jeweled stūpa
5	12	Dragon king's daughter appears, occasionally shown as a buddha
	12	King who becomes servant to seer (collecting firewood and water)
	14	Occasionally includes king with jewel in topknot
	15	Occasionally includes bodhisattvas welling up from ground
6	16	Good physician and sons
	19	Dharma Preacher expounds the teaching
7	20	Bodhisattva Never Disparaging is pursued and attacked
	22	Śākyamuni Buddha stands to stroke the head of a bodhisattva
	23	Occasionally a bodhisattva burns arms or body
	24	Bodhisattva Fine Sound creates many lotuses
8	25	Bodhisattva Sound Observer (Avalokiteśvara) saves the imperiled, especially those afloat at sea, pushed off mountains, or encircled by armed enemies
	27	Two princes perform magical feats and emit fire and water from their bodies

While the earliest extant example of a printed Chinese frontispiece dates to 868, printed scriptures greatly increased later. The entire canon was first printed between 972 and 983; four more sets followed by the end of the Song dynasty (960–1279); another four (one in Tangut) appeared in the

Yuan dynasty (1279–1368); and two editions were printed in Korea in the eleventh and thirteenth centuries. Although the Japanese did not print the entire canon until the seventeenth century, they imported Chinese printed versions as early as the eleventh century.

The Song and Yuan styles of frontispieces were used in both printed and hand-painted versions of the *Lotus*. Rather than being rolled, the Song and Yuan sūtra scrolls were generally folded in accordion fashion to form a booklet. The rectangular frontispiece had the title of the scripture on the right edge and was framed by a decorative band, an element that the Japanese usually omitted. The composition of the frontispieces belonged to the second type, in which the preaching scene appeared on the right and the parables and stories on the left. In comparison to many extant Japanese frontispieces based on earlier models, the Song and Yuan frontispieces paid greater attention to the narrative aspects and details of the *Lotus*'s stories, and they increased the number of illustrated scenes from the sūtra. They also presented the preaching scene in great detail and with many more figures in the assembly. For example, the frontispiece for fascicle 1 in Song- and Yuan-style frontispieces illustrated not only children building sand stūpas but also people painting and carving buddha images, bodhisattvas practicing in quiet areas among the trees, and the Buddha emitting a ray of light from between his brows to illuminate the heavens and hells along with the inhabitants of the six realms of rebirth.

Korean and Japanese artists followed these models in producing frontispieces in hand-painted versions using gold and silver on dark-blue paper as in the earlier examples. The Korean versions produced in the Koryŏ period are especially beautiful. Indeed, Korean histories record that thirty-five Korean calligraphers were sent to China to copy sūtras in gold and silver script in 1290, and additional calligraphers went in 1298, 1302, and 1304. Extant Korean examples, such as the frontispiece (produced ca. 1340) to fascicle 2 of the *Lotus* in the folded-booklet scroll now in the Metropolitan Museum of Art (fig. 6.4), display detailed narratives of the burning house and prodigal son stories. They also include a preaching scene consisting of fifteen figures surrounding the Buddha, who sits on a large, elaborate dais. What is characteristic of the Korean frontispiece, however, is that nearly the entire surface is filled with gold patterns: the robes of the figures, the tile flooring of the dais, the brocades of the altar table, and even the ground itself are all embellished with minute patterns in rich gold. There is almost no plain surface, and the indigo paper acts only as an accent to the golden surface. This gold is balanced

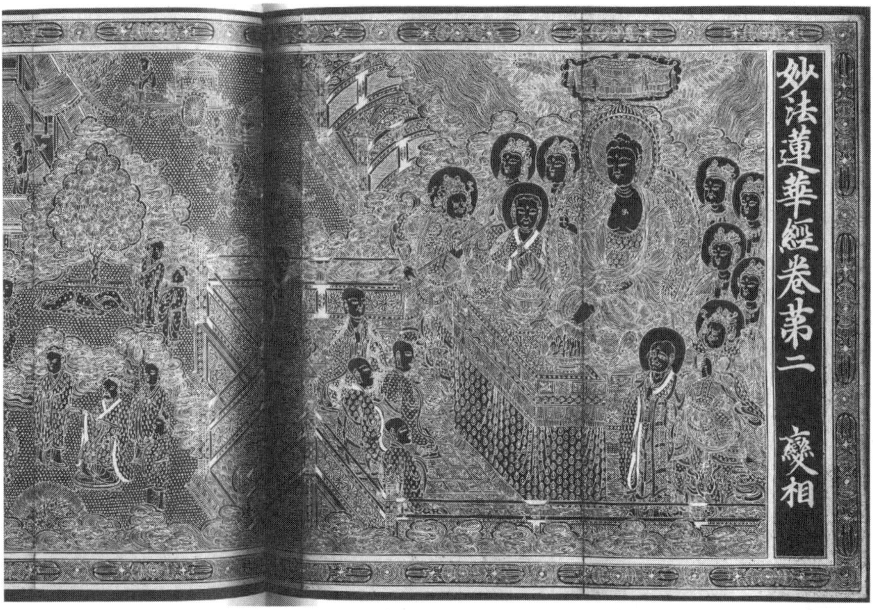

FIGURE 6.4 *Lotus Sūtra*: frontispiece to fascicle 2. Manuscript, folding booklet, gold and silver on indigo-dyed mulberry paper, 33 x 11.4 cm. Ca. 1340 (Koryŏ period).

THE METROPOLITAN MUSEUM OF ART, NEW YORK. PURCHASE, LILA ACHESON WALLACE GIFT, 1994 (1994.207). IMAGE ©THE METROPOLITAN MUSEUM OF ART.

by the elegant script in silver that is used for the text and the title at the right edge of the frontispiece.[14]

While some Korean patrons delighted in elaborate gold and silver frontispieces, the Japanese aristocrats of the late Heian and Kamakura periods began to replace the conventional renderings with ones that more freely interpreted the contents of the *Lotus*. The frontispieces of these "decorative" sūtra scrolls, so called to distinguish them from the more standard religious subjects and styles, included (1) scenes that incorporated Japanese settings and figures; (2) themes borrowed from nonscriptural sources, especially Japanese poetry on the *Lotus* or miracle tales about the *Lotus*; and even (3) subject matter that seemed to have no apparent connection to the sūtra. Many of the paintings in this decorative tradition were copied in the single-chapter-per-scroll format rather than the single-fascicle-per-scroll format of most orthodox versions.

Two of the most famous decorated sūtra scrolls are the *Heike nōkyō* (*Sūtra Dedicated by the Heike Clan*) and the *Kunōji Lotus Sūtra*.[15] The *Heike* sūtra was sponsored by Taira Kiyomori in 1164 out of gratitude for his family's prosperity and was copied in the one-chapter-per-scroll format along with four additional sūtras. The *Kunōji Lotus Sūtra* was sponsored in 1141 by Emperor Toba, Empress Bifukumon'in, and others to form a mutual bond or connection with the Buddha to gain merit. The copying of sūtras to form a bond (Ja.: *kechien kyō*) was popular not only among the upper classes but also among less affluent devotees, who pooled their more meager resources to fund productions of scrolls, sculptures, and paintings. The freedom to interpret the teachings in terms compatible with specific times and places can be seen at the very beginning of the *Heike* scrolls, in the frontispiece to Chapter 1. Rather than starting with a formal assembly of the Buddha, attendants, and audience of nuns, monks, and laypeople, the *Heike* frontispiece portrays a peaceful landscape full of flowering plants and trees, a brushwood fence, and a mansion lacking a roof so that we can see inside. This technique of the "blown-off roof" is a common device used in secular hand scrolls of the time. Inside the house a courtier is reading a scripture, a nun is holding a tray of altar items, and a court woman has taken a scroll from a sūtra box. Outside a monk sits in prayer underneath a bamboo shelter. All are dressed in twelfth-century costumes and are portrayed in a style common to that era's pictorial hand scrolls of court life, such as illustrations of *The Tale of Genji*, the novel written in the eleventh century by Lady Murasaki. Thus, at first glance, this painting seems to represent a secular genre scene. However, hidden in the landscape of the garden are words from Chapter 1 of the *Lotus* referring to the four classes of believers who "through practice had attained the path" (Hurvitz, 5). Complementing the line of characters written into the landscape, the four classes of followers—nuns, monks, laymen, and laywomen—are represented by the four figures. The painting is, in other words, faithful to the text, but interprets it in a contemporary way that explicitly connects the ancient *Lotus* to the present time.

Painters also based their illustrations on sources outside the *Lotus*. In Japan, Buddhist poetry was written in both Chinese and Japanese, and about half the poems were based on specific scriptures, the *Lotus* being preeminent among them. Series of poems on the twenty-eight chapters of the *Lotus* became popular with such renowned poets as Fujiwara Shunzei (1114–1204) and Saigyō (1118–1190).[16] Perhaps the most famous example of a frontispiece based on a poem is the frontispiece to Chapter 5, "Medicinal Herbs," of the *Kunōji* scrolls. Orthodox frontispieces to Chapter 5 usually displayed farmers in their fields during a rainstorm. The *Kunōji* frontispiece presents two Japanese aristocrats huddled under an umbrella in the rain. The field contains a tree and plants, a half-buried wheel, luggage, a crane, and three birds flying across the sky. The painting uses the style and some of the techniques, such as abbreviated facial features (a line for the eye, a hook for the nose), common to secular narrative hand scrolls. This painting is a poem-picture (Ja.: *uta e*) based on a poem by Fujiwara Shunzei. The author underscores the point of the *Lotus* that, like the rain, the Buddha's grace falls on everyone without discrimination.

Harusame wa	The spring rains
Konomo kanomo no	Soak this face and that face,
Kusa mo ki mo	The grass and the trees,
WAkeZU MIDORI NI	Dyeing them all green
Somuru narikeri	Without distinction.[17]

However, the painter has done more than present a picture of contemporary figures in a rainstorm based on a poem. He has also created a rebus, or pictophone, in which objects such as the half-buried wheel (*wa*), crane (*tsu* or *zu*), three birds (*midori*), and luggage (*ni*) make up syllables of the fourth line of the poem, while the other lines, such as "this face and that face" or "the grass and the trees," have been made into pictures. Pictures are read as sounds, sounds are written as pictures. Pictures drawn with characters written to look like reeds, rocks, or birds were called "reed-hand pictures" (*ashide e*), and the other technique was known as "pictures read for sound" (*jion e*). Their employment demonstrated an intimate knowledge of the scripture's meaning, skill in the arts of painting and poetry, and a delight in subtle playfulness typical of the Heian court.[18]

Miracle tales also provided a basis for frontispiece illustrations in the decorative tradition. Both the Chinese and Japanese compiled anthologies of *jātaka* tales, folk tales, and legends of *Lotus* devotees and their experiences. The frontispiece to Chapter 25 in the *Heike* sūtra contains a narrative of the *Valāhasa jātaka*, in which the Buddha, in a former life, is a white horse that saves a band of shipwrecked traders, a story that does not appear in the *Lotus* itself.[19]

The third category of illustration in the decorative tradition uses secular subject matter that has no direct connection to the sūtra. Although there are few extant examples of this category, records refer to the practice. For example, in a late twelfth-century manuscript, there is mention of a *Lotus Sūtra* copied in the one-chapter-per-scroll format that had frontispieces based on *The Tale of Genji*. One of the few extant examples is the "fan-shaped sūtra" (Ja.: *senmen kyō*), dedicated at Shitennōji by Empress Kaya-no-in (d. 1156), Empress Bifukumon'in, and Emperor Toba in 1152. The *Lotus* was copied over colorful paintings on fan-shaped paper and then folded into booklets. The text is written in lines that become smaller at the bottom of the fan, and the ink characters are replaced with gold ones when the writing covers a black area of the paintings. The paintings under the copied scripture include genre scenes of women hanging clothes, visiting the village well, and shopping, as well as aristocrats practicing calligraphy and undertaking other tasks. There are also landscapes, birds, and flowers. The covers of the booklets depict the *rākṣasa* daughters, or female demons, mentioned in Chapter 26 of the *Lotus*, but here they are beautiful women dressed in Japanese court robes. The fan sūtras may have been written on recycled paper, that is, written over paintings belonging to Empress Kaya-no-in or someone close to her. On the other hand, these works may also have expressed the idea that, just as the text is superimposed over scenes of everyday life, so too does the sacred realm of the *Lotus* overlie our ordinary realm.

JEWELED STŪPA MAṆḌALAS: PAINTINGS AS EQUAL TO THE TRANSCRIBED TEXT

Writing the *Lotus* in the shape of a stūpa magnified merit by simultaneously completing two acts encouraged by the *Lotus*: copying the text and erecting a stūpa. The Japanese paintings known as jeweled stūpa maṇḍalas arrange the characters of the text of each fascicle in the shape of a nine-story pagoda in the center of a large hanging scroll (fig. 6.5). The two buddhas, Many Jewels and Śākyamuni, appear in the open doorway on the first floor. All the characters are transcribed crisply, but they are written sideways, upside down, and upright, following the shape of the pagoda and rendering the text unreadable. Thus, the talismanic quality of the text supersedes its readability.

To transmit the content of the scripture, Japanese painters added illustrations at the sides, top, and bottom of the pagoda. The text and illustrations are in gold and silver on indigo paper in the style of the standard frontispiece paintings. However, because they bear the narrative burden, these illustrations are more descriptive and detailed. The ten-scroll set at Danzan Jinja contains 215 narrative episodes, and a set in eight scrolls at Ryūhonji contains 120. By contrast, a standard set of *Lotus* frontispieces has only about 20 episodes. Clearly, the large format and the lack of read-

FIGURE 6.5 *Jeweled Stūpa Maṇḍala* (Ja.: *Kinji hōtō mandara*), in gold script. *Lotus Sūtra*: fascicle 1. Hanging scroll, gold and silver on blue paper, 110 x 58.8 cm. Thirteenth century (Kamakura period).

RYŪHONJI, KYOTO, JAPAN.

able text in the pagoda-style painting encouraged the painters to elaborate on stories that had rarely been illustrated, such as the scene of the buddhas extending their tongues to the Brahmā Heaven described in Chapter 21 (Hurvitz, 263).

A comparison of the conventional frontispiece of fascicle 7 to the illustrations of fascicle 7 on the jeweled stūpa maṇḍala from Ryūhonji demonstrates the greater detail of pictorial narration on the maṇḍala. Frontispieces sometimes include the story from the chapter on Bodhisattva Medicine King, showing that he has burned his arms as an offering to the buddha. The Ryūhonji scroll includes the burning of the arms but also adds the building of stūpas for the relics of a buddha as well as all the similes from this chapter illustrating the benefits of the sūtra (Hurvitz, 273–74), such as a child finding a mother, a patient finding a doctor, or a naked man finding clothes. Similarly, fascicle 2 includes not only the parables of the burning house and the prodigal son but also the difficulties of such things as birth, old age, sickness, and death in this transient world (fig. 6.6). The Ryūhonji scrolls narrate the text in much greater detail, their tenfold increase in vignettes replacing the need for written details.

In comparison to standard frontispieces, the jeweled stūpa maṇḍalas also pay greater attention to hell scenes. The *Lotus Sūtra* mentions hells only peripherally, but the jeweled stūpa maṇḍalas include scenes of the six realms, particularly hell, based on the descriptions by Genshin (942–1017) in his *Essentials for Rebirth in the Pure Land* (*Ōjōyōshū* [completed in 985]). While the subject of hells was often a special concern of the Pure Land traditions, the Ryūhonji work connects hell imagery with the *Lotus* and elaborates on the details of, for example, demons boiling sinners in large pots or drinking the blood of a wounded man; a lust-ridden, naked man climbing a tree of swordlike branches to reach a beautiful woman; and hungry ghosts gnawing on human bones.

Although there are only a few extant examples of jeweled stūpa maṇḍalas in China, records mention the existence of such works from the tenth through the twentieth centuries. Chinese examples of other sūtras written or printed in the shape of pagodas exist, and Dunhuang manuscripts include a stūpa-shaped, readable *Heart Sūtra* from the tenth century. Korean examples exist, too, including a jeweled stūpa maṇḍala of the *Lotus* in gold script on deep-blue silk dated 1369. The Korean painting has the entire scripture written on one hanging scroll in the shape of a seven-story pagoda with two buddhas on the first floor and a single buddha in each of the doorways of the six other stories. Bodhisattvas, protective deities, and buddhas line the sides of the pagoda, arranged in

FIGURE 6.6 Detail of *Jeweled Stūpa Maṇḍala* (Ja.: *Kinji hōtō mandara*), in gold script. *Lotus Sūtra*: fascicle 1. Hanging scroll, gold and silver on blue paper, 110 x 58.8 cm. Thirteenth century (Kamakura period).

RYŪHONJI, KYOTO, JAPAN.

symmetrical fashion at the edge of each roof and the foundation platform. But, unlike the Japanese versions, there are no narrative illustrations.

Artists formed pictures from lines of scripture also in later Japan. The Japanese literatus painter Tanomura Chikuden (1777–1835), influenced by Chinese printed examples, copied the *Diamond Sūtra* in the shape of a pagoda. Katō Nobukiyo (1734–1810) used the lines of the *Lotus* to produce a series of fifty paintings of the five hundred arhats (Ja.: *rakan*).[20] Each hanging scroll has ten arhats, whose robed figures and surrounding landscape and architecture are all depicted with words of the *Lotus*. At first glance, the images look like an ordinary painting. Only upon closer examination does one see that what appears like lines, forms, and shading are all produced by Chinese characters in ink and color. The theme of five hundred arhats, typically used in art related to the Zen schools, is an appropriate subject for the *Lotus* text because of their appearance in Chapter 8, "Receipt of Prophecy by Five Hundred Disciples." Like the jeweled stūpa maṇḍalas in gold script, the paintings of the five hundred arhats blur the distinction between picture and text, making the text function as picture and the picture as text.

TRANSFORMATION PICTURES: PAINTINGS AS TEXT

Transformation tableaux or pictures (Ch.: *bianxiang*, Ja.: *hensō*) are paintings that visualize the scripture's content either without the presence of any text or with only brief excerpts written within cartouches. Eugene Wang argues that it is misleading to call the transformation tableaux "illustrations" because the term implies complete subservience to the text, whereas the transformation tableaux often diverged from a single written source and followed both artistic and textual precedents.[21] Nevertheless, most of the scenes adhered closely to the scriptural source. Indeed, one could argue that faithful adherence to content was more critical precisely because the full written text was absent.

Transformation pictures are found in various formats, including hanging scrolls, murals, and hand scrolls. The large size of many allowed them to function as a central image of worship, but they were primarily didactic. Their large surface also allowed the depiction of so many episodes that some scholars suggest that a professional narrator was needed to explain the contents of the painting. Such is the case for the twenty-two large hanging scrolls of the *Lotus Sūtra* at Honpōji (fig. 6.7). In transformation tableaux in Chinese cave temples, on the other hand, poor lighting

FIGURE 6.7 *Lotus Sūtra* transformation tableau (Ja.: *hensō*): scenes from "Medicinal Herbs." Hanging scroll, fifth scroll in a set of twenty-two. Colors on silk, 187–191.2 x 124.8–127 cm. 1326–1328 (Kamakura period).

HONPŌJI, TOYAMA PREFECTURE, JAPAN. IMPORTANT CULTURAL PROPERTY.

and other conditions may have made the works less accessible to a large audience and professional narrators.

Chinese artists produced numerous transformation pictures, but most were destroyed by fire, wars, and persecutions. Fortunately, the murals and sculptures that decorated cave-temple sites along the trade routes from northern India through central Asia and into China remain. Sites such as Binglingsi and Maijishan (Gansu, China), Yungang (Shanxi), and Longmen (Henan) preserve murals and sculptures recording the development of Buddhism and its art. The most important among the cave sites with murals, because of their scale, condition, and length of active production, are the Mogao caves near Dunhuang. Similar cave chapels have been excavated at smaller sites nearby, such as the Yulin caves and the caves at Xiqianfodong (Gansu). The Mogao cave chapels, sometimes referred to as the Thousand Buddha Caves, total about 600, more than 480 of which are decorated with murals painted on a clay ground that was applied to the stone walls of the chapel. Most also have painted clay sculptures, which, with the murals, create a vivid three-dimensional realm of sacred space. Paintings and sculptures at Dunhuang were commissioned as early as the fourth century and as late as the twentieth century, but the majority date from the Tang dynasty. Many have argued that, despite their provincial location, paintings at Dunhuang need to be placed in a metropolitan context and that they reflect the content and styles sponsored by the upper classes in major urban centers.[22] Thus, Dunhuang provides an excellent view of the development of the large-scale Chinese transformation tableaux of the *Lotus Sūtra*.

The Dunhuang cave temples originated as meditative spaces for monks modeled after Indian and central Asian prototypes. Soon, however, wealthy merchants, important local families, community leaders, and even groups of ordinary devotees began to sponsor the construction and decoration of cave temples for many of the same reasons that they sponsored sūtra copying. The donors commissioned works in order to gain merit for themselves and the immediate past seven generations of their families, secure protection against natural disasters and illness, request the birth of sons, pray for safe pregnancies, gain protection and prosperity of the nation, pacify the spirits of the dead, and express gratitude for benefits received.

Murals related to the *Lotus* at Dunhuang date from the sixth century, with the earliest, in Cave 285, dated 538–539. However, this painting of the two buddhas from the chapter on "The Apparition of the Jeweled Stūpa" does not function in a narrative way and is therefore discussed in the following section on emblematic paintings. The more comprehensive transformation tableaux of the *Lotus Sūtra* are found in at least seventy-five caves, ranging from the Sui dynasty (561–618) through the Song dynasty.

The *Lotus* murals of the Sui and early Tang (581–712) include illustrations from no more than four or five chapters. Sui murals are restricted to the sloped sides of the ceiling, while early Tang ones are generally placed along the upper walls. Cave 303, for example, displays only scenes from Chapter 25, and Cave 331 displays scenes from five chapters. In most, the apparition of the jeweled stūpa remains a prominent theme.

The Dunhuang *Lotus* tableaux from the High Tang reach a new level of skill and complexity. The murals present scenes from as many as fifteen different chapters. The episodes are often placed in landscape settings, which also function to separate the scenes. The painting is lively and colorful, and the narrative sense is increased. The north wall of Cave 23 portrays Chapter 5, "Medicinal Herbs," and shows rain falling not only on plants and trees but also on farmers cultivating their fields and shouldering bundles of grain, and on a farmer's family having a picnic on the banks between rice paddies. Below this is a visualization of Chapter 2, with figures playing music and children building sand stūpas (fig. 6.8). These scenes could easily be mistaken for a genre illustration of farmers celebrating a prosperous harvest. Depictions of Chapter 7, "Parable of the Conjured City," in Cave 217, and the perils described in Chapter 25, "Bodhisattva Sound Observer," in Cave 45, are particularly noteworthy for their integration of landscape and figures in narrative sequences. In the High Tang, artists transformed the realm of the scripture into scenes of a familiar world that created an intimate connection between the viewer and the painting.

By the middle and late Tang (766–907), the number of illustrations of *Lotus* chapters had increased, but the selections had become more conventionalized and thus more easily identifiable. Not surprisingly in these unsettled times of strife, there was an increase in the number of illustrations of the story from Chapter 14 of the king who rewards his soldiers with many goods, including a precious pearl from his topknot. These vignettes feature realistic details in the armor, weapons, and mounts of the soldiers. The military families who controlled Dunhuang in the ninth and tenth centuries (the Zhangs and Caos) were enthusiastic patrons, and it may be that military subjects reflected their interests and experiences. As other scholars have noted, they were particularly interested in scriptures stressing filial piety and retribution according to one's deeds.[23]

Also at this time, the compositions became standardized into three types. The first type places the Buddha and a large assembly of attendants and audience in the center and arranges narrative episodes from the stories

FIGURE 6.8 *Lotus Sūtra* tableau (Ja.: *hensō*): scenes from "Medicinal Herbs" (above) and "Expedient Devices" (below). Wall painting. Mid-eighth century (Tang dynasty). North wall, Mogao Cave 23, Dunhuang, Gansu, China.

FROM DUNHUANG YANJIUSUO, ED., *DUNHUANG MOGAOKU*, 5 VOLS., ZHONGGUO SHIKU (BEIJING: WENWU CHUBANSHE, 1982–1987), 3, PLATE 161.

of the *Lotus* around this preaching scene. Examples include Caves 138, 144, 154, 196, and 472. The second type divides the surface into upper and lower halves, with a composition similar to the first type in the upper half and a series of rectangular panels, like four hanging scrolls, in the bottom half. Often these four panels contain only scenes from Chapter 25, on Bodhisattva Sound Observer. Caves in this second category include 12, 159, 231, 232, and 237. The third type of composition presents a *Lotus* assembly of the Buddha preaching at the center and illustrations of the various chapters on four sides, but it places this array on the trapezoidal slopes of the ceiling, reminiscent of the placement common in Sui-dynasty cave temples. Examples include Caves 85 and 156.

Cave murals from the Five Dynasties (907–960) and Song periods continue with conventionalized scenes from the *Lotus*. They tend to use the rectangular, vertical compositions similar to hanging-scroll formats, sometimes with four panels on the upper half of the wall and four along the bottom half, as in Cave 76, while many others continue the first type of composition, as in Caves 4, 6, 61, 98, 108, 146, and 261. A new compositional arrangement can also be found, in which the preaching scene of the Buddha and his attendants is placed in the center of the mural, flanked on two sides by a large group of deities, as in Caves 55 and 454.

The general content of the cave murals near Dunhuang from the Sui to Song dynasties is summarized in the accompanying chart. The range of content and dates of the murals in just this one area attest to the popularity of representations of the *Lotus Sūtra* in China and to the continuing power of the *Lotus* to inspire devotees and artists.

PAINTINGS OF THE *LOTUS SŪTRA* AT DUNHUANG

CHAPTER	SUI (561–618)	EARLY TANG (618–713)	HIGH TANG (713–781)	MID TANG (781–848)	LATE TANG (848–907)	FIVE DYNASTIES (907–960)	SONG (960–1279)	TOTAL SCENES
1. INTRODUCTION	420	331, 335	23, 31, 74, 103, 217	154, 159, 231, 237, 432, 472	12, 85, 138, 144, 156, 196, 232, Y36	4, 6, 61, 98, 108, 146, 261	55, 76, 431, 449, 454	*34*
2. EXPEDIENT DEVICES	420		23, 103, 217	31, 154, 159, 231, 237, 472	12, 38, 85, 138, 144, 156, 196, 232, Y36	6, 61, 98	55, 449, 454	*25*

PAINTINGS OF THE *LOTUS SŪTRA* *(continued)*

CHAPTER	SUI (561–618)	EARLY TANG (618–713)	HIGH TANG (713–781)	MID TANG (781–848)	LATE TANG (848–907)	FIVE DYNASTIES (907–960)	SONG (960–1279)	TOTAL SCENES
3. PARABLE	419, 420		23,103, 217	154,159, 231, 237, 472	12, 85, 138, 144, 156, 196, 232, Y36	4, 6, 61, 98, 108, 146, 261, 396	55, 76, 431, 449, 454	*31*
4. BELIEF AND UNDER-STANDING			23, 217	159, 231, 237, 472	12, 85, 138, 144, 156, 196, 232, 459, Y36	4, 6, 61, 98, 108, 146, 261, 396	55, 76, 431, 449, 454	*28*
5. MEDI-CINAL HERBS			23	159, 231, 237	12, 85, 138, 468	6, 61, 98, 396	55, 76, 431, 449	*16*
6. BESTOW-AL OF PROPHECY				154, 231		146	76	*4*
7. PARABLE OF CONJURED CITY	419	202	23, 103, 217	31, 159, 231, 237	12, 85, 138, 144, 196	6, 61, 98, 108	55, 76, 431, 449	22
8. RECEIPT OF PROPH-ECY BY 500 DISCIPLES				154, 159, 231, 237	85, 144	61, 98, 108	55, 76, 98	*12*
9. PROPH-ECIES CON-FERRED ON LEARNERS AND ADEPTS					85	61, 146		*3*
10. PREACHERS OF DHARMA			23, 103	159	85			*4*
11. APPARI-TION OF JEWELED STŪPA	276, 277, 394, 420	68, 202, 331, 332, 335, 340, 341, 371, 431, 441	23, 27, 31, 45, 46, 48, 49, 208, 215, 217, 374, 444	31, 154, 159, 231, 237, 361	12, 14, 85, 138, 141, 144, 156, 196, 232, 468, Y36	6, 61, 98, 108, 146	55, 76, 368, 431, 449, 454	*54*
12. DEVA-DATTA		331, 335	23, 31, 103, 217	154, 159, 231, 237	12, 85, 138, 144, 156, 196, Y36	6, 61, 98, 108, 146	55, 76, 431, 449, 454	*27*

PAINTINGS OF THE *LOTUS SŪTRA* (continued)

CHAPTER	SUI (561–618)	EARLY TANG (618–713)	HIGH TANG (713–781)	MID TANG (781–848)	LATE TANG (848–907)	FIVE DYNASTIES (907–960)	SONG (960–1279)	TOTAL SCENES
13. FORTITUDE						61		*1*
14. COMFORTABLE CONDUCT			217	154, 159, 231, 237	12, 85, 138, 144, 154, 156, 196, Y36	6, 61, 98, 108, 146, 396	431, 449	*21*
15. WELLING UP OUT OF EARTH		31, 202, 331, 335	31	154, 159, 231, 237	12, 85, 138, 144, 154, 156, 196, Y36	6, 61, 98, 108, 146, 198	55, 76, 431, 449	*27*
16. LIFE SPAN OF THUS COME ONE				159, 231, 237	85, 156	6, 61, 98	449	*9*
17. DISCRIMINATION OF MERITS					85			*1*
18. MERITS OF APPROPRIATE JOY			31, 217	159		6, 61, 98, 146		*7*
19. MERITS OF DHARMA PREACHER					85			*1*
20. BODHISATTVA NEVER DISPARAGING				154, 159, 231, 237	12, 85, 144, 154, 156, Y36	6, 61, 108, 146	55, 76	*16*
21. SUPERNATURAL POWERS OF THUS COME ONE			23, 217		85		76	*4*
22. ENTRUSTMENT			23, 103, 217		85			*4*
23. FORMER AFFAIRS OF BODHISATTVA MEDICINE KING			23, 31, 103, 217	31, 154, 159, 231, 237	12, 85, 138, 144, 154, 156, 196, Y36	6, 61, 98, 146	55, 76	*23*
24. BODHISATTVA FINE SOUND		331		231	85	61, 108	76	*6*

PAINTINGS OF THE *LOTUS SŪTRA* (*continued*)

CHAPTER	SUI (561–618)	EARLY TANG (618–713)	HIGH TANG (713–781)	MID TANG (781–848)	LATE TANG (848–907)	FIVE DYNASTIES (907–960)	SONG (960–1279)	TOTAL SCENES
25. GATEWAY OF BODHISATTVA WHO OBSERVES SOUNDS OF WORLD	303, 420		23, 45, 74, 126, 205, 217, 444	7, 112, 185, 231, 361, 468, 472, X18	8, 12, 14, 18, 85, 128, 141, 156, 196, 232, 468, Y36	6, 61, 108, 128, 261, 288, 345	55, 76, 141, 368, 454, Y38	*42*
26. DHĀRAṆĪ				231	12, 85	61		*4*
27. FORMER AFFAIRS OF KING FINE ADORNMENT			23, 103, 217	231, 237	12, 85, 156, 196, Y36	6, 61, 98, 108, 146	431	*16*
28. ENCOURAGEMENTS OF BODHISATTVA UNIVERSALLY WORTHY		331	23, 31, 103, 217	231	12, 85	6, 61		*10*

Numbers refer to cave temples at three sites near Dunhuang: Mogao caves (e.g., 420), Yulin caves (e.g., Y36), and Xiqianfo caves (e.g., X18). Identification of specific chapters are tentative, based on the tables in Shi Pingting and He Shizhe, "Dunhuang bihuazhong de *Fahua jing* bian chutan," in *Dunhuang Mogaoku*, Dunhuang shiku, 5 vols., ed. Dunhuang wenwu yanjiusuo (Beijing: Wenwu chubanshe, 1982–1987), 3:191; and He Shizhe, ed., *Fahua jing huajuan*, Dunhuang shiku quanji 7 (Hong Kong: Shangwu yinshuguan, 1999), 250.

I thank Jimmy Yu (Department of Religion, Florida State University) for his help in compiling and checking several references in this table.

Japanese artists also produced transformation tableaux of the *Lotus*, usually on hanging scrolls or as murals in temples. These works were public as opposed to the more private format of hand scrolls. Like the *Lotus* transformation tableaux in China, the Japanese compositions often included preaching scenes with the Buddha, attendants, and audience, and they arranged episodes from individual chapters in horizontal registers or in a circular pattern around the preaching scene. The works were sometimes used as the main image for the temple, but they also served a didactic purpose and generally contained cartouches with brief excerpts from the text or titles of the chapters to assist in identification.

Among the Japanese transformation paintings, one of the earliest is the hanging scroll known as the *Fundamental Maṇḍala of the Lotus Hall*

(*Hokkedō konpon mandara*), originally belonging to the *Lotus* Hall of Tōdaiji. This painting was produced in 746 for a *Lotus* convocation at Tōdaiji. Although it is in poor condition, one can see that it reflects a Tang painting and compositional style featuring Śākyamuni preaching to an assembly at Vulture Peak amid a detailed landscape. Pavilions, visible at the upper left, represent an unidentified element from the text. While the bottom is damaged, scholars speculate that additional illustrations appeared there. Another single hanging scroll on silk and in colors, from Kaijūsenji, selects scenes from only three chapters: a preaching scene and hell scenes from Chapter 1, two scenes from the chapter on the "Apparition of the Jeweled Stūpa," and one illustration of the bodhisattvas from underground from Chapter 15. In both painting style and the restricted number of illustrations, the Kaijūsenji work retains traces of the Heian style.[24]

More typical of the Japanese transformation tableaux of the twelfth through fourteenth centuries are sets of hanging scrolls or murals that comprised such a large number of episodes that a professional narrator was sometimes used to explain them. Examples include: (1) eight wall paintings in the pagoda of Saimyōji (one per fascicle); (2) a set of seven hanging scrolls in color on silk (one scroll has illustrations from two fascicles), now at the Nara National Museum; (3) a set of four hanging scrolls, dated 1335, in color on silk from Honkōji (two fascicles per scroll); and (4) a set of twenty-two scrolls in colors on silk, with nearly one scroll for each chapter, from Honpōji, dated 1326–1328.

While these works exhibit many differences, they also share some common features, particularly in the choice of subject matter. They include, for example, a large number of scenes used in frontispieces, but these episodes are more narrative and detailed. Second, they include new representations previously unseen in Japanese illustrations of the *Lotus*. The Honkōji scrolls, for example, include a scene of the ten daughters of rākṣasas about to attack men weighing rice with false measures, as mentioned in Chapter 26, and the Honpōji scrolls include the thirty-three transformations of the bodhisattva Sound Observer and the fulfillment of the prophecy to Śāriputra that he would become a buddha. Several of these works also include stories not found in the *Lotus Sūtra* itself. The Honpōji scrolls, for example, feature an incident in the life of the disciple Maudgalyāyana; the work in the Nara National Museum depicts the birth of the Buddha and his anointment by dragons; and the Honkōji set includes incidents from the life of Śākyamuni's son and a jātaka tale. Finally, it should be noted that, as in the jeweled stūpa maṇḍalas, all the transformation paintings in Japan emphasize illustrations of the six paths of transmigration, particularly the hells.[25] The Honpōji set places most of these scenes along the bottom edge of the scroll; this arrangement follows Buddhist cosmology and allows viewers to see more easily the paintings' gruesome but enthralling details.[26]

Lotus transformation tableaux from China and Japan tend to be encyclopedic in their coverage, but another group of transformation paintings focus on a single bodhisattva or a limited number of deities. These works are perhaps best represented by paintings of the bodhisattvas Sound Observer and Universally Worthy. Chapter 25 of the *Lotus* was so popular that it was often copied independently and treated as a separate scripture, entitled *The Sūtra on Sound Observer*, particularly in China. Indeed, paintings of this bodhisattva are ubiquitous among Dunhuang wall paintings and banner paintings. The Dunhuang murals, such as in Cave 45, and hanging scrolls generally place Bodhisattva Sound Observer in the center, flanked by a series of perils such as a man falling from a cliff or being thrown into a pit of fire, while portraits of donors are pictured below the main scenes. The narrative episodes are generally accompanied by cartouches with brief excerpts from the text. Many date from the tenth century, attesting to this bodhisattva's continued popularity after the Tang period. An excellent example, in the Fogg Art Museum, has an eleven-headed, six-armed Bodhisattva Sound Observer, who holds a sun, moon, rosary, and lasso in four of his six arms and is flanked by an abbreviated version of the perils. At the bottom are pictures of a donor and a Thousand-Armed Bodhisattva Sound Observer.[27] The figure dominates the vignettes and clearly is the focus of the painting.

In Japan, one of the most popular deities from the *Lotus* was Bodhisattva Universally Worthy (Samantabhadra), the focus of Chapter 28 and the closing sūtra, who was considered a protector to all who receive and honor the *Lotus Sūtra*. In frontispieces, he usually appears before a reclusive monk in a cave. In hanging-scroll paintings, he appears both alone and together with the ten female demons, who, in Chapter 26, "Dhāraṇī," pledge to protect the devotees of the *Lotus*.[28] Paintings of the bodhisattva Universally Worthy and the ten female demons are attested in records from the mid-twelfth century; the earliest extant version is a late twelfth-century hanging scroll at Rozanji. At times the female demons and Bodhisattva Universally Worthy are joined by two additional bodhisattvas, two guardian kings, and young boys holding a banner. Universally Worthy always sits atop a six-tusked elephant, while the ten demonesses are painted sometimes in Chinese court costumes and in some works appear as long-haired beauties in Japanese court robes. The possibility of women becoming buddhas is expounded in Chapter 12, "Devadatta," and the large number of images of Bodhisattva Universally Worthy and the ten female demons, who could protect all beings without discrimination, may have reflected the aristocratic sponsors' desire to emphasize the value of women. The many paintings of Bodhisattva Sound Observer, Bodhisattva Universally Worthy, and the ten female demons shift the emphasis from comprehensive narration to specific images for worship, reflecting the impact of deity cults.

IMAGES AS EMBLEMS OF THE ENTIRE TEXT

Images from the *Lotus* do not, of course, always function as didactic illustrations or narratives of the text. Rather, the images can be symbolic or emblematic of the scripture as a whole. Works that represent the scripture as a whole without a sense of specific narrative and that clearly belong to this category include esoteric maṇḍalas. Such cosmograms are characterized by the diagrammatic arrangement of their subject matter and were used chiefly by the Shingon and Tendai schools. The *Lotus* maṇḍalas were the main images in the *Lotus Sūtra* ritual (*Hokke hō*), an esoteric rite that was based on instruction manuals brought back to Japan from China as early as 847.[29] *Lotus* maṇḍalas arranged deities (or Sanskrit letters representing deities) in three concentric squares. In the innermost one, the buddhas Many Jewels and Śākyamuni sit in the center of an eight-petaled lotus, upon which sit the eight great bodhisattvas, while the four great disciples sit at the four corners of the inner square. In the middle square are sixteen bodhisattvas, and the outermost square contains the four guardian kings, the eight classes of beings, and the four great kings of knowledge (*vidyārājas*). Like most esoteric maṇḍalas, this presents a hierarchical diagram of deities symbolizing doctrinal ideas rather than narrating the scripture's stories.

The most popular image associated with the *Lotus Sūtra* in China prior to the seventh century was that of the two buddhas, Many Jewels and Śākyamuni, from Chapter 11, "Apparition of the Jeweled Stūpa." The earliest extant mural (ca. 420) appears at Binglingsi in Cave 169; it was sponsored by a group of monks, one of whom was a student of Kumārajīva. The two buddhas are surrounded by images of the one thousand buddhas, and the inscription makes clear that these represent the magically conjured buddhas who were emanations of Śākyamuni (Hurvitz, 169–70).

FIGURE 6.9 *Śākyamuni and Prabhūtaratna (Many Jewels).* Bronze sculpture, 4⅞ x 2¼ x 1⅛ in. (12.4 x 5.7 x 2.9 cm.). Chinese, Northern Wei dynasty.

THE NELSON-ATKINS MUSEUM OF ART, KANSAS CITY, MISSOURI. PURCHASE, NELSON TRUST, 45–29. PHOTOGRAPH BY JAMISON MILLER.

More ubiquitous, however, are the sculpted images of the two buddhas in the early cave chapels, such as those in Cave 80 at Maijishan, Caves 6 and 22 at Yungang, and Niche 130 of the Guyang Cave at Longmen. The sculpted images of the two buddhas may be surrounded by the thousand buddha images, but, more important, they often place Maitreya Buddha above or to their side. The real point of this group of buddhas, representing the past (Many Jewels), present (Śākyamuni), and future (Maitreya), is to symbolize the eternal presence of the Buddha and the idea of the unity of all time and all realms. As Eugene Wang has noted, "Different time frames and spatial realms . . . were compressed into one [seamless] continuum."[30] More than mere illustration, this grouping summarizes one of the most important points of the scripture and as such signifies the profundity of the whole text.

With some notable exceptions, sculpture tended to be used as an emblem, not didactic illustration, of scripture. The exceptions include stone stelae, which are particularly versatile because one side can have an emblematic representation of deities (the two buddhas, for example) while the reverse side can hold vignettes of specific chapters. A fragmentary stele dated 425 from Wanfosi, in Chengdu (Sichuan), with detailed depictions of the perils and images of the various manifestations of Bodhisattva Sound Observer, is claimed to be the first extant representation of Chapter 25 of the *Lotus*.[31] However, freestanding works such as the famous cast bronze of the two buddhas (dated 518) in the Musée Guimet (similar in subject to the Nelson-Atkins statue reproduced in fig. 6.9) or Śākyamuni triads with Bodhisattva Universally Worthy on an elephant and Bodhisattva Mañjuśrī atop a lion are all inspired by the *Lotus Sūtra*. These independent works spur devotion to the *Lotus* more than they expound its contents.

This brief overview of art associated with the *Lotus Sūtra* makes clear that East Asian Buddhists went far beyond the sūtra's simple exhortation to draw images with fingernails and pile up sand stūpas. Buddhists in China, Korea, and Japan developed a range of genres, styles, materials, and thematic treatments to fulfill the sūtra's call to preserve, protect, and expound the scripture. Devotees understood the scripture variously as a text to be read for meaning, as a powerful talisman for protection against misfortune, as narrative illustration, and as symbolic idea. As they gave form to their understandings using strands of silk, ink, pigment, lacquer, metal, clay, stone, and even pebbles, they fulfilled the proclamation of the *Lotus* itself that it was the king of all sūtras.

NOTES

1. Originally translated in twenty-seven chapters written in seven scrolls or fascicles, Kumārajīva's work was modified by the early seventh century with the addition of the Devadatta chapter, bringing the total to twenty-eight chapters, which were divided into seven or eight fascicles.
2. William H. McCullough and Helen Craig McCullough, trans., *A Tale of Flowering Fortunes*, 2 vols. (Stanford, Calif.: Stanford University Press, 1980), 2:505; Willa J. Tanabe, *Paintings of the Lotus Sutra* (New York: Weatherhill, 1988), 40–43.
3. Ōyama Ninkai, ed., *Shakyō, Nihon no bijutsu*, no. 156 (Tokyo: Shibundō, 1979), 22–25; Edwin O. Reischauer, trans., *Ennin's Diary: The Record of a Pilgrimage to China in Search of the Law* (New York: Ronald Press, 1955), 254.
4. Youngsook Pak, "The Korean Art Collection in the Metropolitan Museum of Art," in *Arts of Korea*, ed. Judith G. Smith (New York: Metropolitan Museum of Art, 1998), 437.
5. Donald E. Gjertson, "The Lotus Sutra and Popular Faith in Medieval China" (unpublished paper, University of Massachusetts, Amherst, n.d. [ca. 1966]), 15.
6. Eugene Y. Wang, *Shaping the Lotus Sutra: Buddhist Visual Culture in Medieval China* (Seattle: University of Washington Press, 2005), 124.
7. Miyeko Murase, "Kuan-Yin as Savior of Men: Illustration of the Twenty-fifth Chapter of the Lotus Sūtra in Chinese Painting," *Artibus Asiae* 331, no. 2 (1971): 39.
8. Tanabe, *Paintings of the Lotus Sutra*, 37.
9. The *Sūtra of Immeasurable Meanings* (*Wuliangyi jing, Taishō shinshū daizōkyō*, 100 vols., ed. Takakusu Junjirō, Watanabe Kaigyoku, and Ono Gemmyō [1924–1934; repr., Taibei: Xinwenfeng chuban gongsi, 1974] [hereafter abbreviated as *T*], no. 276, trans. Dharmāgatayaśas [Tanmoqietuoyeshe, ca. 481]) came to be regarded as the introductory sūtra to the *Lotus*, and the *Sūtra on the Method of Contemplating Bodhisattva Universally Worthy* [*Samantabhadra*] (*Guan Puxian pusa xingfa jing*, *T* no. 277, trans. Dharmamitra [Tanwumiduo, 356–442]), as its concluding sūtra. Together they make up the "threefold *Lotus Sūtra*." No Sanskrit version is extant for either the introductory or the concluding sūtra, and the circumstances of their compilation remain unclear.
10. For recent research on the practice of the burial of scriptures, see D. Max Moerman, "The Archaeology of Anxiety: An Underground History of Late Heian Religion," in *Heian Japan: Centers and Peripheries*, ed. Mikael Adolphson, Edward Kamens, and Stacie Yamamoto, 245–71 (Honolulu: University of Hawai'i Press, 2007).
11. For examples of stones and tiles from sūtra burials, see Nara kokuritsu hakubutsukan, ed., *Hokekyō no bijutsu* (Nara: Nara kokuritsu hakubutsukan, 1979), 200–202.
12. Kōsen Nishiyama and John Stevens, trans., *A Complete English Translation of Dōgen Zenji's Shōbōgenzō (The Eye and Treasury of the True Law)*, 4 vols. (Sendai: Daihokkaikaku, 1975–1983), 1:122.
13. See discussion of examples in Tanabe, *Paintings of the Lotus Sutra*, 56; and, more generally, John Kieschnick, "Blood Writing in Chinese Buddhism," *Journal of the International Association of Buddhist Studies* 23, no. 2 (2000): 177–94.
14. For information on gold and silver sūtras of the Koryŏ period, see Judith G. Smith, ed., *Arts of Korea* (New York: Metropolitan Museum of Art, 1998), 172–73, 436–39.

See also Ōyama, *Shakyō*, 27–29; and Youngsook Pak, "Illuminated Buddhist Manuscripts in Korea," *Oriental Art* 33, no. 4 (winter 1987–88): 357–74.

15. For illustrations of the *Kunōji Lotus Sūtra* and the *Heike nōkyō*, see Kurata Bunsaku and Tamura Yoshirō, eds., *Hokekyō no bijutsu* (Tokyo: Kōsei shuppansha, 1981), plate 83, plates 48–53, respectively.
16. For the development of *Lotus*-related poetry in Japan, see Shōzen Yamada, "Poetry and Meaning: Medieval Poets and the *Lotus Sutra*," in *The Lotus Sutra in Japanese Culture*, ed. George J. Tanabe Jr. and Willa Jane Tanabe, 95–118 (Honolulu: University of Hawai'i Press, 1989).
17. *Chōshū eisō*, Fujiwara Shunzei (Tokyo: Koten bunko, 1994), 79. Joshua Mostow omits the final *no* in the second line in his excellent discussion of the poem-pictures, as does Shirahata Yoshi (Joshua S. Mostow, "Painted Poems, Forgotten Words: Poem-Pictures and Classical Japanese Literature," *Monumenta Nipponica* 47, no. 3 [autumn 1992]: 323–46; Shirahata Yoshi, *Yamoto e* [Kyoto: Kawahara shoten, 1967], 129–31). The word *tree* in the third line was probably pronounced "ko" in classical Japanese rather than, in the modern pronunciation, "ki."
18. For discussion of poem-paintings and frontispieces, see Tanabe, *Paintings of the Lotus Sutra*, 66–73; Julia Meech-Pekarik, "Disguised Scripts and Hidden Poems in an Illustrated Heian Sutra: *Ashide-e* and *Uta-e* in the Heike Nōgyō," *Archives of Asian Art* 31 (1977): 52–75; and William R. LaFleur, *The Karma of Words: Buddhism and the Literary Arts in Medieval Japan* (Los Angeles: University of California Press, 1983), 94–95.
19. Julia Meech-Pekarik, "The Flying White Horse: Transmission of the Valāhasa Jātaka Imagery from India to Japan," *Artibus Asiae* 431, no. 2 (1981–82): 111–28.
20. Miyeko Murase, *Bridge of Dreams: The Mary Griggs Burke Collection of Japanese Art* (New York: Metropolitan Museum of Art, 2000), 274–75.
21. Wang, *Shaping the Lotus Sutra*, 74–75; Hung Wu, "What Is *Bianxiang*?—On the Relationship between Dunhuang Art and Dunhuang Literature," *Harvard Journal of Asiatic Studies* 52, no. 1 (June 1992): 111–92.
22. Wang, *Shaping the Lotus Sutra*, 122.
23. Marsha Weidner, ed., *Latter Days of the Law: Images of Chinese Buddhism 850–1850* (Lawrence: Spencer Museum of Art, University of Kansas, 1994), 132–33.
24. Bunsaku Kurata and Yoshirō Tamura, eds., *Art of the Lotus Sutra: Japanese Masterpieces*, trans. Edna B. Crawford (Tokyo: Kōsei, 1987), plates 23 and 24.
25. Representations of the six paths of transmigration greatly increased after the appearance, in 985, of Genshin's *Essentials for Rebirth in the Pure Land* (*Ōjō yōshū*), which described the six paths in great detail. This work was of critical importance to the development of beliefs about paradise. Hōnen (1133–1212), for example, wrote four commentaries on it. Although images of the six paths increased with the development of the Pure Land school, Genshin's vivid descriptions, especially of hells, informed many late Heian and Kamakura paintings regardless of the sectarian alliances of the patrons.
26. For more detailed discussion, see Tsugio Miya, "Pictorial Art of the *Lotus Sutra* in Japan," in Tanabe and Tanabe, *The Lotus Sutra in Japanese Culture*, 81–86.
27. For further discussion of Chinese works, see Murase, "Kuan-Yin as Savior of Men," 39–74.
28. Nicole Fabricand-Person, "Demonic Female Guardians of the Faith: The *Fugen Jūrasetsunyo* Iconography in Japanese Buddhist Art," in *Engendering Faith: Women*

and Buddhism in Premodern Japan, ed. Barbara Ruch, 343–82 (Ann Arbor: Center for Japanese Studies, University of Michigan, 2002); Fabricand-Person, "Filling the Void: The *Fugen Jūrasetsunyo* Iconography in Japanese Buddhist Art" (Ph.D. diss., Princeton University, 2001).

29. For more on this ritual, see Lucia Dora Dolce, "Esoteric Patterns in Nichiren's Interpretation of the Lotus Sutra" (Ph.D. diss., University of Leiden, 2002), 215–84.
30. Wang, *Shaping the Lotus Sutra*, 55.
31. Ibid., 219–25.

[7]

BODILY READING OF THE *LOTUS SŪTRA*

Ruben L. F. Habito

ONE OF THE most influential scriptures in East Asian history, the *Lotus Sūtra* has been received and read in different ways by Buddhist followers through the ages. This essay focuses on "bodily reading of the *Lotus*" (*Hokke shikidoku*), a term associated with the life and teachings of the thirteenth-century Japanese Buddhist prophet Nichiren (1222–1282).[1] In the opening section, I present a rough sketch of how the *Lotus Sūtra* was received, read, and regarded in Buddhist history as a scripture imbued with both spiritual and worldly powers.[2] In the next two sections, I lay out the philosophical and religious underpinnings of Nichiren's way of reading the *Lotus*, gleaned from his own writings, and consider some of its hermeneutical implications. In conclusion, I look at some modern Japanese Buddhists influenced by Nichiren and analyze briefly how their own readings of the sūtra framed their self-understanding and worldview.

THE POWER OF THE BOOK

An underlying theme of the *Lotus Sūtra*, beginning with Chapter 10, concerns upholding and propagating the sūtra as the direct way to supreme, perfect enlightenment (Skt.: *anuttarasamyaksaṃbodhi*). This teaching played a key role in Nichiren's doctrine, which focuses on the *Lotus Sūtra*'s salvific power, accessed by individuals through the recitation of its title (Ja.: *daimoku*).

Chapter 10 of the *Lotus*, "Preachers of Dharma," signals a shift away from a motif appearing in the first nine chapters, in which venerating stūpas containing the Buddha's relics is enumerated as one of the forms of practice leading to enlightenment. For example, Chapter 2, "Expedient Devices," says, "When the buddhas have passed into extinction, / Persons who make offerings to their *śarīras* [bodily relics], / Shall erect myriads of millions of kinds of *stūpas* [reliquary structures] / . . . Persons like these / Have all achieved the buddha path" (Hurvitz, 36). But from Chapter 10 on, the *Lotus Sūtra* itself is equated with the body of the Tathāgata and presented as an object of veneration in its own right. For example, among several passages in this chapter referring to the sūtra's reception and propagation, we read:

> If a good man or good woman shall receive and keep, read and recite, explain, or copy in writing a single phrase of the *Scripture of the Dharma Blossom*, or otherwise and in a variety of ways make offerings to the scriptural roll with flower perfume, necklaces, powdered incense, perfumed paste, burnt incense, silk banners and canopies, garments, or music, or join palms in reverent worship, that person is to be looked up to and exalted by all the worlds, showered with offerings fit for a Thus Come One. Let it be known that that person is a great bodhisattva who, having achieved anuttarasamyaksaṃbodhi, taken pity on the living beings, and vowed to be reborn here, is preaching the *Scripture of the Blossom of the Fine Dharma* with breadth and discrimination.
>
> (HURVITZ, 160)

Several other passages enumerate these meritorious acts (keeping the sūtra, reading it, expounding it, and so forth) destining the practitioner to supreme, perfect enlightenment, and they, too, emphasize the same underlying attitude of devoted reception and readiness to proclaim the *Lotus Sūtra*'s teaching.[3]

Such devoted reception of the *Lotus Sūtra*, leading to its proclamation and exposition, calls forth the very presence of the Buddha himself in bodily form:

> Wherever it may be preached, or read, or recited, or written, or whatever place a roll of this scripture may occupy, in all those places one is to erect a stūpa of the seven jewels, building it high and wide and with impressive decoration. There is no need even to lodge śarīras in it. What is the reason? Within it there is already a whole body of the Thus Come One. This stūpa is to be showered with offerings, humbly venerated, held in solemn esteem, and praised with all manner of flowers, scents, necklaces, silk banners and canopies, music skillfully sung and played. If there are persons who can see this stūpa and worship and make offerings to it, be it known that these persons are all close to anuttarasamyaksaṃbodhi.
>
> (HURVITZ, 163)

The significant point to note here is the identification of the sūtra's physical scrolls with the body of the Tathāgata (Thus Come One), deserving the very same reverence and veneration. Through such veneration of the sūtra text, manifested in the meritorious acts this passage enumerates, the devotee is destined to realize supreme, perfect enlightenment. The key phrase "no need even to lodge śarīras in it" marks the transition from the first part of the *Lotus,* which includes veneration of the Buddha's relics as a way to enlightenment, to the second part, which emphasizes instead the importance of upholding the sūtra and expounding it on behalf of others as the cause for enlightenment. In short, it is now the physical text of the *Lotus Sūtra* that is venerated, on the same level as the relics of the Tathāgata, and considered as no less—or perhaps even more—soteriologically efficacious.[4]

The underlying attitude prescribed in the series of meritorious acts directed toward the sūtra (including reading it) is one of accepting and upholding it with reverence and devotion. It is the devoted reception of the *Lotus*, upholding it as the beacon and guide of one's life and religious practice, that ensures achieving supreme, perfect enlightenment. And this devoted acceptance is inseparable from the readiness to proclaim its teaching to all, so that they may also accept it and attain enlightenment themselves.

Thus, in the *Lotus* itself, reading the sūtra is to be understood in terms of this total attitude of devoted reception and willingness to offer oneself for its propagation. This attitude of upholding (Skt.: *dhāraṇā*) scriptures as the efficient cause for attaining supreme enlightenment is also taught in the Mahāyāna Perfection of Wisdom (*prajñāpāramitā*) literature. Some sūtras in this group are thought to have been composed earlier than the *Lotus* and may well have influenced it in this regard. Certain passages in the *Eight Thousand Verse Prajñāpāramitā Sūtra* on the merits of upholding and reading the sūtra in fact closely resemble those in the *Lotus*.[5] Through the centuries in East Asia, however, the Perfection of Wisdom sūtras have not been as popular as the *Lotus* as a focus of devotion and veneration.[6]

In sūtras such as these, upholding a scriptural text—that is, accepting it with devotion and reverence—is said not only to ensure one's realization of supreme, perfect enlightenment but also to yield various kinds of merit and worldly benefit. This view opens the way to a significant line of development regarding the reading of sūtras. I refer here to the practice of reciting *dhāraṇīs* (incantations), a practice that flowered later, especially in the context of esoteric Buddhism.

Chapter 21 of the Sanskrit *Lotus Sūtra* (Chapter 26 in Kumārajīva's Chinese version) deals with various dhāraṇīs, whose recitation is considered efficacious for achieving different kinds of worldly benefit. These benefits include the prevention or cure of illnesses, protection from dangers and calamities, and so on. Some scholars consider this chapter, as well as other passages including references to dhāraṇīs, to be a later addition to the text. Be that as it may, the significant point in this chapter is that the protection from various calamities ensured by reciting the dhāraṇīs is bestowed on those practitioners who maintain an attitude of upholding the sūtra.[7] The connection underscored here by the common linguistic root between "upholding" the sūtra (dhāraṇā) and "incantatory phrases" imbued with spiritual power (dhāraṇīs) would figure prominently in Nichiren's understanding of the power of chanting the daimoku of the *Lotus Sūtra*.

We also find a tradition, especially prominent in East Asian Buddhism, of reading and reciting sūtras, a practice deemed particularly effective in transferring merit to the deceased, as well as bringing about worldly benefit for the reader or reciter and for those to whom he or she wishes to transfer the merits of this practice.[8] Reading and reciting the *Lotus Sūtra* were widely conducted as popular devotional practices in China, Korea, and Japan, for example, in association with the cult of the bodhisattva Guanyin (Korean: Kwan Um, Ja.: Kannon). Worship of Guanyin was also expressed in chanting the "great compassion dhāraṇī" (Ch.: *dabei zhou* or *dabei xin tuoloni*), which was said to confer various kinds of worldly benefit on the reciter.[9]

One indicator of how the *Lotus Sūtra* was received and read is the eleventh-century Japanese tale collection *Miraculous Tales of the Lotus Sūtra from Japan* (*Dainihonkoku Hokekyō kenki*, or simply *Hokke genki*). Many of these stories center on the practice of *Lotus Sūtra* recitation as conducted by holy ascetics (Ja.: *hijiri*). These are individuals who have withdrawn from the mainstream of society as well as from established Buddhist institutions and who endeavor to live the teaching of the *Lotus*. The stories in this collection relate wondrous episodes of healing, superhuman acts of valor, and other kinds of miraculous phenomena that occur for the benefit of individuals in situations of distress or need—all attributed to the power of the *Lotus Sūtra* as mediated by the devoted ascetic, who has accumulated untold merit through his sūtra recitation.[10]

When Nichiren came upon the scene in thirteenth-century Japan, there was thus already a well-established tradition of special reverence for the *Lotus* as a religious icon endowed with power, capable of dispensing spiritual and worldly benefits to devotees who follow its prescribed practices of upholding, reading, reciting, expounding, and copying the sūtra text.[11] For Nichiren, reciting the title of the sūtra (*Myōhō renge kyō,* the title as translated by Kumārajīva in its Japanese pronunciation) encompassed all these practices. In Nichiren's teaching, chanting the title assumes a twofold efficacy: it ensures both the attainment of perfect enlightenment and also protection from harm as well as other kinds of worldly benefit. Nichiren's emphasis on the practice of reciting the sūtra's title, which he developed over the course of his career, brings together the *Lotus Sūtra*'s own teaching on upholding the sūtra as the path of attaining enlightenment and well-established thinking concerning the power of incantatory phrases (dhāraṇī) to bring about worldly benefit. Nichiren was heir both to the popular tradition, found across social levels, that regards the *Lotus* as a sacred object imbued with miraculous and salvific powers, and to the intellectual tradition of *Lotus*-based metaphysics as expounded by Tiantai masters in China and continued in the Japanese Tendai school by Saichō (766 or 767–822) and his successors at the Tendai center on Mount Hiei. In short, Nichiren united the traditions of devotional practice and theoretical speculation centered on the sūtra in an integrated vision grounded in religious praxis. His "bodily reading" of the *Lotus* opens the horizon of his comprehensive religious vision of the universe, as laid out in his teaching on the "three thousand realms in a single thought-moment" (*ichinen sanzen*).[12]

NICHIREN'S RELIGIOUS VISION AND BODILY READING OF THE *LOTUS SŪTRA*

One of Nichiren's early treatises, *On Protecting the Country* (*Shugo kokka ron*), written in 1259, sets forth a systematic account of his religious project: propagating faith in the *Lotus Sūtra* as the only effective way for ensuring the protection of the land and the salvation of the people. Nichiren composed this treatise after more than twenty years of spiritual pursuit that involved sojourns for study at the great Tendai monastery on Mount Hiei as well as other major religious centers of the period, where he had pored over sūtras and commentaries. His central purpose in this quest was to determine which among the many Buddhist scriptures and schools of Buddhist thought handed down through China and Korea to Japan represented Śākyamuni's supreme teaching.

The following passage from *On Protecting the Country* offers us an initial insight into how Nichiren understood the practice of reading the *Lotus Sūtra*:

> The Great Teacher Miaole [Zhanran] writes: "If foolish and ignorant persons of the latter age practice the *Lotus Sūtra*, they will behold the bodhisattva Universally Worthy (Skt.: Samantabhadra), as well as the buddha Many Jewels (Prabhūtaratna) and the buddhas of the ten directions," thus proclaiming that [the *Lotus*] represents the easy path. He also says, "Even with a dispersed mind, without entering into *samādhi* [concentration], one should recite the *Lotus Sūtra*, and, whether sitting, standing, or walking, one should single-mindedly keep the words of the *Lotus Sūtra* in mind." The point of this commentarial passage is that [the *Lotus*] was intended to save the foolish and ignorant persons of the final age [of the dharma]. "Dispersed mind" is the opposite of "mind in samādhi." To "recite the *Lotus Sūtra*" refers to one who reads and recites the eight scrolls, or one scroll, or one letter, or one stanza, or one verse, or its title [daimoku], or to one in whom arises a single moment of rejoicing [at hearing even one verse of the sūtra], up to the fiftieth person in succession. "Sitting, standing, or walking" means that one does not discriminate among the four postures. "Single-mindedly" refers neither to the mind of samādhi nor to the mind as universal principle, but to the single thought of a mind ordinarily dispersed in everyday life. To keep the "words of the *Lotus Sūtra* in mind" means that the words of this sūtra are different from those of all other sūtras. Even if one reads only a single character, the eighty thousand treasure chambers of characters [that compose the Buddha's teachings] are thereby included, as are the merits of all buddhas.[13]

Elsewhere in the same treatise, Nichiren affirms the idea that "practicing the *Lotus*" in and of itself is "beholding the Buddha." Citing Chapter 28, on the bodhisattva Universally Worthy, he says: "Again, it is written, 'If there is anyone who can receive and keep, read and recite, recall properly, cultivate and practice, and copy this *Lotus Sūtra*, know that such a person has seen Śākyamuni Buddha, that he might have heard this sūtra preached from the Buddha's very mouth. Let it be known that such a person has made offerings to Śākyamuni Buddha.' According to this passage, the *Lotus Sūtra* and Śākyamuni Buddha are one and the same."[14]

This, then, is the first point we can note about Nichiren's understanding of reading the *Lotus Sūtra*: to do so is no less than to be placed in the presence of Śākyamuni Buddha, the World-Honored One. In other words, the *Lotus Sūtra* was, for Nichiren, the very embodiment of Śākyamuni himself, meriting the same homage and devotion. To read the *Lotus Sūtra*, then, is not simply to peruse the words of the text in order to understand what meaning is conveyed, but rather to engage oneself in an entire cycle of acts that issue from the fundamental attitude of receiving and keeping the sūtra, including reciting, copying, expounding it to others, doing homage to it with offerings of flowers and incense, and so on.[15] To uphold the *Lotus Sūtra* is, by that very act, to receive and keep Śākyamuni Buddha himself in one's heart and being.

It is significant that the Śākyamuni Buddha referred to here is not the historical Gautama but rather the Awakened One who occupies a realm beyond history—that is, the primordial buddha revealed in Chapter 16 of the *Lotus*, "Life Span of the Thus Come One," who chooses to reenter history and engage in human events in order to save living beings from their state of misery and dissatisfaction. He is the constantly abiding Śākyamuni, the father of the world, who, as depicted in Chapter 3 of the sūtra, beholds his children trapped in a burning house and offers all kinds of expedient devices to free them.

A second vital point in Nichiren's understanding of the practice of reading the *Lotus* is his assertion that reading even one word of the sūtra is equivalent to reading the contents of the "eighty thousand treasure chambers" that make up the entirety of the Buddha's teachings and includes the merits of all buddhas. In affirming this, Nichiren simply draws on the teaching of the *Lotus* itself, which, as we have seen, asserts that the sūtra text is equal to the Buddha himself. Nichiren's exposition of the character *myō* (Ch.: *miao*, "fine" or "wondrous") in *Myōhō renge kyō*, the five-character title of the sūtra in Kumārajīva's translation, develops the sūtra's teaching on this point: "The character *myō* derives from *sad* in the language of India and is rendered *miao* in Chinese. *Myō* means 'endowed,' and 'endowed' has the meaning of 'complete and perfect.' Every character of the *Lotus Sūtra*, each single one, contains within it all the other 69,384 characters that compose the sūtra, just as one drop of water from the great ocean contains water from all rivers [that flow into the ocean], or as a single wish-fulfilling jewel, though only the size of a mustard seed, can shower on one all the treasures of all wish-fulfilling jewels."[16]

This notion that "one contains all" derives from Mahāyāna tradition; it is expounded, for example, in the *Flower Garland* (Skt.: *Avataṃsaka*) *Sūtra* and was developed in different ways by Chinese and Korean Buddhist commentators. One significant exposition of this idea is the Tiantai master Zhiyi's (538–597) concept of "three thousand realms in a single thought-moment" (Ch.: *yinian sanqian*, Ja.: *ichinen sanzen*), which Nichiren adopted as the central feature of his own religious understanding of reality. Nichiren refers specifically to this notion of "three thousand realms in a single thought-moment" in many of his writings, most famously in his major treatise *On the Contemplation of the Mind and the Object of Worship (Kanjin honzon shō*), a work that he himself described as addressing "the sole important matter in my life."[17] For Nichiren, the principle of ichinen sanzen was the basis for the teaching that all sentient beings have the potential for buddhahood. He describes this principle as "the father and mother of all buddhas" and the "seed of buddhahood."[18] For Nichiren, this seed of buddhahood was not merely an abstract principle but assumed concrete form in the practice of chanting the daimoku, being equated in his thought with the five characters of the sūtra's title. Nichiren writes, "Manifesting great compassion for those who do not know this three thousand realms in a single thought-moment, the Buddha wrapped up this gem in a five-character phrase, which he placed around the necks of the childish beings of the latter age."[19]

Reciting the five-character phrase *Myōhō renge kyō*—preceded by *Namu*, indicating an attitude of veneration and homage—thus becomes the concrete vehicle by which the principle of the three thousand realms in a single thought-moment is activated and realized. What easier way could there be to realizing buddhahood, Nichiren argued, than by reciting this phrase, which contains within itself all the treasures of the universe and all the truths in the teachings of all buddhas?

Nichiren himself not only recited the title with this understanding but also habitually read the sūtra text. Throughout the major part of his career, he carried with him a manuscript of the *Lotus* that he continually annotated in his own hand, inserting relevant passages from the Tiantai commentaries or from other sūtras. This annotated *Lotus Sūtra* served him as a concordance for use in his own preaching and writing. For his followers, he prescribed the simple recitation of the title, expressing homage and veneration. As noted, in Nichiren's understanding, this simple recitation opens to the reciter the infinite treasure store contained in the *Lotus*; it destines that person to supreme enlightenment and also assures the reciter of untold merit and worldly benefit.

Nichiren presented this practice as especially suited to a particular place within this earthly realm (the Sahā World), namely, the country of Japan, and to a given time in history, that is, the period of the Final Dharma age—in other words, Nichiren's own country and historical time. This represents a third important point to be noted in Nichiren's understanding of reading and practicing the *Lotus Sūtra*: his acute consciousness of the significance of the time and the place where that reading and practice were to be conducted.

The age of the Final Dharma (*mappō*) was believed by many people of Nichiren's time to have begun in 1052, that is, two thousand years after the Buddha's final *nirvāṇa,* which was then thought to have occurred in 949 B.C.E.[20] The Final Dharma age was seen as a period of history when human beings, burdened by evil karma, would no longer be able to attain enlightenment through the traditional disciplines of meditation and precept observance. In Nichiren's understanding, the evil age after the Buddha's nirvāṇa was a time when people who think they are acting in accord with the dharma of Śākyamuni are in fact going against it, even persecuting those who are its true bearers, a time when many who appear to uphold the dharma actually malign and despise it. The *Lotus Sūtra,* he said, predicts precisely this situation where it states, "This scripture has many enemies even now, when the Thus Come One is present. How much more so after his nirvāṇa!" (Hurvitz, 162–63, slightly modified.) Behind Nichiren's claim we must note the widespread reception accorded in his day to the exclusive Pure Land teaching of Hōnen (1133–1212), who stressed abandoning all practices in favor of the *nenbutsu* (recitation of the buddha Amida's name). From the standpoint of the *Lotus,* as expounded in the Tendai teachings that Nichiren accepted and further developed, in this degenerate age, only the *Lotus Sūtra* could truly lead to liberation. Thus, engaging in practices such as the nenbutsu prescribed by Hōnen and his Pure Land followers was not only fruitless but also tantamount to slandering the true dharma.

Nichiren saw the *Lotus Sūtra* as uniquely suited not only to the present time but also to a particular place, that is, his country of Japan. We find this in his teaching on the "five points," or five perspectives from which he explained the superior efficacy of the *Lotus Sūtra*: the teaching, the capacity, the time, the country, and the sequence of propagation. The people of Japan, Nichiren asserts, have a capacity "suited solely to the [teaching of the] *Lotus.*"[21] In short, Nichiren understood himself to be located in the place to which reading the *Lotus Sūtra* was best suited and in the specific time in history when it was most efficacious. Yet he also saw that very place and time as characterized by slander of the dharma, by a widespread abandonment of faith in the *Lotus Sūtra* in favor of Hōnen's nenbutsu and other practices.

This brings us to a fourth point concerning Nichiren's teaching about reading and practicing the *Lotus.* Because he saw the *Lotus Sūtra* as uniquely efficacious for his time and place, and yet ignored in favor of practices he deemed inferior or useless, he called upon his followers to join him in denouncing other teachings and proclaiming the sole efficacy of the *Lotus,* even at the risk of their lives. For example, he wrote, "No matter what great good deeds one may perform, even if one reads and copies the entire *Lotus Sūtra* a thousand or ten thousand times or masters the contemplation of three thousand realms in a single thought-moment, should one fail to denounce the enemies of the *Lotus Sūtra*, one will not be able to attain the way."[22]

In other words, in a situation where the sūtra is misunderstood, made light of, or maligned, true practitioners will not be content to ignore this fact and keep their practice of the *Lotus* to themselves. Rather, moved by compassion, they will regard such slanders with utmost seriousness and will not hesitate to denounce them. Nichiren continued, "To illustrate, if a court official, even one who may have served ten or twenty years, knows that an enemy of the ruler is in the vicinity but neither reports that person nor feels personal enmity toward him, then not only will the merits gained by that official [in his years of service] be erased, but he will instead be held liable for a crime."[23]

I have identified four critical points in Nichiren's understanding of what reading the *Lotus Sūtra* entails. First, reading the sūtra is equal to encountering Śākyamuni face-to-face, in effect entering the very presence of the Buddha. Second, to read and recite even a single phrase of the sūtra is to be assured of attaining enlightenment as well as receiving various kinds of worldly benefit. And the single phrase that is most appropriate for reading and recitation is the title of the sūtra, which encompasses all the *Lotus Sūtra*'s meritorious contents. Third, reading the sūtra is an act that takes place in the context of a specific time and place, which in effect calls for a reading of the *Lotus Sūtra* that correlates its teachings with contemporary events and situations. And fourth, beyond the acts of mental or verbal reading or recitation, true followers of the *Lotus* are enjoined to lay down their very lives if need be for its propagation and the realization of its message in this world.

PRACTICING THE *LOTUS* AND ENGAGING THE WORLD

In *On Protecting the Country*, in setting forth his religious vision based on the teaching of the *Lotus Sūtra*, Nichiren notes that he "looks at and listens to current social conditions" and correlates what he sees and hears of the actual events of his time with Buddhist scripture.[24] He opens his famous treatise *On Bringing Peace to the Land by Establishing the True Dharma (Risshō ankoku ron)*, written in 1260, by vividly depicting the social chaos evident to anyone at the time, noting, for example, the "oxen and horses lying dead in the streets, skeletons sprawled in all directions."[25] At that time, natural disasters such as earthquakes and deteriorating social conditions resulting from famine, epidemics, and internecine warfare all contributed to a general sense of insecurity. As he explains in this treatise, Nichiren sought the causes of this turmoil as well as possible solutions by reading Buddhist scriptures, trying to correlate the situation he observed with the teachings of the *Lotus* and other sūtras. He concluded that the fundamental cause of the people's suffering lay in neglect and slander of Śākyamuni's dharma as embodied in the *Lotus Sūtra*. Nichiren believed that this slander of the true dharma was being perpetrated in large measure through the spread of Hōnen's teaching of relying solely on reciting the name of Amida Buddha. On the basis of his studies, Nichiren understood Amida Buddha to be merely one of the many emanations of the transhistorical, primordially awakened Śākyamuni. To focus one's devotion on one or another of the primordial buddha's emanations without regard for the true source constituted, for Nichiren, a slight to Śākyamuni Buddha himself and was tantamount to slandering the true dharma. Moreover, the fact that the political authorities and military rulers allowed this practice to spread was, in his eyes, no less than official sanction of such slander.

Having arrived at the conclusion that the cause of chaos and suffering lay in this flagrant slander of the true dharma, he deemed that the next logical step was to put a stop to this state of affairs, and he spared no effort toward that objective. Nichiren wrote and presented *On Bringing Peace to the Land by Establishing the True Dharma* to the ruling authorities precisely to convince them to take the necessary steps that would ease the prevailing social turmoil by attacking the root of the problem. In this treatise, Nichiren drew on several scriptures with the theme of nation protection, such as the *Sūtra of the Golden Light* (Ch.: *Jinguangming jing*, Ja.: *Konkōmyō kyō*) and the *Sūtra for Humane Kings* (Ch.: *Renwang jing*, Ja.: *Ninnō kyō*), which detail the misfortunes that will befall a country where the true dharma is neglected or disparaged. Based on these passages, Nichiren predicted that two further disasters—foreign invasion and strife within the ruling clan—would occur if the present situation were allowed to persist. Throughout his life, Nichiren maintained this interpretive stance, continually turning to the *Lotus* to shed light on the social and political events of his time, interpreting them in the light of the *Lotus* and other sūtras, and also reading the sūtras in the light of what he saw happening around him.

Both of the calamities Nichiren predicted in fact materialized. In 1268, ambassadors from the Mongol empire delivered a written message demanding that Japan submit to Mongol overlordship; when these demands were refused, Mongol forces attempted to invade Japan, in 1274 and again in 1281. The Mongol threat represented the gravest danger Japan as a nation had ever faced. And even while under this external threat, political intrigues within the ruling families of the time, highlighted by the 1271 rebellion of Hōjō Tokisuke, the shogunal regent's half brother, plunged the entire country into a state of turmoil and uncertainty. Nichiren saw these events as fulfillment of "predictions" found in the sūtras he had cited in *On Bringing Peace to the Land by Establishing the True Dharma*, and they reconfirmed his convictions about the truth of the *Lotus Sūtra*, the misfortunes that arise from slandering it, and the accuracy of his reading of the Buddhist scriptures guided by the *Lotus* teaching.

Nichiren's public pronouncements and actions—in particular, his admonishing political and military authorities to take specific measures to stop what he saw as slander of the dharma—clearly derived from this religious conviction, based on his reading of the *Lotus Sūtra* in the light of the events of his day. His actions also led to his arrest and exile by the authorities. Nichiren's experiences of persecution further reaffirmed his conviction of the truth of his teaching and the accuracy of his own reading of the *Lotus Sūtra*. His fundamental attitude came to be manifested in and through this cross-reading of the *Lotus* with the events of his day and the general situation of his time: his was not a disinterested, objective reading but a thoroughly committed stance that presupposed his readiness to give his life for the dharma, "not begrudging even bodily life" (Hurvitz, 186; see also 190, 223). Nichiren cites this phrase from the *Lotus Sūtra* time and again in his many writings as exemplifying the stance of selfless dedication that the *Lotus Sūtra* itself requires. He maintained this position throughout his career, enduring repeated trials and hardships for the dharma's sake.

Among the persecutions Nichiren endured in spreading his *Lotus* teaching was exile to the small northern island of Sado (from 1271 to 1274), a sentence ordered by Japan's ruling authorities on a man they considered a nuisance and a challenge to their authority. During his stay on this desolate island, Nichiren undertook a period of self-examination, reflecting on the events of his life that had led to his present isolation and suffering. It was during this time that his sense of his own calling as a practitioner of the *Lotus* came to him in full clarity, confirming him in all that he had said and done since commencing his public career. A passage from the *Nirvāṇa Sūtra*, which Nichiren considered a "sister sūtra" to the *Lotus*, goes into particular detail about persecutions and sufferings that will inevitably be the lot of those who propagate the dharma. Nichiren took such passages as a mirror of his own life, affirming their correspondence to his own experience:

By now all my doubts have melted away, and the tens of thousands of barriers have been overcome. Let me match each phrase of the sūtra with my own bodily experience. [The *Nirvāṇa Sūtra* says,] "You will be despised, etc." And the *Lotus Sūtra* says, "You will be despised, hated, envied, etc." In the past twenty years this is exactly the kind of treatment I have received—contempt and arrogance. [Again, the *Nirvāṇa Sūtra* says,] "You will have an ugly appearance." Or, "You will be poorly clad." This is what happened to me. "You will be poorly fed." This is what happened to me. "You will seek worldly wealth in vain." This happened to me. "You will be born to a poor family." This happened to me. "You will meet with persecution from rulers, etc." This happened to me. Who could doubt these words of the sūtra? The *Lotus Sūtra* says, "You will be banished time and again." And the same passage refers to many similar evils.[26]

In short, Nichiren came to a deep personal realization that what he had read in the *Lotus Sūtra* had been actualized in his own life experience and, at the same time, that his own life experience was nothing less than the materialization and authentication of the sūtra's words. Nichiren's bodily reading of the *Lotus Sūtra* can thus be described as a circular hermeneutic, in which the text and the reader authenticate and bear witness to each other in the very act of reading. This is not "reading" in the ordinary sense of reading in order to ascertain meaning from the words of a text seen against its context, but an act whereby the reader—in this case, Nichiren—is authenticated in his self-understanding as the one referred to by the text itself. And at the same time, the *Lotus Sūtra*, which predicts that one who propagates its teaching in the evil age after the Buddha's nirvāṇa will meet with grave trials, is authenticated precisely as the events it refers to come to pass in the lived experience of Nichiren. "Looking at the present society," he wrote, "is there anyone other than Nichiren who is maligned and despised, hit with sticks, and so forth, on behalf of the *Lotus Sūtra*? Indeed, if it were not for Nichiren, this entire passage of prediction would be false."[27]

The same point is emphasized in a letter to Toki Jōnin, one of Nichiren's closest followers, written soon after Nichiren had completed his pivotal treatise *The Opening of the Eyes* (*Kaimoku shō*, 1272) and while still in exile on Sado Island:

[Chapter 10] of the *Lotus Sūtra* says, "Even if in the conflagration at the *kalpa*'s end / One should carry dry grass on one's back / And enter the flame, yet not be burnt, / That would not be difficult. / But after my final nirvāṇa, / If

> one can hold this scripture / And preach it to even one person, / *That* is difficult." It is Nichiren himself to whom these words refer. [Chapter 11] says, "There will be ignorant people who will slander and malign us, / And beat us with swords and staves." And again, the Buddha makes a prediction, saying: "In the fifth five hundred years after my final nirvāṇa, there will be a practitioner of the *Lotus* who will be subjected to slanderous treatment by ignorant persons; who will be struck with swords and sticks and stones and bricks; and who will be exiled and condemned to death." Now if it were not for me, Nichiren, all these predictions of Śākyamuni, Many Jewels, and the buddhas of the ten directions would be great lies.[28]

Nichiren's bodily reading of the *Lotus Sūtra* also underlay his identification with specific figures in the *Lotus Sūtra*. During his exile to Sado, Nichiren began to speak of himself as a forerunner of Bodhisattva Superior Conduct (Skt.: Viśiṣṭacāritra, Ja.: Jōgyō), the leader of the bodhisattvas who emerge from beneath the earth and are charged by Śākyamuni with the mission of propagating the *Lotus Sūtra* in the latter evil age after his nirvāṇa. Nichiren also identified himself with Bodhisattva Never Disparaging (Skt.: Sadāparibhūta, Ja.: Jōfukyō), described in Chapter 20 of the *Lotus Sūtra*, who was reviled and persecuted in his propagation of the dharma—an identification reflecting Nichiren's own experiences of adversity in declaring the *Lotus Sūtra*'s message.

In short, in Nichiren's reading, his experience of encountering persecutions and hardships in propagating the *Lotus Sūtra* thus becomes the very confirmation of the truth of the sūtra's teachings, as its words are realized in his own person. In this sense Nichiren understood himself as embodying the dharma as taught in the *Lotus Sūtra*. This was the source of the joy he often wrote of, which pervaded his being even in the midst of tribulations, despite his failure to gain a hearing from Japan's leaders or to convert more than a handful of followers. This apparent failure at obtaining external results led, in 1274, to his self-imposed retreat at Mount Minobu, in Kai province, where he spent his final years. During this last period of his life at Mount Minobu, he looked back at the main events of his career, especially the trials and hardships he had endured in propagating the *Lotus Sūtra*, and wrote: "Oh, what a joy it is to be able to give one's life for the *Lotus Sūtra*! If I can offer up my unworthy head, it will be like trading sand for gold, or exchanging a stone for a pearl."[29]

In his musings during this last period of his life, Nichiren reconfirmed the direction he had taken since the early years of his religious career. He had come to understand the various events and persons in his life as actualizing what had already been expounded in the *Lotus Sūtra*. He wrote:

> Oh, what great joy! King Dan endured the harsh training of the hermit Ashi and thereby obtained the merits of the *Lotus Sūtra*, and Bodhisattva Never Disparaging was beaten by the sticks of arrogant monks, thus winning praise as a practitioner of the one vehicle. And now, Nichiren, born in the Final Dharma age and propagating the five characters *Myōhō renge kyō*, is also subjected to the same treatment. In the more than 2,200 years since the Buddha's final nirvāṇa, perhaps not even the Great Teacher Tiantai [Zhiyi] was able to put into practice the sūtra passage that says, "The whole world will resent the dharma and will find it very hard to believe." And regarding the passage "They will be banished time and again," it is Nichiren alone who has fulfilled it. The Buddha has conferred the prediction that anyone who receives and keeps even a single stanza or a single verse of this sūtra will achieve buddhahood. This refers to myself. There is not the slightest doubt of my attaining supreme, perfect enlightenment. Thus, the regent Hōjō Tokimune himself [who persecuted me] has been my worthy friend in the dharma. [The warrior official] Taira no Saemon [who had me arrested and banished to Sado] is to me as Devadatta was to Śākyamuni. The nenbutsu followers are like Kokalika, and the vinaya followers are like the monk Sunakṣatra [both enemies of Śākyamuni Buddha]. Śākyamuni's lifetime on earth is right now. Now is Śākyamuni's lifetime on earth. This is the very essence of the *Lotus* that teaches the true aspect of the dharmas and their ultimate consistency from beginning to end.[30]

Nichiren thus read every event of his life and every element surrounding it as a fulfillment of particular predictions made in the *Lotus Sūtra*. Conversely, he read the *Lotus Sūtra* text as the very mirror of events happening in his life. We can also gain a glimpse of Nichiren's inner life throughout all his vicissitudes in a passage from another treatise written at Mount Minobu, in which he recalled the public pronouncements he had made to the authorities on three separate occasions, pointing out that his predictions of internal rebellion and invasion from abroad had been fulfilled. Nichiren wrote: "These three pronouncements were not made by myself, Nichiren. They were solely made by the spirit of Śākyamuni Tathāgata that entered my own body. As for me, I am beside myself with joy. The great matter of the three thousand realms in a single thought-moment taught in the *Lotus Sūtra* is none other than this."[31]

This passage recalls the four points concerning how Nichiren understood what the practice of reading the *Lotus Sūtra* involves. These four points illuminate and frame the course of Nichiren's career, which was thoroughly grounded, empowered, and propelled by his habitual reading of the sūtra .

First, an awareness of Śākyamuni Buddha's living presence accompanies Nichiren throughout the vicissitudes of his career. He was assured of this through his habitual way of reading the sūtra not just in a conceptual manner but in an immediate and experiential, bodily manner. His major treatises and numerous letters to his followers overflow with this awareness that one could well describe as mystical.[32]

Second, this awareness was grounded in Nichiren's experience of what one could call a "cosmic plenitude" accompanying his every thought, word, and action on behalf of the *Lotus Sūtra.* Based on the teaching of ichinen sanzen, which he understood as representing the core of the sūtra, every thought (or word, or deed) contains in itself the whole of the three thousand realms. For Nichiren, what most clearly manifested this cosmic plenitude was nothing other than the act of reciting the title of the *Lotus Sūtra*. His message was simple: uphold the *Lotus* and express this devoted acceptance in reciting the sūtra's five-character title. But underlying this simplicity is an intricate vision of ultimate reality that unfolds as one delves further into the various levels of this doctrine of cosmic plenitude in a single thought, a doctrine informed and brought to life by Nichiren's own mystical awareness.

Third, what I refer to as Nichiren's mystical awareness, embracing the sense of Śākyamuni's abiding presence together with the experience of cosmic plenitude, is realized in a given historical time (the Final Dharma age) and a specific geographical location (Japan), in response to concrete events and situations that evoked and activated the power of the *Lotus Sūtra*. Nichiren's response to these situations and events as a practitioner of the *Lotus* led to persecution, which, being predicted in the *Lotus Sūtra* itself, further confirmed for him the truth of its teaching and deepened him in his mystical awareness.

Fourth, Nichiren's lifelong conduct was clearly informed by an underlying willingness to give up even body and life in propagating the *Lotus Sūtra*'s message. This total dedication to the *Lotus* infused him with a sense of joy, peace, and fulfillment, in spite of the sufferings and hardships that his commitment entailed.

These four points, describing Nichiren's understanding of what reading the *Lotus Sūtra* involves, constitute the central elements of his religious message. These are elements that he actualized and embodied in his own life and career and that may be characterized from beginning to end as a thoroughgoing bodily reading of the sūtra. This understanding is what empowered Nichiren to engage the society of his day, seeing both the events occurring before his eyes as already predicted in the *Lotus* and other sūtras and these scriptural predictions as authenticated by actual events. This mutual authentication of prediction (in the text) and event (in the actual world) served to reconfirm Nichiren in his self-understanding as a votary of the *Lotus*, that is, as one in and through whom the *Lotus Sūtra* comes to be embodied in the world.

READING THE *LOTUS SŪTRA* AFTER NICHIREN

After his death, Nichiren's work of propagating the *Lotus Sūtra* was taken up by a small band of loyal disciples, and through the centuries his followers grew to form a powerful Buddhist sect in Japan that now bears his name. And in the late nineteenth and early twentieth centuries, several new religious movements, most notably Reiyūkai, Risshō Kōseikai, and Sōka Gakkai, also drew inspiration from Nichiren's teaching.[33] Also during this period, several thinkers influenced by Nichiren's teachings came to prominence in Japanese intellectual and political circles.[34]

This surge in interest in Nichiren and his message centered on the *Lotus Sūtra* during the period of Japan's modernization has been termed "Nichirenism" (*Nichiren-shugi*), a social and intellectual movement in which three modes of thinking can be distinguished.[35] The first and perhaps the predominant mode of Nichirenism, in the years before World War II, is associated with ultranationalistic and Japanocentric ideas that accompanied the imperialistic and militaristic fervor of those times. A second is connected with a vision of a transnational, ideal world society based on universal principles derived from the *Lotus Sūtra*. A third is oriented more explicitly toward religious practice, as promoted by organized religious bodies drawing on Nichiren's message.

Unquestionably the most prominent representative of the first, nationalistic mode of Nichirenism is Tanaka Chigaku (1861–1931), although several others, influenced chiefly by Tanaka, are also noteworthy.[36] As described in greater detail by Jacqueline I. Stone in chapter 8 of this volume, Tanaka founded the Kokuchūkai (Pillar of the Nation Society), which became the bulwark of Nichiren-inspired nationalism in Japan's modern history. Tanaka encouraged followers to assume Nichiren's attitude of "willingness to offer bodily life" for the *Lotus Sūtra* and to give themselves to the ultimate goal of bringing the entire human race to the "one wondrous path" as laid out in the *Lotus Sūtra*. And in keeping with the nationalism of the times, Tanaka saw Japan as playing a pivotal role in that endeavor. For example, he wrote: "The nation of Japan is indeed entrusted with this heavenly mission of accomplishing the spiritual unification of the whole universe. The whole universe must be brought to unity through Japan. Through Japan, the great spiritual pacification of the entire universe and of all humanity is to be accomplished for all eternity."[37]

Tanaka used military imagery to set forth his vision of the unification of all humanity and the entire universe under the aegis of the *Lotus*, with the great empire of Japan as the leader for the rest of the world. One can immediately see how such thinking served as an ideological buttress for the imperialistic and militaristic designs of Japan's leaders in the years leading up to World War II.[38]

This vision of a universal community uniting all people on earth was taken in another direction by socialist activist and thinker Seno'o Girō (1890–1961), who represents the second, universalistic or humanistic mode of Nichirenism. Although inspired by the ideals of Tanaka Chigaku early in his life, Seno'o later abandoned Tanaka's nationalism when he founded the New Buddhist Youth League (Shinkō Bukkyō Seinen Dōmei), espousing humanist, socialist, pacifist, and democratic ideals based on Buddhist principles. Seno'o regarded Nichiren's life as embodying these principles and called on all Buddhists to unite under Śākyamuni's banner to build a society based on mutual trust and love among human beings. Seno'o condemned capitalism as inconsistent with these principles. He undertook numerous walking pilgrimages throughout the Japanese countryside, calling for a transformation of Japanese society. His slogan was "Carrying the Buddha on our back, let us go out into the streets. Let us go out to the farming and fishing villages!"[39] Seno'o's life and thought became an inspiration to both Nichiren Buddhists and others who, while not necessarily followers of Nichiren, came to espouse socialist ideals and themes in their endeavors to rebuild Japanese society after World War II.

Another figure in the second mode of Nichirenism was Miyazawa Kenji (1896–1933), known as a poet, storyteller, artist, and visionary humanist as well as a peasant organizer. Miyazawa received his inspiration from his reading of the *Lotus Sūtra* and Nichiren's writings. He is often cited as a paradigmatic example of a modern Japanese bodhisattva, living a life of total service to others. This spirit of dedication shines through in his poems and stories, which are still widely read today. Like Seno'o Girō, Miyazawa was first inspired by the teachings of the *Lotus Sūtra* in his youth through his association with Tanaka Chigaku's Pillar of the Nation Society, while he was a student in Tokyo. But also like Seno'o, he later separated himself from Tanaka's group and abandoned the society's nationalistic ideals in favor of a universalist message. Miyazawa returned to his family farm in northeastern Japan, where he lived a life of simplicity and total dedication in service to those around him. His writings, which represent different genres, manifest his magnanimous heart and altruistic spirit. After his death, his work attracted wide attention in Japan and internationally.[40]

Yet another Nichiren-inspired thinker in the universalist mode is Uehara Senroku (1899–1975), historian and noted intellectual who helped establish the Association for People's Culture (Kokumin Bunka Kaigi), a circle influential in the 1950s and early 1960s. Uehara read the *Lotus Sūtra* and Nichiren's writings in the context of what he termed "contemporary global awareness." Uehara laid out a set of methodological guidelines for bringing Nichiren's religious vision to bear on the twentieth-century global context, outlining basic tasks waiting to be accomplished to liberate beings in his contemporary world. Uehara wrote during the Cold War and the early period of Japan's economic boom, also a moment in world history when peoples in many Asian, African, and Latin American countries were beginning to find their voices as they struggled to free themselves from socioeconomic and political structures that were part of their long, colonial past. Inspired by Nichiren's religious vision and that of the *Lotus Sūtra*, Uehara called on his fellow Japanese to take up their "national tasks" in ways that would align them with those peoples in a common endeavor to build a global community founded on peace, justice, and the equality of all.[41] The national tasks Uehara outlined included (1) survival, relating to the establishment of peace and security for the nation and its people, ravaged by defeat in a recent war; (2) livelihood, or the fulfillment of basic needs through agriculture and industry; (3) freedom and equality, involving the assurance of basic human rights for each citizen; (4) progress and prosperity, meaning economic development providing for the people's material, medical, educational, cultural, and other needs; and (5) independence and autonomy, indicating the effective exercise of self-determination, as opposed to remaining under the hegemony of Japan's conquerors, that is, the United States and the Allied powers, the victors in World War II. In outlining these concrete endeavors, Uehara drew inspiration from the teachings of Nichiren and the *Lotus Sūtra*, forging his vision of a Japanese nation and society that would be aligned with peoples throughout the world pursuing similar goals and faced with similar tasks as human beings inhabiting the same planet.

A disciple of Uehara who has continued his work is Maruyama Teruo (b. 1932), a Nichiren priest and religious and social activist. Maruyama has led study groups of activists in Japan working in solidarity with grassroots communities in other Asian countries at tasks of social transformation in their respective local contexts. He has formed alliances with groups in those countries, as well as with local groups in Japan, to address problems of discrimination, economic injustice, and militarization, as well as issues of human rights and environmentalism. Maruyama cooperated with socially engaged Buddhists in Thailand to form a Japan chapter of the International Network of Engaged Buddhists and has also formed alliances with Christian groups in the Philippines actively engaged in sociopolitical, economic, and ecological reform efforts. Observing his own, Japanese society from the perspective of his Asian alliances, Maruyama, like Nichiren in his own time, has taken upon himself the role of a gadfly, harshly criticizing political as well as religious authorities for policies and actions not in consonance with principles of peace, equality, and justice, which he interprets in the light of the *Lotus* teaching. Maruyama thus seeks to carry on the spirit of Nichiren and his bodily reading of the *Lotus Sūtra*.[42]

The third mode of Nichirenism is founded on a specific practice orientation embraced by the new Nichiren- or *Lotus*-based religious movements. In the postwar period, two such groups in particular, Risshō Kōseikai and Sōka Gakkai, grew dramatically in numbers and influence; they also succeeded in establishing communities of devotees in many countries besides their large followings in Japan. These two groups, described in greater detail in chapter 8, ironically remain at odds and have very little official contact with each other, though each seeks in its own way to promote the message of Nichiren and the *Lotus Sūtra* at home and in the international arena, supporting interreligious dialogue and cooperation in tasks aimed at global peace and social and ecological healing.[43]

What all these groups and figures have in common is that they read the *Lotus Sūtra* and Nichiren's writings in the light of contemporary events and, at the same time, interpret those events, both local and global, in the light of the *Lotus Sūtra* and Nichiren's writings. In the context of their respective religious communities and institutions, their readings have inspired them to engage in tasks of social engagement aimed at personal and global transformation, with the aim of realizing a *Lotus* land here on earth. Thus, the bodily reading of the *Lotus Sūtra* that marked Nichiren's life continues to be a living tradition in our times.[44]

NOTES

1. Part of this essay is a revised version of my "Bodily Reading of the *Lotus Sūtra*: Understanding Nichiren's Buddhism," *Japanese Journal of Religious Studies* 26, nos. 3–4 (1999): 281–306. See also my "*Lotus* Buddhism and Its Liberational Thrust: A Rereading of the *Lotus Sutra* by Way of Nichiren," *Ching Feng* 35, no. 2 (June 1992): 85–112; and "Mystico-Prophetic Buddhism of Nichiren," in *Papers of the Henry Luce III Fellows in Theology*, ed. Jonathan Strom, 2:43–62 (Atlanta: Scholar's Press, 1996).
2. For a relevant study of the significance of sacred texts across religious traditions, see Wilfred Cantwell Smith, *What Is Scripture?—A Comparative Approach* (Minneapolis: Fortress Press, 1993).
3. While different passages in the *Lotus* give slightly different versions of the meritorious acts to be directed toward the sūtra, Chinese Tiantai commentators, working from Kumārajīva's translation, usually standardized them as the five practices of (1) upholding the *Lotus*, (2) reading the sūtra, (3) reciting it from memory, (4) explaining (or interpreting) it, and (5) copying it. See chapter 5, n. 7, this volume.
4. See Gregory Schopen's groundbreaking study, "The Phrase *sa pṛthivīpradeśaś caityabhūto bhavet* in the *Vajracchedikā*: Notes on the Cult of the Book in Mahāyāna," 1975, reprinted in Schopen, *Figments and Fragments of Mahāyāna Buddhism in India: More Collected Papers*, Studies in the Buddhist Traditions, 25–62 (Honolulu: University of Hawai'i Press, 2005).
5. Edward Conze, *The Gilgit Manuscript of the Aṣṭadāsasāhasrikā Prajñāpāramitā: Chapters 55 to 70 Corresponding to the 5th Abhisamaya* (Rome: Istituto Italiano per il Medio ed Estremo Oriente, 1962), 76–77, 272–74.
6. An exception is the *Heart Sūtra*, a concise version of the *Prajñāpāramitā* that has been widely revered, memorized, and chanted in a number of meditative and ritual contexts.
7. Ruben L. F. Habito, "*Daimoku* and *Dhāraṇī*: Tracing the Roots of Nichiren's Buddhism," in *Ejima Yasunori hakushi tsuitō ronshū, Kū to jitsuzai*, ed. Ejima Yasunori hakushi tsuitō ronshū kankōkai, 633–43 (Tokyo: Shunjūsha, 2001).
8. The Sanskrit word used here, *vācayati*, means "vocalized reading." In Chinese, *vācayati* is usually translated with the binome *dusong*, whose two characters mean "to read" and "to recite," respectively. See chapter 5 in this volume.
9. Maria Reis-Habito, "The *Great Compassion Dhāraṇī*," in *The Esoteric Buddhist Tradition: Selected Papers from the 1989 Seminar for Buddhist Studies Conference*, ed. Henrik Sorensen, 31–49 (Copenhagen: SBS Monographs, 1994); Chün-fang Yü, *Kuan-yin: The Chinese Transformation of Avalokiteśvara* (New York: Columbia University Press, 2001).
10. Yoshiko K. Dykstra, trans., *Miraculous Tales of the Lotus Sutra from Ancient Japan: The "Dainihonkoku Hokekyōkenki" of Priest Chingen* (Honolulu: University of Hawai'i Press, 1983). See also William E. Deal, "Ascetics, Aristocrats, and the *Lotus Sutra*: The Construction of the Buddhist Universe in Eleventh-Century Japan" (Ph.D. diss., Harvard University, 1988).
11. Jacqueline I. Stone, "Chanting the August Title of the *Lotus Sutra: Daimoku* Practices in Classical and Medieval Japan," in *Re-Visioning "Kamakura" Buddhism*, ed. Richard K. Payne, Kuroda Institute, Studies in East Asian Buddhism 11, 116–66 (Honolulu: University of Hawai'i Press, 1998); Stone, "Not Mere Written Words:

Perspectives on the Language of the *Lotus Sūtra* in Medieval Japan," in *Discourse and Ideology in Medieval Japanese Buddhism*, ed. Richard K. Payne and Taigen Dan Leighton, 160–94 (London: Routledge, 2006).

12. Habito, "*Daimoku* and *Dhāraṇī*."
13. *Shugo kokka ron*, Nichiren (1222–1282), in *Shōwa teihon Nichiren Shōnin ibun*, ed. Risshō daigaku Nichiren kyōgaku kenkyūjo, 4 vols. (Minobu-chō, Yamanashi, Japan: Minobusan Kuonji, 1952–1959; rev. 1988) (hereafter abbreviated as *Teihon*), 1:110–11. All translations from Nichiren's writings are my own, with some indebtedness to other English translations. In this passage, the "fiftieth person in succession" refers to Chapter 18 of the *Lotus*, which explains that the merit gained by even the fiftieth person in succession who hears the sūtra and rejoices appropriately surpasses that of someone who makes offerings to all beings in the universe (Hurvitz, 237). The "four postures" are sitting, standing, walking, and lying down, or, in short, all human behavior. Buddhist monastic traditions prescribe rules of conduct conducive to awakening for each of these postures.
14. *Shugo kokka ron, Teihon* 1:123. The sūtra passage cited is at Hurvitz, 308, slightly modified.
15. This fundamental attitude of "receiving and keeping" (Ch.: *shouchi*, Ja.: *juji*) the *Lotus Sūtra* has been highlighted by Nichiren Buddhist scholars in Japan as a key feature of Nichiren's religious message. The term *juji* derives from the Sanskrit dhāraṇā.
16. "*Hokke* daimoku shō," *Teihon* 1:398.
17. "*Kanjin honzon shō* soejō," *Teihon* 1:702.
18. "Shōmitsu-bō gosho," *Teihon* 1:822; *Kanjin honzon shō, Teihon* 1:711.
19. *Kanjin honzon shō, Teihon* 1:720.
20. Jan Nattier, *Once upon a Future Time: Studies in a Buddhist Prophecy of Decline*, Nanzan Studies in Asian Religions 1 (Berkeley: Asian Humanities Press, 1991).
21. "Nanjō Hyōe Shichirō-dono gosho," *Teihon* 1:324.
22. Ibid., 1:321.
23. Ibid., 1:321–22.
24. *Shugo kokka ron, Teihon* 1:98.
25. *Risshō ankoku ron, Teihon* 1:209.
26. *Kaimoku shō, Teihon* 1:602.
27. Ibid., 1:559. The reference is to Chapter 13 of the *Lotus*, which predicts persecutions that its devotees will encounter in the latter evil age (Hurvitz, 188–90).
28. *Kaimoku shō, Teihon* 1:639. For the sūtra passages referred to, see Hurvitz, 175 and 188, slightly modified. The Buddha's "prediction" cited here summarizes the verse section of Chapter 13, "Fortitude" (Hurvitz, 188–90).
29. *Shuju onfurumai gosho, Teihon* 2:963. The reference is to Nichiren's near beheading in 1271, at the time of his second arrest and exile.
30. Ibid., 2:971.
31. *Senji shō, Teihon* 2:1054.
32. By the term "mystical," I refer to a kind of human experience marked by both transcendence and immanence, numinosity and immediacy. In Nichiren's case, the transcendent dimension is the cosmic plenitude that encompasses all the myriad things of the universe ("the three thousand realms," or *sanzen*), while the immanent dimension is the single thought-moment (*ichinen*), in which the transcendent is encapsulated.
33. For a brief, introductory account of these groups, see Ruben L. F. Habito, "*Lotus* Buddhism after Nichiren," in *Experiencing Buddhism: Ways of Wisdom and Com-*

passion (New York: Orbis Books, 2005), 181–86, with bibliographical notes.

34. Ruben L. F. Habito, "Uses of Nichiren in Modern Japanese History," *Japanese Journal of Religious Studies* 26, nos. 3–4 (1999): 423–39. This essay reviews two volumes of essays in Japanese that highlight Nichiren's influence since the beginning of Japan's modern period (from 1868).

35. I am taking the term *Nichirenism* in its broadest sense to mean "political thought inspired by Nichiren," with at least three lines of development as described here. The term is also sometimes used in a narrower sense, corresponding only to the first of these three modes. See Tamura Yoshirō, "Kindai Nihon no ayumi to Nichiren-shugi," in *Nihon kindai to Nichiren-shugi*, ed. Tamura Yoshirō and Miyazaki Eishū, Kōza Nichiren 4 (Tokyo: Shunjūsha, 1972), 2–7; as well as the summary in Habito, "Uses of Nichiren," 424.

36. Among them are the Nichiren Buddhist priest Honda Nisshō (1867–1931), the military officers Ishiwara (sometimes read Ishihara) Kanji (1889–1949) and Kita Ikki (1883–1937), and Inoue Nisshō (1886–1967), a lay Nichiren devotee who espoused fascist ideas.

37. Tanaka Chigaku, "On the Renovation of Our Sect," cited in Habito, "Uses of Nichiren," 427.

38. George J. Tanabe Jr., "Tanaka Chigaku: The *Lotus Sutra* and the Body Politic," in *The Lotus Sutra in Japanese Culture*, ed. George J. Tanabe Jr. and Willa Jane Tanabe, 191–208 (Honolulu: University of Hawai'i Press, 1989).

39. Seno'o Girō, "New Buddhism toward the Transformation of Society," cited in Habito, "Uses of Nichiren," 430.

40. Miyazawa Kenji's major works are now available in English translation. A catalog can be found at www.kenji-world.net /english/index.html.

41. Uehara Senroku's *Collected Works* have been published in recent years in a twenty-eight-volume series. In English, see Ruben L. F. Habito, entry on Uehara Senroku in *Great Thinkers of the Eastern World*, ed. Ian McGreal, 391–94 (San Francisco: HarperCollins, 1994). See also Ulrich Dehn's habilitation thesis "Die geschichtliche Perspektive des japanischen Buddhismus: Am Beispiel Uehara Senroku" (Mainz, 1995). The main points of this study are summarized in Ulrich Dehn, "Towards a Historical Consciousness of Japanese Buddhism: Uehara Senroku," *Japanese Religions* 17, no. 2 (July 1992): 126–41.

42. For Maruyama's vision of sociopolitical engagement inspired by Nichiren's teaching, see Maruyama Teruo, *Tatakau bukkyō* (Tokyo: Hōzōkan, 1990).

43. On Risshō Kōseikai, see *Dharma World: For Living Buddhism and Interfaith Dialogue*, a bimonthly journal in English published at the group's headquarters in Tokyo and distributed internationally. On Sōka Gakkai, see, for example, David Machacek and Bryan Wilson, eds., *Global Citizens: The Soka Gakkai Movement in the World* (New York: Oxford University Press, 2000).

44. For examples of readings of the *Lotus* in the light of present-day global issues, see the essays in Gene Reeves, ed., *A Buddhist Kaleidoscope: Essays on the Lotus Sutra* (Tokyo: Kōsei, 2002).

[8]

REALIZING THIS WORLD AS THE BUDDHA LAND

Jacqueline I. Stone

THE *LOTUS SŪTRA* is famous for its promise that eventually all beings shall become buddhas. And, in the long history of its reception, the *Lotus Sūtra* has often been understood as related not only to the buddhahood or enlightenment of individual practitioners but also to the enlightenment of their larger, objective world: the land or realm. Although not fully elaborated in the sūtra itself, ideas about this world as a buddha realm represent an important strand of *Lotus Sūtra* thought, one that developed chiefly, although not exclusively, in Japan. In this chapter I consider how the *Lotus Sūtra* came to be read as teaching that the buddha land is inseparable from this present world and how some of its major interpreters understood this idea. Tracing this particular strand of the *Lotus Sūtra*'s interpretive history offers insight into both the astonishingly diverse readings that this single sūtra has inspired as well as the hermeneutical processes by which Buddhist texts undergo continual reinterpretation in different cultural contexts and historical circumstances.

THE NOTION OF THE BUDDHA'S CONSTANT PRESENCE AS SEEN IN THE *LOTUS SŪTRA*

It is basic to Buddhist cosmology that Gautama, or Śākyamuni, is the teacher for our own, Sahā World during the present world cycle; he is the Buddha who appeared here and taught the dharma for the liberation of all. The *Lotus Sūtra* affirms this understanding in the verse section of Chapter 3, "Parable," in which Śākyamuni states, "Now these three spheres [that compose the world] / Are all my possession. / The living beings within them / Are all my children" (Hurvitz, 67).[1] However, the *Lotus Sūtra* goes well beyond this traditional view in asserting that Śākyamuni Buddha is *still* here, constantly abiding in the present world. This remarkable claim occurs in connection with the dramatic revelation in Chapter 16, "The Life

Span of the Thus Come One" (hereafter, "Life Span"), of the Buddha's original awakening in the inconceivably remote past. Here Śākyamuni declares that he had not achieved supreme awakening for the first time during his present lifetime, as everyone had always thought, but countless, inconceivable *kalpas* (eons) ago. Ever since then, he continues, he has been "constantly dwelling in this Sahā world sphere, preaching the dharma, teaching and converting," as well as guiding and benefiting the beings in incalculable other worlds (Hurvitz, 220). From this perspective, the key events of the Buddha's biography—his renouncing the world, awakening under the bodhi tree, and entry into final *nirvāṇa*—were all "skillful means" designed to awaken in living beings a mind that would seek the Buddhist teachings. As the verse section of the same chapter explains, "For the beings' sake, / And as an expedient device, I make a show of nirvāṇa; / Yet in fact I do not pass into extinction / But ever dwell here and preach the dharma" (Hurvitz, 223). Deluded people will not see him, but when those with single-minded resolve desire to behold him, he will appear together with his assembly on Vulture Peak.

In the context in which the *Lotus Sūtra* was compiled, this refiguring of the Buddha as awakened since the remotest past and constantly teaching in both this and other worlds would appear to be one of several innovations in Mahāyāna thought, such as nonabiding nirvāṇa (Skt.: *apratiṣṭhitanirvāṇa*) or notions of the Buddha as an omnipresent dharma body (*dharmakāya*), that attempt to reinterpret the Buddha not as departed into final nirvāṇa, as the Indian Buddhist mainstream maintained, but as in some sense still accessible and responsive to devotees. In the case of the *Lotus Sūtra*, Śākyamuni's revelation of his awakening in the remotest past in effect transforms him from the traditional model of a buddha who appears, teaches, and then departs into a Mahāyāna bodhisattva who elects not to enter nirvāṇa at all but to remain active in this saṃsāric world for living beings' sake. At the same time, however, in its claim that this refigured Buddha constantly abides in this world, the "Life Span" chapter also introduces the notion of a buddha realm that is in some sense immanent in the present world, although radically different from our ordinary experience of it in being free from decay, danger, and suffering. As the verse section reads, "When the beings see the kalpa ending / And being consumed by a great fire, / This land of mine is perfectly safe, / . . . Variously adorned with gems, / As well as jeweled trees with many blossoms and fruits, / Wherein the beings play and amuse themselves; / . . . My pure land is not destroyed" (Hurvitz, 224). Some commentators have taken the "pure land" referred to in this passage to mean an ideal realm set apart from our own world, while others have understood it as immanent in this very world, although not experienced by those whose perception is deluded.[2] In the *Lotus Sūtra* itself, the idea of the immanent buddha realm is not developed doctrinally, nor is it linked to notions of an ideal Buddhist society. Nonetheless, it proved foundational for later readings of the sūtra as teaching the possibility of a "this-worldly" buddha land.

THE BUDDHA LAND AND UNIVERSAL NONDUALITY

A common theme in Mahāyāna philosophical thought is that this world and the pure land are not, ultimately, separate places but are in fact nondual: a deluded mind sees the world as a place of suffering, while an awakened person sees it as the buddha realm.[3] A related idea held that the specific pure lands of Amitābha (Ja.: Amida) and other buddhas were not only superior worlds in which devotees might be reborn but realms that could be accessed by accomplished meditators.[4] In East Asia, such thinking, while by no means confined to the *Lotus Sūtra*, came to be linked to the *Lotus* in specific ways by developments within the Tiantai tradition of Chinese Buddhism, which takes the *Lotus Sūtra* as its central scripture. As noted in chapter 1 of this volume, one problem that engaged medieval Chinese Buddhist exegetes across divisions of school and lineage was how to conceptualize the relationship of the mind or principle (*li*) with the concrete observable phenomena of the world (*shi*). An extremely sophisticated approach to this question was put forth by the Tiantai patriarch Zhiyi (538–597). Drawing on Mahāyāna notions of emptiness and nonduality, Zhiyi held that all phenomena, being devoid of independent substance, constantly interpenetrate and include one another without losing their individual identity, a concept succinctly expressed in the famous statement, "There is not a single color or scent that is not the middle way."[5] Zhiyi developed this concept, as an object for advanced meditation, into a complex, architectonic model of reality known as the "three thousand realms in a single thought-moment" (Ch.: *yinian sanqian*, Ja.: *ichinen sanzen*), according to which one's mind and the entire cosmos are mutually encompassing. In this model, good and evil, delusion and awakening, subject and object, and all the levels of sentient existence, from hell beings, hungry ghosts, and animals up through bodhisattvas and buddhas, as well as their corresponding lands or environments, are inherent in every moment of consciousness.[6] Integral to Zhiyi's schema was the inseparability or nonduality of living beings and the realm of the insentient container world that they inhabit.[7]

The concept of the inseparability of person and land, or of the living subject and his or her objective world, was further developed by the sixth Tiantai patriarch Zhanran (711–782) as the "nonduality of primary and dependent [karmic] recompense," one of "ten nondualities" elaborated in his commentary on Zhiyi's analysis of the *Lotus Sūtra*.[8] The idea here is that the cumulative effects of one's deeds find expression both as "primary recompense"—the physical and mental workings that compose a person or living subject—and simultaneously as that individual's environment, or "dependent recompense," and that person and environment are ultimately nondual. Since the land is thus held to reflect the life state of living beings, the world of hell dwellers would be hellish, while the world of a fully awakened person would by definition be a buddha land. Commenting from this perspective on Zhiyi's principle, Zhanran wrote: "You should know that one's person and land are [both] the single thought-moment comprising three thousand realms. Therefore, when one attains the way, in accordance with this principle, one's body and mind in that moment pervade the dharma realm."[9]

Zhanran also contributed to thinking about the innate buddha realm by proposing that even insentient beings such as rocks and trees possess the buddha nature.[10] In so doing, he was participating in a broader effort on the part of Chinese Buddhist thinkers to extend the potential for buddhahood as universally as possible. More specifically, his doctrine may be understood as a development of Zhiyi's teaching that living beings and their objective environments, in all states of existence from hell dwellers to bodhisattvas and buddhas, are inherent in the mind at each thought-moment. "Every blade of grass, tree, pebble, and particle of dust is perfectly endowed with buddha nature," Zhanran wrote. "The practitioner of the perfect teaching, from beginning to end, knows that ultimate principle is nondual, and that there are no objects apart from mind. Who then is sentient? What then is insentient? Within the assembly of the *Lotus*, there is no discrimination."[11] Although the buddhahood of insentient beings had been proposed earlier, by the Sanlun scholar Jizang (549–623) and others, Zhanran's is the name most closely associated with this doctrine. Against the position of the Huayan and other rival schools, which generally confined the potential for enlightenment to sentient beings, Zhanran asserted that insentient beings also have the nature of suchness and, therefore, the potential for buddhahood—thus in effect claiming superior inclusivity for Tiantai. Zhanran played a critical role in the formation of Tiantai sectarian identity, and through him, notions of the potential buddhahood of the insentient environment became linked firmly to the *Lotus Sūtra* and the Tiantai school.

In this way, Tiantai scholars of medieval China elaborated sophisticated doctrines of the nonduality of the living subject and his or her objective container world, implying that the condition of the land mirrors the delusion or enlightenment of living beings: when the individual practitioner achieves awakening, that person's world becomes the buddha land. Such thinking remained largely at the level of theoretical speculation; buddhahood was not seriously envisioned as a goal most practitioners were likely to attain in this lifetime. Nonetheless, in principle, these ideas had the effect of valorizing the present, phenomenal world, not as a place of suffering to be escaped but as inseparable from the realm of ultimate principle.

Japanese commentators also read the *Lotus Sūtra* in terms of a nondual reality in which this world is inseparable from the buddha land, but they carried this line of interpretation in new directions. As noted in the first chapter of this volume, Tendai Buddhism in Japan quickly came to be differentiated from its parent, continental Tiantai, by its incorporation of esoteric Buddhism. The cosmic buddha of the esoteric teachings—Mahāvairocana in Sanskrit, or Dainichi in Japanese—is understood not as a person, whether historical or mythic, but as the dharma realm or universe itself: all forms are his body, all sounds are his speech, all thoughts are his mind. Or, alternatively, the same six elements of earth, water, fire, wind, space, and mind make up the body and mind of both the cosmic buddha and the practitioner; thus there is originally no distinction between them. This inherent identity of the practitioner's body, speech, and mind with those of the cosmic buddha could, it was said, be manifested in the performance of the "three mysteries"—the use of *mudrās*, or scripted symbolic gestures, the chanting of *mantras* (incantations), and visualization exercises—thus "realizing buddhahood with this very body" (Ja.: *sokushin jōbutsu*). In the Tendai esoteric teachings (Taimitsu), the cosmic buddha is identified with the primordially enlightened Śākyamuni of the "Life Span" chapter, and his realm—that is, the entire universe—is conceived in maṇḍalic terms as an ever-present, ongoing *Lotus Sūtra* assembly.[12]

Under the influence of Tendai esotericism, during Japan's medieval period (roughly, twelfth through sixteenth centuries), the *Lotus Sūtra* itself came to be read from the perspective of "original enlightenment" (*hongaku*), which was understood as the deep message of the origin teaching (*honmon*), or latter fourteen chapters of the sūtra.[13] According to original enlightenment doctrine, buddhahood is not a potential to be realized as the final result of practice but the true state of all things just as they are, although ordinary, deluded people do not realize this. Thus practice is redefined not as a means to an end but as the vehicle for accessing an enlightenment that in some sense is already present. And of course, from this perspective, this world is already the buddha land, a concept sometimes expressed metaphorically in the phrase "the assembly on Sacred Vulture Peak is solemnly present and has not yet dispersed." Secret initiations into medieval Tendai monastic teaching lineages sometimes ritually enacted this metaphor. An example can be found in the "precept initiation" (*kai kanjō*), a transmission of the secret meaning of the precepts as conducted by the Tendai Kurodani lineage. In this initiation ceremony, master and disciple share the same seat and are of equal status, like the two buddhas Śākyamuni and Many Jewels (Skt.: Prabhūtaratna) seated together as described in the "Apparition of the Jeweled Stūpa" chapter of the *Lotus Sūtra*. An early description of the rite says that, unlike the ordinary ceremony of conferring the precepts, this initiation does not have the meaning of transmission in a linear sequence from the Buddha through a line of successive patriarchs. Rather, in accordance with the teaching that "the assembly on Sacred Vulture Peak is solemnly present and has not yet dispersed," master and disciple are manifested as the two buddhas in the jeweled stūpa, and the mythic time when the *Lotus Sūtra* was expounded is manifested in the present.[14] This particular ritual provides but one instance in broader understandings of the realm of the primordially enlightened Śākyamuni of the *Lotus Sūtra* as an ever-present, maṇḍala-like reality that one can enter through ritual practice, meditative insight, or faith.

GROUNDING THE BUDDHA LAND IN NATURE, GEOGRAPHY, AND NATION

Whether understood as a potential to be achieved in the future or as an originally inherent reality to be realized in the act of practice, interpretations of the immanent buddha realm discussed thus far all rest on notions of a universal, nondual ground: when the individual realizes enlightenment, so does that person's land. At the same time, the *Lotus Sūtra* in premodern Japan was also grounded in more concrete ways that associated its teachings with specific sites. Like notions of nonduality, these interpretive moves were not confined to the *Lotus Sūtra* but nonetheless played an important role in its reception.

Buddhahood and the Realm of Nature

One way of grounding the immanent buddha land suggested in the *Lotus Sūtra* was by associating it with the natural realm, an idea often expressed via the doctrine of "the attainment of buddhahood by grasses and trees" (*sōmoku jōbutsu*). In both Shingon and Tendai circles, the claim that grasses and trees can attain buddhahood was at first asserted as a specific instance of the larger, universalistic position that all beings have the buddha nature. Kūkai (774–835), originator of the Japanese Shingon school, argued that insentient plants and trees are composed of the same five elements as the body of the cosmic buddha and are therefore indistinguishable from the dharma body, or ultimate principle. Saichō (766 or 767–822), who established the Japanese Tendai school, maintained—against the position of the Hossō (Ch.: Faxiang) school, which restricted the potential for buddhahood to sentient beings of particularly acute capacity—that grasses and trees can attain buddhahood. Thus, this claim, like that of Zhanran, began as an attempt to extend the implications of Mahāyāna inclusivism and originally had little to do with what we would call "nature" over and against the realm of culture and civilization. But where Zhanran and other Chinese exegetes had argued that insentient beings manifest enlightenment in response to the enlightenment of living beings, in Japan this doctrine assumed a more specific focus on plant life and the natural world. Japanese Tendai commentators after Saichō insisted that grasses and trees, of their own volition, can aspire to enlightenment, engage in practice, and realize awakening. "Grasses, trees, the land itself: all will become buddhas," wrote the Tendai thinker Annen (841–?), in a phrase echoed frequently in literary sources.[15] Annen never fully clarified what this assertion meant, but a later text explains it in this way: "Grasses and trees already have the four aspects of emergence, abiding, change, and extinction. These are [respectively] the awakening of aspiration, the cultivation of practice, the realization of enlightened wisdom [*bodhi*], and the nirvāṇa of grasses and trees. How could they not be sentient beings?"[16] Here the realization of buddhahood by grasses and trees is understood as their natural life cycle of sprouting, blossoming, maturing, and withering. This represents a reading from the position of original enlightenment, in which, to enlightened eyes, the arising and perishing of all phenomena just as they are is none other than the true face of reality.

Outside Buddhist scholastic circles, medieval poets and playwrights often understood the realization of buddhahood by grasses and trees as an important teaching of the *Lotus Sūtra*. The spirit of a plant, tree, or flower achieving release from saṃsāric suffering and attaining buddhahood by the power of the *Lotus Sūtra* was a recurrent theme in Noh drama. Such plays were often linked thematically to Chapter 5 of the *Lotus Sūtra*, "Medicinal Herbs," in which grasses and trees of different kinds grow to different heights according to their capacity but are all nourished by the same rain. In the sūtra itself, this parable serves as a metaphor for the essential unity underlying the multiplicity of the Buddha's teachings. In Noh plays, however, it was taken literally to mean that plants can achieve liberation.[17] In the words of one scholar, literary appropriations of this theme "historically 'fixed' a lasting nexus between Buddhism and nature in the popular consciousness of the Japanese people" and helped to establish ideas of the natural realm as a site of unsurpassed religious value.[18]

The Lotus Sūtra *and Sacred Geography*

The *Lotus Sūtra* was also connected to the establishment of sacred sites. The term "flying mountains" has been used to describe the identification of particular mountains in Japan—usually important Buddhist practice sites—as equivalent, or in some sense even identical, to sacred mountains on the Asian continent; such mountains were often said literally to have flown to Japan.[19] Hiei, Ōmine, Kasagi, and other locations of mountain ascetic practice were all at times identified with Vulture Peak, where the ever-abiding Śākyamuni Buddha is said constantly to preach the *Lotus Sūtra*.[20] Mount Hiei, in particular, as the site of the head Tendai monastery Enryakuji, was frequently equated in medieval Tendai records of oral transmissions with both Vulture Peak in India and with Mount Tiantai, headquarters of the parent tradition, in China. All three sites, it was frequently noted, lay to the northeast of the capital in their respective countries and thus constituted centers of nation protection that could block the evil influences thought to gain ingress from that unlucky direction. "Therefore," to quote one such text, "the transmission [of the *Lotus Sūtra*] through the three countries [of India, China, and Japan] always takes place on Sacred Vulture Peak. Our mountain [Hiei] is to be understood as the site of 'the assembly on Sacred Vulture Peak [that] is solemnly present and has not yet dispersed.'"[21] Identifying Mount Hiei with the realm of the *Lotus* assembly not only transposed the world of the sūtra to Japan but also underscored the authority of this leading Buddhist center.

Another form of sacred place was the geographic maṇḍala, in which specific landscapes were identified with the realms of particular buddhas and bodhisattvas; to visit such sites was thus to enter a buddha realm. The

Yoshino and Kumano regions of Japan's Kii Peninsula, for example, both famed areas of pilgrimage and mountain ascetic practice, were identified, respectively, with the Diamond World (Skt.: Vajradhātu, Ja.: Kongōkai) and the Womb World (Skt.: Garbhadhātu, Ja.: Taizōkai) maṇḍalas of esoteric Buddhism. The *Lotus Sūtra* was also projected onto certain topographies in this fashion. For example, according to one tradition, Kunisaki Peninsula, in Kyushu, another major site for mountain ascetic practice, had twenty-eight temples representing the sūtra's twenty-eight chapters; its eight major valleys corresponded to the sūtra's eight scrolls; and it enshrined more than 69,380 buddha images, one for each character of the sūtra.[22] This spatializing of the *Lotus* in effect enabled the practitioner to "read" the sūtra corporally through the physical act of traversing the pilgrimage route.

The Lotus *as a Nation-Protecting Sūtra*

As early as the eighth century, well before the formation of medieval pilgrimage routes or scholarly arguments about the buddhahood of plants, the *Lotus Sūtra* was starting to be linked with another specific site—Japan itself. This began in connection with the adoption of the *Lotus* as a "nation-protecting sūtra" (*chingo kokka kyō*), a role it had never been assigned in any official way on the East Asian mainland. Nation-protecting sūtras, as the name suggests, were scriptures ritually recited for the protection of the realm. This practice was seldom explicitly linked to doctrinal concepts such as the nonduality of person and land but rather represented a thaumaturgical expectation of the protective power of Buddhist ritual, entertained by people at all social levels. Two of the sūtras most widely employed for this purpose in China and the Korean kingdoms were the *Sūtra for Humane Kings* (Ch.: *Renwang jing*) and the *Sūtra of the Golden Light* (Skt.: *Suvarṇaprabhāsa-sūtra*, Ch.: *Jinguangming jing*). Both have content relevant to the theme of nation protection. The *Sūtra for Humane Kings* deals with Buddhist statecraft and qualities of virtuous rule, while the *Sūtra of the Golden Light* promises that the four heavenly kings will guard over that country where the dharma is correctly upheld. In Japan, these two sūtras were integrated into court rites for the welfare of the realm and were lectured upon in the palace and the provinces for that purpose beginning in the late seventh century.[23] Unlike these two sūtras, however, the *Lotus Sūtra* has no content specifically related to issues of nation protection or Buddhist kingship. Why, then, was it adopted for this purpose?

One reason has to do with the establishment of provincial temples, especially provincial convents for nuns. In 741, Emperor Shōmu, a devout

Buddhist, gave orders to establish a network of provincial temples: one monastery and one nunnery to be built in each province for the welfare of the realm. He was actively assisted in this endeavor by his consort, Empress Kōmyō. The provincial monasteries were known as "temples for the four heavenly kings' protection of the country by the *Sūtra of the Golden Light*," while the nunneries were termed "temples for eradicating sin by the *Lotus Sūtra*." The monks and nuns of these temples were to perform recitation each month of the *Golden Light* and *Lotus* sūtras, respectively.[24] Until recently, scholars assumed that nuns were assigned to recite the *Lotus Sūtra* because of the connection between their status as women and the episode of the dragon king's daughter and her gender transformation described in Chapter 12 of the *Lotus*, "Devadatta" (see chapter 3 in this volume). Scholars also understood the provincial nunneries in terms of later, medieval Japanese views of women as carrying an especially heavy karmic burden that they needed to eradicate in order to attain liberation. However, recent scholarship has shown that in eighth-century Japan, the chapter on Devadatta and the dragon king's daughter was not well known. The story of the dragon girl and her change into male form began to attract sustained attention only from the ninth century on, and concepts of female gender as an obstacle to liberation had yet to gain currency. One theory suggests that Empress Kōmyō, who was instrumental in establishing the provincial nunneries, was inspired by news of a *Lotus* hall for practicing the *Lotus samādhi* (Ch.: *Fahua sanmei*, Ja.: *Hokke zanmai*)—a Tiantai contemplation ritual aimed at eradicating one's karmic hindrances—erected by imperial decree at the elite convent Anguosi in the capital of Tang China at Luoyang during the Kaiyuan era (713–741). If this theory is correct, then the sins that the nuns of early Japanese provincial convents were to expiate through their recitation of the *Lotus Sūtra* were not their personal "sins" as women but the transgressions of the people as a whole.[25] In any event, via the nuns' component of the provincial temple system, the *Lotus* came to be associated with the theme of nation protection.

The Tendai founder Saichō also played a role in establishing the *Lotus* as a nation-protecting sūtra. At the monastery he founded on Mount Hiei, Saichō instituted two courses of study: one curriculum grounded in esoteric Buddhism and the other in study and meditation based on the *Lotus Sūtra* and traditional Tiantai teachings. Those who followed the latter course, he stipulated, should be able to recite and lecture upon the *Lotus*, *Golden Light*, and *Humane Kings* sūtras for the protection of the nation.[26] At least in part as a result of Saichō's influence, the *Lotus Sūtra* soon formally joined the *Golden Light* and *Humane Kings* sūtras, forming a triad of nation-protecting scriptures. By 877, a court edict required provincial lecture masters to know and be able to recite all three.[27]

A KARMIC LINK TO JAPAN?

Nation-protecting sūtras were thought to extend their protective power to any country where they were revered and recited. But there was a sense in which the *Lotus Sūtra* came to be thought of as specifically connected to Japan, an idea that may have originated with Saichō. On the one hand, Saichō saw the *Lotus Sūtra* as universal and all-inclusive. In establishing Tendai as an independent school, he sought to encompass esoteric ritual, Tendai meditation, precept observance, Zen practice, and indeed, the whole of Buddhism within the framework of the one vehicle of the *Lotus Sūtra*, which he understood as the only true perfect teaching. At the same time, however, in advocating the *Lotus Sūtra* and the Tendai teachings, he argued that the *Lotus* was particularly suited to his own time and place. "If we speak of the age," he wrote, "it is the end of the age of the Semblance Dharma and the beginning of the age of the Final Dharma [*mappō*]. If we inquire about the land we live in, it is to the east of China. . . . If we ask about the people to whom this teaching is to be preached, they are those born in a time of strife when the five defilements prevail."[28] Zhiyi and other Chinese exegetes had attributed differences among Buddhist teachings to the Buddha's accommodation of his preaching to the varying receptivities of his hearers. Saichō linked this issue of differences in receptivity to the country as a whole: the people of Japan, he asserted, have faculties according specifically with the perfect teaching, that is, the *Lotus Sūtra*. He wrote, "In our realm of Japan, faculties suited to the perfect teaching have already matured. The perfect teaching has finally arisen."[29]

The notion of a special connection between the *Lotus Sūtra* and a particular country might, on first encounter, seem peculiar, especially in light of the sūtra's universalistic assertion that "all shall attain the buddha way." However, from early on Japanese Buddhists were acutely conscious of their country's marginal position as a small island literally on the edge of the Buddhist world, far removed from Buddhism's birthplace in India and from the age of the historical Buddha, as seen in the recurring phrase "a peripheral land in the latter age" (*masse hendo*). Claims that particular scriptures, holy beings, or revered teachers had strong karmic ties to Japan are found throughout premodern Japanese Buddhist discourse. These Japan-centered representations work to overcome the sense of spatial and temporal separation from Buddhism's source by suggesting that the dharma still flourishes and enlightenment can still be achieved—even (or at times, especially) in the distant land of Japan and in a latter age.[30] Saichō's argument for a particular relationship between the *Lotus Sūtra* and Japan must be understood in this light. This alleged connection served not only to overcome a sense of separation in time and space from the historical Śākyamuni but in effect also endowed Japan with a special status as the place where the *Lotus Sūtra*, the Buddha's most profound teaching, would flourish. "The age of the [other,] provisional teachings has already drawn to a close, [like the sun] setting in the west," Saichō wrote. Then, he predicted, "The sun of the true teaching will now arise in [this] eastern land."[31]

The idea that Japan enjoys a distinctive connection to the *Lotus Sūtra* was reiterated by later Tendai thinkers, including Annen and Genshin (942–1017).[32] Such claims served not only to promote the authority of the Tendai school, which claimed the *Lotus Sūtra* as its fundamental scripture, but also to accord Japan an important, even central place within the Buddhist world.

THE *LOTUS SŪTRA*, JAPAN, AND NICHIREN

Unquestionably the single most influential figure in that strand of interpretation associating the *Lotus Sūtra* with the buddhahood of the land is Nichiren (1222–1282). Originally a Tendai monk, Nichiren is famous for having initiated one of the so-called "single practice" movements of Japan's Kamakura period (1185–1333). The claim of these movements, that a single form of practice can liberate all, was strongly rooted in Tendai ideas about the one vehicle and, in Nichiren's case, was explicitly connected to the *Lotus Sūtra*. Nichiren inherited the Tendai position that regards the *Lotus Sūtra* as the Buddha's ultimate teaching and all others as provisional, and he maintained that only the *Lotus* leads to liberation now in the age of the Final Dharma, in which he and his contemporaries believed themselves to be living. Nichiren also advocated the universal chanting of the sūtra's *daimoku* (title), in the formula *Namu myōhō renge kyō*, grounding the practice doctrinally in the origin teaching (*honmon*), or latter fourteen chapters of the sūtra, which he understood as specifically intended by the Buddha for this age.[33] Nichiren eventually brought together virtually all preexisting associations of the *Lotus Sūtra* with the land or realm and assimilated them to his claim for the exclusive validity of the *Lotus* in the present age.

The nonduality of living beings and their container world was an important concept for Nichiren from the outset, one that he developed from the perspectives both of traditional Tiantai/Tendai teachings about the interpenetration of the mind and all phenomena and of esoteric Buddhism. A passage from his first extant essay, written when he was twenty-one, reads in part: "When we attain the awakening of the *Lotus Sūtra*, our own person—composed of body and mind, and subject to birth and extinction—is precisely unborn and unperishing. And the land is also thus. [When we so awaken,] the oxen, horses, and six kinds of domestic animals in this land are all buddhas, and the grasses and trees, sun and moon, are all sage beings."[34] In his early writings, Nichiren deployed this idea against the Pure Land teachings of his day and their ethos of "shunning this defiled world and aspiring to the pure land" by seeking birth after death in the western realm of the Buddha Amida:

> QUESTION: Toward which pure land should one who practices the *Lotus Sūtra* aspire?
> ANSWER: The "Life Span" chapter, the heart and core of the twenty-eight chapters of the *Lotus Sūtra*, states, "I [Śākyamuni] have been constantly dwelling in this Sahā World." It also states, "I constantly abide here." And again it states, "This land of mine is secure and peaceful." According to these passages, the Buddha of the perfect teaching in his original ground, enlightened since the remotest past, abides in this world. Why should one abandon this world and aspire to another land? The place where one who practices the *Lotus Sūtra* dwells should be regarded as the pure land.[35]

Nichiren also developed the idea that the immanent buddha realm is an ever-present reality that one can enter through faith. In his major work, *On the Contemplation of the Mind and the Object of Worship* (*Kanjin honzon shō*), he writes: "The Sahā World of the present moment, which is the original time [of Śākyamuni Buddha's enlightenment in the remotest past], is the constantly abiding pure land, separated from the three disasters and beyond [the cycle of] the four kalpas. Its buddha has not already entered nirvāṇa in the past, nor is he yet to be born in the future. And his disciples are of the same essence. This [world] is none other than the three realms, which encompass the three thousand realms of one's mind."[36]

This constantly abiding pure land is the very realm depicted on Nichiren's great maṇḍala, the calligraphic object of worship (*honzon*) he devised, which represents in Chinese characters and Sanskrit letters the assembly of the *Lotus Sūtra* on Vulture Peak, where the ever-present Śākyamuni preaches to his auditors (fig. 1.1). For Nichiren, faith in the *Lotus Sūtra* thus collapses all temporal and spatial separation between the Buddha and the devotee;

by upholding the sūtra and chanting its daimoku, one can immediately enter into the *Lotus* assembly and dwell in the Buddha's presence.

Nichiren further drew on associations of the *Lotus Sūtra* with nation protection, linking them explicitly to Tendai thinking about the nonduality of person and land and adapting them to his exclusive advocacy of the *Lotus*. Since person and land are nondual, Nichiren held, the truth and efficacy of one's religious practice will be expressed in the outer conditions of one's land and society. Japan in his day was ravaged by a number of calamities, including famine, earthquakes, epidemics, and the threat of invasion by the Mongols. Nichiren saw these disasters as resulting from widespread slander of the dharma—willful rejection of the *Lotus Sūtra* in favor of what he viewed as inferior, provisional teachings no longer suited to human capacity in the Final Dharma age. Nichiren develops this theme in his famous treatise *On Bringing Peace to the Land by Establishing the True Dharma* (*Risshō ankoku ron*), submitted in 1260 to the government. In it he rebuked the Kamakura shogunate for its support of monks who promoted teachings that, from Nichiren's perspective, were no longer efficacious. The solution to the country's troubles was, to his mind, crystal clear: "Now with all speed you must simply reform your faith and at once devote it to the single good of the true vehicle. Then the threefold world will all become the buddha land, and could a buddha land decline? The ten directions will all become a treasure realm, and how could a treasure realm be destroyed?"[37]

The conviction that only the *Lotus Sūtra* could save the people as a whole underlay Nichiren's choice of the practice of *shakubuku* (cutting off and subduing attachments), a confrontational method of teaching the dharma by explicitly rebuking wrong views or attachment to provisional teachings. As discussed by Ruben L. F. Habito in chapter 7 of this volume, Nichiren's criticism of other forms of Buddhism—and of government officials for supporting them—provoked the anger of shogunal officials and influential religious leaders, and he and his community met with repeated persecutions. Nichiren stressed the need to defy even the ruler himself if he opposes the *Lotus Sūtra*.[38] In this context, Nichiren invoked traditional Buddhist cosmology and the idea of Śākyamuni Buddha as lord of the Sahā World to insist that the authority of the dharma, and of the *Lotus Sūtra* in particular, transcends worldly power: "[The Indian world-ruling deities] Brahmā and Indra govern the domain of our true father, Śākyamuni Tathāgata, and protect those who support monks of the true dharma. Vaiśravana and the others of the four heavenly kings who rule over and protect the four quarters serve as gatekeepers to Brahmā and Indra, while the monarchs of the four continents are vassals to Vaiśravana and the other heavenly kings. The ruler of Japan is not even equal to a vassal of the wheel-turning monarchs of the four continents. He is just an island chief."[39]

As we have seen, by teaching that establishing the true dharma would bring peace to the land, Nichiren explicitly united several distinct strands of Buddhist doctrine concerning the nonduality of sentient beings and the realms they inhabit, along with the perceived powers of Buddhist ritual to benefit the country, all in the service of his *Lotus* exclusivism. A striking characteristic of his approach was his insistence that the immanence of the buddha land in this world was not only to be realized subjectively, in the faith or meditative insight of individual practitioners, but also to be actualized in the outer world: "When all people throughout the land enter the one buddha vehicle, and the wonderful dharma [of the *Lotus*] alone flourishes, because the people all chant *Namu myōhō renge kyō*, the wind will not thrash the branches nor the rain fall hard enough to break the earth. The age will become like the reigns of [the Chinese sage-kings] Yao and Shun. In the present life, inauspicious calamities will be banished, and the people will obtain the art of longevity. . . . There can be no doubt of the sūtra's promise of 'peace and security in the present world.' "[40]

This seems to suggest a conviction on Nichiren's part that faith in the *Lotus Sūtra* could bring about an age of harmony with nature, just rule, and, in some sense, a transcending of impermanence. In his teaching, manifesting the buddha land in this world becomes a concrete goal of practice; to work for its realization is the responsibility of *Lotus* devotees. A marginal, often persecuted figure with only a small following in his own time, Nichiren himself had to abandon expectations that this goal would be achieved any time soon. Nonetheless, he introduced into the tradition of *Lotus Sūtra* interpretation what might be called a millennial element, a prophecy or vision of an ideal world, based on the spread of exclusive faith in the *Lotus Sūtra*, to be realized at some future time.

As noted, Nichiren inherited from Saichō and other Tendai predecessors the idea of a specific connection between the *Lotus Sūtra* and Japan. "Japan is a country where people have faculties related solely to the *Lotus Sūtra*," he wrote. "If they practice even a phrase or verse of it, they are certain to attain the way, because it is the teaching to which they have a connection. . . . As for the chanting of Amida Buddha's name [*nenbutsu*] and other good practices, Japan has no connection to them."[41] Especially later in his life, Nichiren assimilated the connection between the *Lotus Sūtra* and Japan to his claims for the exclusive efficacy of the daimoku. This trend paralleled his growing sense of himself as the bearer of a new teaching, one suited for the age of the Final Dharma, grounded solely in the origin teaching and distinguished in significant ways from earlier Tendai. Elaborating on Saichō's analogy of the sunset and sunrise, noted previously, he wrote, "The moon appears in the west and illuminates the east, while the sun emerges from the east and shines toward the west. The same is true of the buddha-dharma. In the True and Semblance Dharma ages, it moved from west to east, but in the Final Dharma age, it will return from east to west." In that age, Nichiren added, "the buddhadharma will surely emerge from the eastern land of Japan."[42] Nichiren's understanding of Japan's connection to the *Lotus Sūtra*, like that of Saichō before him, was embedded in a premodern discourse about Japan's place in Buddhist cosmology, a discourse routinely deployed by Buddhist leaders to argue the superior relevance of their own practices, doctrines, or institutions. In the modern period, however, Nichiren's vision of Japan as the source of a new buddhadharma was appropriated in the service of a different agenda altogether, one no medieval figure could likely have imagined.

THE *LOTUS SŪTRA* AND MODERN JAPANESE NATIONALISM

For roughly six centuries after Nichiren's death, his vision of establishing the buddha land in this world through the spread of the *Lotus Sūtra* remained for his followers an abstract ideal, with little serious expectation of its imminent fulfillment. At the beginning of the twentieth century, however, that vision was for the first time assimilated to concrete social and political agendas, closely allied to that era's nationalistic and expansionist aims. Nichiren's conception also acquired a strongly millenarian character as a religious ideal that would actually materialize in the foreseeable future. The emphasis in modern Nichiren Buddhist thought on concrete social action owes much to Buddhist modernism, a broader trend among both Asian and Western Buddhist interpreters that rejected traditional emphases on detached self-cultivation and rites for the deceased and sought instead to reorient Buddhist practice toward practical social engagement. Japanese Buddhist modernizers of the late nineteenth and early twentieth centuries, however, faced particular challenges, as Buddhism came under attack from the new Meiji government (1868–1912), which promoted state Shinto as the nation's ideological basis. The nation's leaders were determined to forge the country into a modern state, able to hold its own against Western powers, and Buddhist leaders of all sects strove to refigure their tradition as compatible with the goals of modernizing and nation building, and in time, with Japan's own imperialist ventures.[43] Throughout Japan's modern imperial period (1895–1945), the majority of Buddhist and other religious institutions generally supported the expansion of empire by promoting patriotism and loyalty to the emperor among their followers, sending chaplains abroad to minister to Japanese troops, and missionizing in subjugated territories. In this sense, the nationalistic orientation of modern *Lotus Sūtra* or Nichiren Buddhist interpreters was not unique. Nonetheless, they had inherited, as part of their doctrinal tradition, Nichiren's teaching of establishing the buddha land in the present world and his prophecy that the true dharma would one day emerge from Japan. At the time, these elements were susceptible to interpretation in the light of nationalistic aims and in turn imbued those aims with a millennial fervor.

Modern readings of the *Lotus Sūtra* and of Nichiren that emerged at this time are often collectively termed "Nichirenism" (*Nichiren-shugi*), meaning not the traditional Nichiren Buddhism of temples and priests (although Nichirenism enjoyed some support from that quarter) but a popular Nichiren doctrine welded to lay Buddhist practice and modern national aspirations.[44] (This Japan-centered use of the term corresponds to the first of the three modes of Nichirenism discussed in chapter 7 of this volume.) Of the clerics, sectarian scholars, and prominent lay leaders who contributed to the formation of nationalistic Nichirenism, I consider here only one of the most influential, Tanaka Chigaku (1861–1939), who in fact coined the term.[45] Tanaka abandoned his training for the Nichiren sect priesthood to become a lay evangelist, and in 1881, he founded a society, later reorganized as the Kokuchūkai, or "Pillar of the Nation Society" (after Nichiren's words, "I will be the pillar of Japan") to promote his ideology of Nichirenism. Eventually he won support from ranking government officials, army officers, leading intellectuals, and members of the public.[46]

Tanaka may have been the first *Lotus Sūtra* devotee to formulate a modern reading of the "this-worldly" buddha land. His 1901 *Restoration of Our [Nichiren] Sect* (*Shūmon no ishin*) sets forth an astonishing plan, complete with a detailed fifty-year timetable, for converting first Japan and then the world to the *Lotus Sūtra* and Nichiren's teaching. Some aspects of Tanaka's vision described in this tract now strike us as far-fetched, such as his prediction that, in two or three decades, Nichirenist sympathizers would dominate both houses of the Diet and make Nichiren Buddhism the national religion.[47] Yet *Restoration of Our Sect* also shows that Tanaka, alert to the trend of the times, was a shrewd innovator in proselytizing methods. His recommendations included moving preaching activities out of temples and into public auditoriums; organizing nursing corps and charitable hospitals to be run by the sect; publishing a daily newspaper and evangelical materials in vernacular Japanese; investing the sect's capital to make Nichiren Buddhism a significant economic force; and establishing colonies of Nichiren adherents in overseas countries as bases for global evangelizing.[48]

Tanaka's language in *Restoration of Our Sect* illustrates both his religious nationalism and the growing militancy of his Nichirenist interpretations: "Nichiren is the general of the army that will unite the world. Japan is his headquarters. The people of Japan are his troops; teachers and scholars of Nichiren Buddhism are his officers. The Nichiren creed is a declaration of war, and shakubuku is the plan of attack. . . . The faith of the *Lotus* [*Sūtra*] will prepare those going into battle. Japan truly has a heavenly mandate to unite the world."[49]

From around the time of the Russo-Japanese War (1904–1905), the *Lotus Sūtra* became increasingly fused in Tanaka's thought with the idea of the Japanese national essence or polity (*kokutai*), the ideological pillar of Meiji nationalism. "The truth contained in the *Lotus Sūtra* and the Japanese national essence form one another, like front and back, and are mutually dependent, like essence and function. Truly, this is the great way of non-duality," he wrote.[50] Tanaka even developed a Japan-centered hermeneutic by which he read the entire *Lotus Sūtra* as a revelation of the nation's destiny. For example, the word "thus" in "Thus have I heard" in the sūtra's opening passage he interpreted as the Japanese national essence, and "I heard" as practicing the great way of loyalty to the nation. Tanaka interpreted the "heavenly drums [that] resound of their own accord" when the Buddha begins to preach as heralding Japan's mission of world unification; the sūtra's reference, in Chapter 14, to the wheel-turning sage-king as foreshadowing the military might of the Meiji emperor; and the Buddha's demonstration of his supernatural powers as Japan's military victories against China and Russia.[51]

The buddhahood of the land, in the sense of peace, just rule, and the manifestation of the *Lotus Sūtra*'s blessings in all spheres of human activity, was something Nichiren himself had envisioned. But neither Nichiren nor his medieval followers had understood this goal as necessarily allied to any specific regime or form of government. For these earlier figures, any ruler—whether emperor or shogun—who upheld the *Lotus Sūtra* would serve its realization. For Tanaka, however, the buddhahood of the land was to be exemplified, mediated, and extended to all humanity by the modern imperial Japanese state. And Tanaka's vision of a world united under the *Lotus Sūtra*—equated in his reading with the Japanese national essence—was congruent with that state's own imperialistic agenda of a world united under Japanese rule. In particular, by identifying the *Lotus Sūtra* with the Japanese national essence, Tanaka elevated a particular nation's polity to the status of universal truth. This philosophical move legitimated unreserved support for the imperial system and abolished the critical distance that Nichiren and his early tradition had maintained toward rulers who do not embrace the *Lotus Sūtra*. It also conflated the spread of the *Lotus Sūtra* by shakubuku with the expansion of Japanese hegemony and legitimated armed aggression on the Asian mainland. Wartime Nichirenism serves as a sobering reminder that religion has been used to legitimate some deeply troubling agendas, and Buddhism is no exception.

Chilling and repugnant as his views may seem today, Tanaka is nonetheless important to the history of the *Lotus Sūtra*'s reception as the first person to directly associate its teaching of the immanent buddha land with a specific social and political agenda. His nationalistic Nichirenism represents, one might say, an early form of modern *Lotus*-based "socially engaged Buddhism," although that term usually carries assumptions of Buddhist universalism and nonviolence. Tanaka may also have been the first religious leader in modern Nichiren Buddhist history to have conceived the worldwide spread of the *Lotus Sūtra* not as a remote ideal but as a target within actual reach. In this regard, his activities may have exerted a considerable if indirect impact on contemporary movements of lay Nichiren Buddhism, even those that vehemently reject his values.

THE POSTWAR *LOTUS SŪTRA*

Today, *Lotus*-inspired visions of a this-worldly buddha land continue to be linked to concrete agendas of social activism, as discussed in chapter 7 of this volume. Since Japan's defeat in 1945, however, these agendas no longer entail military conquest but rather urge nuclear disarmament and the establishment of global peace. The aim of a harmonious society based on Buddhist ideals is of course by no means confined to *Lotus Sūtra* devotees but is advocated by many Japanese religious bodies, including traditional Buddhist sects and new religious movements, several of which support the United Nations as nongovernmental organizations (NGOs) and promote international relief and local welfare work. However, world peace as a goal to be achieved through Buddhist practice has been most explicitly articulated in the Japanese context by movements associated with the *Lotus Sūtra* and Nichiren. Like the Nichirenism of the earlier, modern imperial period, these movements draw creatively on Nichiren's doctrines of establishing peace in the realm through faith in the *Lotus Sūtra* and realizing a this-worldly buddha realm, but they refigure them in the light of postwar pacifistic ideals.[52] Different *Lotus*-related groups offer variations on this theme. As examples, let us look briefly at two prominent lay Buddhist movements that achieved their major growth in the postwar decades: Sōka Gakkai and Risshō Kōseikai, the two largest of Japan's so-called "new religions."

Both groups hold NGO status in the United Nations and also mobilize their members for volunteer welfare work: Kōseikai has been especially active in famine relief, while Sōka Gakkai has since the 1970s carried out grassroots efforts for "peace education" and, more recently, established the Toda Institute for Global Peace and Policy Research to promote collaboration among peace researchers, policy makers, and activists. In 1964, in a highly controversial move, it also founded a political party, the Komeitō or Clean Government Party, to implement Buddhist ideals in politics.[53] Despite their activism, however, both groups hold social welfare activities to be secondary to the fundamental transformation of character—the "human revolution," in Sōka Gakkai terms, or "reformation of the mind," in Risshō Kōseikai parlance—said to come about through practice of the *Lotus Sūtra*, on which world peace in any real sense must depend. Both hold that war and other social evils have their roots in the greed, anger, and delusion of individuals. It is therefore individual efforts in self-cultivation and promoting harmony in everyday relations—rather than diplomatic or political efforts—that will fundamentally establish world peace. To quote Ikeda Daisaku (1928–), president of Sōka Gakkai International: "The individual human revolution will never stop with just that person. It represents a moment that surely encompasses all humanity. . . . As a single drop of water or speck of dust, each of you must win the trust of those around you, acting on the basis of our common humanity, and steadily advance the movement of a new awakening of life. Your own awakening will give rise to the next awakened person, who in turn will be followed by two, three, and ten in succession, becoming a great ocean of nirvāṇa and a great mountain of wondrous enlightenment, just as Nichiren teaches."[54]

Working to establish world peace is, in other words, conceived of as an integral part of each individual member's Buddhist practice. In the ethos of these lay movements, the humblest actions and interactions of daily life, performed conscientiously and with a sense of that greater purpose, all become bodhisattva practice and karmic causes linked directly to the realization of a better world: what governments and diplomacy have failed to accomplish, ordinary believers are in fact achieving. It is here, in the heightened sense of personal meaning, with the conviction that one has a larger mission to fulfill, that these movements have exerted their chief appeal.

Interestingly, despite this shared ethos, these two groups embrace radically different understandings of what it means to practice the *Lotus Sūtra*. Sōka Gakkai's position is exclusivistic and maintains that only the spread of Nichiren's teachings, as interpreted by its own organizational lineage, can bring about world peace. Sōka Gakkai ultimately blamed the sufferings sustained during Japan's misguided militarist ventures and even Japan's eventual defeat on adherence to other, false religions. This conviction underlay the organization's aggressive missionizing in the postwar decades. Risshō Kōseikai, on the other hand, has taken an ecumenical approach. Its cofounder and longtime president Niwano Nikkyō (1906–1999) went so far as to claim that "*Lotus Sūtra*" is not a proper noun but the fundamental truth—God, Allah, or the one vehicle—at the heart of all great religions.[55] Niwano himself tirelessly promoted worldwide interfaith dialogue for peace.

Niwano's popular lectures on the *Lotus Sūtra* vividly show how the sūtra has become associated in the postwar and contemporary periods with the aim of global peace. "The whole *Lotus Sūtra* embodies an ideology of peace," he asserted.[56] From this hermeneutical perspective, Niwano read specific passages and parables from the sūtra as teaching how peace is to be achieved. For example, Śākyamuni Buddha's gratitude toward his vindictive cousin Devadatta for favors in a prior life teaches one to break the cycle of enmity by refusing to bear grudges. The parable of the medicinal herbs, which receive the same rain but grow to different heights in accord with their capacity, teaches that differences among nations must be respected; developing nations must not be arbitrarily expected to emulate the industrial model of developed nations. In the parable of the magically conjured city, the long, steep path represents "the long history of mankind's suffering caused by war, starvation, poverty, the violation of human rights, and so on." The conjured city itself symbolizes temporary peace—the physical cessation of war. The place of jewels, the real goal of the journey, is "the reformation of one's mind by religion" that must underlie lasting peace.[57] Niwano explains the envisioned results of this "reformation of the mind" in his interpretation of Chapter 21 of the *Lotus Sūtra*, "Supernatural Powers of the Thus Come One," in which the Buddha opens unobstructed passage among the worlds in the ten directions, as though they were a single buddha land (Hurvitz, 264). This foretells, Niwano writes, that "a world of great harmony will appear when all nations, all races, and all classes come to live in accordance with the one truth, so that discrimination among them vanishes, discord and fighting do not occur, and all the people work joyfully, enjoy their lives, and promote culture. In short, the whole world will become one buddha-land. Organizationally speaking, it can be said that the buddha-land means the formation of a world federation."[58]

Niwano is here interpreting the very passage that Tanaka Chigaku, earlier in the same century, had read as presaging world unification under the Japanese empire. Few examples could better illustrate how quickly, under the right circumstances, scriptural understandings can shift, and how the same text can be enlisted to support radically different agendas.

We have seen some of the ways in which the *Lotus Sūtra*'s references to this world as the realm of Śākyamuni Buddha have been understood: as an aspect of nondual reality to be discerned through meditation; in terms of thaumaturgical rites of nation protection; as a valorization of nature and sacred geography; in the light of claims for a specific connection to Japan; as a millennial vision of an ideal society; and in terms of a range of modern social and political agendas, from militant imperialism to world peace. What are we to make of so many different, even contradictory, readings of a single text?

As Chapter 1 of this volume notes, some scholars have argued that the *Lotus Sūtra*, lacking clear propositional content, is like an empty container that later readers have filled with their own interpretations. The *Lotus Sūtra*'s wealth of mythic imagery, and its relative paucity of explicit doctrine, may indeed have rendered it exceptionally open to multiple readings. But this is far from the whole story. Interpretation of the *Lotus Sūtra*—or of any scripture—does not take place solely in the encounter between reader and text but is also shaped by multiple, interrelated contexts. First, there is the complex diachronic context of received tradition: devotees, practitioners, and scholars bring to their reading elements drawn from the accretions of previous interpretations. Nichiren's understanding of the immanent buddha realm, for example, was not formed only by his personal reading of the *Lotus Sūtra* text but was mediated by Tiantai/Tendai doctrines of the nonduality of person and land and the buddhahood of the insentient. Similarly, later interpretations were influenced by Nichiren's own teaching and his prophecy that the ideal buddha land would one day be realized in this world. Such layers of interpretation do not necessarily accumulate in a simple linear fashion. Some, like Zhiyi's concept of the three thousand realms in a single thought-moment, came directly out of the work of *Lotus Sūtra* interpretation, while others, such as notions of nation protection, emerged independently of the *Lotus Sūtra* and were only later assimilated to it. Over time, particular strands of the received interpretive tradition are internalized and naturalized, to the point that they become "obviously" what the sūtra is about. Indeed, for many devotees, the term "*Lotus Sūtra*" may serve less as the name of a scripture than as a referent for ideas or aims that may have little direct relation to the sūtra text but that later came to be associated with it.

Of the many received layers of sūtra interpretation, which elements are selected, which rejected, and how any individual element is understood at a given time are all shaped by synchronic contexts: historical and political circumstances, intellectual assumptions, social trends, and the hopes and desires of the sūtra's devotees. Thus, at different junctures, it has appeared obvious that the *Lotus Sūtra* foretells Japanese imperial conquest, or that it contains a blueprint for global peace. Particular readings cease to be obvious when the concerns, assumptions, or worldviews that once informed them no longer hold sway, although the possibility for their revival always remains. A literal reading of the "realization of buddhahood by grasses and trees," for example, more congruent with medieval sensibilities than with modern ones, has long since fallen by the wayside; nonetheless, one could readily imagine its being revived with a postmodern twist in the service of a Buddhist environmental ethic. To gain insight into why people have interpreted the *Lotus Sūtra*'s immanent buddha realm in so many ways, it is necessary to be familiar with not only the sūtra text itself but also the sūtra's history of interpretation and the circumstances that have shaped that process over time.

NOTES

1. The "three spheres" are the realms of desire, form, and formlessness that constitute the world in Buddhist cosmology, from the lowest reaches of the hells to the highest heavens.
2. Tsumori Kiichi, "Ryōzen jōdo shinkō no keifu," *Nichiren kyōgaku kenkyūjo kiyō* 15 (1988): 23–51.
3. This idea is vividly illustrated in the opening chapter of the *Vimalakīrtinirdeśa*. See Robert A. F. Thurman, trans., *The Holy Teaching of Vimalakīrti: A Mahāyāna Scripture* (University Park: Pennsylvania State University Press, 1976), 18–19.
4. Stephan Beyer, "Notes on the Vision Quest in Early Mahāyāna," in *Prajñāpāramitā and Related Systems: Studies in Honor of Edward Conze*, ed. Lewis Lancaster with Luis O. Gómez, Berkeley Buddhist Studies Series 1, 329–40 (Berkeley: Institute of

East Asian Studies, 1977); and Paul Harrison, "Mediums and Messages: Reflections on the Production of Mahāyāna Sūtras," *Eastern Buddhist*, n.s., 35, nos. 1–2 (2003): 115–47, especially 117–22.

5. *Mohe zhiguan*, Zhiyi (538–597), *Taishō shinshū daizōkyō*, 100 vols., ed. Takakusu Junjirō, Watanabe Kaigyoku, and Ono Gemmyō (1924–1934; repr., Taibei: Xinwenfeng chuban gongsi, 1974) (hereafter abbreviated as *T*) no. 1911, 46:1c24–25; Paul L. Swanson, trans., *The Great Cessation-and-Contemplation (Mo-ho chih-kuan)* (Tokyo: Kōsei, 2004), 21, CD-ROM, also available at Swanson's Web site under "Staff" at http://www.ic.nanzan-u.ac.jp/SHUBUNKEN/staff/staff.htm. See also Neal Donner and Daniel B. Stevenson, *The Great Calming and Contemplation: A Study and Annotated Translation of the First Chapter of Chih-i's "Mo-ho chih-kuan,"* Kuroda Institute, Classics in East Asian Buddhism (Honolulu: University of Hawai'i Press, 1993), 112–13. This oft-quoted passage is actually from the preface by Zhiyi's disciple Guanding.
6. On the three thousand realms in a single thought-moment, see Kanno Hiroshi, *Ichinen sanzen to wa nani ka* (Tokyo: Daisan bunmeisha, 1992). In English, see Jacqueline I. Stone, *Original Enlightenment and the Transformation of Medieval Japanese Buddhism*, Kuroda Institute, Studies in East Asian Buddhism 12 (Honolulu: University of Hawai'i Press, 1999), 178–81.
7. *Mohe zhiguan*, *T* 46:54a3–6. Here Zhiyi explains that good and evil lands, like the beings who inhabit them, equally possess the ten suchnesses or universal characteristics into which he analyzes the "true aspect of the dharmas" (Ch.: *zhufa shixiang*, Ja: *shohō jissō*).
8. *Fahua xuanyi shiqian*, Zhanran (711–782), *T* no. 1717, 33:919a26–b10.
9. *Zhiguan fuxingzhuan hongjue*, Zhanran (711–782), *T* no. 1912, 46:295c23–24.
10. Zhanran developed this concept most fully in his *Diamond Scalpel* (*Jingang bei*, *T* no. 1932). An English translation and annotation appear in Linda Penkower, "T'ien-t'ai during the T'ang Dynasty: Chan-jan and the Sinification of Buddhism" (Ph.D. diss., Columbia University, 1993), 360–556.
11. *Jingang bei*, *T* 46:784b21, 785b8–9; trans., from Penkower, "T'ien-t'ai during the T'ang Dynasty," 510, 525, slightly modified.
12. The actual term "pure land of Sacred [Vulture] Peak" (Ja.: *Ryōzen jōdo*) may have first been used by the Tendai founder Saichō (766 or 767–822), who employs it to refer to the pure land of the primordially enlightened Śākyamuni and as equivalent to "the truth that is the highest meaning" (*Naishō buppō sōjō kechimyaku fu*, Saichō, in *Dengyō Daishi zenshū*, ed. Hieizan Senshūin fuzoku Eizan gakuin, 5 vols. [Tokyo: Sekai seiten kankō kyōkai, 1989] [hereafter abbreviated as *DDZ*], 1:215). From at least the ninth century, the "pure land of Sacred Vulture Peak" was also occasionally envisioned as a postmortem destination; see Tsumori, "Ryōzen jōdo shinkō no keifu," 33–37.
13. Stone, *Original Enlightenment*, especially 24–27, 170–72, 353.
14. *Enkai jūrokujō*, Kōen (1263–1317), in *Zoku Tendaishū zensho*, ed. Tendai shūten hensanjo (Tokyo: Shunjūsha, 1989), *Enkai* 1:88–91; see also Stone, *Original Enlightenment*, 135–37.
15. *Shinjō sōmoku jōbutsu shiki*, Annen (841–?), reproduced in Sueki Fumihiko, *Heian shoki bukkyō shisō no kenkyū* (Tokyo: Shunjūsha, 1995), 713. Annen presents this famous statement as a quotation from the *Zhongyin jing* (Zhu Fonian [fourth century], *T* no. 385), but it does not appear in extant versions of that text. See also Fabio Rambelli, "The Buddhist Philosophy of Objects and the Status of Inanimate Entities,"

in his *Buddhist Materiality: A Cultural History of Objects in Japanese Buddhism*, Asian Religions and Cultures (Stanford, Calif.: Stanford University Press, 2007), 11–57. Rambelli's book provides a comprehensive bibliography on this topic.

16. *Sōmoku hosshin shugyō jōbutsu ki*, attributed to Ryōgen (912–985) but quite probably a later work (ca. twelfth to fourteenth centuries), in *Dainihon bukkyō zensho*, 151 vols. (Tokyo: Bussho kankōkai, 1912–1922), 24:345a. See Sueki, *Heian shoki bukkyō shisō no kenkyū*, 416–17.
17. Donald H. Shively, "Buddhahood for the Nonsentient: A Theme in Nō Plays," *Harvard Journal of Asiatic Studies* 20, nos. 1–2 (1957): 135–61.
18. William R. LaFleur, "Saigyō and the Buddhist Value of Nature," *History of Religions* 13, no. 2 (1973): 93–128; 13, no. 3 (1974): 227–48. The quotation is in 13, no. 2 (1973): 93.
19. Allan G. Grapard, "Flying Mountains and Walkers of Emptiness: Toward a Definition of Sacred Space in Japanese Religions," *History of Religions* 20, no. 3 (1982): 195–221.
20. Tsumori, "Ryōzen jōdo shinkō no keifu," 30–31.
21. *Keiran jūyōshū*, comp. Kōshū (1276–1350), *T* no. 2410, 76:860a26–27.
22. Allan G. Grapard, "The Textualized Mountain—Enmountained Text: The *Lotus Sutra* in Kunisaki," in *The Lotus Sutra in Japanese Culture*, ed. George J. Tanabe Jr. and Willa Jane Tanabe (Honolulu: University of Hawai'i Press, 1989), 172–73. East Asian tradition long maintained that Kumārajīva's *Lotus Sūtra* contains 69,384 characters. However, no extant version has precisely that number, although the sūtra does comprise approximately 70,000 characters; see Kabutogi Shōkō, *Hokke hangyō no kenkyū* (Tokyo: Daitō shuppansha, 1982), 322–25.
23. Marinus Willem de Visser, *Ancient Buddhism in Japan: Sutras and Ceremonies in Use in the Seventh and Eighth Centuries* A.D. *and Their History in Later Times*, 2 vols. (Leiden: Brill, 1935), 1:13, 14, 116–17.
24. The imperial orders concerning the provincial temple system are summarized in De Visser, *Ancient Buddhism in Japan*, 2:646–48.
25. Katsuura Noriko, "*Hokke* metsuzai no tera to Rakuyō Ankokuji *Hokke* dōjō: Ama to amadera no Nittō hikaku kenkyū no kadai," *Shiron* 46 (1993): 1–18; Kazuhiko Yoshida, "The Enlightenment of the Dragon King's Daughter in the *Lotus Sutra*," translated and adapted by Margaret H. Childs, in *Engendering Faith: Women and Buddhism in Premodern Japan*, ed. Barbara Ruch, (Ann Arbor: Center for Japanese Studies, University of Michigan, 2002), 304–5. A connection between the adoption of the *Lotus Sūtra* and its perceived powers of eradicating sin was also suggested by De Visser, *Ancient Buddhism in Japan*, 2:653. On the *Lotus* samādhi, see Daniel B. Stevenson, "The Four Kinds of Samādhi in Early T'ien-t'ai Buddhism," in *Traditions of Meditation in Chinese Buddhism*, ed. Peter N. Gregory, Kuroda Institute, Studies in East Asian Buddhism 4, 45–97 (Honolulu: University of Hawai'i Press, 1986).
26. *Sange gakushōshiki*, *DDZ* 1:12; see also Paul Groner, *Saichō: The Establishment of the Japanese Tendai School*, Berkeley Buddhist Studies Series 7 (Berkeley: Center for South and Southeast Asian Studies, 1984; repr., Honolulu: University of Hawai'i Press, 2000), 120–21.
27. *Fusō ryakki*, Kōen (?–1169), in *Shintei zōho kokushi taikei*, ed. Kuroita Katsumi and Kokushi taikei henshūkai, represented by Maruyama Jirō, 66 vols. (Tokyo: Yoshikawa kōbunkan, 1929–1966), 12:125, entry for 5/9; and *Ruijū sandaikyaku*, author unknown, ibid., 25:51–52.

28. *Hokke shūku, DDZ* 3:251; trans. Groner, *Saichō*, 170, modified. The *Lotus Sūtra* says that buddhas appear in a world stained by the five defilements—of the kalpa, the passions, the beings, views, and life span (Hurvitz, 30, slightly modified). On Saichō's views of the *Lotus Sūtra* and Japan, see Groner, *Saichō*, 170, 174–76, 181–82.
29. *Ehyō Tendaishū, DDZ* 3:343.
30. For an overview of such claims, see Mark L. Blum, "The *Sangoku-Mappō* Construct: Buddhism, Nationalism, and History in Medieval Japan," in *Discourse and Ideology in Medieval Japanese Buddhism*, ed. Richard K. Payne and Taigen Dan Leighton, 31–51 (London: Routledge, 2006).
31. *Shugo kokkai shō, DDZ* 2:234.
32. *Futsūju bosatsukai kōshaku*, Annen, *T* no. 2381, 74:757c24; *Ichijō yōketsu*, Genshin (942–1017), *T* no. 2370, 74:351a3.
33. *Namu myōhō renge kyō* represents full scholarly transliteration of the daimoku, but slightly differing pronunciations are used among some contemporary groups; see chapter 1, n. 72, in this volume.
34. *Kaitai sokushin jōbutsu gi*, Nichiren (1222–1282), in *Shōwa teihon Nichiren Shōnin ibun*, ed. Risshō daigaku Nichiren kyōgaku kenkyūjo, 4 vols. (Minobu-chō, Yamanashi, Japan: Minobusan Kuonji, 1952–1959; rev. 1988) (hereafter abbreviated as *Teihon*), 1:14.
35. *Shugo kokka ron, Teihon* 1:129. For the quotations from the *Lotus Sūtra*, see Hurvitz, 220, 223, and 224, modified. In his later years, Nichiren interpreted Vulture Peak, where Śākyamuni Buddha continually preaches the *Lotus Sūtra*, as the postmortem destination of *Lotus* devotees. However, Nichiren posits this postmortem pure land not in opposition to the pure land to be realized in this world but as an extension of it, to encompass the deceased faithful; see Stone, *Original Enlightenment*, 292–94.
36. *Kanjin honzon shō, Teihon* 1:712. The "four kalpas" are the eons of formation, stability, decline, and extinction. The "three realms" refer to the division of all phenomena into the five *skandhas*, living beings, and their lands, a fundamental component principle of the three thousand realms in a single thought-moment.
37. *Risshō ankoku ron, Teihon* 1:226.
38. See Jacqueline I. Stone, "When Disobedience Is Filial and Resistance Is Loyal: The *Lotus Sutra* and Social Obligations in the Medieval Nichiren Tradition," in *A Buddhist Kaleidoscope: Essays on the Lotus Sutra*, ed. Gene Reeves, 261–81 (Tokyo: Kōsei, 2002).
39. "Hōmon mōsarubekiyō no koto," *Teihon* 1:448. Parenthetically, between 1932 and 1944, at the height of militant nationalism, the Japanese Home Ministry and the Ministry of Education repeatedly demanded the deletion from Nichiren's writings of this and other passages—eventually totaling more than two hundred—that were deemed disrespectful to imperial authority; see Cheryl M. Allam, "The Nichiren and Catholic Confrontation with Japanese Nationalism," *Buddhist-Christian Studies* 10 (1990): 35–84, especially 56–58.
40. *Nyosetsu shugyō shō, Teihon* 1:733; Hurvitz, 96, modified.
41. "Nanjō Hyōe Shichirō-dono gosho," *Teihon* 1:324.
42. *Kenbutsu mirai ki, Teihon* 1:741, 742; see also "Soya Nyūdō-dono gari gosho," *Teihon*, 1:909. A more detailed discussion of this topic would take into consideration Nichiren's mandate for the future establishment of an ordination platform of the origin teaching as a central place of practice for the entire world, to be erected by official edict once the rulers of Japan had embraced faith in the *Lotus Sūtra*. See

Pier P. Del Campana, trans., "*Sandaihihō-shō*: An Essay on the Three Great Mysteries by Nichiren," *Monumenta Nipponica* 26, no. 1 (1971): 205–24; and Jacqueline I. Stone, "'By Imperial Edict and Shogunal Decree': Politics and the Issue of the Ordination Platform in Modern Lay Nichiren Buddhism," in *Buddhism in the Modern World: Adaptations of an Ancient Tradition*, ed. Steven Heine and Charles S. Prebish, 192–219 (New York: Oxford University Press, 2003).

43. On the Meiji-period refiguration of Japanese Buddhism, see James Edward Ketelaar, *Of Heretics and Martyrs in Meiji Japan: Buddhism and Its Persecution* (Princeton, N.J.: Princeton University Press, 1990).

44. On Nichirenism, see Gerald Scott Iguchi, "Nichirenism as Modernism: Imperialism, Fascism, and Buddhism in Modern Japan" (Ph.D. diss., University of California, San Diego, 2006); Ōtani Eiichi, *Kindai Nihon no Nichiren-shugi undō* (Kyoto: Hōzōkan, 2001); and Tokoro Shigemoto, *Kindai shakai to Nichiren-shugi* (Tokyo: Hyōronsha, 1972).

45. On Tanaka, see Iguchi, "Nichirenism as Modernism," 67–121; Edwin B. Lee, "Nichiren and Nationalism: The Religious Patriotism of Tanaka Chigaku," *Monumenta Nipponica* 30, no. 1 (1975): 19–35; and George J. Tanabe Jr., "Tanaka Chigaku: The *Lotus Sutra* and the Body Politic," in Tanabe and Tanabe, *Lotus Sutra in Japanese Culture*, 191–208.

46. Some of the better-known figures influenced to some extent by Tanaka include the religious studies scholar Anesaki Masaharu (1873–1949), instrumental in introducing Japanese religion to the West; Inoue Nisshō (1886–1967), agrarian reformer, a lay Nichiren devotee, and founder of the civilian terrorist organization Ketsumeidan (League of Blood); and General Ishiwara (also read Ishihara) Kanji (1889–1949), operations officer of the Guangdong Army, whose role in precipitating the 1931 Japanese invasion of Manchuria seems to have been inspired by his apocalyptic reading of Tanaka's nationalistic teachings on Nichiren and the *Lotus Sūtra*. The literary figures Takayama Chōgyū (1871–1902) and Miyazawa Kenji (1896–1933) were also briefly drawn to Tanaka, though they eventually rejected his nationalistic views.

47. In 1923 Tanaka did in fact found a political party and ran, unsuccessfully, for a Diet seat, an early attempt to realize the aim of a *Lotus*-centered society via modern political processes; see Ōtani, *Kindai Nihon no Nichiren-shugi undō*, 297–98, 322–29.

48. Tanaka's appendix to *Shūmon no ishin* (1901), in *Shishiō zenshū*, ed. Shishiō zenshū kankōkai, 36 vols. (Tokyo: Shishiō bunkō, 1931–1938), 7:93–134; see also Lee, "Nichiren and Nationalism," 26–27.

49. *Shūmon no ishin*, 7:16; translation from Lee, "Nichiren and Nationalism," 26.

50. Tanaka Chigaku, *Honge kyōhan Hokke hakkō*, in *Tanaka Chigaku jiden*, 10 vols. (Tokyo: Shishiō bunkō, 1936), 7:163.

51. Ibid., 7:102, 103, 155, 107; see also the discussion in George J. Tanabe Jr., "Tanaka Chigaku," 202–4.

52. Robert Kisala, *Prophets of Peace: Pacifism and Cultural Identity in Japan's New Religions* (Honolulu: University of Hawai'i Press, 1999); Jacqueline I. Stone, "Japanese *Lotus* Millennialism: From Militant Nationalism to Contemporary Peace Movements," in *Millennialism, Persecution, and Violence: Historical Cases*, ed. Catherine Wessinger, 261–80 (Syracuse, N.Y.: Syracuse University Press, 2000); and Stone, "Nichiren's Activist Heirs: Sōka Gakkai, Risshō Kōseikai, Nipponzan Myōhōji," in *Action Dharma: New Studies in Engaged Buddhism*, ed. Christopher

Queen, Charles Prebish, and Damien Keown, 63–94 (New York: RoutledgeCurzon, 2003).

53. On Kōmeitō, see Hiroshi Aruga, "Soka Gakkai and Japanese Politics," in *Global Citizens: The Soka Gakkai Buddhist Movement in the World*, ed. David Machacek and Bryan Wilson, 97–127 (New York: Oxford University Press, 2000); Robert Kisala, "Sōka Gakkai, Kōmeitō, and the Separation of Religion and State in Japan," *Bulletin of the Nanzan Institute for Religion and Culture* 18 (spring 1994): 7–17; and Daniel A. Métraux, *The Soka Gakkai Revolution* (Lanham, Md.: University Press of America, 1994), 39–69.
54. Ikeda Daisaku, "Ikeda kaichō no gosho kōgi: *Senjishō*," *Daibyakurenge* 320 (November 1977): 170–71.
55. Nikkyō Niwano, *A Buddhist Approach to Peace*, trans. Masuo Nezu (Tokyo: Kōsei, 1977), 68, 71.
56. Ibid., 63; see also chaps. 2 and 3.
57. Ibid., 59–60.
58. Ibid., 65.

TRANSLATIONS OF THE *LOTUS SŪTRA* INTO EUROPEAN LANGUAGES

Listings are arranged alphabetically by translator.

Borsig, Margareta von. *Sūtra von der Lotosblume des wunderbaren Gesetzes*. Darmstadt, Ger.: Wissenschaftliche Buchgesellschaft, 1993. German translation of Kumārajīva's version as contained in the *Taishō* canon.

Buddhist Text Translation Society. *The Wonderful Dharma Lotus Flower Sutra, Translated into Chinese by Tripitaka Master Kumarajiva of Yao Ch'in*. 10 vols. San Francisco: Sino-American Buddhist Association, Buddhist Text Translation Society, 1977–1982. Titles of each of the volumes are not consistent, and the cover lists Tripitaka Master Hua (from Hsüan-hua, the Wade-Giles form of Xuanhua) as the main author. Some library catalogs credit individual members of the translation committee (Bhikshuni Heng Yin or Upasika Kuo-lin Lethcoe) as the translators of different volumes. This is an English translation of Kumārajīva's version as contained in the *Taishō* canon. The volumes include extensive commentary by the modern Chinese monk Xuanhua (1918–1995). Xuanhua emigrated to the United States and founded the Dharma Realm Buddhist Association, which carries out educational and scholarly efforts through the Buddhist Text Translation Society.

Burnouf, Eugène. *Le lotus de la bonne loi; traduit du sanscrit, accompagné d'un commentaire et de vingt et un mémoires relatifs au bouddhisme*. Paris: Imprimerie Nationale, 1852. Reprint, Paris: Librairie d'Amérique et d'Orient, Adrien Maisonneuve, J. Maisonneuve, 1973. The first complete translation of the *Lotus Sūtra* into a Western language. Translated from twelfth-century Sanskrit manuscripts preserved in Nepal and procured, in 1837, by Brian Houghton Hodgson for the Société Asiatique. Burnouf's translation was completed by 1840 but not published until after his death. Includes extensive annotation (pp. 285–434) discussing textual variants, comparison with the Tibetan translation of the *Lotus*, and philological questions, plus another twenty-one chapters discussing deities, doctrines, and terms in the text.

Deeg, Max. *Das Lotos-Sūtra, übersetzt von Max Deeg, mit einer Einleitung von Max Deeg und Helwig Schmidt-Glintzer*. Darmstadt, Ger.: Wissenschaftliche Buchgesellschaft, 2007. German translation of Kumārajīva's text from the *Taishō* canon. Deeg renders into German most words that Kumārajīva translates into Chinese (exceptions include Avalokiteśvara) and gives Sanskrit transliteration (phonetic transcription) for words that Kumārajīva transliterates.

Hurvitz, Leon. *Scripture of the Lotus Blossom of the Fine Dharma (The Lotus Sūtra), Translated from the Chinese of Kumārajīva*. Records of Civilization: Sources and

Studies 94, Translations from the Asian Classics. New York: Columbia University Press, 1976; rev. ed., 2009. Hurvitz translates Kumārajīva's Chinese version, based on a Japanese critical edition of the text published in 1891. Hurvitz compares Kumārajīva's Chinese to a late Sanskrit version of the text, offering comments or translations of the Sanskrit in footnotes (or, in Chapter 5, in the body of the text) wherever the two diverge. The translation is considered among the most accurate and consistent, on a word-by-word basis, of the English translations of Kumārajīva's text. Hurvitz renders into English any word that Kumārajīva translates into Chinese (including most proper names), and he gives in Sanskrit any word that Kumārajīva transliterates. One exception is the word *dharma*, which Kumārajīva translates into Chinese (*fa*, "law" or "doctrine") but which Hurvitz renders in Sanskrit as "dharma." Hurvitz's extensive glossary consists of words in romanized Sanskrit. In the original edition (1976), the few words in Chinese that appear in his notes, introduction, and glossary are given in a modified form of the Wade-Giles system of romanization; in the revised, second edition (2009), they have been converted to the Pinyin system. The revised edition contains other small revisions and an updating of copyediting style, and its pagination differs slightly from that of the first edition.

Katō, Bunnō. *Myōhō-Renge-Kyō: The Sutra of the Lotus Flower of the Wonderful Law.* Revised by W. E. Soothill and Wilhelm Schiffer. Tokyo: Risshō kōseikai, 1971. The original translation was completed in 1930 by Katō, revised first by Soothill and later by Schiffer. In the preface but not on the title page, Yoshirō Tamura is also credited with assisting in the revision. This is a translation of Kumārajīva's Chinese version. Most words translated in the original are translated into English, and most words given in transliteration in the original are rendered in Sanskrit, including the *dhāraṇīs* (spells).

Katō, Bunnō, Yoshirō Tamura, and Kōjirō Miyasaka. *The Threefold Lotus Sutra: Innumerable Meanings, The Lotus Flower of the Wonderful Law, and Meditation on the Bodhisattva Universal Virtue.* Revised by W. E. Soothill, Wilhelm Schiffer, and Pier P. Del Campana. New York: Weatherhill / Tokyo: Kōsei, 1975. Reproduces, with only slight typographical emendation, the *Lotus* translation credited to Katō, *Myōhō-Renge-Kyō*, with the addition of *The Sūtra of Innumerable Meanings* (*Wuliangyi jing*) and *The Sūtra of Visualizing the Bodhisattva Universally Worthy* (*Guan Puxian pusa jing*), two texts traditionally regarded as a preface and conclusion to the *Lotus.*

Kern, [Jan] H[endrik]. *Saddharma-Puṇḍarīka or The Lotus of the True Law.* The Sacred Books of the East 21. Oxford: Clarendon Press, 1884. Reprint, New York: Dover, 1963. Also available online at http://www.sacred-texts.com/bud/lotus/index.htm and http://lotus.nichirenshu.org/lotus/sutra/english/kern/kerndex.htm. This is a translation of the Sanskrit version of the text in a twelfth-century Nepalese manuscript kept in the library of Cambridge University. The notes make frequent reference to Burnouf's French translation of a similar Sanskrit manuscript.

Kubo, Tsugunari, and Akira Yuyama. *The Lotus Sutra, Translated from the Chinese of Kumārajīva (Taishō, Volume 9, Number 262).* BDK English Tripiṭaka 13-I. Berkeley: Numata Center for Buddhist Translation and Research, 1993. Kubo and Yuyama translate Kumārajīva's Chinese version (dated 406) based on a Japanese edition printed in 1263 (the Kasuga edition), which is close to the modern scholarly edition in the *Taishō* canon. Their translation is in many ways the most thorough, up-to-date, and philologically precise translation of the text, although the book (in accord with the goals of the publisher) does not include footnotes. For reconstruction of proper names, Kubo and Yuyama sometimes follow the version of the text contained in early Indian manuscripts from central Asia and the later Tibetan translation of the *Lotus.* They consistently render all proper names in Sanskrit form (for example, Avalokiteśvara, Rājagṛha) rather than in English ("He Who Observes the Sounds of the World," "Vulture Peak"). In addition, they translate into English (for example, "highest complete enlightenment") some forms that appear in Kumārajīva's version as transliterations of Sanskrit sounds (*anuttarasamyaksaṃbodhi*).

Murano, Senchu. *The Sutra of the Lotus Flower of the Wonderful Dharma.* Revised by Daniel B. Montgomery. 2nd ed. Tokyo: Nichiren Shu Headquarters, 1991. The first edition (1974) was translated during 1960–1964 with the support of the Bollingen Foundation. This is an English translation of Kumārajīva's Chinese version, based on a Japanese edition printed in 1263 (the Kasuga edition), which is close to the modern scholarly edition in the *Taishō* canon. Most words translated into Chinese in Kumārajīva's original are translated into English, and most words transliterated by Kumārajīva are rendered in Sanskrit, with the exception of dhāraṇīs, which are given in their Japanese pronunciation. Exceptions to these rules are explained systematically in the translator's note (pp. xv–xvi).

Reeves, Gene. *The Lotus Sutra: A Contemporary Translation of a Buddhist Classic.* Boston: Wisdom Publications, 2008. English translation of Kumārajīva's version, often following the glosses and notes provided in a 1976 Japanese edition of Kumārajīva's original. Intended for nonspecialist readers, the book includes few Buddhist technical terms and simplifies the spelling of Sanskrit words. Includes *The Sūtra of Innumerable Meanings* (*Wuliangyi jing*) and *The Sūtra on the Visualization of the Bodhisattva Universally Worthy* (*Guan Puxian pusa jing*), two texts traditionally regarded as a preface and conclusion to the *Lotus.*

Robert, Jean-Noël. *Le sûtra du Lotus: Suivi du Livre des sens innombrables et du Livre de la contemplation de Sage-Universel.* L'espace intérieur. Paris: Fayard, 1997. French translation of Kumārajīva's version as contained in the *Taishō* canon. Robert translates into French many terms that the original presents as transliteration of the Sanskrit, such as "formule détentrice," for dhāraṇī, and "Don des Dieux," for Devadatta. The syllables of the dhāraṇīs themselves are presented in their traditional Japanese pronunciation. Includes *The Sūtra of Innumerable Meanings* (*Wuliangyi jing*) and *The Sūtra on the Visualization of the Bodhisattva Universally Worthy* (*Guan Puxian pusa jing*), two texts traditionally regarded as a preface and conclusion to the *Lotus.*

Soothill, W[illiam] E[dward]. *The Lotus of the Wonderful Law, or, The Lotus Gospel, Saddharma pundarīka sūtra, Miao-fa lien hua ching.* Oxford: Clarendon Press, 1930. Reprint, London: Curzon Press / Atlantic Highlands, N.J.: Humanities Press International, 1987. Bunnō Katō is credited as cotranslator in the preface and introduction but not on the title page. The original edition claims that it is the first Western translation of the Chinese. This is a highly abridged translation of Kumārajīva's version; it is superseded by revised and unabridged translations under Katō's name.

Watson, Burton. *The Lotus Sutra.* Translations from the Asian Classics. New York: Columbia University Press, 1993. Online version at http://lotus.nichirenshu.org/lotus/sutra/english/watson/indxwatson.htm. Abridged in Burton Watson, trans., *The Essential Lotus: Selections from the Lotus Sutra,* Translations from the Asian Classics (New York: Columbia University Press, 2002). Watson translates Kumārajīva's Chinese version, based on a modern Japanese recension of Kumārajīva's text dated 1961. Watson explicitly follows the interpretation of the text by Nichiren (1222–1282) and Zhiyi (538–597) as understood by the modern Nichiren group Sōka Gakkai. The translation is the most elegant and natural sounding of the English translations. As in Hurvitz's translation, Chinese words are usually translated into English, and words that are transcriptions of Sanskrit sounds in the original are transliterated into Sanskrit. Watson translates the word *fa* (Skt.: dharma) in the original variously as "Dharma," "doctrine," "Law," "phenomena," or "teachings," depending on context. Watson's translation of technical terms sometimes diverges from standard usage in the field of Buddhist studies; for example, Watson's "true entity of all phenomena" (*zhufa shixiang*) is usually translated as "true aspect of the *dharmas* [constituents of existence]." In romanizing foreign words, Watson uses a simplified form for Sanskrit (for example, Shakyamuni for Śākyamuni, Rajagriha for Rājagṛha) and employs the Wade-Giles system for the few Chinese words included in his introduction and glossary.

Watson, Burton. *The Lotus Sutra and Its Opening and Closing Sutras*. Tokyo: Soka Gakkai, 2009. Based on a Chinese version of the threefold *Lotus Sūtra* published by Sōka Gakkai in 2002, this represents a slightly revised version of Watson's earlier translation (see preceding entry) with the addition of *The Sūtra of Innumerable Meanings* (*Wuliangyi jing*, translated by Watson as the *Innumerable Meanings Sutra*) and *The Sūtra on the Visualization of the Bodhisattva Universally Worthy* (*Guan Puxian pusa jing*, translated by Watson as the *Sutra on How to Practice Meditation on Bodhisattva Universally Worthy*). Watson has designed his translation for readers with no special background in Asian religion. As in his earlier translation, Sanskrit words are given in simplified form. The Wade-Giles system of romanizing Chinese words used in his earlier version has been replaced here with the Pinyin system, and the translation of some technical terms has been revised (e.g., *zhufa shixiang* is now "the true aspect of all phenomena"). This new translation by Watson is forthcoming as the present volume goes to press.

CROSS-REFERENCES TO CITATIONS OF THE *LOTUS SŪTRA*

Listed here are cross-references to facilitate comparing citations of the *Lotus Sūtra* in this book with the English translation of the text by Leon Hurvitz (both 2009 and 1976 editions), used as the standard for this volume; the 1993 English translation by Burton Watson (both full and abbreviated versions); and the original text of Kumārajīva's Chinese version (in the *Taishō* canon).

THIS BOOK PAGE	HURVITZ 2009 TRANS. PAGE	HURVITZ 1976 TRANS. PAGE	WATSON 1993 TRANS. PAGE	WATSON ABBREV. TRANS. PAGE	TAISHŌ ED., VOL. 9, PAGE
CHAPTER 1					
18	68-69	74	71	49	15a
20	38	41	41	19	9b3
45	176	193	180	78	34b
45	159, 242, 263	174, 264, 286	161, 251, 272	NA, NA, NA	30c, 47c, 51c
49	287-89	311-13	298-300	119-21	56c-57a
53, n. 10	49, 88, 135, 146	51, 96, 148, 158	49, 93, 135, 144	27, NA, NA, NA	11a, 18c, 25c, 27c
55, n. 38	146	159	145	NA	27c
58, n. 60	22-23	22-23	24	2	5c
60, n. 84	71	76	73	51	15b
CHAPTER 2					
62	22	22	22	1	5b-c
62	25-27	25-27	26-29	4-7	6a-7a
63	25	25	27	5	6a
65	28	29	30	8	7a

THIS BOOK PAGE	HURVITZ 2009 TRANS. PAGE	HURVITZ 1976 TRANS. PAGE	WATSON 1993 TRANS. PAGE	WASON ABBREV. TRANS. PAGE	TAISHŌ ED., VOL. 9, PAGE
65	28-29	29	31	9	7a
65	29	30	31	9	7a
68	30	30-31	32	10	7b
68	36-38	37-40	38-41	16-19	8c-9b
68	42	45	44-45	22-23	10a
68	47-53	49-56	47-54	25-32	10b-12a
69	55-57	58-60	56-58	34-36	12c
69	57-60	61-64	59-62	37-40	12c
70	79-82	85-89	81-86	NA	17a-b
71	95-97	101-3	97-100	NA	19a-c
71	100-2	107-9	103-4	NA	20a-b
71	103 (Skt. only)	110 (Skt. only)	NA	NA	NA
72	103-7 (Skt. only)	111-15 (Skt. only)	NA	NA	NA
72	159	174	160-61	58-59	30c
73	151	164-65	150-51	NA	29a
73	136-37	148-49	136-37	NA	26a
74	164	180	162	64-65	31c-32a
75	163	178	165	63	31b
75	206-7	225-26	212-13	88-89	40a
76	219	237	225	101	42b
76	220-21	238-40	225-27	101-3	42b-c
76	221-23	240-41	227-29	103-5	43a-b
76	221	240	227	103	43a
77	263	286	273	NA	51c
77	169-71	185-87	172-75	70-73	33b
81, n. 3	32-33	33-34	34-36	12-14	8a
82, n. 6	189	205-6	193-94	NA	36c

CHAPTER 3

91	35	37	37	15	8a
91	51	53	51	29	11b

THIS BOOK PAGE	HURVITZ 2009 TRANS. PAGE	HURVITZ 1976 TRANS. PAGE	WATSON 1993 TRANS. PAGE	WATSON ABBREV. TRANS. PAGE	TAISHŌ ED., VOL. 9, PAGE
91	192	209	197	NA	37a
92	159	174	160-61	58-59	30c
92	3	1	3	NA	1c
92	3	1	4	NA	2a
93	3-4	1-2	4	NA	2a
93	186-88	202-4	190-92	NA	36a
93	187	203	191	NA	36a-b
94	146, 269	159, 293	145, 281	NA, NA	27c, 53a
94	275	300	287	NA	54b
94	192	209	197	NA	37b
94	307	334	321	NA	61b
95	160	175	161	59	30c
95	229	249	237	NA	44c
96	184	200-1	188	86	35c
96	184	201	188	86	35c
96	184	201	188	86	35c
98	47	49	48	26	10c
98	82-83	89	85	NA	17b
98	89	97	93	NA	18c
98	90	97	94	NA	18c
99	36	38-39	39	17	8c
99	159	174	160	58	30c
100	43-44	47	46	24	10b
100	28	29	30	8	7a
101	28	29	30	8	7a
101	71-72	77	73-74	51-52	15b
103, n. 17	3	1	4	NA	1c
104, n. 20	304	330	318	NA	60c
104, n. 22	192	209	197	NA	37b
105, n. 29	78-79	84-85	81	NA	16b-c
CHAPTER 4					
109	270	294-95	281	NA	53b
109-10	271	295	282	NA	53b

THIS BOOK PAGE	HURVITZ 2009 TRANS. PAGE	HURVITZ 1976 TRANS. PAGE	WATSON 1993 TRANS. PAGE	WATSON ABBREV. TRANS. PAGE	TAISHŌ ED., VOL. 9, PAGE
110	271	295	283	NA	53b
111	272	297	284	NA	53c
111	273	297-98	285	NA	54a
112	273	298	285	NA	54a
112	273	298	285	NA	54a
116	183-85	200-1	188	86	35c
116	250	273	255	NA	49b

CHAPTER 5

133	163	178-79	165	63	31c
147	164, 306	180, 333	162, 320	65, NA	32a, 61a-b
147	223-25, 232	242-44, 252	229-332, 240	105-8, NA	43b-44a, 45b
147	307	334	322	NA	61c
147	307	335	322	NA	61c
147	275	300	287	NA	54c
149, n. 7	159–61	174-76	161	59	30c
149, n. 7	162-63	178-79	165	63	31b-c
149, n. 7	188	204	193	NA	36b
149, n. 7	233	253	242	NA	45c
149, n. 7	242-43	264-65	251-52	NA	47c
149, n. 7	245	267	254	NA	48a-b
149, n. 7	250	273	259-60	NA	49b
149, n. 7	251-53	275-76	261-63	NA	49c
149, n. 7	264-65	288	274	NA	52a

CHAPTER 6

153	251	275	261	NA	49c
153	265-66	289	275	NA	52b
153	161	176	162	60	31a

THIS BOOK PAGE	HURVITZ 2009 TRANS. PAGE	HURVITZ 1976 TRANS. PAGE	WATSON 1993 TRANS. PAGE	WATSON ABBREV. TRANS. PAGE	TAISHŌ ED., VOL. 9, PAGE
153	37	39	39	17	9a
154	163	178	165	63	31b
163	5	4	6	NA	2b
167	263	286	273	NA	51c
167	273-74	298-99	286	NA	54b
180	169-70	186	174	72	33a

CHAPTER 7

187	36	38-39	38-39	16-17	8c
187	160	175	162	60	30c
187	163	178-79	165	63	31c
194	162-63	178	164	62	31b
197	186, 190, 223	202, 206, 242	191, 194, 230	NA, NA, 106	36a, 36c, 43b
207, n. 13	237	259-60	247	NA	46c
207, n. 14	308	335	323	NA	61c-62a
207, n. 27	188-90	205-6	194	NA	36b
207, n. 28	175, 188	192, 205	179, 193	77, NA	34a, 36b
207, n. 28	188-90	205-6	194	NA	36b

CHAPTER 8

209	67	72	69	47	14c
210	220	238	225-26	101-2	42b
210	223	242	229	105	43b
210	224	243	230	106	43c
230	264	287	273	NA	52a
234, n. 28	30	31	32	10	7b
234, n. 35	220, 223, 224	238, 242, 243	225-26, 229, 230	101-2, 105, 106	42b, 43b, 43c
234, n. 40	96	102	99	NA	19b

CHARACTER GLOSSARY

Amida 阿弥陀
Anesaki Masaharu 姉崎正治
Anguosi 安國寺
Annen 安然
ashide e 草手絵
benmen 本門
bianxiang 變相
Bifukumon'in 美福門院
Binglingsi 炳靈寺
Cao 曹
Chan 禪
Chegwan 諦觀
chi 持
chi *Fahua jing* 持法華經
Chingen 鎮源
chingo kokka kyō 鎮護国家経
chū 中
Ch'ungnyŏl 忠烈
dabei xin tuoloni 大悲心陀羅尼
dabei zhou 大悲呪
daimandara 大曼荼羅
daimoku 題目
Dainichi 大日
Dainihonkoku Hokekyō kenki 大日本国法華経験記
Danzan Jinja 談山神社
Daoshi 道世
di'erdi 第二諦
Dōgen 道元
dun 頓
Dunhuang 敦煌
dunjiao 頓教
dunwu 頓悟
dusong 讀誦
Eijitsu 睿実
Enchin 円珍
Ennin 円仁
Enryakuji 延暦寺
Fahua chanfa 法華懺法
Fahua sanmei 法華三昧
Fahua wenju 法華文句
Fahua xuanyi 法華玄義
fangbian 方便
Faxiang 法相
Fayun 法雲
fengsong 諷誦
fenke 分科
Fujiwara Michinaga 藤原道長
Fujiwara Michitaka 藤原道隆
Fujiwara Motohira 藤原基衡
Fujiwara Shunzei 藤原俊成
gan 感
ganying 感應
Genji 源氏
Genshin 源信
gohonzon 御本尊
goji hakkyō 五時八教
gon 権
gongyang 供養
Gonzō 勤操
Goreizei 後冷泉
Guanding 灌頂
Guanshiyin 觀世音
Guanyin 觀音
Guanzizai 觀自在
guo 果
Guoqingsi 國清寺
Guyang 古陽
Hasedera 長谷寺
Heike nōkyō 平家納経

hensō 変相
Hiei 比叡
hijiri 聖
hōben 方便
hogu kyō 反故経
Hōjō Tokimune 北条時宗
Hōjō Tokisuke 北条時輔
Hokkedō konpon mandara 法華堂根本曼荼羅
Hokke genki 法華験記
Hokke hō 法華法
Hokke metsuzaiji 法華滅罪寺
Hokke shikidoku 法華色読
Hokkeshū 法華宗
Hokke zanmai 法華三昧
Honda Nisshō 本田日生
Hōnen 法然
hongaku 本覚
Honkōji 本興寺
honmon 本門
Honpōji 本法寺
honzon 本尊
Hossō 法相
Huayan 華嚴
Huijin 慧津
Huisi 慧思
Huixiang 惠/慧祥/詳
ichinen sanzen 一念三千
Inoue Nisshō 井上日召
Ishiwara (also read Ishihara) Kanji 石原莞爾
jia 假
jian 漸
Jiangling 江陵
jikidō 直道
jimen 迹門
Jinguangming jing 金光明經
Jingzhou 荊州
jion e 字音絵
jitsu 実
Jiumoluoshi 鳩摩羅什
jiyuan 機緣
Jizang 吉藏
Jōfukyō 常不軽
Jōgyō 上行
juji 受持
Kaijūsenji 海住山寺
kai kanjō 戒潅頂
Kaiyuan 開元
kanbun 漢文
Kannon 観音
Kanzeon 観世音
Kasagi 笠置
Katō Nobukiyo 加藤信清
Kaya-no-in 高陽院
ke 仮
kechien kyō 結縁経
Kegon 華厳
Ketsumeidan 血盟団
Kii 紀伊
Kinji hōtō mandara 金字宝塔曼荼羅
Kita Ikki 北一輝
Kōkō 光孝
Kokuchūkai 国柱会
Kokumin bunka kaigi 国民文化会議
kokutai 国体
Kōmeitō 公明党
Kōmyō 光明
kong 空
Kongōkai 金剛界
kū 空
Kuiji 窺基
Kūkai 空海
Kŭmjawŏn 金字院
Kunisaki 国東
Kunōji 久能寺
Kurodani 黒谷
Kwan Um 觀音
li 理
Lingxiusi 靈修寺
liutong fen 流通分
Longmen 龍門
Luoyang 洛陽
Maijishan 麥積山
mappō 末法
masse hendo 末世辺土
miao 妙
Miaofa lianhua jing 妙法蓮華經
Miaole 妙樂
Miaoshan 妙善
Miaozhi 妙智
michi 道
mikaeshi e 見返し絵
mikkyō 密教
Minobu 身延
Miyazawa Kenji 宮沢賢治
mofa 末法
Mogao 莫高

muyu 木魚
myō 妙
Myōhō renge kyō 妙法蓮華経
Myŏngjong 明宗
namo 南無
namu 南無
Namu *myōhō renge kyō* 南無妙法蓮華経
nanxing 難行
nanxing kuxing 難行苦行
nenbutsu 念仏
Nichiren 日蓮
Nichirenshū 日蓮宗
Nichiren-shugi 日蓮主義
Nipponzan Myōhōji 日本山妙法寺
Niwano Nikkyō 庭野日敬
nyohōgyō 如法経
Ōjōyōshū 往生要集
Ōmine 大峰
panjiao 判教
Putuoshan 普陀山
quan 權
rakan 羅漢
Reiyūkai 霊友会
Renwang jing 仁王經
risshō ankoku 立正安国
Risshō Kōseikai 立正佼成会
Rozanji 廬山寺
rufajing 如法經
Ryōzen jōdo 霊山浄土
Ryūhonji 立本寺
Sado 佐渡
Sagyŏng'wŏn 寫經院
Saichō 最澄
Saigyō 西行
Saimyōji 西明寺
sandi 三諦
Sanlun 三論
santai 三諦
Sengming 僧明
Sengrui 僧叡
Sengxiang 僧祥
senmenkyō 扇面経
Seno'o Girō 妹尾義郎
shakubuku 折伏
shakumon 迹門
shan nanzi 善男子
shan nüren 善女人
Shanxin 善信
shaoshen 燒身
sheshen 捨身
shi (phenomena) 事
shi (real or true) 實
Shingon 真言
Shinkō Bukkyō Seinen Dōmei 新興仏教青年同盟
Shitennōji 四天王寺
Shizong 世宗
shōgun 将軍
shohō jissō 諸法実相
Shōmu 聖武
Shōtoku 聖徳
shou 受
shouchi 受持
shū 宗
Silla 新羅
Sōka Gakkai 創価学会
sokushin jōbutsu 即身成仏
sōmoku jōbutsu 草木成仏
Sōtō 曹洞
Taimitsu 台密
Taira Kiyomori 平清盛
Taira no Saemon 平左衛門
Taizōkai 胎蔵界
Takayama Chogyū 高山樗牛
Tanaka Chigaku 田中智学
Tanomura Chikuden 田能村竹田
Tanyou 曇猷
Tendai 天台
Tianshou 天授
Tiantai 天台
Toba 鳥羽
Tōdaiji 東大寺
Toki Jōnin 富木常忍
Uehara Senroku 上原専禄
Ŭnjawŏn 銀字院
uta e 歌絵
Wanfosi 萬佛寺
Wang Jie 王玠
wangshen 亡身
Wen 文
wushi bajiao 五時八教
wuxing 五性
Wu Zetian 武則天
Xiao Yu 蕭瑀
Xinxing 信行
Xiqianfodong 西千佛洞
Xuanzang 玄奘

xu fen 序分
Yang 煬
Yanshou 延壽
Yao Xing 姚興
Yijing 義淨
yin 因
ying 應
yinian sanqian 一念三千
yiqie seshen sanmei 一切色身三昧
yishen 遺身
Yuezhi 月氏
Yulin 榆林
Yungang 雲岡
Zanning 贊寧
Zen 禅
Zhang 張
Zhanran 湛然
Zhenajueduo 闍那崛多
Zheng'e ji 正訛集
zhengshuo fen 正說分
Zhisheng 智昇
Zhiyi 智顗
zhong 中
Zhu Fahu 竺法護
zhufa shixiang 諸法實相
Zhuhong 袾宏
zifen 自焚
zong 宗
zongchi 總持
Zongxiao 宗曉
zuishang sheng 最上乘

BIBLIOGRAPHY

COLLECTIONS AND THEIR ABBREVIATIONS

Dainihon bukkyō zensho 大日本仏教全書. 151 vols. Tokyo: Bussho kankōkai, 1912–1922. Abbreviated as *DBZ*.

Dainihon zoku zōkyō 大日本続蔵経. Edited by Maeda Eun 前田慧雲 and Nakano Tatsue 中野達慧. 150 vols. Kyoto: Zōkyō shoin, 1905–1912. Abbreviated as *Z*.

Dengyō Daishi zenshū 伝教大師全集. Edited by Hieizan Senshūin fuzoku Eizan gakuin 比叡山専修院附属叡山学院. 5 vols. Tokyo: Sekai seiten kankō kyōkai, 1989. Abbreviated as *DDZ*.

Shintei zōho kokushi taikei 新訂増補国史大系. Edited by Kuroita Katsumi 黒板勝美 and Kokushi taikei henshūkai 国史大系編修会, represented by Maruyama Jirō 丸山二郎. 66 vols. Tokyo: Yoshikawa kōbunkan, 1929–1966.

Shishiō zenshū 師子王全集. Tanaka Chigaku 田中智学 (1861–1939). 36 vols. Edited by Shishiō zenshū kankōkai 師子王全集刊行会. Tokyo: Shishiō bunko, 1931–1938.

Shōwa teihon Nichiren Shōnin ibun 昭和定本日蓮聖人遺文. Edited by Risshō daigaku Nichiren kyōgaku kenkyūjo 立正大学日蓮教学研究所. 4 vols. Minobu-chō, Yamanashi, Japan: Minobusan Kuonji, 1952–1959 ; rev. 1988. Abbreviated as *Teihon*.

Taishō shinshū daizōkyō 大正新修大蔵経. 100 vols. Edited by Takakusu Junjirō 高楠順次郎, Watanabe Kaigyoku 渡辺海旭, and Ono Gemmyō 小野玄妙. 1924–1934. Reprint, Taibei: Xinwenfeng chuban gongsi, 1974. Abbreviated as *T*.

PRIMARY SOURCES

"Chisong *Fahua jing* yi" 持誦法華經儀. Author unknown. In *Miaofa lianhua jing* 妙法蓮華經. Tiantaishan: Tiantaishan guoqing jiangsi fawu liutong chu, n.d.

Chōshū eisō 長秋詠藻. Fujiwara Shunzei 藤原俊成 (1114–1204). Tokyo: Koten bunko, 1994.

Chu sanzang ji ji 出三藏記集. Sengyou 僧祐 (445–518). *T* no. 2145.

Da banniepan jing 大般涅盤經 (*Mahāparinirvāṇa sūtra*). Dharmakṣema (Tanwuchan 曇無讖, 385–433). *T* no. 374.

Da banniepan jing 大般涅盤經 (*Mahāparinirvāṇa sūtra*). Huiyuan 慧遠 (363–443) and Xie Lingyun 謝靈運 (385–433). *T* no. 375.

Dabei jing 大悲經 (*Mahākaruṇāpuṇḍarīka sūtra*). 552. Narendrayaśas (Naliantiyeshe 那連提耶舍, 517–589). *T* no. 380.

Da foding rulai miyin xiuzheng liaoyi zhupusa wanxing shoulengyan jing 大佛頂如來密

因修證了意諸菩薩萬行首楞嚴經 (*Śūraṃgama sūtra*). Attributed to Pāramiti (Banlamidi 般剌蜜帝, fl. ca. 705). *T* no. 945.

Da zhidu lun 大智度論 (*Mahāprajñāpāramitā śāstra*). Kumārajīva (Jiumoluoshi 鳩摩羅什, 344–413, or 350–409). *T* no. 1509.

Ehyō Tendaishū 依憑天台宗. Saichō 最澄 (766 or 767–822). *DDZ* 3.

Enkai jūrokuchō 円戒十六帖. Kōen 興円 (1263–1317). In *Zoku Tendaishū zensho* 続天台宗全書, edited by Tendai shūten hensanjo 天台宗典編纂所, *Enkai* 円戒, 1. Tokyo: Shunjūsha, 1989.

Fahua jing anlexing yi 法華經安樂行義. Huisi 慧思 (515–577). *T* no. 1926.

Fahua jing chiyan ji 法華經持驗記. Zhou Kefu 周克復 (Qing dynasty). *Z* 2b, 7.

Fahua jing xianying lu 法華經顯應錄. 1198. Zongxiao 宗曉 (1151–1214). *Z* 2b, 7.

Fahua jing yiji 法華經義記. Fayun 法雲 (467–529). *T* no. 1715.

Fahua jing zhuanji 法華經傳記. Ca. 754. Sengxiang 僧祥 (dates unknown). *T* no. 2068.

Fahua sanmei chanyi 法華三昧懺儀. Zhiyi 智顗 (538–597). *T* no. 1941.

Fahua wenju ji 法華文句記. Zhanran 湛然 (711–782). *T* no. 1719.

Fahua xuanyi shiqian 法華玄義釋籤. Zhanran 湛然 (711–782). *T* no. 1717.

Fahua yishu 法華義疏. Jizang 吉藏 (549–623). *T* no. 1721.

Fanwang jing 梵網經. Attributed to Kumārajīva (Jiumoluoshi 鳩摩羅什, 344–413, or 350–409). *T* no. 1484.

Fozu tongji 佛祖統紀. Zhipan 智磐 (fl. ca. 1258). *T* no. 2035.

Fusō ryakki 扶桑略記. Kōen 皇円 (?-1169). In *Shintei zōho kokushi taikei* 新訂增補国史大系12.

Futsūju bosatsukai kōshaku 普通授菩薩戒広釈. Annen 安然 (841–?). *T* no. 2381.

Gaoseng zhuan 高僧傳. Huijiao 慧皎 (497–554). *T* no. 2059.

Guan Puxian pusa xingfa jing 觀普賢菩薩行法經. Dharmamitra (Tanwumiduo 曇無密多, 356–442). *T* no. 277.

Guanxin songjing faji 觀心誦經法記. Attributed to Zhiyi 智顗 (538–597) and Zhanran 湛然 (711–782). *Z* 2a, 4.

"*Hokke* daimoku shō" 法華題目抄. Nichiren 日蓮 (1222–1282). *Teihon* no. 44.

Hokke shūku 法華秀句. Saichō 最澄 (766 or 767–822). *DDZ* 3.

"Hōmon mōsarubekiyō no koto" 法門可被申様之事. Nichiren 日蓮 (1222–1282). *Teihon* no. 70.

Hongzan Fahua zhuan 弘贊法華傳. Ca. 706. Huixiang 惠/慧祥/詳 (ca. 639–706). *T* no. 2067.

Ichijō yōketsu 一乗要決. Genshin 源信 (942–1017). *T* no. 2370.

Jingang bei 金剛錍. Zhanran 湛然 (711–782). *T* no. 1932.

Jingang bore boluomi jing 金剛般若波羅蜜經 (*Vajracchedikā*). Kumārajīva (Jiumoluoshi 鳩摩羅什, 344–413, or 350–409). *T* no. 235. Early printed edition, British Library, Or. 8210/P. 2; digitized photographic edition online at http://idp.bl.uk/database/oo_scroll_h.a4d?uid=23815833137;recnum=18824;index=1.

Kaimoku shō 開目抄. Nichiren 日蓮 (1222–1282). *Teihon* no. 98.

Kaitai sokushin jōbutsu gi 戒体即身成仏義. Nichiren 日蓮 (1222–1282). *Teihon* no. 1.

Kaiyuan shijiao lu 開元釋教錄. Zhisheng 智昇 (ca. 669–740). *T* no. 2154.

Kanjin honzon shō 観心本尊抄. Nichiren 日蓮 (1222–1282). *Teihon* no. 118.

"*Kanjin honzon shō* soejō" 観心本尊抄副状. Nichiren 日蓮 (1222–1282). *Teihon* no. 119.

Keiran jūyōshū 渓嵐拾葉集. Kōshū 光宗 (1276–1350). *T* no. 2410.

Kenbutsu mirai ki 顕仏未来記. Nichiren 日蓮 (1222–1282). *Teihon* no. 125.

Lidai sanbao ji 歷代三寶記. 597. Fei Changfang 費長房 (Sui dynasty). *T* no. 2034.

"Li *Fahua jing* yi" 禮法華經儀. Author unknown. In *Miaofa lianhua jing* 妙法蓮華經. Tiantaishan: Tiantaishan guoqing jiangsi fawu liutong chu, n.d.

Li Fahua jing yishi 禮法華經儀式. Attributed to Zhili 知禮 (960–1028). *T* no. 1944.

"Lisong qian guanxiang fa" 禮誦前觀想法. Author unknown. In *Miaofa lianhua jing* 妙法蓮華經. Tiantaishan: Tiantaishan guoqing jiangsi fawu liutong chu, n.d.

Liudu ji jing 六度集經. Kang Senghui 康僧會 (d. 280). *T* no. 152.

Miaofa lianhua jing 妙法蓮華經 (*Saddharmapuṇḍarīka*). Kumārajīva (Jiumoluoshi 鳩摩羅什, 344–413, or 350–409). *T* no. 262. Modern printed edition, Tiantaishan: Tiantaishan guoqing jiangsi fawu liutong chu, n.d.

Miaofa lianhua jing shu 妙法蓮華經疏. Daosheng 道生 (360–434). *Z* 2b, 23.

Miaofa lianhua jing wenju 妙法蓮華經文句. Zhiyi 智顗 (538–597) and Guanding 灌頂 (561–632). *T* no. 1718.

Miaofa lianhua jing xuanzan 妙法蓮華經玄贊. Kuiji 窺基 (632–682). *T* no. 1723.

Mohe zhiguan 摩訶止觀. Zhiyi 智顗 (538–597). *T* no. 1911.

Naishō buppō sōjō kechimyaku fu 内証仏法相承血脈譜. Saichō 最澄 (766 or 767–822). *DDZ* 1.

Nanhai jigui neifa zhuan 南海寄歸內法傳. Yijing 義淨 (635–713). *T* no. 2125.

"Nanjō Hyōe Shichirō-dono gosho" 南条兵衛七郎殿御書. Nichiren 日蓮 (1222–1282). *Teihon* no. 38.

Nittō guhō junrei kōki 入唐求法巡礼行記. Ennin 円仁 (794–864). *DBZ* 113.

Nyosetsu shugyō shō 如説修行抄. Nichiren 日蓮 (1222–1282). *Teihon* no. 124.

Pŏhwa yŏnghŏm chŏn 法華靈驗傳. Yowŏn 義圓 (fl. ca. 1300). *Z* 2b, 7.

Pŏphwakyŏng jiphŏmki 法華經集驗記. Uijŏk 義寂 (ca. 681–705). Manuscript edition, *Tōkyō daigaku toshokan zō: Hokekyō shūkenki* 東京大学図書館蔵—法華經集驗記. Tokyo: Kichō kotenseki kankōkai, 1981.

Risshō ankoku ron 立正安国論. Nichiren 日蓮 (1222–1282). *Teihon* no. 24.

Ruijū sandaikyaku 類聚三代格. Author unknown (mid-Heian period). In *Shintei zōho kokushi taikei* 新訂増補国史大系 25.

Sanbao gantong lu 三寶感通錄. Daoxuan 道宣 (596–667). *T* no. 2106.

Sange gakushōshiki 山家学生式. Saichō 最澄 (766 or 767–822). *DDZ* 1.

Senji shō 選時抄. Nichiren 日蓮 (1222–1282). *Teihon* no. 181.

Shinjō sōmoku jōbutsu shiki 斟定草木成仏私記. Annen 安然 (841–?). Critical edition of the text and modern Japanese gloss in Sueki Fumihiko 末木文美士, *Heian shoki bukkyō shisō no kenkyū* 平安初期仏教思想の研究, 523–653. Tokyo: Shunjūsha, 1995.

"Shōmitsu-bō gosho" 聖密房御書. Nichiren 日蓮 (1222–1282). *Teihon* no. 148.

Shoshū mondō shō 諸宗問答抄. Nichiren 日蓮 (1222–1282). *Teihon* no. 5.

Shugo kokkai shō 守護国界章. Saichō 最澄 (766 or 767–822). *DDZ* 2.

Shugo kokka ron 守護国家論. Nichiren 日蓮 (1222–1282). *Teihon* no. 15.

Shuju onfurumai gosho 種々御振舞御書. Nichiren 日蓮 (1222–1282). *Teihon* no. 176.

Sōmoku hosshin shugyō jōbutsu ki 草木発心修行成仏記. Attributed to Ryōgen 良源 (912–985). *DBZ* 24.

Song gaoseng zhuan 宋高僧傳. Zanning 贊寧 (919–1001). *T* no. 2061.

"Soya Nyūdō-dono gari gosho" 曾谷入道殿許御書. Nichiren 日蓮 (1222–1282). *Teihon* no. 170.

Sui Tiantai Zhizhe dashi biezhuan 隋天台智者大師別傳. Guanding 灌頂 (561–632). *T* no. 2050.

Wuliangyi jing 無量意經. Dharmāgatayaśas (Tanmoqietuoyeshe 曇摩伽陀耶舍, fl. ca. 481). *T* no. 276.

Xu gaoseng zhuan 續高僧傳. Daoxuan 道宣 (596–667). *T* no. 2060.

Yuedeng sanmei jing 月燈三昧經 (*Samādhirāja sūtra*). Narendrayaśas (Naliantiyeshe 那連提耶舍, 517–589). *T* no. 639.

Zheng fahua jing 正法華經 (*Saddharmapuṇḍarīka*). Dharmarakṣa (Zhu Fahu 竺法護, 265–313, or 239–316). *T* no. 263.

Zhiguan fuxingzhuan hongjue 止觀輔行傳弘決. Zhanran 湛然 (711–782). *T* no. 1912.

Zhongyin jing 中陰經. Zhu Fonian 竺佛念 (fourth century). *T* no. 385.

SECONDARY SOURCES

Abbot, Terry Rae. "Vasubandhu's Commentary to the *Saddharmapuṇḍarīka-sūtra*: A Study of Its History and Significance." Ph.D. diss., University of California, Berkeley, 1985.

Akira, Yuyama. *A Bibliography of the Sanskrit Texts of the Saddharmapuṇḍarīkasūtra*. Australian National University, Faculty of Asian Studies, Oriental Monograph Series 5. Canberra: Australian National University Press, 1970.

Allam, Cheryl M. "The Nichiren and Catholic Confrontation with Japanese Nationalism." *Buddhist-Christian Studies* 10 (1990): 35–84.

Ariga Yoshitaka 有賀祥隆. "Hōkekyō e 法華経絵." In *Enryakuji, Onjōji, Saikyōji* 延暦寺園城寺西教寺. *Nihon kobijutsu zenshū* 日本古美術全集 10. Tokyo: Shueisha, 1980.

——. *Hōkekyō e* 法華経絵. *Nihon no bijutsu* 日本の美術, no. 269. Tokyo: Shibundō, 1989.

Aruga, Hiroshi. "Soka Gakkai and Japanese Politics." In *Global Citizens: The Soka Gakkai Buddhist Movement in the World*, edited by David Machacek and Bryan Wilson, 97–127. New York: Oxford University Press, 2000.

Bareau, André. *Les sectes bouddhiques du Petit Véhicule*. Publications de l'École française d'Extrême-Orient 38. Paris: École française d'Extrême-Orient, 1955.

Benn, James A. *Burning for the Buddha: Self-Immolation in Chinese Buddhism*. Kuroda Institute, Studies in East Asian Buddhism 19. Honolulu: University of Hawai'i Press, 2007.

——. "Fire and the Sword: Some Connections between Self-Immolation and Religious Persecution in the History of Chinese Buddhism." In *The Buddhist Dead: Practices, Discourses, Representations*, edited by Bryan J. Cuevas and Jacqueline I. Stone, Kuroda Institute, Studies in East Asian Buddhism 20, 234–65. Honolulu: University of Hawai'i Press, 2007.

——. "Spontaneous Human Combustion: Some Remarks on a Phenomenon in Chinese Buddhism." In *Heroes and Saints: The Moment of Death in Cross-cultural Perspectives*, edited by Phyllis Granoff and Koichi Shinohara, 101–33. Newcastle, UK: Cambridge Scholars Press, 2007.

——. "Where Text Meets Flesh: Burning the Body as an 'Apocryphal Practice' in Chinese Buddhism." *History of Religions* 37, no. 4 (1998): 295–322.

Beyer, Stephan. "Notes on the Vision Quest in Early Mahāyāna." In *Prajñāpāramitā and Related Systems: Studies in Honor of Edward Conze*, edited by Lewis Lancaster with Luis O. Gómez, Berkeley Buddhist Studies Series 1, 329–40. Berkeley: Institute of East Asian Studies, 1977.

Bielefeldt, Carl. "The One Vehicle and the Three Jewels: On Japanese Sectarianism and Some Ecumenical Alternatives." *Buddhist-Christian Studies* 10 (1990): 5–16.

Birnbaum, Raoul. *The Healing Buddha*. Boston: Shambhala, 1979.

Blackstone, Kathryn. *Women in the Footsteps of the Buddha: Struggle for Liberation in the Therīgāthā*. Richmond, UK: Curzon, 1998.

Blum, Mark L. "The *Sangoku-Mappō* Construct: Buddhism, Nationalism, and History in Medieval Japan." In *Discourse and Ideology in Medieval Japanese Buddhism*, edited by Richard K. Payne and Taigen Dan Leighton, 31–51. London: Routledge, 2006.

Borsig, Margareta von. *Sūtra von der Lotosblume des wunderbaren Gesetzes*. Darmstadt, Ger.: Wissenschaftliche Buchgesellschaft, 1993.

Boucher, Daniel. "Buddhist Translation Procedures in Third-Century China: A Study of Dharmarakṣa and His Translation Idiom." Ph.D. diss., University of Pennsylvania, 1996.

——. "Gāndhārī and the Early Chinese Buddhist Translations Reconsidered: The Case of the *Saddharmapuṇḍarīkasūtra*." *Journal of the American Oriental Society* 118, no. 4 (1998): 471–506.

——. "The Textual History of the Rāṣṭrapālaparipṛcchā: Notes on Its Third-Century Chinese Translation." In *Annual Report of the International Research Institute for Advanced Buddhology at Soka University for the Academic Year 2000*, 93–116. Tokyo: The International Research Institute for Advanced Buddhology, Soka University, 2001.

Buddhist Text Translation Society. *The Wonderful Dharma Lotus Flower Sutra, Translated into Chinese by Tripitaka Master Kumarajiva of Yao Ch'in*. 10 vols. San Francisco: Sino-American Buddhist Association, Buddhist Text Translation Society, 1977–1982.

Burnouf, Eugène. *Le lotus de la bonne loi; traduit du sanscrit, accompagné d'un commentaire et de vingt et un mémoires relatifs au bouddhisme*. Paris: Imprimerie Nationale, 1852. Reprint, Paris: Librairie d'Amérique et d'Orient, Adrien Maisonneuve, J. Maisonneuve, 1973.

Buswell, Robert E., Jr., ed. *Chinese Buddhist Apocrypha*. Honolulu: University of Hawai'i Press, 1990.

Buswell, Robert E., Jr., and Robert M. Gimello, eds. *Paths to Liberation: The Mārga and Its Transformations in Buddhist Thought*. Kuroda Institute, Studies in East Asian Buddhism 7. Honolulu: University of Hawai'i Press, 1992.

Campany, Robert F. "The Earliest Tales of the Bodhisattva Guanshiyin." In *Religions of China in Practice*, edited by Donald S. Lopez Jr., 82–96. Princeton, N.J.: Princeton University Press, 1996.

——. "Notes on the Devotional Uses and Symbolic Functions of Sūtra Texts as Depicted in Early Chinese Buddhist Miracle Tales and Hagiographies." *Journal of the International Association of Buddhist Studies* 14, no. 1 (1991): 28–72.

——. "The Real Presence." *History of Religions* 32, no. 3 (1993): 233–72.

——. *Strange Writing: Anomaly Accounts in Early Medieval China*. Albany: SUNY Press, 1996.

Chang, Garma C. C., et al., trans. *A Treasury of Mahāyāna Sūtras: Selections from the Mahāratnakūṭa Sūtra*. University Park: Pennsylvania State University Press, 1983.

Chappell, David, ed. *T'ien-t'ai Buddhism: An Outline of the Fourfold Teachings*. Tokyo: Daiichi shobō, 1983.

Chavannes, Édouard, trans. *Cinq cents contes et apologues extrait du Tripiṭaka chinois*. 4 vols. Paris: Leroux, 1910–1934.

Ch'en, Kenneth K. S. *Buddhism in China: A Historical Survey*. Princeton, N.J.: Princeton University Press, 1964.

Cole, Alan. *Text as Father: Paternal Seductions in Early Mahāyāna Buddhist Literature*. Buddhisms. Berkeley: University of California Press, 2005.

Collins, Steven. *Nirvana and Other Buddhist Felicities: Utopias of the Pali Imaginaire*. Cambridge Studies in Religious Traditions 12. Cambridge: Cambridge University Press, 1998.

——. "On the Very Idea of the Pāli Canon." *Journal of the Pāli Text Society* 15 (1990): 89–126.

Cone, Margaret, and Richard F. Gombrich, trans. *The Perfect Generosity of Prince Vessantara: A Buddhist Epic.* Oxford: Clarendon Press, 1977.

Conze, Edward. *The Gilgit Manuscript of the Aṣṭadāsasāhasrikā Prajñāpāramitā: Chapters 55 to 70 Corresponding to the 5th Abhisamaya.* Rome: Istituto Italiano per il Medio ed Estremo Oriente, 1962.

——. *The Perfection of Wisdom in Eight Thousand Lines and Its Verse Summary.* Wheel Series 1. Bolinas, Calif.: Four Seasons Foundation, 1973.

——. *The Prajñāpāramitā Literature.* Indo-Iranian Monographs 6. The Hague: Mouton, 1960.

Cowell, E. B., et al., ed. and trans. *The Jātaka; or, Stories of the Buddha's Former Births.* 6 vols. Cambridge: Cambridge University Press, 1895–1907.

Cox, Collett. *Disputed Dharmas: Early Buddhist Theories on Existence.* Tokyo: International Institute for Buddhist Studies, 1995.

Davidson, J. Leroy. *The Lotus Sutra in Chinese Art.* New Haven, Conn.: Yale University Press, 1954.

Davidson, Ronald M. "Appendix: An Introduction to the Standards of Scriptural Authenticity in Indian Buddhism." In *Chinese Buddhist Apocrypha,* edited by Robert E. Buswell Jr., 291–325. Honolulu: University of Hawai'i Press, 1990.

Dayal, Har. *The Bodhisattva Doctrine in Buddhist Sanskrit Literature.* London: Paul, Trench, Trubner, 1932.

Deal, William E. "Ascetics, Aristocrats, and the *Lotus Sutra*: The Construction of the Buddhist Universe in Eleventh-Century Japan." Ph.D. diss., Harvard University, 1988.

——. "The *Lotus Sūtra* and the Rhetoric of Legitimation in Eleventh-Century Japan." *Japanese Journal of Religious Studies* 20, no. 4 (1993): 261–96.

Deeg, Max. *Das Lotos-Sūtra, übersetzt von Max Deeg, mit einer Einleitung von Max Deeg und Helwig Schmidt-Glintzer.* Darmstadt, Ger.: Wissenschaftliche Buchgesellschaft, 2007.

Dehn, Ulrich. "Die geschichtliche Perspektive des japanischen Buddhismus: Am Beispiel Uehara Senroku." Habilitation thesis, Mainz, 1995.

——. "Towards a Historical Consciousness of Japanese Buddhism: Uehara Senroku." *Japanese Religions* 17, no. 2 (July 1992): 126–41.

Del Campana, Pier P., trans. "*Sandaihihō-shō*: An Essay on the Three Great Mysteries by Nichiren." *Monumenta Nipponica* 26, no. 1 (1971): 205–24.

Dolce, Lucia. "Awareness of *Mappō*: Soteriological Interpretations of Time in Nichiren." *Transactions of the Asiatic Society of Japan,* 4th ser., 7 (1992): 81–106.

——. "Between Duration and Eternity: Hermeneutics of the 'Ancient Buddha' of the Lotus Sutra in Chih-i and Nichiren." In *A Buddhist Kaleidoscope: Essays on the Lotus Sutra,* edited by Gene Reeves, 223–39. Tokyo: Kōsei, 2002.

——. "Esoteric Patterns in Nichiren's Interpretation of the Lotus Sutra." Ph.D. diss., University of Leiden, 2002.

——. "Reconsidering the Taxonomy of the Esoteric: Hermeneutical and Ritual Practices of the Lotus Sutra." In *The Culture of Secrecy in Japanese Religion,* edited by Bernhard Scheid and Mark Teeuwen, 130–71. London: Routledge, 2006.

Donner, Neal. "Chih-i's Meditation on Evil." In *Buddhist and Taoist Practice in Medieval Chinese Society,* edited by David W. Chappell, Buddhist and Taoist Studies 2, 49–64. Honolulu: University of Hawai'i Press, 1987.

Donner, Neal, and Daniel B. Stevenson, trans. *The Great Calming and Contemplation: A Study and Annotated Translation of the First Chapter of Chih-i's "Mo-ho chih-kuan."* Kuroda Institute, Classics in East Asian Buddhism. Honolulu: University of Hawai'i Press, 1993.

Dudbridge, Glen. *The Legend of Miao-shan*. Oxford Oriental Monographs 1. London: Ithaca Press for the Board of the Faculty of Oriental Studies, Oxford University, 1978.

——. "Miao-shan on Stone: Two Early Inscriptions." *Harvard Journal of Asiatic Studies* 42, no. 2 (1982): 589–614.

Dunhuang yanjiusuo 敦煌研究所, ed. *Dunhuang Mogaoku* 敦煌莫高窟. 5 vols. Zhongguo shiku 中國石窟. Beijing: Wenwu chubanshe, 1982–1987.

Durt, Hubert. "The Offering of the Children of Prince Viśvantara/Sudāna in the Chinese Tradition." *Journal of the International College for Advanced Buddhist Studies (Kokusai bukkyōgaku daigakuin daigaku kenkyū kiyō* 国際仏教学大学院大学研究紀要) 2 (1999): 147–82.

Dykstra, Yoshiko K., trans. *Miraculous Tales of the Lotus Sutra from Ancient Japan: The "Dainihon Hokekyōkenki" of Priest Chingen*. Honolulu: University of Hawai'i Press, 1983.

——. "Tales of the Compassionate Kannon: The *Hasedera Kannon Genki*." *Monumenta Nipponica* 31, no. 2 (1976): 113–43.

Egami Yasushi 江上綏. *Sōshokugyō* 装飾経. *Nihon no bijutsu* 日本の美術, no. 278. Tokyo: Shibundō, 1989.

Elverskog, Johan. *Uygur Buddhist Literature*. Silk Road Studies 1. Turnhout, Belg.: Brepols, 1997.

Fabricand-Person, Nicole. "Demonic Female Guardians of the Faith: The *Fugen Jūrasetsunyo* Iconography in Japanese Buddhist Art." In *Engendering Faith: Women and Buddhism in Premodern Japan*, edited by Barbara Ruch, 343–82. Ann Arbor: Center for Japanese Studies, University of Michigan, 2002.

——. "Filling the Void: The *Fugen jūrasetsunyo* Iconography in Japanese Buddhist Art." Ph.D. diss., Princeton University, 2001.

Faure, Bernard. *The Power of Denial: Buddhism, Purity, and Gender*. Buddhisms. Princeton, N.J.: Princeton University Press, 2003.

Filliozat, Jean. "La mort volontaire par le feu et la tradition bouddhique indienne." *Journal Asiatique* 251, no. 1 (1963): 21–51.

Fronsdal, E. Gil. "The Dawn of the Bodhisattva Path: Studies in a Religious Ideal of Ancient Indian Buddhists with a Particular Emphasis on the Earliest Extant Perfection of Wisdom Sutra." Ph.D. diss., Stanford University, 1998.

Fujii, Nichidatsu. *Buddhism for World Peace*. Translated by Yumiko Miyazaki. Tokyo: Japan-Bharat Sarvodaya Mitrata Sangha, 1980.

——. *Tranquil Is This Realm of Mine: Dharma Talks and Writings of the Most Venerable Nichidatsu Fujii*. Translated by Yumiko Miyazaki. Atlanta: Nipponzan Myōhōji, 2007.

Fujita, Kōtatsu. "One Vehicle or Three?" Translated by Leon Hurvitz. *Journal of Indian Philosophy* 3 (1975): 79–166.

Fukui Fumimasa 福井文雅. "Kōkyō gishiki no soshiki naiyō 講経儀式の組織内容." In *Tonkō to Chūgoku bukkyō* 敦煌と中国仏教, edited by Makita Tairyō 牧田諦亮 and Fukui Fumimasa 福井文雅, Kōza Tonkō 講座敦煌 7, 359–82. Tokyo: Daitō shuppansha, 1984.

Fuse Kōgaku 布施浩岳. *Hokekyō seiritsushi* 法華経成立史. Tokyo: Daitō shuppansha, 1934.

Fussman, Gérard. "Histoire du monde indien." In *Annuaire du Collège de France 1995–1996, Résumé des cours et travaux*, 779–86. Paris: Collège de France, 1996.

Georgieva, Valentina. "Representation of Buddhist Nuns in Chinese Edifying Miracle Tales During the Six Dynasties and the Tang." *Journal of Chinese Religions* 24 (1996): 47–76.

Gernet, Jacques. "Les suicides par le feu chez les bouddhistes chinois de Ve au Xe siècle." In *Mélanges publiés par l'Institut des Hautes Études Chinoises* 2:527–58. Paris: Presses Universitaires de France, 1960.

Giles, Lionel. *Descriptive Catalogue of the Chinese Manuscripts from Tunhuang in the British Museum*. London: The British Museum, 1957.

Gimello, Robert M. "Apophatic and Kataphatic Discourse in Mahāyāna: A Chinese View." *Philosophy East and West* 26, no. 2 (1976): 117–36.

Gjertson, Donald E. "The Lotus Sutra and Popular Faith in Medieval China." Unpublished paper, Amherst: University of Massachusetts, n.d. [ca. 1966].

Gombrich, Richard. "How the Mahāyāna Began." *The Buddhist Forum* 1 (1990): 21–30.

Graham, William. *Beyond the Written Word: Oral Aspects of Scripture in the History of Religion*. Cambridge: Cambridge University Press, 1987.

Grapard, Allan G. "Flying Mountains and Walkers of Emptiness: Toward a Definition of Sacred Space in Japanese Religions." *History of Religions* 20, no. 3 (1982): 195–221.

——. "The Textualized Mountain—Enmountained Text: The *Lotus Sutra* in Kunisaki." In *The Lotus Sutra in Japanese Culture*, edited by George J. Tanabe Jr. and Willa Jane Tanabe, 159–89. Honolulu: University of Hawai'i Press, 1989.

Gregory, Peter N., ed. *Sudden and Gradual: Approaches to Enlightenment in Chinese Thought*. Kuroda Institute, Studies in East Asian Buddhism 5. Honolulu: University of Hawai'i Press, 1987.

Griffiths, Paul. *On Being Buddha: The Classical Doctrine of Buddhahood*. Albany: SUNY Press, 1994.

Groner, Paul. "The Fan-wang ching and Monastic Discipline in Japanese Tendai: A Study of Annen's Futsū jubosatsukai kōshaku." In *Chinese Buddhist Apocrypha*, edited by Robert E. Buswell Jr., 251–90. Honolulu: University of Hawai'i Press, 1990.

——. "The *Lotus Sutra* and Saichō's Interpretation of the Realization of Buddhahood with This Very Body." In *The Lotus Sutra in Japanese Culture*, edited by George J. Tanabe Jr. and Willa Jane Tanabe, 53–74. Honolulu: University of Hawai'i Press, 1989.

——. *Ryōgen and Mt. Hiei: Japanese Tendai in the Tenth Century*. Kuroda Institute, Studies in East Asian Buddhism 15. Honolulu: University of Hawai'i Press, 2002.

——. *Saichō: The Establishment of the Japanese Tendai School*. Berkeley Buddhist Studies Series 7. Berkeley: Center for South and Southeast Asian Studies, 1984. Reprint, Honolulu: University of Hawai'i Press, 2000.

——. "Shortening the Path: Early Tendai Interpretations of the Realization of Buddhahood with This Very Body (*Sokushin Jōbutsu*)." In *The Mārga and Its Transformations in Buddhist Thought*, edited by Robert E. Buswell Jr. and Robert M. Gimello, Kuroda Institute, Studies in East Asian Buddhism 7, 439–74. Honolulu: University of Hawai'i Press, 1992.

Groot, Jan J. M. de, trans. *Le code du Mahâyâna en Chine: Son influence sur la vie monacale et sur le monde laïque*. Amsterdam: Müller, 1893.

Habito, Ruben L. F. "Bodily Reading of the *Lotus Sūtra*: Understanding Nichiren's Buddhism." *Japanese Journal of Religious Studies* 26, nos. 3–4 (1999): 281–306.

——. "*Daimoku* and *Dhāranī*: Tracing the Roots of Nichiren's Buddhism." In *Ejima Yasunori hakushi tsuitō ronshū: Kū to jitsuzai* 江島惠教博士追悼論集—空と実在, edited by Ejima Yasunori hakushi tsuitō ronshū kankōkai 江島惠教博士追悼論集刊行会, 633–43. Tokyo: Shunjūsha, 2001.

——. "*Lotus* Buddhism after Nichiren." In *Experiencing Buddhism: Ways of Wisdom and Compassion*, 181–86. New York: Orbis Books, 2005.

——. "*Lotus* Buddhism and Its Liberational Thrust: A Rereading of the *Lotus Sutra* by Way of Nichiren." *Ching Feng* 35, no. 2 (June 1992): 85–112.

——. "Mystico-Prophetic Buddhism of Nichiren." In *The Papers of the Henry Luce III Fellows in Theology*, edited by Jonathan Strom, 2:43–62. Atlanta: Scholar's Press, 1996.

——. "Uehara Senroku." In *Great Thinkers of the Eastern World*, edited by Ian McGreal, 391–94. San Francisco: HarperCollins, 1994.

——. "Uses of Nichiren in Modern Japanese History." *Japanese Journal of Religious Studies* 26, nos. 3–4 (1999): 423–39.

Habito, Ruben L. F., and Jacqueline I. Stone, eds. *Revisiting Nichiren*. Special issue, *Japanese Journal of Religious Studies* 26, nos. 3–4 (1999).

Harrison, Paul M. "*Buddhānusmṛti* in the *Pratyutpanna-buddha-saṃmukhāvasthita-samādhi-sūtra*." *Journal of Indian Philosophy* 6 (1978): 35–57.

——. "Mediums and Messages: Reflections on the Production of Mahāyāna Sūtras." *Eastern Buddhist*, n.s., 35, nos. 1–2 (2003): 115–47.

——. *The Pratyutpanna Samādhi Sutra Translated by Lokakṣema*. BDK English Tripiṭaka 25–2. Berkeley: Numata Center for Buddhist Translation and Research, 1998.

——. *The Samādhi of Direct Encounter with the Buddhas of the Present: An Annotated English Translation of the Tibetan Version of the "Pratyutpanna-Buddha-Saṃmukhāvasthita-Samādhi-Sūtra" with Several Appendices Relating to the History of the Text*. Studia Philologica Buddhica, Monograph Series 5. Tokyo: International Institute for Buddhist Studies, 1990.

——. "Searching for the Origins of the Mahāyāna: What Are We Looking For?" *Eastern Buddhist*, n.s., 28, no. 1 (1995): 48–69.

——. "Who Gets to Ride in the Great Vehicle? Self-Image and Identity among the Followers of the Early Mahāyāna." *Journal of the International Association of Buddhist Studies* 10, no. 1 (1987): 67–89.

Hazama, Jikō. "The Characteristics of Japanese Tendai." *Japanese Journal of Religious Studies* 14, nos. 2–3 (1987): 101–11.

He Shizhe 賀世哲, ed. *Fahua jing huajuan* 法華經畫卷. Dunhuang shiku quanji 敦煌石窟全集 7. Hong Kong: Shangwu yinshuguan, 1999.

Hinüber, Oskar von. "The Foundation of the Bhikkhunīsaṃgha: A Contribution of the Earliest History of Buddhism." In *Annual Report of the International Research Institute for Advanced Buddhology at Soka University for the Academic Year 2007*, 3–29. Tokyo: The International Research Institute for Advanced Buddhology, Soka University, 2008.

——. *A Handbook of Pāli Literature*. Berlin: de Gruyter, 1996.

Hirakawa, Akira, trans. *Monastic Discipline for the Buddhist Nuns: An English Translation of the Chinese Text of the Mahāsāṃghika-Bhikṣuṇī-Vinaya*. Tibetan Sanskrit Works Series 21. Patna, India: Kashi Prasad Jayaswal Research Institute, 1982.

——. "The Rise of Mahāyāna Buddhism and Its Relationship to the Worship of Stūpas." Translated by Taitetsu Unno. *Memoirs of the Research Department of the Tōyō Bunkō*, no. 22 (1963): 57–106.

Holt, John Clifford. *Buddha in the Crown: Avalokiteśvara in the Buddhist Tradition of Sri Lanka*. New York: Oxford University Press, 1991.

Hubbard, Jamie. *Absolute Delusion, Perfect Buddhahood: The Rise and Fall of a Chinese Heresy.* Nanzan Library of Asian Culture and Religion. Honolulu: University of Hawai'i Press, 2001.

——. "Buddhist-Buddhist Dialogue? The *Lotus Sutra* and the Polemic of Accommodation." *Buddhist-Christian Studies* 15 (2005): 118–36.

Hurvitz, Leon. *Chih-i (538–597): An Introduction to the Life and Ideas of a Chinese Buddhist Monk. Mélanges chinois et bouddhiques* 12. Brussels: Institut Belge des Hautes Études Chinoises, 1962.

——. "The Lotus Sūtra in East Asia: A Review of *Hokke shisō.*" *Monumenta Serica* 29 (1970–1971): 697–762.

——. *Scripture of the Lotus Blossom of the Fine Dharma (The Lotus Sūtra), Translated from the Chinese of Kumārajīva.* Records of Civilization: Sources and Studies 94, Translations from the Asian Classics. New York: Columbia University Press, 1976; rev. ed., 2009.

Ibuki Atsushi 伊吹敦. "Tōsō Eshō ni tsuite 唐僧慧祥について." *Waseda daigaku daigakuin bungaku kenkyū kiyō, bessatsu: Tetsugaku-shigaku hen* 早稲田大学大学院文学研究紀要別冊: 哲学史学編 14 (January 1987): 33–45.

Iguchi, Gerald Scott. "Nichirenism as Modernism: Imperialism, Fascism, and Buddhism in Modern Japan." Ph.D. diss., University of California, San Diego, 2006.

Ikeda Daisaku 池田大作. "Ikeda kaichō no gosho kōgi: *Senjishō*" 池田会長の御書講義—選時抄. *Daibyakurenge* 大白蓮華 320 (November 1977): 163–72.

Jan, Yün-hua. "Buddhist Self-Immolation in Medieval China." *History of Religions* 4, no. 2 (1965): 243–65.

Jong, J. W. de. "The Lotus Sutra." Review of *The Lotus Sutra*, by Burton Watson. *Eastern Buddhist*, n.s., 28, no. 2 (1995): 303–4.

——. "Lotus Sūtra: Scripture of the Lotus Blossom of the Fine Dharma." Review of *Scripture of the Lotus Blossom of the Fine Dharma (The Lotus Sūtra)*, by Leon Hurvitz. *Eastern Buddhist*, n.s., 10, no. 2 (1977): 169–74.

——. "Myōhō-renge-kyō: The Sutra of the Lotus Flower of the Wonderful Law." Review of *Myōhō-Renge-Kyō: The Sutra of the Lotus Flower of the Wonderful* Law, by Bunnō Katō, and *The Sutra of the Lotus Flower of the Wonderful Dharma*, by Senchu Murano. *Eastern Buddhist*, n.s., 8, no. 2 (1975): 154–59.

Kabutogi Shōkō 兜木正亨. *Hokke hangyō no kenkyū* 法華版経の研究. Tokyo: Daitō shuppansha, 1982.

——. *Hokke shakyō no kenkyū* 法華写経の研究. Tokyo: Daitō shuppansha, 1983.

Kamens, Edward. "Dragon-Girl, Maidenflower, Buddha: The Transformation of a Waka Topos, 'The Five Obstructions.'" *Monumenta Nipponica* 53, no. 2 (winter 1993): 389–442.

Kanno Hiroshi 菅野博史. "Chinese Buddhist Sutra Commentaries of the Early Period." In *Annual Report of the International Research Institute for Advanced Buddhology at Soka University for the Academic Year 2002*, 301–20. Tokyo: The International Research Institute for Advanced Buddhology, Soka University, 2003.

——. "A Comparison of Zhiyi's and Jizang's Views of the *Lotus Sūtra*: Did Zhiyi, After All, Advocate a 'Lotus Absolutism'?" In *Annual Report of the International Research Institute for Advanced Buddhology at Soka University for the Academic Year 1999*, 125–47. Tokyo: The International Research Institute for Advanced Buddhology, Soka University, 2000.

——. "A General Survey of Research Concerning Chinese Commentaries on the *Lotus*

Sūtra." In *Annual Report of the International Research Institute for Advanced Buddhology at Soka University for the Academic Year 2006*, 417–44. Tokyo: The International Research Institute for Advanced Buddhology, Soka University, 2007.

——. *Ichinen sanzen to wa nani ka* 一念三千とは何か. Tokyo: Daisan bunmeisha, 1992.

——. "An Overview of Research on Chinese Commentaries of the *Lotus Sūtra*." *Acta Asiatica, Bulletin of the Institute of Eastern Culture* 66 (1994): 87–103.

——. "The Practice of Bodhisattva Never Disparaging in the *Lotus Sūtra* and Its Reception in China and Japan." *Journal of Oriental Studies* 12 (2002): 104–22.

——. "The Reception of *Lotus Sūtra* Thought in China." *Journal of Oriental Studies* 11 (2001): 106–22.

——. "The Three Dharma Wheels of Jizang." In *Buddhist and Indian Studies in Honour of Professor Dr. Sodo Mori*, edited by Publication Committee for Buddhist and Indian Studies in Honour of Professor Dr. Sodo Mori, 399–412. Hamamatsu, Japan: International Buddhist Association, 2002.

Karashima, Seishi. *A Glossary of Dharmarakṣa's Translation of the Lotus Sutra*. Bibliotheca Philologica et Philosophica Buddhica 1. Tokyo: The International Research Institute for Advanced Buddhology, Soka University, 1998.

——. *A Glossary of Kumārajīva's Translation of the Lotus Sutra*. Bibliotheca Philologica et Philosophica Buddhica 4. Tokyo: The International Research Institute for Advanced Buddhology, Soka University, 2001.

——. *The Textual Study of the Chinese Versions of the Saddharmapuṇḍarīkasūtra in the Light of the Sanskrit and Tibetan Versions*. Bibliotheca Indologica et Buddhologica 3. Tokyo: Sankibō Press, 1992.

——. "Who Composed the Lotus Sutra? Antagonism between Wilderness and Village Monks." In *Annual Report of the International Research Institute for Advanced Buddhology at Soka University for the Academic Year 2000*, 143–79. Tokyo: The International Research Institute for Advanced Buddhology, Soka University, 2001.

Katō, Bunnō. *Myōhō-Renge-Kyō: The Sutra of the Lotus Flower of the Wonderful Law*. Revised by W. E. Soothill and Wilhelm Schiffer. Tokyo: Risshō kōseikai, 1971.

Katō, Bunnō, Yoshirō Tamura, and Kōjirō Miyasaka, trans. *The Threefold Lotus Sutra: Innumerable Meanings, The Lotus Flower of the Wonderful Law, and Meditation on the Bodhisattva Universal Virtue*. Revised by W. E. Soothill, Wilhelm Schiffer, and Pier P. Del Campana. New York: Weatherhill/Tokyo: Kōsei, 1975.

Katsuura Noriko 勝浦令子. "*Hokke* metsuzai no tera to Rakuyō Ankokuji *Hokke* dōjō: Ama to amadera no Nittō hikaku kenkyū no kadai" 法華滅罪之寺と洛陽安国寺法華道場—尼と尼寺の日唐比較研究の課題. *Shiron* 史論 46 (1993): 1–18.

Kawakatsu Kenryō 川勝賢亮. *Tahōtō to Hokke shisō* 多宝塔と法華思想. Tokyo: Tōkyōdō shuppan, 1984.

Kern, [Jan] H[endrik], trans. *Saddharma-Puṇḍarīka or The Lotus of the True Law*. The Sacred Books of the East 21. Oxford: Clarendon Press, 1884. Reprint, New York: Dover, 1963. Also available online at http://www.sacred-texts.com/bud/lotus/index.htm and http://lotus.nichirenshu.org/lotus/sutra/english/kern/kerndex.htm.

Kern, [Jan] Hendrik, and B. Nanjio. *Saddharmapuṇḍarīka*. Bibliotheca Buddhica 10. Tokyo: Meicho fukyūkai, 1977.

Ketelaar, James E. *Of Heretics and Martyrs in Meiji Japan: Buddhism and Its Persecution*. Princeton, N.J.: Princeton University Press, 1990.

Kieschnick, John. "Blood Writing in Chinese Buddhism." *Journal of the International Association of Buddhist Studies* 23, no. 2 (2000): 177–94.

——. *The Eminent Monk: Buddhist Ideals in Medieval Chinese Hagiography*. Kuroda Institute, Studies in East Asian Buddhism 10. Honolulu: University of Hawai'i Press, 1997.

——. *The Impact of Buddhism on Chinese Material Culture*. Buddhisms. Princeton, N.J.: Princeton University Press, 2003.

Kikutake Jun'ichi 企救岳順一 and Yoshida Hiroshi 吉田弘. *Kōrai butsuga* 高麗仏画. Tokyo: Asahi shinbunsha, 1981.

Kim, Ha Poong. "Fujii Nichidatsu's *Tangyō-Raihai*: Bodhisattva Practice for the Nuclear Age." *Cross Currents* (summer 1986): 193–203.

Kim, Young-ho. *Tao-sheng's Commentary on the Lotus Sūtra: A Study and Translation*. SUNY Series in Buddhist Studies. Albany: SUNY Press, 1990.

Kim, Yung-Hee. *Songs to Make the Dust Dance: The Ryōjin hishō of Twelfth-Century Japan*. Los Angeles: University of California Press, 1994.

Kisala, Robert. *Prophets of Peace: Pacifism and Cultural Identity in Japan's New Religions*. Honolulu: University of Hawai'i Press, 1999.

——. "Sōka Gakkai, Kōmeitō, and the Separation of Religion and State in Japan." *Bulletin of the Nanzan Institute for Religion and Culture* 18 (spring 1994): 7–17.

Kleine, Christoph. "'The Epitome of the Ascetic Life': The Controversy over Self-Mortification and Ritual Suicide as Ascetic Practices in East Asian Buddhism." In *Asceticism and Its Critics: Historical Accounts and Comparative Perspectives*, edited by Oliver Freiberger, 153–77. Oxford: Oxford University Press, 2006.

Komatsu Shigemi 小松茂美. *Heike nōkyō no kenkyū* 平家納経の研究. 3 vols. Tokyo: Kodansha, 1976.

Kōsei Publications. *Dharma World: For Living Buddhism and Interfaith Dialogue*. A bimonthly journal in English published at Risshō Kōseikai headquarters in Tokyo and distributed internationally.

Kubo, Tsugunari, and Akira Yuyama. *The Lotus Sutra, Translated from the Chinese of Kumārajīva (Taishō, Volume 9, Number 262)*. BDK English Tripiṭaka 13–I. Berkeley: Numata Center for Buddhist Translation and Research, 1993.

Kurata Bunsaku 倉田文作 and Tamura Yoshirō 田村芳朗, eds. *Hōkekyō no bijutsu* 法華経の美術. Tokyo: Kōsei shuppansha, 1981.

Kurata, Bunsaku, and Yoshirō Tamura. *Art of the Lotus Sutra: Japanese Masterpieces*. Translated by Edna B. Crawford. Tokyo: Kōsei, 1987.

Kyōto kokuritsu hakubutsukan 京都国立博物館. *Heike nōkyō to Itsukushima no hihō* 平家納経と厳島の秘宝. Kyoto: Kōrinsha, 1972.

——. *Kokyō zuroku* 古経図録. Kyoto: Benridō, 1964.

——. *Sanjūrokunin kashū to Kunōji kyō* 三十六人歌集と久能寺経. Kyoto: Benridō, 1953.

LaFleur, William R. *The Karma of Words: Buddhism and the Literary Arts in Medieval Japan*. Los Angeles: University of California Press, 1983.

——. "Saigyō and the Buddhist Value of Nature." *History of Religions* 13, no. 2 (November 1973): 93–128; 13, no. 3 (February 1974): 227–48.

Lamotte, Étienne. *History of Indian Buddhism: From the Origins to the Śaka Era*. Translated by Sara Webb-Boin. Louvain, Belg.: Peeters Press, 1988.

——. *Le traité de la grande vertu de sagesse de Nāgārjuna (Mahāprajñāpāramitāśāstra)*. 5 vols. Publications de l'Institut orientaliste de Louvain 25–26. Louvain, Belg.: Université de Louvain, Institut orientaliste, 1944–1980.

Lee, Edwin B. "Nichiren and Nationalism: The Religious Patriotism of Tanaka Chigaku." *Monumenta Nipponica* 30, no. 1 (1975): 19–35.

Leighton, Taigen Dan. *Visions of Awakening Space and Time: Dōgen and the Lotus Sutra*. New York: Oxford University Press, 2007.

Levering, Miriam L. "The Dragon Girl and the Abbess of Mo-Shan: Gender and Status in the Ch'an Buddhist Tradition." *Journal of the International Association of Buddhist Studies* 5, no. 1 (1982): 19–35.

——. "Is the Lotus Sutra 'Good News' for Women?" In *A Buddhist Kaleidoscope: Essays on the Lotus Sutra*, edited by Gene Reeves, 469–91. Tokyo: Kōsei, 2002.

Ling, Trevor O. *The Buddha: Buddhist Civilization in India and Ceylon*. Harmondsworth, U.K.: Penguin Books, 1976.

Lopez, Donald S., Jr. "Authority and Orality in the Mahāyāna." *Numen* 42 (1995): 21–47.

——, ed. *Buddhist Hermeneutics*. Kuroda Institute, Studies in East Asian Buddhism 6. Honolulu: University of Hawai'i Press, 1988.

Lu, Yang. "Narrative and Historicity in the Buddhist Biographies of Early Medieval China: The Case of Kumārajīva." *Asia Major*, 3rd ser., 17, no. 2 (2004): 1–43.

Luk, Charles (Lu Kuan Yü), trans. *The Śuraṅgama Sūtra (Leng Yen Ching)*. London: Rider, 1966.

Luo Zhufeng 羅竹風 et al., eds. *Hanyu dacidian* 漢語大詞典. 13 vols. Hong Kong: Sanlian shudian / Shanghai: Shanghai cishu chubanshe, 1987–1995.

Machacek, David, and Bryan Wilson, eds. *Global Citizens: The Soka Gakkai Movement in the World*. New York: Oxford University Press, 2000.

Mair, Victor H. "Buddhism and the Rise of the Written Vernacular: The Making of National Languages." *Journal of Asian Studies* 53, no. 3 (1994): 707–51.

——. "Written Aspects of Chinese Sūtra Lectures (chiang-ching-wen)." *Hanxue yanjiu* 漢學研究 4, no. 2 (December 1988): 311–34.

Mallmann, Marie-Thérèse de. *Introduction à l'étude d'Avalokiteśvara*. Annales du Musée Guimet, Bibliothèque d'études 57. Paris: Presses Universitaires de France, 1967.

Maruyama Teruo 丸山照雄. *Tatakau bukkyō* 闘う仏教. Tokyo: Hōzōkan, 1990.

Matsubara, Saburō, and Terukazu Akiyama. *Arts of China*. Vol. 2, *Buddhist Cave Temples: New Researches*. Translated by A. C. Soper. Tokyo: Kodansha, 1969.

McCullough, William H., and Helen Craig McCullough, trans. *A Tale of Flowering Fortunes: Annals of Japanese Aristocratic Life in the Heian Period*. 2 vols. Stanford, Calif.: Stanford University Press, 1980.

Meech-Pekarik, Julia. "Disguised Scripts and Hidden Poems in an Illustrated Heian Sutra: *Ashide-e* and *Uta-e* in the Heike Nōgyō." *Archives of Asian Art* 31 (1977): 52–75.

——. "The Flying White Horse: Transmission of the Valāhasa Jātaka Imagery from India to Japan." *Artibus Asiae* 43, no. 1/2 (1981–82): 111–28.

——. "Taira Kiyomori and the Heike Nōgyō." Ph.D. diss., Harvard University, 1976.

Métraux, Daniel A. *The Soka Gakkai Revolution*. Lanham, Md.: University Press of America, 1994.

Miya Tsugio 宮次男. *Kinji hōtō mandara* 金字宝塔曼荼羅. Tokyo: Yoshikawa kōbunkan, 1976.

——. "Pictorial Art of the *Lotus Sutra* in Japan." In *The Lotus Sutra in Japanese Culture*, edited by George J. Tanabe Jr. and Willa Jane Tanabe, 75–94. Honolulu: University of Hawai'i Press, 1989.

Mizuno Seiichi 水野清一 and Nagahiro Toshio 長広敏雄. *Ryūmon sekkutsu no kenkyū* 龍門石窟の研究. Tokyo: Zayūhō kankōkai, 1941.

——. *Unkō sekkutsu* 雲崗石窟. 16 vols. Kyoto: Kyōto daigaku jinbun kagaku kenkyūjo, 1951–1956.

Mochizuki Shinkō 望月信亨. *Bukkyō daijiten* 仏教大辞典. Rev. ed. 10 vols. Kyoto: Seikai seiten kankō kyōkai, 1954–1963.

Moerman, D. Max. "The Archaeology of Anxiety: An Underground History of Heian Religion." In *Heian Japan: Centers and Peripheries*, edited by Mikael Adolphson, Edward Kamens, and Stacie Yamamoto, 245–71. Honolulu: University of Hawai'i Press, 2007.

——. "Passage to Fudaraku: Suicide and Salvation in Premodern Japanese Buddhism." In *The Buddhist Dead: Practices, Discourses, Representations*, edited by Bryan J. Cuevas and Jacqueline I. Stone, Kuroda Institute, Studies in East Asian Buddhism 20, 266–96. Honolulu: University of Hawai'i Press, 2007.

Mostow, Joshua S. "Painted Poems, Forgotten Words: Poem-Pictures and Classical Japanese Literature." *Monumenta Nipponica* 47, no. 3 (autumn 1992): 323–46.

Murano, Senchu, trans. *The Sutra of the Lotus Flower of the Wonderful Dharma*. Tokyo: Nichren Shu Headquarters, 1974. Reprinted with revisions by Daniel B. Montgomery. Tokyo: Nichiren Shu Headquarters, 1991.

Murase, Miyeko. *Bridge of Dreams: The Mary Griggs Burke Collection of Japanese Art*. New York: Metropolitan Museum of Art, 2000.

——. "Kuan-Yin as Savior of Men: Illustration of the Twenty-fifth Chapter of the Lotus Sūtra in Chinese Painting." *Artibus Asiae* 33, no. 1/2 (1971): 39–74.

Murcott, Susan. *The First Buddhist Women: Translations and Commentaries on the Therigatha*. Berkeley: Parallax Press, 1991.

Musée Guimet. *Rarities of the Musée Guimet*. New York: Asia Society, 1975.

Nakamura, Kyoko Motomochi, trans. *Miraculous Stories from the Japanese Buddhist Tradition: The "Nihon ryōiki" of the Monk Kyōkai*. Cambridge, Mass.: Harvard University Press, 1973.

Nara kokuritsu hakubutsukan 奈良国立博物館. *Hōkekyō no bijutsu* 法華経の美術. Nara: Nara kokuritsu hakubutsukan, 1979.

Nattier, Jan. *A Few Good Men: The Bodhisattva Path according to "The Inquiry of Ugra (Ugraparipṛcchā)."* Studies in the Buddhist Traditions. Honolulu: University of Hawai'i Press, 2003.

——."Gender and Awakening: Sexual Transformation in Mahāyāna Sūtras." Unpublished ms.

——. "A Greater Awakening." *Tricycle: The Buddhist Review* 15, no. 3 (2006): 65–69.

——. *Once upon a Future Time: Studies in a Buddhist Prophecy of Decline*. Nanzan Studies in Asian Religions 1. Berkeley: Asian Humanities Press, 1991.

Ng, Yu-kwan. *T'ien-t'ai Buddhism and Early Mādhyamika*. Honolulu: Tendai Institute of Hawai'i, Buddhist Studies Program, University of Hawai'i, 1993.

Nishimoto Teruma 西本照真. *Sangaikyō no kenkyū* 三階教の研究. Tokyo: Shunjūsha, 1998.

Nishiyama, Kōsen, and John Stevens, trans. *A Complete English Translation of Dōgen Zenji's Shōbōgenzō (The Eye and Treasury of the True Law)*. 4 vols. Sendai: Daihokkaikaku, 1975–1983.

Niwano, Nikkyō. *Buddhism for Today: A Modern Interpretation of The Threefold Lotus Sutra*. Translated by Kōjirō Miyasaka. Tokyo: Kōsei, 1976.

——. *A Buddhist Approach to Peace*. Translated by Masuo Nezu. Tokyo: Kōsei, 1977.

Norman, K. R., trans. *Elders' Verses*. 2 vols. London: Luzac, 1969–1971.

——. trans. *The Group of Discourses (Sutta-nipāta)*. 2 vols. London: Pali Text Society, 1995.

——. *Pāli Literature: Including the Canonical Literature in Prakrit and Sanskrit of All the Hīnayāna Schools of Buddhism*. Wiesbaden, Ger.: Harrassowitz, 1983.

Ōchō, Enichi. "The Beginnings of Buddhist Tenet Classification in China." *Eastern Buddhist*, n.s., 14, no. 2 (1981): 7–94.

Ogiwara (Wogihara), Unrai, and C. Tsuchida, eds. *Saddharmapuṇḍarīka-sūtram: Romanized and Revised Text of the Bibliotheca Buddhica Publication by Consulting a Skt. Ms. and Tibetan and Chinese Translations.* 1935, 1958. Reprint, Tokyo: Sankibō Buddhist Book Store, 1994.

Ohnuma, Reiko. "Dehadāna: The 'Gift of the Body' in Indian Buddhist Narrative Literature." Ph.D. diss., University of Michigan, 1997.

——. "Gift." In *Critical Terms for the Study of Buddhism*, edited by Donald S. Lopez Jr., 103–23. Chicago: University of Chicago Press, 2005.

——. "The Gift of the Body and the Gift of the Dharma." *History of Religions* 37, no. 4 (1998): 323–59.

——. *Head, Eyes, Flesh, and Blood: Giving Away the Body in Indian Buddhist Literature.* New York: Columbia University Press, 2007.

——. "The Story of Rūpāvatī: A Female Past Birth of the Buddha." *Journal of the International Association of Buddhist Studies* 23, no. 1 (2007): 103–45.

Ōtani Eiichi 大谷栄一. *Kindai Nihon no Nichiren-shugi undō* 近代日本の日蓮主義運動. Kyoto: Hōzōkan, 2001.

Ōyama Ninkai 大山仁快. *Shakyō* 写経. *Nihon no bijutsu* 日本の美術, no. 156. Tokyo: Shibundō, 1979.

Pak, Youngsook. "Illuminated Buddhist Manuscripts in Korea." *Oriental Art* 33, no. 4 (winter 1987–1988): 357–74.

——. "The Korean Art Collection in the Metropolitan Museum of Art." In *Arts of Korea*, edited by Judith G. Smith, 402–49. New York: Metropolitan Museum of Art, 1998.

Pal, Pratapaditya, and Julia Meech-Pekarik. *Buddhist Book Illumination.* New York: Ravi Kumar, 1988.

Pandey, Rajyashree. *Writing and Renunciation in Medieval Japan: The Works of the Poet-Priest Kamo no Chōmei.* Ann Arbor: Center for Japanese Studies, University of Michigan, 1998.

Pas, Julian F. *Visions of Sukhāvatī: Shan-tao's Commentary on the Kuan Wu-liang shou-fo ching.* SUNY Series in Buddhist Studies. Albany: SUNY Press, 1995.

Peach, Lucinda Joy. "Social Responsibility, Sex Change, and Salvation: Gender Justice in the Lotus Sutra." In *A Buddhist Kaleidoscope: Essays on the Lotus Sutra*, edited by Gene Reeves, 437–67. Tokyo: Kōsei, 2002.

Pelliot, Paul. *Les grottes de Touen-Houang: Peintures et sculptures des époques des Wei, des T'ang et des Song.* 6 vols. Paris: Librairie Paul Geuthner, 1914–1924.

Penkower, Linda. "Making and Remaking Tradition: Chan-Jan's Strategies toward a T'ang T'ien-t'ai Agenda." In *Tendai Daishi kenkyū: Tendai Daishi sen yonhyakunen go-onki kinen shuppan* 天台大師研究—天台大師千四百年御遠忌記念出版, edited by Tendai Daishi kenkyū henshū iinkai 天台大師研究編集委員会, 1338–1289 (reverse pagination). Kyoto: Tendai gakkai, 1997.

——. "T'ien-t'ai during the T'ang Dynasty: Chan-jan and the Sinification of Buddhism." Ph.D. diss., Columbia University, 1993.

Potter, Karl H. *Presuppositions of India's Philosophies.* Westport, Conn.: Greenwood Press, 1963.

Powers, John. *Hermeneutics and Tradition in the Saṃdhinirmocana-sūtra.* Leiden: Brill, 1993.

Prip-Møller, Johannes. *Chinese Buddhist Monasteries: Their Plan and Its Function as a Setting for Buddhist Monastic Life.* Hong Kong: Hong Kong University Press, 1982.

Prochnau, William W. *Once Upon a Distant War*. New York: Vintage, 1995.

Pye, Michael. *Skilful Means: A Concept in Mahayana Buddhism*. London: Duckworth, 1978; 2nd ed., London: Routledge, 2003.

Rambelli, Fabio. *Buddhist Materiality: A Cultural History of Objects in Japanese Buddhism*. Asian Religions and Cultures. Stanford, Calif.: Stanford University Press, 2007.

Ray, Reginald A. *Buddhist Saints in India: A Study in Buddhist Values and Orientations*. New York: Oxford University Press, 1994.

Reeves, Gene, ed. *A Buddhist Kaleidoscope: Essays on the Lotus Sutra*. Tokyo: Kōsei, 2002.

——. *The Lotus Sutra: A Contemporary Translation of a Buddhist Classic*. Boston: Wisdom, 2008.

Reischauer, Edwin O., trans. *Ennin's Diary: The Record of a Pilgrimage to China in Search of the Law*. New York: Ronald Press, 1955.

Reis-Habito, Maria. "The *Great Compassion Dhāraṇī*." In *The Esoteric Buddhist Tradition: Selected Papers from the 1989 Seminar for Buddhist Studies Conference*, edited by Henrik Sorensen, 31–49. Copenhagen: SBS Monographs, 1994.

Robert, Jean-Noël. *Le sûtra du Lotus: Suivi du Livre des sens innombrables et du Livre de la contemplation de Sage-Universel*. L'espace intérieur. Paris: Fayard, 1997.

Robinson, Richard H. *Early Mādhyamika in India and China*. Madison: University of Wisconsin Press, 1967.

Robinson, Richard H., Willard L. Johnson, and Thanissaro Bhikkhu. *Buddhist Religions: A Historical Introduction*. 5th ed. Belmont, Calif.: Wadsworth, 2005.

Rosenfield, John M., and Elizabeth ten Grotenhuis. *Journey of the Three Jewels: Japanese Buddhist Paintings from Western Collections*. New York: Asia Society, 1979.

Sadakata, Akira. *Buddhist Cosmology: Philosophy and Origin*. Translated by Gaynor Sekimori. Tokyo: Kōsei, 1997.

Saddhatissa, H. *The Birth-Stories of the Ten Bodhisattvas and the Dasabodhisattuppattikathā: Being a Translation and Edition of the Dasabodhisattuppattikathā*. London: Pali Text Society, 1975.

Sangren, P. Steven. "Female Gender in Chinese Religious Symbols: Kuan Yin, Ma Tsu, and the 'Eternal Mother.'" *Signs* 9, no.1 (1983): 4–25.

Schopen, Gregory. *Figments and Fragments of Mahāyāna Buddhism in India: More Collected Papers*. Studies in the Buddhist Traditions. Honolulu: University of Hawai'i Press, 2005.

——. "The Phrase *sa pṛthivīpradeśaś caityabhūto bhavet* in the *Vajracchedikā*: Notes on the Cult of the Book in Mahāyāna." 1975. Reprinted in Gregory Schopen, *Figments and Fragments of Mahāyāna Buddhism in India: More Collected Papers*, Studies in the Buddhist Traditions, 25–62. Honolulu: University of Hawai'i Press, 2005.

Schroeder, John W. *Skillful Means: The Heart of Buddhist Compassion*. Honolulu: University of Hawai'i Press, 2001.

Sharf, Robert H. *Coming to Terms with Chinese Buddhism: A Reading of the "Treasure Store Treatise."* Kuroda Institute, Studies in East Asian Buddhism 14. Honolulu: University of Hawai'i Press, 2002.

Shi Pingting 施萍婷 and He Shizhe 贺世哲. "Dunhuang bihuazhong de *Fahua jing* bian chutan 敦煌壁画中的法华经变初探." In *Dunhuang Mogaoku* 敦煌莫高窟, 5 vols., edited by Dunhuang yanjiusuo 敦煌研究所, Zhongguo shiku 中國石窟, 3:177–91. Beijing: Wenwu chubanshe, 1987.

Shih, Robert, trans. *Biographies des moines éminents de Houei-Kiao: Kao seng tchouan, traduites et annotées par Robert Shih*. Bibliothèque du Muséon 54. Louvain, Belg.: Institut orientaliste, Bibliothèque de l'Université, 1968.

Shinohara, Koichi. "Guanding's Biography of Zhiyi, the Fourth Chinese Patriarch of the Tiantai Tradition." In *Speaking of Monks*, edited by Phyllis Granoff and Koichi Shinohara, 97–232. Oakville, Ont.: Mosaic Press, 1992.

——. "The Maitreya Image in Shicheng and Guanding's Biography of Zhiyi." In *From Benares to Beijing: Essays on Buddhism and Chinese Religion in Honour of Prof. Jan Yün-hua*, edited by Koichi Shinohara and Gregory Schopen, 203–28. Oakville, Ont.: Mosaic Press, 1991.

Shiori, Ryōdō. "The Meaning of the Formation and Structure of the *Lotus Sutra*." Translated by George J. Tanabe Jr. In *The Lotus Sutra in Japanese Culture*, edited by George J. Tanabe Jr. and Willa Jane Tanabe, 15–36. Honolulu: University of Hawai'i Press, 1989.

Shirahata Yoshi 白畑よし. *Yamato e* やまと絵. Kyoto: Kawahara shoten, 1967.

Shively, Donald H. "Buddhahood for the Nonsentient: A Theme in Nō Plays." *Harvard Journal of Asiatic Studies* 20, nos. 1–2 (1957): 135–61.

Silk, Jonathan A. "What, If Anything, Is Mahāyāna Buddhism? Problems of Definitions and Classifications." *Numen* 49 (2002): 76–109.

Smith, Judith G., ed. *Arts of Korea*. New York: Metropolitan Museum of Art, 1998.

Smith, Wilfred Cantwell. *What Is Scripture?—A Comparative Approach*. Minneapolis: Fortress Press, 1993.

Soothill, W[illiam] E[dward]. *The Lotus of the Wonderful Law, or, The Lotus Gospel, Saddharma pundarīka sūtra, Miao-fa lien hua ching*. Oxford: Clarendon Press, 1930. Reprint, London: Curzon Press / Atlantic Highlands, N.J.: Humanities Press International, 1987.

Sponberg, Alan. "Attitudes toward Women and the Feminine in Early Buddhism." In *Buddhism, Sexuality, and Gender*, edited by José Ignacio Cabezón, 3–36. Albany: SUNY Press, 1992.

Sponberg, Alan, and Helen Hardacre, eds. *Maitreya, the Future Buddha*. Cambridge: Cambridge University Press, 1988.

Stein, Rolf A. "Avalokiteśvara/Kouan-yin, un exemple de transformation d'un dieu en déesse." *Cahiers d'Extrême-Asie* 2 (1986): 17–77.

Steuber, Jason. "Shakyamuni and Prabhutaratna in 5th and 6th Century Chinese Buddhist Art at the Nelson-Atkins Museum of Art." *Arts of Asia* 36, no. 2 (March-April 2006): 85–103.

Stevenson, Daniel B. "The Four Kinds of Samādhi in Early T'ien-t'ai Buddhism." In *Traditions of Meditation in Chinese Buddhism*, edited by Peter N. Gregory, Kuroda Institute, Studies in East Asian Buddhism 4, 45–97. Honolulu: University of Hawai'i Press, 1986.

——. "Tales of the Lotus Sūtra." In *Buddhism in Practice*, edited by Donald S. Lopez Jr., 427–51. Princeton, N.J.: Princeton University Press, 1995.

——. "Where Meditative Theory Meets Practice: Requirements for Entering the 'Halls of Contemplation/Penance' (観/懺堂) in Tiantai Monasteries of the Song." *Tendai gakuhō, tokubetsugō: Kokusai Tendai gakkai ronshū* 天台学報, 特別号—国際天台学会論集 (October 2007): 71–142.

——. "Zhiyi: The Lotus Samādhi Rite of Repentance." In *Sources of Chinese Tradition*, 2nd ed., edited by Wm. Theodore de Bary and Irene Bloom, 1:462–67. New York: Columbia University Press, 1999.

Stevenson, Daniel B., and Hiroshi Kanno. *The Meaning of the Lotus Sūtra's Course of*

Ease and Bliss: An Annotated Translation and Study of Nanyue Huisi's (515–577) "Fahua jing anlexing yi." Bibliotheca Philologica et Philosophica Buddhica 9. Tokyo: The International Research Institute for Advanced Buddhology, Soka University, 2006.

Stone, Jacqueline I. "By Imperial Edict and Shogunal Decree: Politics and the Issue of the Ordination Platform in Modern Lay Nichiren Buddhism." In *Buddhism in the Modern World: Adaptations of an Ancient Tradition*, edited by Steven Heine and Charles S. Prebish, 192–219. New York: Oxford University Press, 2003.

——. "Chanting the August Title of the *Lotus Sūtra*: *Daimoku* Practices in Classical and Medieval Japan." In *Re-Visioning "Kamakura" Buddhism*, edited by Richard K. Payne, Kuroda Institute, Studies in East Asian Buddhism 11, 116–66. Honolulu: University of Hawai'i Press, 1998.

——. "Giving One's Life for the *Lotus Sūtra* in Nichiren's Thought." Unpublished ms.

——. "Inclusive and Exclusive Perspectives on the One Vehicle." *Dharma World* 26 (1999): 20–25.

——. "Japanese *Lotus* Millennialism: From Militant Nationalism to Contemporary Peace Movements." In *Millennialism, Persecution, and Violence: Historical Cases*, edited by Catherine Wessinger, 261–80. Syracuse, N.Y.: Syracuse University Press, 2000.

——. "Nichiren's Activist Heirs: Sōka Gakkai, Risshō Kōseikai, Nipponzan Myōhōji." In *Action Dharma: New Studies in Engaged Buddhism*, edited by Christopher Queen, Charles Prebish, and Damien Keown, 63–94. New York: RoutledgeCurzon, 2003.

——. "Not Mere Written Words: Perspectives on the Language of the *Lotus Sūtra* in Medieval Japan." In *Discourse and Ideology in Medieval Japanese Buddhism*, edited by Richard K. Payne and Taigen Dan Leighton, 160–94. London: Routledge, 2006.

——. *Original Enlightenment and the Transformation of Medieval Japanese Buddhism.* Kuroda Institute, Studies in East Asian Buddhism 12. Honolulu: University of Hawai'i Press, 1999.

——. "When Disobedience is Filial and Resistance is Loyal: The *Lotus Sutra* and Social Obligations in the Medieval Nichiren Tradition." In *A Buddhist Kaleidoscope: Essays on the Lotus Sutra*, edited by Gene Reeves, 261–81. Tokyo: Kōsei, 2002.

Strong, John S. "The Buddha's Funeral." In *The Buddhist Dead: Practices, Discourses, Representations*, edited by Bryan J. Cuevas and Jacqueline I. Stone, Kuroda Institute, Studies in East Asian Buddhism 20, 32–59. Honolulu: University of Hawai'i Press, 2007.

——. *The Legend and Cult of Upagupta: Sanskrit Buddhism in North India and Southeast Asia.* Princeton, N.J.: Princeton University Press, 1992.

——. *Relics of the Buddha.* Buddhisms. Princeton, N.J.: Princeton University Press, 2004.

Sueki Fumihiko 末木文美士. "Annen: The Philosopher Who Japanized Buddhism." *Acta Asiatica* 66 (1994): 69–86.

——. *Heian shoki bukkyō shisō no kenkyū* 平安初期仏教思想の研究. Tokyo: Shunjūsha, 1995.

Suguro, Shinjo. *Introduction to the Lotus Sutra*. Translated by Nichiren Buddhist International Center. Fremont, Calif.: Jain, 1998.

Sullivan, Michael. *The Cave Temples of Maichishan*. London: Farber & Farber, 1969.

Suwa Gijun 諏訪義純. *Chūgoku nanchō bukkyōshi no kenkyū* 中国南朝仏教史の研究. Kyoto: Hōzōkan, 1997.

Swanson, Paul L. *Foundations of T'ien-t'ai Philosophy: The Flowering of the Two Truths Theory in Chinese Buddhism*. Nanzan Studies in Religion and Culture 9. Berkeley: Asian Humanities Press, 1989.

——, trans. *The Great Cessation-and-Contemplation (Mo-ho chih-kuan)*. Tokyo: Kōsei, 2004. CD-ROM. Also available online at Swanson's Web site under "Staff" at http://www.ic.nanzan-u.ac.jp/SHUBUNKEN/staff/staff.htm.

——. "Understanding Chih-i: Through a Glass, Darkly?" *Journal of the International Association of Buddhist Studies* 17, no. 2 (1994): 337–60.

Takakusu, Junjirō. *Record of the Buddhist Religion as Practised in India and the Malay Archipelago (A.D. 671–695) by I-tsing*. London: Clarendon Press, 1896.

Tamura Yoshirō 田村芳朗. "Kindai Nihon no ayumi to Nichiren-shugi" 近代日本の歩みと日蓮主義. In *Nihon kindai to Nichiren-shugi* 日本近代と日蓮主義, edited by Tamura Yoshirō 田村芳朗 and Miyazaki Eishū 宮崎英修, *Kōza Nichiren* 4 講座日蓮, 1–17. Tokyo: Shunjūsha, 1972.

Tanabe, George J., Jr. "Tanaka Chigaku: The *Lotus Sutra* and the Body Politic." In *The Lotus Sutra in Japanese Culture*, edited by George J. Tanabe Jr. and Willa Jane Tanabe, 191–208. Honolulu: University of Hawai'i Press, 1989.

Tanabe, George J., Jr., and Willa Jane Tanabe, eds. *The Lotus Sutra in Japanese Culture*. Honolulu: University of Hawai'i Press, 1989.

Tanabe, Willa Jane. "The Lotus Lectures: *Hokke Hakkō* in the Heian Period." *Monumenta Nipponica* 39, no. 4 (1984): 394–407.

——. *Paintings of the Lotus Sutra*. New York: Weatherhill, 1988.

Tanaka Chigaku 田中智学. *Honge kyōhan Hokke hakkō* 本化教判法華八講. In *Tanaka Chigaku jiden* 田中智学自伝 7. 10 vols. Tokyo: Shishiō bunkō, 1936.

——. *Shūmon no ishin* 宗門之維新. 1901. In *Shishiō zenshū* 師子王全集, 36 vols., edited by Shishiō zenshū kankōkai 師子王全集刊行会, 7. Tokyo: Shishiō bunkō, 1931–1938.

Thurman, Robert A. F., trans. *The Holy Teaching of Vimalakīrti: A Mahāyāna Scripture*. University Park: Pennsylvania State University Press, 1976.

Tokoro Shigemoto 戸頃重基. *Kindai shakai to Nichiren-shugi* 近代社会と日蓮主義. Tokyo: Hyōronsha, 1972.

Tōkyō kokuritsu hakubutsukan 東京国立博物館. *Kunōji kyō* 久能寺経. Tokyo: Tōkyō kokuritsu hakubutsukan, 1978.

Tōkyō teikoku hakubutsukan 東京帝国博物館. *Kinbusen no kyōzuka ibutsu no kenkyū* 金峰山の経塚遺物の研究. Tokyo: Tōkyō teikoku hakubutsukan, 1937.

Tsumori Kiichi 都守基一. "Ryōzen jōdo shinkō no keifu" 霊山浄土信仰の系譜. *Nichiren kyōgaku kenkyūjo kiyō* 日蓮教学研究所紀要 15 (1988): 23–51.

Tyler, Royall, trans. *The Tale of Genji*. 2 vols. New York: Viking, 2001.

Verellen, Franciscus. "'Evidential Miracles in Support of Taoism': The Inversion of a Buddhist Apologetic Tradition in Late Tang China." *T'oung Pao* 78 (1992): 218–63.

Visser, Marinus Willem de. *Ancient Buddhism in Japan: Sutras and Ceremonies in Use in the Seventh and Eighth Centuries A.D. and Their History in Later Times*. 2 vols. Leiden: Brill, 1935.

Waley, Arthur. *A Catalogue of Paintings Recovered from Tun-huang by Sir Aurel Stein*. London: British Museum, 1931.

Wang, Eugene Y. *Shaping the Lotus Sutra: Buddhist Visual Culture in Medieval China*. Seattle: University of Washington Press, 2005.

Watson, Burton, trans. *The Essential Lotus: Selections from the Lotus Sutra*. Translations from the Asian Classics. New York: Columbia University Press, 2002.

——. *The Lotus Sutra*. Translations from the Asian Classics. New York: Columbia University Press, 1993. Also available online at http://lotus.nichirenshu.org/lotus/sutra/english/watson/indxwatson.htm.

——. *The Vimalakirti Sutra*. New York: Columbia University Press, 1996.

Weidner, Marsha, ed. *Latter Days of the Law: Images of Chinese Buddhism 850–1850*. Lawrence: Spencer Museum of Art, University of Kansas, 1994.

Welch, Holmes. *The Practice of Chinese Buddhism*. Cambridge, Mass.: Harvard University Press, 1967.

Whitfield, Roderick. *The Art of Central Asia: The Stein Collection in the British Museum*. 3 vols. Tokyo: Kodansha International, 1982–1985.

——. *Cave Temples of Mogao: Art and History on the Silk Road*. Los Angeles: Getty Conservation Institute and the J. Paul Getty Museum, 2000.

——. *Dunhuang, Caves of the Singing Sands: Buddhist Art from the Silk Road*. London: Textile and Art Publications, 1995.

Wilson, Liz. *Charming Cadavers: Horrific Figurations of the Feminine in Indian Buddhist Hagiographic Literature*. Chicago: University of Chicago Press, 1996.

——. "Human Torches of Enlightenment: Autocremation and Spontaneous Combustion as Marks of Sanctity in South Asian Buddhism." In *The Living and the Dead: Social Dimensions of Death in South Asian Religions*, edited by Liz Wilson, 29–50. Albany: SUNY Press, 2003.

Wong, Dorothy C. *Chinese Steles: Pre-Buddhist and Buddhist Use of a Symbolic Form*. Honolulu: University of Hawai'i Press, 2004.

Wu, Hung. "What Is *Bianxiang*?—On the Relationship between Dunhuang Art and Dunhuang Literature." *Harvard Journal of Asiatic Studies* 52, no. 1 (June 1992): 111–92.

Yamada, Isshi. *Karuṇāpuṇḍarīka: The White Lotus of Compassion*. 1968. Reprint, New Delhi: Heritage, 1989.

Yamada, Shōzen. "Poetry and Meaning: Medieval Poets and the *Lotus Sutra*." In *The Lotus Sutra in Japanese Culture*, edited by George J. Tanabe Jr. and Willa Jane Tanabe, 95–117. Honolulu: University of Hawai'i Press, 1989.

Yamato Bunkakan 大和文華館, ed. *Kōrai butsuga* 高麗仏画. Kyoto: Yamato bunkakan, 1978.

Yampolsky, Philip B. *The Platform Sutra of the Sixth Patriarch*. New York: Columbia University Press, 1967.

Yoshida, Kazuhiko. "The Enlightenment of the Dragon King's Daughter in *The Lotus Sutra*." Translated and adapted by Margaret H. Childs. In *Engendering Faith: Women and Buddhism in Premodern Japan*, edited by Barbara Ruch, 297–324. Ann Arbor: Center for Japanese Studies, University of Michigan, 2002.

Yü, Chün-fang. *Kuan-yin: The Chinese Transformation of Avalokiteśvara*. New York: Columbia University Press, 2001.

Ziporyn, Brook. *Evil and/or/as the Good: Omnicentrism, Intersubjectivity, and Value Paradox in Tiantai Buddhist Thought*. Cambridge, Mass.: Harvard University Asia Center, 2000.

Zürcher, Erik. "Late Han Vernacular Elements in the Earliest Buddhist Translations." *Journal of the Chinese Language Teachers Association* 13, no. 3 (1977): 177–203.

——. "A New Look at the Earliest Chinese Buddhist Texts." In *From Benares to Beijing: Essays on Buddhism and Chinese Religion in Honour of Prof. Jan Yün-hua*, edited by Koichi Shinohara and Gregory Schopen, 277–304. Oakville, Ont.: Mosaic Press, 1991.

Zwilling, Leonard. "Homosexuality as Seen in Indian Buddhist Texts." In *Buddhism, Sexuality, and Gender*, edited by José Ignacio Cabezón, 203–14. Albany: SUNY Press, 1992.

CONTRIBUTORS

James A. Benn is associate professor in the Department of Religious Studies, McMaster University, where he teaches Buddhism and Chinese religions. He is the author of *Burning for the Buddha: Self-Immolation in Chinese Buddhism* (Honolulu: University of Hawai'i Press, 2007). His current research focuses on the religious and cultural aspects of the history of tea in China.

Carl Bielefeldt is professor of religious studies and director of the Ho Center for Buddhist Studies at Stanford University. He is the author of *Dōgen's Manuals of Zen Meditation* (Berkeley: University of California Press, 1988) and other works on medieval Japanese Buddhism. He serves as the editor of the Sōtō Zen Text Project.

Ruben L. F. Habito is professor of world religions and spirituality at the Perkins School of Theology, Southern Methodist University. A longtime scholar of Nichiren, he coedited *Revisiting Nichiren*, a special issue of the *Japanese Journal of Religious Studies* (1999). His books include *Experiencing Buddhism: Ways of Wisdom and Compassion* (New York: Orbis Books, 2005) and *Healing Breath: Zen for Christians and Buddhists in a Wounded World* (Somerville, Mass.: Wisdom Publications, 2006).

Jan Nattier is research professor of Buddhist studies at the International Research Institute for Advanced Buddhology, Soka University, Tokyo. She is the author of *Once upon a Future Time: Studies in a Buddhist Prophecy of Decline* (Berkeley: Asian Humanities Press, 1991), awarded the Gustav O. Arlt Prize; *A Few Good Men: The Bodhisattva Path according to "The Inquiry of Ugra (Ugraparipṛcchā)"* (Honolulu: University of Hawai'i Press, 2003); and *A Guide to the Earliest Chinese Buddhist Translations* (Tokyo: The International Research Institute for Advanced Buddhology, Soka University, 2008).

Daniel B. Stevenson is associate professor and chair of the Department of Religious Studies at the University of Kansas. He has published extensively on the Chinese Tiantai and Pure Land traditions, with an emphasis on the areas of ritual, exegetical, and institutional history. His interests lie in the social and cultural processes at work behind the construction of religious identities in traditional China.

Jacqueline I. Stone is professor of Japanese religions in the Religion Department of Princeton University. She is the author of *Original Enlightenment and the Transformation of Medieval Japanese Buddhism* (Honolulu: University of Hawai'i Press, 1999), which received the American Academy of Religion Award for Excellence in the Study of Religion (Historical Studies). Her current research interests include Buddhism and national identity in premodern and modern Japan and the history of the Nichiren Buddhist tradition.

Willa Jane Tanabe is professor emerita of Japanese art history and former dean of the School of Hawaiian, Asian, and Pacific Studies at the University of Hawai'i. Her publications include *Paintings of the Lotus Sutra* (New York: Weatherhill, 1988), (coeditor) *The Lotus Sutra in Japanese Culture* (Honolulu: University of Hawai'i Press, 1989), and contributions to *Sacred Treasures of Mount Kōya* (Honolulu: Koyasan Reihokan Museum, 2002).

Stephen F. Teiser is D. T. Suzuki Professor in Buddhist Studies at Princeton University. His book on art of the otherworld, *Reinventing the Wheel: Paintings of Rebirth in Medieval Buddhist Temples* (Seattle: University of Washington Press, 2006), was awarded the Prix Stanislas Julien by the Institut de France. He is currently writing about Chinese Buddhist ritual based on early manuscripts.

INDEX

Italic page numbers refer to figures.